Springer Texts in Business and Economics

Springer Texts in Business and Economics (STBE) delivers high-quality instructional content for undergraduates and graduates in all areas of Business/Management Science and Economics. The series is comprised of self-contained books with a broad and comprehensive coverage that are suitable for class as well as for individual self-study. All texts are authored by established experts in their fields and offer a solid methodological background, often accompanied by problems and exercises.

Daleik A. Vaughn

Essentials of Residential Property Management

Managing Single-Family Homes, Multi-Family Homes, and Community Associations

Springer

Daleik A. Vaughn
Adjunct Professor, Residential Property Management
at H. Wayne Huizenga College of Business and Entrepreneurship
Nova Southeastern University
Fort Lauderdale, FL, USA

ISSN 2192-4333 ISSN 2192-4341 (electronic)
Springer Texts in Business and Economics
ISBN 978-3-031-92328-9 ISBN 978-3-031-92329-6 (eBook)
https://doi.org/10.1007/978-3-031-92329-6

This Springer imprint is published by the registered company Springer Nature Switzerland AG
The registered company address is: Gewerbestrasse 11, 6330 Cham, Switzerland

Preface

Welcome to this comprehensive guide on Residential Property Management, a resource crafted to equip property managers, students, and professionals with the knowledge and tools necessary to excel in the dynamic field of property management. This book covers an array of topics, including the management of single-family homes, manufactured home parks, and multifamily residences. It delves into the intricacies of maintenance, resident relations, financial management, and legal compliance, providing a holistic approach to property management education.

Over the past few decades, the property management industry has undergone significant transformations. Advancements in technology, evolving legal frameworks, and shifting market demands have reshaped the responsibilities and challenges faced by property managers. This book not only addresses these changes but also anticipates future trends, ensuring that readers are well-prepared to navigate the complexities of modern property management. By integrating practical examples, case studies, and up-to-date industry practices, this guide offers a practical, hands-on approach to learning.

The aim of this book is to provide a solid foundation in the principles and practices of property management while also offering advanced strategies for addressing specific challenges. Whether you are a seasoned professional looking to refine your skills or a student just beginning your journey in property management, this book is designed to meet your needs. Each chapter is structured to build on the previous one, gradually expanding your knowledge and competence in various aspects of property management.

Special emphasis is placed on legal compliance and risk management, areas that are critical to the successful operation of any residential property. Detailed discussions on US federal and state laws, fair housing regulations, and risk management strategies are included to ensure that you are well-informed and capable of making sound decisions. Additionally, the book explores the impact of technology on property management, offering insights into how digital tools and smart home technology can enhance efficiency and resident satisfaction.

We hope this book serves as a valuable resource in your professional development and helps you achieve excellence in the field of residential property management. By embracing the best practices and principles outlined in these pages, you will be better equipped to manage properties effectively, ensure resident satisfaction, and maintain legal and ethical standards. Thank you for choosing this guide as your companion in the ever-evolving world of property management.

Fort Lauderdale, FL, USA Daleik A. Vaughn

The original version of the book was inadvertently published without the backmatter (Glossary and Answer key). The backmatter has now been included in the book.

Acknowledgments

This book would not have been possible without the guidance, support, and contributions of many individuals and resources.

First and foremost, I would like to express my deepest gratitude to Ines Flores Vaughn, CPA, whose expertise in financial management and accounting brought invaluable insights.

I am also profoundly grateful to Leila A. Vaughn, PhD, for her thoughtful critiques and academic perspective. Her detailed reviews helped shape the structure and depth of the book, ensuring it aligns with the needs of students and instructors. Her commitment to academic rigor and clarity has elevated the quality of this work.

Additionally, I would like to acknowledge the use of ChatGPT, as a resource in drafting, refining, and organizing various sections and alt text of this book. While every effort was made to ensure the content aligns with my professional knowledge and experience, the use of AI technology played a supporting role in the writing process.

Finally, I am grateful to Springer Nature and the peer reviewers whose feedback has been instrumental in shaping this manuscript into its final form. Their thoughtful comments and suggestions have ensured that this book serves as a comprehensive and practical guide for students and professionals entering the field of residential property management.

Competing Interests The author has no competing interests to declare that are relevant to the content of this manuscript.

Contents

1 **Understanding Residential Property Management** 1

2 **Managing Single-Family Homes** 25

3 **Introduction to Managing Timeshares** 61

4 **Introduction to Manufactured Home Parks** 85

5 **Managing Multifamily Residences** 107

6 **General Property Management** 193

Answer Key 303

Glossary of Key Terms 319

About the Author

Daleik A. Vaughn MBA, LCAM, CMCA, is a seasoned property management professional with over 16 years of experience in the industry. Throughout his career, Mr. Vaughn has demonstrated exceptional proficiency in managing a diverse portfolio of properties, including income generating single-family homes and multifamily residences as well as not-for-profit community associations. His extensive knowledge and hands-on approach have enabled him to successfully navigate the complexities of property management and property value enhancement.

In addition to his practical experience, Mr. Vaughn holds the credentials of a Florida & Michigan Real Estate Broker, Florida Licensed Community Association Manager (LCAM), and Certified Manager of Community Associations (CMCA). These certifications reflect his commitment to maintaining high standards of professionalism and his dedication to continuous learning in the field of real estate property management. Daleik's expertise spans various aspects of the industry, including resident relations, maintenance coordination, construction project management, financial management, and legal compliance.

Mr. Vaughn currently serves as the Regional Director with a leading property management firm, where he oversees the management of residential and commercial properties, ensuring operational excellence and adherence to best practices. His role involves strategic planning, team leadership, and the implementation of innovative solutions to meet the evolving needs of property owners and residents. Under his leadership, properties have consistently achieved financial stability, resident retention, and overall satisfaction.

Beyond his professional practice, Mr. Vaughn is also Adjunct Professor of Residential Property Management in the Huizenga College of Business and Entrepreneurship at Nova Southeastern University. In this capacity, he shares his wealth of knowledge and industry insights with the next generation of property managers. His teaching approach combines theoretical frameworks with real-world applications, providing students with a comprehensive understanding of the field. Mr. Vaughn's passion for education and mentorship has made him a respected figure among his students and peers, contributing significantly to the advancement of property management education.

1 Understanding Residential Property Management

1.1 Learning Objectives

By the end of this unit, students will be able to:

- *Understand the Importance and Scope of Residential Property Management*
  - Define the role of residential property management in maintaining and enhancing property value.
  - Identify the various responsibilities and challenges involved in managing residential properties.
- *Describe the Role of a Residential Property Manager*
  - Explain the day-to-day duties and long-term responsibilities of a residential property manager.
  - Understand the manager's role in balancing resident satisfaction with property owner expectations.
- *Classify Different Types of Residential Properties*
  - Differentiate between single-family homes, multifamily residences, and manufactured home parks.
  - Explain the unique challenges and opportunities associated with managing each type of residential property.
- *Identify the Key Skills and Qualities of Successful Property Managers*
  - Highlight essential skills such as communication, organization, and problem-solving.
  - Understand the importance of ethical behavior and conflict resolution in property management.
- *Explore the Rise of Professional Property Management*
  - Trace the historical growth and development of property management as a profession.
  - Discuss how industry standards and practices have evolved over time.

D. A. Vaughn, *Essentials of Residential Property Management*, Springer Texts in Business and Economics, https://doi.org/10.1007/978-3-031-92329-6_1

- *Recognize the Role of Professional Trade Organizations*
  - Identify key trade organizations, such as Institute of Real Estate Management (IREM), NARPM, & CAI, that support property management professionals.
  - Explain how these organizations provide training, certification, and networking opportunities.
- *General Business Economy*
  - Analyze the key economic factors influencing residential real estate.
  - Explain the impact of seasonal variations and cyclic fluctuations on the real estate market.
- *Examine the Economics of Property Management*
  - Analyze how property management contributes to the financial success of residential real estate investments.
  - Understand the impact of effective management on revenue, expenses, and overall property performance.
- *Understand the Evolution of Residential Property Management*
  - Discuss the key trends and technological advancements shaping the future of residential property management.
  - Explain how changing resident expectations and market conditions are influencing modern property management practices.

By achieving these learning objectives, students will gain a solid foundation in the principles and practices of residential property management, preparing them for more advanced topics and real-world application.

1.2 Key Terms

By the end of this unit, students will be familiar with the following key terms:

Building Owners and Managers Association (BOMA)
Business Cycle
Certified Property Manager (CPM)
Community Association Institute (CAI)
Human Resources Management (HRM)
National Apartment Association (NAA)
National Association of Residential Property Managers (NARPMs)
Property Management
Property Classifications.
Single-Family Home
Manufactured Home Park
Multifamily Residences

1.3 Overview

Property management is a crucial aspect of real estate, encompassing the oversight, operation, and maintenance of residential, commercial, and industrial properties. The primary objective of property management is to ensure the optimal performance of the property, which includes maintaining its physical condition, enhancing its market value, and/or maximizing its income potential. Residential property management focuses on managing properties where individuals and families reside, including single-family homes, multifamily residences, and manufactured home parks.

The role of a residential property manager is multifaceted, involving a blend of administrative, financial, and operational tasks. From finding and screening residents to handling maintenance requests and ensuring compliance with local laws, property managers wear many hats. Effective property management requires a combination of organizational skills, knowledge of the real estate market, and the ability to communicate effectively with residents, owners, and service providers.

1.4 Importance and Scope of Residential Property Management

Residential property management is vital for several reasons. It ensures that properties are well-maintained, which in turn helps preserve and increase their value. This is important not only for the property owners, who benefit from higher rental income and property appreciation, but also for the residents, who enjoy a safe and comfortable living environment.

The scope of residential property management extends beyond just maintaining the physical structure of a property. It also involves financial management, including budgeting, rent and maintenance fee collection, along with financial reporting. Additionally, property managers are often tasked with marketing vacant units, conducting resident screenings, and handling lease agreements. By taking on these responsibilities, property managers provide a valuable service to property owners, allowing them to focus on other aspects of property ownership.

Moreover, residential property management plays a significant role in ensuring compliance with local, state, and federal regulations. Property managers must stay informed about changes in housing laws and regulations to avoid legal issues that could arise from noncompliance. This includes understanding landlord-tenant laws, community association laws, fair housing regulations, and safety standards.

1.5 Understanding Residential Property Classifications

Residential properties can be broadly classified into three categories: single-family homes, manufactured home parks, and multifamily residences. Each of these classifications has unique characteristics and management requirements.

1.5.1 Single-Family Homes

Single-family homes are standalone properties designed to accommodate one family. These properties are typically owned by individual investors or homeowners who rent them out as income-generating assets. Managing single-family residences involves a range of tasks, including marketing the property to attract qualified residents, screening potential tenants, handling maintenance requests, and ensuring timely rent collection. Property managers must also oversee lease agreements, ensure legal compliance with landlord-tenant laws, and address any issues related to property damage or resident disputes.

One of the key challenges of managing single-family homes is the individualized nature of maintenance and repairs, as each property may have unique needs based on its age, condition, and location. Additionally, property managers must ensure consistent rental income, as vacancies in single-family homes can result in 100% revenue loss for that specific property until a new tenant is secured. Despite these challenges, single-family homes often appeal to residents seeking privacy, larger living spaces, and the experience of traditional homeownership without the long-term commitment.

1.5.2 Manufactured Home Parks

Manufactured home parks consist of multiple manufactured homes situated on leased land, offering an affordable housing option for many residents. These parks often feature communal amenities such as playgrounds, laundry facilities, and clubhouses, which enhance the sense of community among residents. Property management in manufactured home parks involves maintaining common areas, managing utilities, enforcing park rules, and ensuring compliance with local, state, and federal regulations.

A unique aspect of managing manufactured home parks is the dual responsibility of overseeing both the individual homes (when they are park-owned) and the overall park infrastructure, including roads, utility systems, and shared facilities. In many cases, residents own their homes while renting the land, adding complexity to the property manager's role. Managers must navigate issues related to land leases, resident-owned homes, and park-owned rental units, ensuring that both the physical environment and community operations are managed effectively.

1.5.3 Multifamily Residences

Multifamily properties include apartment buildings, condominium associations, cooperatives, homeowner associations (HOAs), and timeshares. These properties house multiple families in separate units within a single structure or complex, but the property management responsibilities can vary significantly depending on the type of multifamily property. While both apartment buildings and community associations fall under the multifamily umbrella, the scope of duties, legal obligations, and stakeholder relationships differ substantially between the two.

Managing Apartment Buildings

Property managers responsible for apartment buildings typically work on behalf of a property owner or real estate investment group. Their primary objective is to maximize the property's profitability through effective tenant management, rent collection, leasing, and maintenance operations. This role involves overseeing multiple leases, marketing vacant units, screening prospective tenants, enforcing lease agreements, and addressing tenant concerns. Apartment managers are also responsible for ensuring high occupancy rates, minimizing vacancies, and managing turnover efficiently.

In terms of financial management, apartment property managers handle operating budgets, control expenses, and ensure rent is collected on time. They manage accounts payable and receivable, oversee vendor contracts for services like landscaping and security, and provide regular financial reports to property owners. Maintenance responsibilities include routine upkeep of building systems ((heating ventilation, air condition (HVAC), plumbing, electrical), addressing emergency repairs, and ensuring common areas are clean and well-maintained. Because apartment buildings are often income-generating properties, managers focus heavily on maximizing revenue while controlling costs to increase the property's net operating income (NOI).

Unlike community associations, apartment property managers have more direct control over decision-making since they report to a property owner or management company rather than a board of directors. This allows for quicker decision-making processes related to leasing strategies, capital improvements, or operational changes.

Managing Community Associations: Condominiums, Cooperatives, HOAs, and Timeshares

On the other hand, property managers who oversee community associations—including condominiums, cooperatives, HOAs, and timeshares—operate within a more complex governance structure. Instead of managing tenants, these managers work with unit owners and boards of directors elected by the community. Their role is to enforce the community's governing documents, such as bylaws, covenants, conditions, and restrictions (CC&Rs), and association rules.

One of the primary responsibilities in community association management is facilitating board operations. Property managers assist the board with strategic planning, budget development, and financial reporting. They manage association assessments (similar to dues) rather than rent, and they oversee reserve funds designated for long-term repairs and capital projects. Delinquency management involves following collection procedures for unpaid assessments, which can differ significantly from traditional rent collection practices.

Maintenance responsibilities focus on common areas and shared amenities rather than individual units. This includes managing swimming pools, fitness centers, clubhouses, landscaping, and infrastructure like elevators, roofs, and parking garages. In condominiums and cooperatives, the association may also be

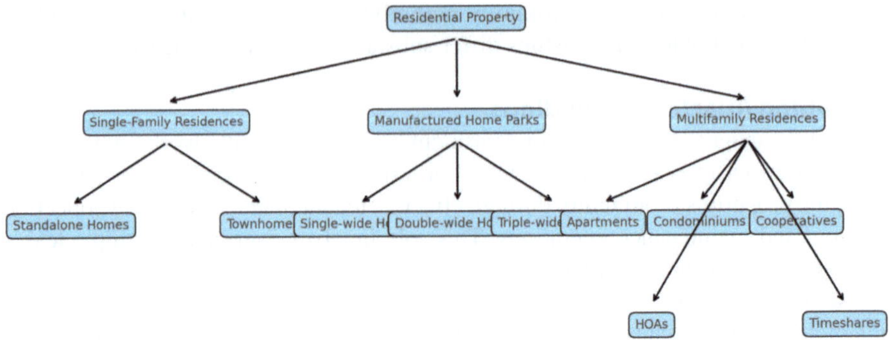

Fig. 1.1 Residential property categories

responsible for maintaining building exteriors and structural components, depending on the governing documents.

For timeshares, management becomes even more specialized. Property managers must handle reservations, manage high turnover rates, and maintain amenities to hospitality standards. They also coordinate with timeshare boards, handle owner relations, and manage financial aspects such as maintenance fees, special assessments, and exchange program partnerships.

A key difference in community association management is the emphasis on resident relations in the context of ownership, not tenancy. Managers often mediate disputes between owners, enforce rules and regulations consistently, and ensure compliance with legal requirements at the state and federal levels, such as fair housing laws. They must also navigate complex legal issues related to association governance, voting procedures, and compliance with nonprofit corporation statutes in many jurisdictions (Fig. 1.1).

1.6 The Role of a Residential Property Manager

A residential property manager's role can be divided into several key areas: administrative, financial, maintenance, and resident relations.

1.6.1 Administrative Responsibilities

Administrative responsibilities form the backbone of effective property management, supporting both the operational and strategic functions of managing residential and commercial properties. Property managers are responsible for maintaining accurate and organized records, handling communications with residents, vendors, and stakeholders, and ensuring that all necessary documentation is up-to-date and compliant with legal and regulatory requirements. This includes managing lease agreements, vendor contracts, insurance policies, meeting minutes (in the case of community associations), and regulatory compliance documents. An organized administrative system facilitates routine operations, aids in informed decision-making, and improves the efficiency of property management activities while ensuring that essential documentation is available for legal matters.

1.6.2 Financial Management

Financial responsibilities are a critical component of property management, serving as the foundation for maintaining the economic health and long-term sustainability of residential properties. This responsibility is universal across all forms of residential property management, whether managing single-family homes, income-generating multifamily properties, or community associations such as condominiums, cooperatives, and homeowners' associations (HOAs). Regardless of the property type, effective financial management ensures that properties remain profitable, financially stable, and/or capable of meeting both short-term obligations and long-term capital needs.

For single-family homes and income-generating multifamily properties, property managers are tasked with setting competitive rental rates based on market analysis, local demand, and property features. This process involves evaluating comparable properties, considering vacancy rates, and adjusting rents periodically to reflect market conditions. Timely rent collection is another core responsibility, with property managers enforcing lease agreements to ensure consistent cash flow. This includes issuing late notices, applying late fees when necessary, and managing the eviction process in cases of nonpayment, all while adhering to local landlord-tenant laws. On the expense side, property managers must control costs related to maintenance, utilities, insurance, and property taxes, ensuring that the property operates efficiently without unnecessary financial strain.

In community associations, such as condominiums, cooperatives, and HOAs, financial management focuses on assessments rather than rent collection. Property managers are responsible for preparing annual budgets, setting assessment rates, and ensuring timely collection of dues from unit owners. Delinquency management is equally important in this context, as unpaid assessments can significantly impact the association's ability to fund operations, reserve accounts, and capital improvement projects. Additionally, community associations often require property managers to oversee reserve funds designated for long-term repairs and replacements, which involves strategic financial planning and periodic reserve studies to assess future funding needs.

1.6.3 Maintenance and Repairs

Maintenance and repairs are fundamental components of property management, serving as one of the most visible and impactful responsibilities across all property types. Whether managing single-family homes, multifamily residences, community associations, or commercial properties, the core objective remains the same: to ensure that the property is safe, functional, and aesthetically pleasing. Proper maintenance not only preserves the physical integrity of the property but also enhances its value and contributes significantly to resident satisfaction.

The responsibility for maintenance is universal, though it may vary in scope and complexity depending on the type of property. For single-family homes, property managers often coordinate routine tasks such as landscaping, HVAC servicing, and roof inspections, while also handling unexpected repairs like plumbing leaks or appliance malfunctions. In multifamily residences, the scale increases with shared systems and common areas, requiring regular upkeep of lobbies, hallways, elevators, and exterior spaces. Community associations, such as HOAs and condominiums, add another layer of complexity, as managers must oversee the maintenance of common amenities like pools, clubhouses, and recreational facilities, while also ensuring compliance with association rules and regulations. Even in commercial properties, although the tenant responsibilities may differ, property managers must still maintain structural elements, mechanical systems, and common areas to support business operations and meet safety standards.

A proactive approach to maintenance is critical. This involves scheduling regular inspections to identify potential issues before they escalate into costly repairs. Routine tasks, such as gutter cleaning, HVAC filter replacements, and fire safety system checks, should be part of a comprehensive preventive maintenance plan. In addition, property managers must be prepared to respond swiftly to emergency repairs, such as water leaks, electrical failures, or safety hazards, to minimize disruptions and ensure resident safety. Establishing relationships with reliable contractors and vendors is key to addressing both routine and urgent maintenance needs efficiently.

1.6.4 Resident Relations

Building and maintaining positive relationships with residents is a cornerstone of successful property management. Whether managing single-family homes, income-generating multifamily properties, or community associations such as condominiums, cooperatives, and homeowners' associations (HOAs), the ability to foster strong resident relations is universal and critical to the long-term success of any residential property. Effective resident relations not only enhance the living experience for residents but also contribute to property value, financial stability, and the overall reputation of the community or rental property.

1.7 Key Skills and Qualities of Successful Property Managers

Property management is a multifaceted profession that demands a wide range of skills and qualities to effectively oversee residential properties. Successful property managers are not only responsible for maintaining the physical condition of the properties they manage but also for fostering positive relationships with tenants, ensuring financial stability, and navigating legal and regulatory frameworks. To excel in this role, property managers must demonstrate expertise in several critical areas, including organizational skills, communication skills, problem-solving abilities, real estate market knowledge, attention to detail, financial acumen, and legal knowledge. Each of these qualities contributes to a manager's ability to provide exceptional service and maximize the value of the properties under their care.

1.7.1 Organizational Skills

Property managers must possess exceptional organizational skills to handle the diverse responsibilities that come with managing residential properties. A single day might involve coordinating maintenance schedules, processing tenant applications, preparing financial reports, and responding to emergency repairs. Without strong organizational skills, managing these tasks efficiently and effectively would be impossible.

Effective property managers are adept at prioritizing their workload, using tools like property management software, calendars, and task management systems to stay on top of deadlines and commitments. They must also be skilled at managing multiple properties simultaneously, which requires tracking individual property needs and tenant requirements. Additionally, organizational skills are critical for maintaining accurate records, such as lease agreements, maintenance logs, and financial documents, all of which are essential for regulatory compliance and efficient operations.

1.7.2 Communication Skills

Clear and effective communication is at the heart of property management. Property managers interact with a variety of stakeholders, including property owners, tenants, contractors, and regulatory authorities. The ability to convey information concisely and professionally is essential for building trust and fostering positive relationships.

For tenants, property managers serve as the primary point of contact for concerns ranging from maintenance requests to lease renewals. Strong communication skills enable managers to listen actively, empathize with tenant concerns, and provide clear solutions. For property owners, managers must communicate financial performance, maintenance updates, and market trends in a way that demonstrates their expertise and instills confidence. Additionally, effective communication is critical when negotiating contracts with vendors or resolving disputes, as it ensures that all parties understand their responsibilities and expectations.

1.7.3 Problem-Solving Abilities

The unpredictable nature of property management means that challenges can arise at any moment. Whether it's handling a burst pipe, mediating a dispute between tenants, or addressing a sudden vacancy, property managers must be resourceful and proactive problem solvers. The ability to assess a situation, identify potential solutions, and implement an effective resolution is one of the most valuable skills a property manager can possess.

Problem-solving also involves anticipating potential issues before they escalate. For example, a property manager might notice signs of wear and tear during routine inspections and schedule preventative maintenance to avoid costly repairs. Similarly, staying informed about local market trends and tenant preferences allows managers to proactively address potential turnover by updating amenities or adjusting marketing strategies.

1.7.4 Knowledge of the Real Estate Market

A deep understanding of the real estate market is critical for property managers, as it directly impacts their ability to attract tenants, set competitive rental rates, and advise property owners on investment strategies. Market knowledge encompasses awareness of local rental trends, demographic shifts, and economic conditions, all of which influence property demand and value.

For instance, a property manager who understands that demand for pet-friendly rentals is increasing may recommend adding pet amenities to attract a broader tenant base. Similarly, staying informed about new developments or infrastructure projects in the area can help managers anticipate changes in property values or rental demand. This knowledge not only benefits property owners but also positions the manager as a trusted advisor, enhancing their professional reputation.

1.7.5 Attention to Detail

Property management involves numerous details that, if overlooked, can lead to significant consequences. From ensuring lease agreements are accurate and legally compliant to monitoring maintenance schedules and following up on tenant requests, attention to detail is a crucial quality for successful property managers.

This skill is particularly important in financial management, where even small errors in budgeting, rent collection, or expense tracking can have serious implications. Similarly, attention to detail is essential for conducting property inspections, as identifying minor issues early can prevent larger problems down the line. By maintaining a meticulous approach to their work, property managers can ensure that operations run smoothly and that properties remain in excellent condition.

1.7.6 Financial Acumen

Property management is as much about managing finances as it is about managing people and properties. Property managers are responsible for creating and adhering to budgets, collecting rents and assessments, paying bills, and preparing financial reports for property owners. Strong financial acumen allows managers to maximize property profitability or sustainability while ensuring that expenses are kept under control.

A property manager with financial expertise can analyze income and expense statements to identify opportunities for cost savings or revenue growth. For example, they might negotiate better terms with vendors, implement energy-efficient upgrades to reduce utility costs, or optimize rental pricing based on market conditions. Additionally, financial acumen is essential for managing reserve funds, planning for capital improvements, and ensuring compliance with tax obligations.

1.7.7 Legal Knowledge

The legal landscape of property management is complex and constantly evolving. Property managers must have a thorough understanding of landlord-tenant laws, fair housing regulations, zoning codes, and building safety standards to ensure compliance and avoid legal disputes. Ignorance of these laws can result in costly fines, reputational damage, and potential lawsuits.

For example, fair housing laws prohibit discrimination based on protected characteristics such as race, religion, or disability. A property manager must ensure that their leasing practices, advertising, and tenant interactions comply with these regulations. Similarly, managers must understand the legal requirements for handling security deposits, drafting lease agreements, and initiating evictions. Staying informed about changes in local, state, and federal laws is critical for maintaining compliance and protecting the interests of property owners and tenants.

1.8 The Rise of Professional Property Management

1.8.1 Origins of Property Management

The roots of property management can be traced back to the early twentieth century when the rapid urbanization and industrialization in the United States created a demand for rental housing. Landlords, often owning multiple properties, realized the need for professional assistance in managing their properties, leading to the emergence of property management as a profession. Initially, property management services were informal, but as the rental market grew, so did the need for standardized practices and professional oversight.

1.8.2 Post-World War II Boom

After World War II, the United States experienced a significant housing boom, with millions of veterans returning home and starting families. This period saw the expansion of suburban neighborhoods and the construction of multifamily housing complexes. The increased complexity and scale of property portfolios required more sophisticated management techniques, prompting the growth of professional property management companies. During this time, the role of property managers evolved from simple caretakers to comprehensive managers of real estate investments.

1.8.3 Modern Property Management

Today, property management is a sophisticated industry employing advanced technology, professional standards, and specialized knowledge. Modern property managers handle a wide range of tasks, including marketing, leasing, maintenance, financial management, and legal compliance. The profession has grown to encompass various property types, including residential, commercial, and industrial properties. The increasing complexity of real estate investments and tenant expectations has further solidified the importance of professional property management.

1.9 Professional Property Management Trade Organizations

1.9.1 Institute of Real Estate Management (IREM)

Founded in 1933, IREM is one of the most prominent trade organizations for property managers. It offers educational programs, certifications, and resources to enhance the skills and knowledge of property management professionals. The Certified Property Manager (CPM) designation is one of IREM's most recognized certifications, signifying a high level of expertise and professionalism in property management.

1.9.2 National Association of Residential Property Managers (NARPMs)

NARPM is dedicated to single-family residential property management. Established in 1988, it provides networking opportunities, educational resources, and certifications such as the Residential Management Professional (RMP) and Master Property Manager (MPM). NARPM focuses on promoting ethical and professional standards among residential property managers.

1.9.3 Building Owners and Managers Association International (BOMA)

BOMA, founded in 1907, serves commercial property managers and building owners. It offers advocacy, education, and information to its members. BOMA's designations, such as the Real Property Administrator (RPA) and Facilities Management Administrator (FMA), are highly respected in the commercial property management industry. BOMA also plays a significant role in influencing legislation and policies affecting commercial real estate.

1.9.4 National Apartment Association (NAA)

The NAA represents the interests of multifamily housing professionals, including property managers, owners, and suppliers. It provides a wide range of educational opportunities, industry research, and networking events. The NAA's Certified Apartment Manager (CAM) and National Apartment Leasing Professional (NALP) certifications are widely recognized in the apartment industry. The organization also advocates for policies that benefit the multifamily housing sector.

1.9.5 Community Association Institute (CAI)

Founded in 1973, the CAI is a prominent trade organization dedicated to the needs of community associations, including homeowners associations (HOAs), condominium associations, and cooperatives. CAI provides extensive educational resources, certification programs, and advocacy services to support the effective management and governance of community associations. Key certifications offered by CAI include the Association Management Specialist (AMS), and Professional Community Association Manager (PCAM). CAI also plays a critical role in shaping public policy and promoting best practices in community association management.

1.9.6 Community Association Managers International Certification Board (CAMICB)

The CAMICB is a leading organization dedicated to upholding the highest standards of professionalism, integrity, and knowledge in community association management. Its mission is to ensure that managers are equipped to effectively oversee residential communities and adhere to ethical practices. CAMICB offers the Certified Manager of Community Associations (CMCA®) certification, the only internationally accredited credential in the field. This program sets a benchmark for excellence, providing community association managers with the knowledge and tools needed to excel in their roles and maintain the trust of the communities they serve.

1.10 General Business Economy

Understanding the economics of property management is crucial for professionals in the residential real estate industry. The performance of residential properties is closely tied to broader economic trends, which influence everything from rental rates and occupancy levels to property values and investment opportunities. A comprehensive understanding of these economic factors enables property managers to make informed decisions, anticipate market shifts, and develop strategies that enhance the value and profitability of residential properties.

1.10.1 Factors Influencing the Residential Real Estate Economy

Interest Rates: Interest rates significantly affect the cost of borrowing for both homebuyers and real estate investors. When interest rates are low, borrowing becomes more affordable, leading to increased demand for homes and investment properties. This can result in higher property values, increased development activity, and greater competition in rental markets. Conversely, higher interest rates can dampen demand, slowing down property sales and affecting rental markets by reducing the pool of qualified buyers and increasing rental vacancies.

Inflation: Inflation impacts the cost of goods and services, including construction materials, labor, and property maintenance. As inflation rises, operating costs for property managers also increase, which may necessitate higher rental rates to maintain profitability. However, if wages do not keep pace with inflation, it can lead to affordability issues for tenants, potentially increasing turnover rates and vacancy levels. Property managers must carefully balance rent adjustments with market conditions to avoid pricing out potential residents.

Employment Rates: The employment rate is a critical driver of the housing market. High employment levels generally correlate with strong demand for housing, as people have stable incomes to support rent or mortgage payments. This stability encourages consumer confidence, driving demand for both rental properties and homeownership. Conversely, high unemployment can lead to increased vacancies, downward pressure on rental rates, and higher delinquency rates as tenants struggle to meet financial obligations.

Demographic Trends: Changes in population size, age distribution, household composition, and migration patterns influence housing demand. For example, an influx of young professionals into urban areas can increase demand for apartments, while aging populations may drive demand for senior living communities or age-restricted housing. Additionally, trends such as remote work have shifted demand toward suburban and rural areas, affecting rental and property values in previously underdeveloped regions.

Government Policies and Regulations: Tax incentives, zoning laws, rent control regulations, and housing subsidies can have significant effects on the residential real estate market. Policies that promote homeownership or affordable housing can stimulate demand, while restrictive regulations may limit development opportunities. For example, rent control laws can cap potential rental income, influencing investment decisions, while tax credits for energy-efficient buildings can encourage sustainable property development.

Supply and Demand: The basic economic principle of supply and demand governs the real estate market. An oversupply of residential units can lead to higher vacancy rates and reduced rental income, as property managers may need to lower rents or offer concessions to attract tenants. Conversely, limited supply coupled with high demand can drive up property values and rents, creating competitive markets where affordability becomes a concern. Property managers must monitor local supply dynamics to adjust pricing strategies and marketing efforts effectively.

Consumer Confidence: Consumer confidence reflects the overall optimism or pessimism that individuals feel about the state of the economy, which directly influences their spending and investment decisions. High consumer confidence often correlates with increased demand for housing, as people are more willing to buy homes or commit to long-term leases. In contrast, during periods of low confidence, potential renters or buyers may delay moving decisions, leading to slower market activity.

Technological Advancements: Technological innovations are reshaping the residential real estate landscape. The rise of property technology (PropTech) solutions, such as smart home devices, virtual tours, and online leasing platforms, affects how properties are marketed, managed, and maintained. Property managers who embrace these technologies can improve operational efficiency, reduce costs, and enhance the resident experience, giving them a competitive edge in the market.

Global Economic Events: Global events, such as pandemics, financial crises, or geopolitical conflicts, can have far-reaching impacts on the residential real estate economy. For instance, the COVID-19 pandemic significantly altered housing demand, shifting preferences toward larger spaces and remote work accommodations. Global supply chain disruptions can also affect construction timelines and costs, influencing housing supply and affordability.

1.10.2 Seasonal Variations in the Residential Real Estate Economy

Seasonal variations are predictable fluctuations that occur within the real estate market throughout the year. These changes are influenced by weather, school calendars, holidays, and cultural factors.

- *Spring and Summer:* Typically, the residential real estate market experiences a surge in activity during spring and summer. Families prefer to move during these seasons to avoid disrupting the school year, and favorable weather conditions make it easier to relocate. This period often sees higher property sales, increased rental turnover, and higher rental rates.
- *Fall and Winter:* The market tends to slow down in the fall and winter, particularly in colder climates. Fewer people are willing to move during the holiday season or in inclement weather. Property managers may face longer vacancy periods and may need to offer incentives to attract tenants during these months.

1.10.3 Cyclic Fluctuations in the Residential Real Estate Economy

Cyclic fluctuations refer to the broader economic cycles that influence the real estate market over several years. These fluctuations are driven by changes in the overall economy and follow four distinct phases of the *business cycle*:

Expansion: This phase is characterized by economic growth, low unemployment, rising incomes, and increased consumer confidence. In real estate, expansion leads to higher demand for housing, rising property values, increased construction activity, and higher rental rates. Property managers may experience high occupancy rates and strong revenue growth during this phase.

Recession: A recession occurs when economic growth slows or contracts, leading to higher unemployment, reduced consumer spending, and declining business investment. The real estate market often sees decreased demand, falling property values, and higher vacancy rates during a recession. Property managers may need to adjust rental rates, offer concessions, and focus on resident retention strategies.

Contraction: This phase represents a prolonged period of economic decline following a recession. Property values may continue to fall, construction activity slows, and financial institutions may tighten lending criteria. Property managers face challenges such as managing distressed properties, dealing with delinquent residents, and maintaining property values in a depressed market.

Revival (or Recovery): During the revival phase, the economy begins to recover from the downturn. Employment rates improve, consumer confidence returns, and demand for housing increases. Property managers can capitalize on this phase by adjusting rental rates, reducing vacancies, and preparing properties to meet renewed market demand (Fig. 1.2).

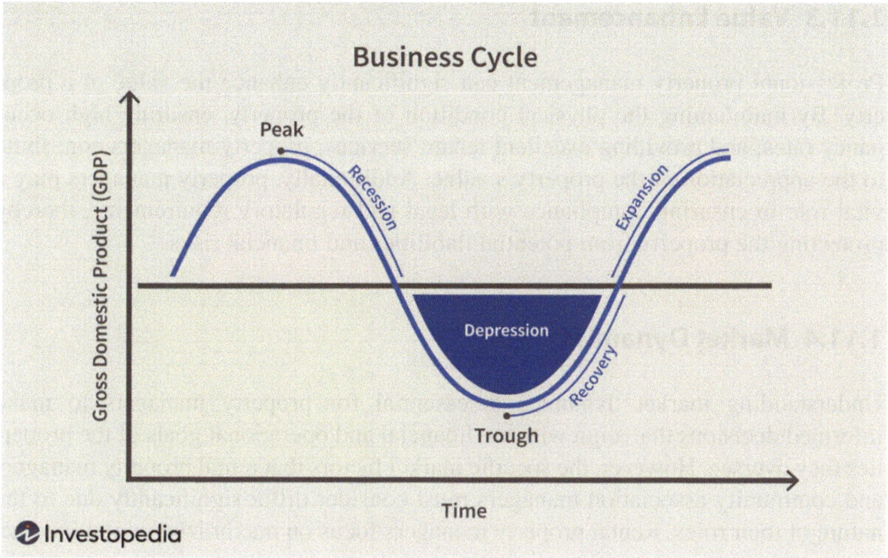

Fig. 1.2 The business cycle. (Business cycle graph. Image by Julie Bang © Investopedia 2019—https://www.investopedia.com/terms/b/businesscycle.asp)

1.11 The Economics of Property Management

1.11.1 Revenue Generation

Property management generates revenue primarily through fees charged for managing properties. These fees can be a percentage of the rental income, a flat fee, or a combination of both. Property managers also earn revenue from leasing commissions, late fees, and service charges for maintenance and repairs. Effective property management can enhance rental income by maintaining high occupancy rates, optimizing rental rates, and minimizing vacancies.

1.11.2 Cost Management

One of the critical roles of property managers is to manage costs effectively. This includes negotiating favorable service contracts, implementing preventive maintenance programs, and efficiently handling repairs and improvements. Cost management also involves budgeting for operating expenses, utilities, property taxes, insurance, and marketing. Effective cost control contributes to the overall profitability of the property.

1.11.3 Value Enhancement

Professional property management can significantly enhance the value of a property. By maintaining the physical condition of the property, ensuring high occupancy rates, and providing excellent tenant services, property managers contribute to the appreciation of the property's value. Additionally, property managers play a vital role in ensuring compliance with legal and regulatory requirements, thereby protecting the property from potential liabilities and financial risks.

1.11.4 Market Dynamics

Understanding market dynamics is essential for property managers to make informed decisions that align with the financial and operational goals of the properties they oversee. However, the specific market factors that rental property managers and community association managers must consider differ significantly due to the nature of their roles. Rental property managers focus on maximizing rental income, occupancy rates, and tenant satisfaction, while community association managers prioritize maintaining property values, ensuring resident satisfaction, and managing common area expenses. Developing a deep understanding of market dynamics tailored to each management type allows property managers to adapt strategies that meet the unique demands of their properties.

1.11.5 Market Dynamics for Rental Property Managers

Rental property managers need a thorough understanding of local rental markets, including trends in rental rates, occupancy levels, and tenant preferences. Key aspects of market dynamics for rental properties include:

- *Rental Rates and Pricing Strategy:* Rental property managers must analyze market data to set competitive rental rates that attract quality tenants while maximizing income. Understanding the supply and demand for rental units in the area, as well as the rental rates of comparable properties, is crucial for effective pricing.
- *Tenant Preferences and Amenities:* Managers must stay updated on what amenities and features are in demand, such as in-unit washers and dryers, modern finishes, and technology-driven services like high-speed Internet or smart home systems. Adjusting offerings based on these trends can enhance tenant retention and justify higher rental rates.
- *Economic and Demographic Trends:* Rental managers should track local economic indicators, such as job growth, population changes, and the development of new housing projects, as these factors directly impact tenant demand and rental property profitability.

1.11.6 Market Dynamics for Community Association Managers

Community association managers, on the other hand, must focus on maintaining the long-term value of the community and managing the interests of resident owners. Key aspects of market dynamics for community associations include:

- *Property Value Trends:* Understanding how the broader real estate market impacts home values within the community is essential. Managers should be aware of local sales data, the quality of nearby developments, and the availability of amenities that could affect property values.
- *Homeowner Expectations and Preferences:* Managers should stay attuned to resident expectations for community upkeep, amenities, and services. Understanding these preferences helps in planning capital improvements, setting realistic budgets, and maintaining a positive community image.
- *Regulatory and Legislative Changes:* Community association managers need to be aware of any changes in local or state regulations that could affect property governance or maintenance standards, as these changes can have a direct impact on budgeting and community planning.

By distinguishing these market dynamics, property managers in both rental and community association settings can implement strategies that are responsive to their unique market conditions, thereby ensuring the success and sustainability of the properties they manage.

1.12 The Evolution of Residential Property Management

The field of residential property management has evolved significantly over the years. Traditionally, property management was a hands-on, labor-intensive job that required property managers to be physically present on-site. However, advancements in technology have transformed the industry, making it more efficient and streamlined.

1.12.1 Technology and Property Management

The advent of property management software has revolutionized the way property managers operate. These software solutions offer a range of features, including tenant and new owner screening, rent collection, maintenance tracking, and financial reporting. By automating many of the routine tasks, property management software allows property managers to focus on more strategic aspects of their job.

1.12.2 Online Marketing and Tenant Acquisition

For rental communities, the internet has also changed the way properties are marketed and tenants are acquired. Online listing platforms and social media have become essential tools for reaching potential tenants. Property managers can now advertise vacancies, conduct virtual tours, and even complete lease agreements online. This not only broadens the pool of potential tenants but also makes the leasing process more convenient and efficient.

1.12.3 Improving Communication

Digital communication tools, including email, tenant portals, and mobile apps, facilitate better communication between property managers, tenants, and maintenance staff. These tools ensure timely responses to inquiries, efficient dissemination of information, and a centralized platform for all communication records.

1.12.4 Enhancing Security

Technology plays a crucial role in enhancing security through advanced access control systems, surveillance cameras, and alarm systems. These technologies help monitor property premises, control access, and respond promptly to security breaches, ensuring a safer environment for tenants.

1.13 Summary

Understanding residential property management is the foundation for successfully managing properties. It involves a combination of administrative, financial, maintenance, and tenant relations tasks, all aimed at ensuring the optimal performance of the property. By mastering these areas and staying informed about industry trends and advancements, property managers can provide exceptional service to property owners and tenants alike.

The role of professional property management trade organizations, such as CAI, IREM, NARPM, BOMA, and NAA, cannot be overstated. These organizations offer essential resources, certifications, and networking opportunities that elevate the standards and practices within the industry. Their contributions ensure that property managers are well-equipped to handle the challenges of managing various types of properties, from single-family homes to large multifamily complexes.

The economics of property management underscores the importance of effective cost management, revenue generation, and value enhancement. Property managers play a crucial role in maintaining and increasing the financial performance and market value of properties through strategic planning, efficient operations, and a deep understanding of market dynamics.

In summary, residential property management is a multifaceted profession that requires a blend of technical knowledge, interpersonal skills, and strategic thinking. By mastering the principles outlined in this chapter, property managers can effectively enhance property value, ensure resident satisfaction, and navigate the complexities of the real estate market. As we move forward in this book, we will continue to build on these foundational concepts, exploring more specific aspects of property management and their practical applications.

1.13.1 Looking Forward

The following chapters will delve deeper into the specifics of managing different types of residential properties, including single-family residences, timeshares, manufactured home parks, and multifamily residences. Each property type has its unique challenges and requirements, and understanding these nuances is key to effective property management. Whether you are a seasoned property manager or new to the field, this book will provide valuable insights and practical advice to help you succeed in residential property management.

1.14 Review Questions

1. *What is one of the primary objectives of residential property management?*
   (A) Minimizing tenant interactions
   (B) Ensuring the optimal performance of the property
   (C) Reducing property taxes
   (D) Increasing property insurance costs
2. *Why is it important for property managers to understand local landlord-tenant laws?*
   (A) To minimize their workload
   (B) To prevent legal disputes and ensure smooth operations
   (C) To increase rent arbitrarily
   (D) To avoid paying property taxes
3. *Which period saw a significant housing boom in the United States that expanded the role of property managers?*
   (A) The Great Depression
   (B) Post-World War II
   (C) The Industrial Revolution
   (D) The Civil Rights Movement
4. *What does the Institute of Real Estate Management (IREM) offer to property managers?*
   (A) Legal representation
   (B) Educational programs and certifications
   (C) Property insurance
   (D) Landscaping services

5. *How do property managers primarily generate revenue?*
   (A) Through property taxes
   (B) By selling property
   (C) Through management fees and leasing commissions
   (D) By offering legal advice
6. *What is the significance of professional property management trade organizations?*
   (A) They provide landscaping services
   (B) They offer essential resources, certifications, and networking opportunities
   (C) They manage tenant disputes directly
   (D) They increase property taxes
7. *Why is understanding market dynamics crucial for rental property managers?*
   (A) To avoid tenant complaints
   (B) To set competitive rental rates and develop effective marketing strategies
   (C) To reduce property insurance costs
   (D) To simplify legal compliance
8. *What is the role of the National Association of Residential Property Managers (NARPMs)?*
   (A) Managing commercial properties
   (B) Representing single-family residential property managers
   (C) Offering property tax reductions
   (D) Providing construction services
9. *What is the major benefit of effective cost management in property management?*
   (A) Increasing tenant turnover
   (B) Minimizing expenses while ensuring property upkeep
   (C) Ignoring maintenance needs
   (D) Arbitrarily increasing rents
10. *Why is the growth of professional property management important in the modern real estate market?*
    (A) It reduces the need for tenant interactions
    (B) It increases the complexity and professionalism required to manage properties effectively
    (C) It simplifies the property sale process
    (D) It decreases the need for property maintenance
11. *Which of the following characteristics is typically associated with the Expansion phase of the business cycle?*
    (A) High unemployment rates and reduced consumer spending
    (B) Declining property values and increased foreclosures
    (C) Increased consumer confidence and rising property values
    (D) Tightened lending criteria and distressed properties
12. *During which phase of the business cycle are property managers most likely to experience challenges related to managing distressed properties and dealing with delinquent residents?*
    (A) Expansion
    (B) Recession

(C) Revival
(D) Contraction

13. *Which of the following strategies should rental property managers prioritize during a Recession to maintain occupancy rates?*
    (A) Increase rental rates to maximize revenue
    (B) Offer rental concessions and focus on resident retention
    (C) Expand construction projects to meet growing demand
    (D) Reduce marketing efforts to cut costs
14. *What typically occurs during the Revival (or Recovery) phase of the business cycle?*
    (A) Property values continue to decline, and financial institutions tighten lending criteria
    (B) Employment rates improve, consumer confidence returns, and housing demand increases
    (C) The economy contracts further, leading to higher vacancy rates
    (D) Construction activity slows down, and rental rates decrease
15. *Which of the following is a key indicator that the economy is in the Contraction phase of the business cycle?*
    (A) Rising incomes and strong consumer spending
    (B) Declining property values and reduced construction activity
    (C) Increased demand for housing and high occupancy rates
    (D) Rapid job growth and increasing investment in real estate

Managing Single-Family Homes 2

2.1 Learning Objectives

By the end of this unit, students will be able to:

- *Understand Key Responsibilities and Challenges*
  - Identify the primary responsibilities of managing single-family homes, such as property maintenance, tenant relations, and financial management.
  - Discuss the unique challenges of managing scattered-site properties and maintaining owner-tenant satisfaction.
- *Draft and Manage Effective Lease Agreements*
  - Outline essential elements of a single-family home lease agreement, including lease terms, rent payment policies, maintenance obligations, and termination clauses.
  - Recognize the key differences between single-family home leases and multifamily or apartment leases.
- *Implement Marketing and Tenant Acquisition Strategies*
  - Develop targeted marketing strategies to attract quality tenants, focusing on property-specific features and local market trends.
  - Utilize screening criteria to select reliable tenants while adhering to fair housing laws and regulations.
- *Navigate Legal and Risk Management Issues*
  - Understand the importance of complying with landlord-tenant laws, fair housing regulations, and other legal requirements specific to single-family home management.
  - Describe risk management strategies, including proper insurance coverage and handling security deposits legally.

By mastering these objectives, students will gain a comprehensive understanding of the complexities involved in managing single-family rental properties and be

D. A. Vaughn, *Essentials of Residential Property Management*, Springer Texts in Business and Economics, https://doi.org/10.1007/978-3-031-92329-6_2

equipped to optimize operations, maintain compliance, and enhance the overall management process.

2.2 Key Terms

By the end of this chapter, students will be familiar with the following key terms:

Background Check
Credit Check
Compliance
Emergency Repairs
Eviction
Fair Housing Act (FHA)
Landlord-Tenant Law
Lease Agreement
Liability Insurance
Maintenance Plan
Preventive Maintenance
Property Maintenance
Rental Market Analysis
Repair Request
Safety Protocols
Security Deposit
Tenant Relations
Tenant Screening

2.3 Overview

This unit provides a comprehensive exploration of the key elements involved in managing single-family homes, focusing on day-to-day operations, maintenance, repairs, and legal considerations. It outlines the critical skills and strategies property managers need to effectively oversee single-family homes, addressing both the practical and legal aspects of their role.

Managing single-family homes requires property managers to handle diverse responsibilities, ranging from tenant relations and rent collection to property inspections and lease administration. A well-rounded approach is necessary to meet both the expectations of the property owner and the needs of tenants. A primary focus is ensuring the property is maintained in excellent condition to preserve its value and enhance tenant satisfaction. These chapters delve into rental market analysis, tenant relations, and the management contract, providing a foundation for the successful operation of single-family rental properties.

Maintenance and repairs are another key aspect covered in these chapters. Property managers are responsible for ensuring that the property remains safe, functional, and aesthetically appealing. This requires the ability to prioritize maintenance tasks, respond quickly to repair requests, and coordinate routine inspections. Property managers must also be well-versed in preventive maintenance, which helps reduce long-term repair costs and extends the life of critical systems within the home. The importance of setting clear maintenance expectations with tenants and working with reliable contractors is also highlighted.

Finally, the legal aspects of managing single-family homes are explored in detail. Property managers must navigate a complex landscape of legal requirements, including landlord-tenant laws, fair housing regulations, and lease agreements. Understanding these legal obligations is crucial to minimizing liability and protecting the interests of both the owner and tenants. These chapters emphasize the importance of having well-drafted management contracts, adhering to legal requirements, and ensuring compliance with local and state regulations.

2.4 Managing Single-Family Homes

2.4.1 The Management Contract for Single-Family Homes

In residential property management, the management contract is a legally binding agreement that outlines the responsibilities and expectations between the property owner and the property manager. For single-family homes, this contract plays a critical role in defining the scope of services, establishing the relationship between the two parties, and ensuring the property is managed efficiently. The management contract not only helps protect both parties legally but also sets the foundation for how the property will be maintained, rented, and handled over the course of the agreement. This section will delve into the purpose of the contract and highlight key elements specific to the management of single-family homes.

Purpose of the Contract

The primary purpose of the management contract for single-family homes is to clearly outline the roles and responsibilities of the property manager and the property owner. It serves as a framework to ensure the property is operated in accordance with the owner's goals and that legal obligations are met. For single-family homes, this often includes maintaining the property in good condition, ensuring rent is collected promptly, and securing high-quality tenants who will preserve the property's value.

Additionally, the management contract provides protection for both parties. Property owners benefit from knowing that their investment will be handled professionally, while property managers gain clarity on what is expected of them, reducing the risk of disputes or misunderstandings. The contract also helps define the financial arrangement, detailing how and when the property manager will be compensated. This is particularly important for single-family homes, where managing one property at a time might involve less volume but often requires a highly personalized approach.

Key Elements of the Management Contract

Scope of Services: For single-family homes, the management contract will specify the exact services the property manager will provide. This may include *tenant screening* and selection, rent collection, maintenance coordination, property inspections, and marketing the property for rent. The scope of services should be tailored to the needs of the owner and the specific nature of the property. For example, in a single-family home, property managers are often tasked with maintaining curb appeal, handling landscaping services, and conducting regular inspections of home systems such as HVAC and plumbing to ensure long-term functionality.

Term of the Agreement: The term of the management contract defines how long the agreement will be in effect. This could range from 1 year to an open-ended agreement, depending on the preferences of the owner and the manager. Some contracts for single-family homes include provisions for early termination, allowing either party to end the agreement with proper notice.

Fees and Compensation: The compensation structure for managing single-family homes is typically a percentage of the monthly rent, but flat-rate agreements can also be used. The contract will clearly state how and when the property manager will be paid. Other fees, such as leasing fees, renewal fees, or fees for coordinating major repairs, should also be detailed in this section. Single-family home management contracts might also specify reimbursement policies for expenses incurred while managing the property, such as marketing or maintenance expenses.

Maintenance and Repairs: In single-family home management, the manager is often responsible for coordinating routine and *emergency repairs*. The contract will define how maintenance requests will be handled and outline any limits on spending authority. For example, it may state that the property manager can authorize repairs under a certain dollar amount without prior approval, while repairs exceeding that amount will require the owner's consent. This ensures that the home is well-maintained while keeping the owner informed and involved in major decisions.

Owner Responsibilities: While the property manager handles most day-to-day operations, the management contract will also outline the owner's responsibilities. For single-family homes, this might include ensuring that the property complies with all legal requirements, such as zoning laws or health and safety regulations, and providing funds for necessary repairs or renovations. Owners may also be required to maintain adequate insurance coverage, including liability and property damage insurance.

Tenant Management: For single-family homes, tenant relations are particularly important. The management contract should outline how tenants will be screened and what qualifications are necessary for lease approval, ensuring that tenants who respect the property are selected. Additionally, the contract will include provisions on lease enforcement, tenant disputes, and eviction procedures. Given the personal nature of single-family home rentals, where properties are often in residential neighborhoods, tenant quality and the enforcement of lease terms are critical to maintaining property value.

Legal Compliance and Liability: Both the property manager and the owner must ensure compliance with local, state, and federal laws, including fair housing regulations, landlord-tenant laws, and property maintenance codes. The management contract will specify that the property manager is responsible for keeping the property in compliance, while the owner must provide the resources needed for legal obligations. Liability clauses may also be included to protect both parties from damages arising from the other's negligence or failure to fulfill the contract.

Reporting and Financial Accountability: Accurate financial reporting is essential in single-family home management. The management contract will outline how often the property manager will provide the owner with financial reports, such as income statements, expense reports, and a breakdown of repair costs. Additionally, the contract may require that rent payments be transferred to the owner within a specified timeframe and that all financial records be kept up to date for auditing purposes.

2.5 Responsibilities and Challenges

Managing single-family homes presents a unique set of responsibilities and challenges that distinguish it from managing multifamily units or large apartment complexes. Property managers overseeing single-family homes must be adept at addressing the specific needs of individual homeowners while maintaining a high level of service to attract and retain quality tenants. Below are the key responsibilities and challenges property managers face in this sector.

2.5.1 Responsibilities

Tenant Relations and Communication: One of the primary responsibilities of managing single-family homes is building and maintaining strong relationships with tenants. Property managers must address tenant concerns promptly, ensuring that issues like maintenance requests, disputes, or lease renewals are handled smoothly. The personal nature of single-family home rentals often means tenants expect more individualized attention than they might in larger, multifamily properties.

Property Maintenance and Inspections: Ensuring that single-family homes are well-maintained is critical to preserving the property's value and keeping tenants satisfied. Property managers are responsible for coordinating regular maintenance, such as lawn care, HVAC servicing, and seasonal upkeep. Routine inspections are also essential to identify any potential problems before they escalate, ensuring that plumbing, roofing, and electrical systems are functioning properly. Preventive maintenance can help avoid costly repairs down the line, and property managers must be diligent in scheduling these tasks.

Marketing and Tenant Placement: Attracting quality tenants for single-family homes requires strategic marketing efforts, such as creating compelling listings, using online rental platforms, and ensuring the property is presented in its best light. Property managers are responsible for handling the entire tenant placement process, including screening applicants, conducting background and *credit checks*, and ensuring that tenants meet the owner's criteria. Given the personal and often higher-value nature of single-family homes, finding responsible tenants is crucial.

Rent Collection and Financial Reporting: A critical responsibility of single-family home management is ensuring that rent is collected on time and that the property's finances are managed effectively. Property managers must establish efficient rent collection processes, handle any late payments, and maintain accurate financial records for owners. They are also responsible for providing detailed financial reports, including income and expense statements, to help owners understand the financial health of their investment.

2.5.2 Challenges

Customization and Personalization: Single-family home tenants often expect a more personalized level of service compared to those in larger apartment buildings. This can be time-consuming for property managers, as they may need to address specific tenant requests, such as coordinating specific maintenance services, or accommodating more flexible lease terms. Property managers must balance this level of service with maintaining operational efficiency.

Higher Maintenance Costs and Expectations: Unlike multifamily properties where maintenance can be more centralized, single-family homes often require more individualized attention, which can lead to higher maintenance costs. Property managers must be skilled in coordinating services like landscaping, pest control, and snow removal, all while managing tenants' high expectations for property upkeep. Additionally, single-family homes are more likely to experience wear and tear over time, requiring proactive measures to avoid major repairs.

Vacancy and Turnover: Vacancy in a single-family home can be particularly challenging since there is only one source of rental income. Property managers must work quickly to fill vacancies when they occur, but it can take longer to find new tenants for single-family homes compared to apartments, where turnover is more frequent. Vacancy periods can significantly impact the property's profitability, so property managers need to ensure marketing efforts and tenant placements are highly efficient.

Legal and Compliance Requirements: Managing single-family homes requires a thorough understanding of local landlord-tenant laws, fair housing regulations, and lease agreements. Property managers must stay updated on legal changes to ensure compliance, which can vary based on the property's location. Additionally, ensuring that the property adheres to zoning laws, building codes, and safety standards is crucial in avoiding legal liabilities.

Managing single-family homes requires a delicate balance of personalized tenant care, meticulous property maintenance, and strategic financial management, all while navigating challenges unique to this type of property. Property managers must be adaptable, resourceful, and proactive to ensure the long-term success of single-family home investments.

2.6 Rental Market Analysis

Understanding the Market: Conducting a thorough rental market analysis is essential for setting competitive rental rates, attracting quality tenants, and making informed management decisions. Key elements of rental market analysis include:

Comparative Market Analysis (CMA): Research current rental rates for similar properties in the area. This helps ensure your rates are competitive while maximizing revenue.

Occupancy Rates: Monitor occupancy rates in the local market to gauge demand. High occupancy rates may indicate a strong rental market, while low rates could signal oversupply.

Demographics: Analyze the demographics of the area to understand the needs and preferences of potential tenants. Factors such as age, income levels, and family size can influence marketing strategies and property amenities.

Trends and Forecasts: Stay informed about market trends and forecasts. Economic conditions, new construction, and changes in local regulations can impact the rental market.

Adjusting Strategies: Based on your market analysis, adjust your marketing, pricing, and property management strategies to align with market conditions and tenant expectations. This proactive approach can help maintain high occupancy rates and tenant satisfaction.

2.7 Understanding the Tenant Demographics

Understanding tenant demographics is crucial for successfully managing single-family homes. Unlike multifamily housing or apartment complexes, the tenant profile for single-family homes tends to be more specific and varies based on several factors, including location, size, and amenities offered by the property. By understanding these demographics, property managers can tailor their strategies to attract and retain tenants, ensuring the long-term success of the property.

2.7.1 Common Tenant Profiles

Families with Children: One of the most common tenant groups in single-family homes is families, particularly those with children. These tenants often seek the space, privacy, and neighborhood amenities that single-family homes typically offer, such as proximity to good schools, parks, and family-friendly communities. Single-family homes are attractive to families because they often feature more living space, backyards, and garages, making them ideal for raising children. Additionally, parents are likely to prioritize stability, meaning families may be inclined to sign longer leases and establish roots in the community.

Young Professionals and Couples: Another growing demographic for single-family homes is young professionals and couples, particularly those who may be transitioning from apartment living but are not yet ready to purchase a home. These tenants typically look for well-maintained homes in desirable locations, often near city centers or employment hubs. Single-family homes offer them more space and privacy compared to apartments, and they may value features such as home offices, modern appliances, and proximity to entertainment, shopping, and dining options. Young professionals and couples might also view renting a single-family home as a stepping stone toward homeownership, making them highly motivated to maintain the property well.

Empty Nesters and Retirees: Empty nesters and retirees are another key tenant demographic for single-family homes. These individuals are often downsizing from larger homes but still want the space and independence that single-family homes provide. They typically seek quiet neighborhoods, easy access to healthcare facilities, and homes that require minimal upkeep. Single-story homes with accessible features, such as ramps or grab bars in bathrooms, may be particularly appealing to retirees. Property managers may find that this demographic values long-term stability, with a preference for multi-year leases.

Long-Term Renters: Long-term renters, those who prefer the flexibility of renting over homeownership, are also a significant demographic for single-family homes. These tenants may have financial reasons for renting or may value the mobility that renting offers. They typically seek properties in stable, quiet neighborhoods and prioritize homes that offer comfort and convenience without the burdens of homeownership, such as paying for major repairs or being locked into a mortgage.

2.7.2 Tailoring Property Management to Tenant Demographics

Each of these demographics comes with its own set of needs and expectations, which property managers must address to attract and retain quality tenants. For families, proximity to good schools and safe neighborhoods is a top priority, so property managers should highlight these aspects when marketing single-family homes. Young professionals and couples may be drawn to homes with modern amenities and easy access to urban areas, while empty nesters and retirees may value homes with low maintenance requirements and accessibility features. Long-term renters typically value stability and convenience, so offering flexible leasing options and efficient maintenance services can make a property more appealing to this group.

2.8 Marketing and Tenant Acquisition

Marketing and tenant acquisition for single-family homes require a tailored approach that addresses the specific needs of prospective tenants and highlights the unique features of the property. Unlike multifamily properties, where apartments may share common amenities, single-family homes offer a distinct living experience, often attracting tenants seeking more privacy, space, and a residential neighborhood setting. Understanding these dynamics is crucial for successfully marketing single-family homes and securing high-quality tenants.

2.8.1 Highlighting the Unique Features of Single-Family Homes

Single-family homes often appeal to tenants who prioritize privacy, outdoor space, and a more residential lifestyle. As a result, marketing efforts should focus on showcasing features that differentiate single-family homes from apartments or condominiums. This could include:

- *Yard and Outdoor Space:* Emphasize the size and appeal of the yard, whether it's a fenced-in backyard, patio, or garden space. Outdoor areas are especially attractive to families with children, tenants with pets, or those who enjoy outdoor activities.
- *Garage and Parking:* Many single-family homes come with garages or dedicated parking spaces, which are a significant draw for tenants who value secure, convenient parking. Highlighting ample parking space can make the property more attractive, especially in areas where parking is limited.
- *Room to Grow:* Single-family homes often feature multiple bedrooms, larger kitchens, and living spaces that are more suitable for growing families or professionals seeking extra space for home offices.
- *Privacy and Independence:* Single-family homes generally offer more privacy than apartments or townhouses, with no shared walls or communal spaces. This

feature should be emphasized for tenants who value a quieter, more independent living environment.

2.8.2 Targeting the Right Demographics

When marketing a single-family home, understanding the likely tenant demographics is essential for targeting the right audience. As discussed earlier in this section, single-family homes often attract:

- *Families with Children:* Families seek homes in residential neighborhoods with access to good schools, parks, and family-friendly amenities. Marketing efforts should include proximity to schools, playgrounds, and safe walking paths, as these are critical factors for families.
- *Young Professionals and Couples:* For couples or professionals looking for more space but not yet ready to buy, single-family homes offer flexibility and room for a home office or entertainment space. Highlighting easy access to commuter routes, nearby shops, restaurants, and entertainment venues can attract this demographic.
- *Empty Nesters and Retirees:* Empty nesters or retirees often seek smaller, single-story homes with less upkeep but still want the privacy and independence that single-family homes provide. Marketing that focuses on ease of maintenance, single-level living, and quiet neighborhoods can appeal to this group.

2.8.3 Creating a Strong Online Presence

Most potential tenants start their property search online, so having a strong online presence is crucial for marketing single-family homes. Property managers should ensure that the property is listed on multiple rental platforms, such as Zillow, Realtor.com, and Trulia, to reach a broad audience. Listings should include high-quality photos of the home, detailed descriptions of its features, and information about the surrounding neighborhood.

In addition to traditional listing sites, social media platforms such as Facebook and Instagram can be used to showcase the property. Posting virtual tours, home walkthroughs, or engaging with local community pages can help generate interest and reach a wider audience.

2.8.4 Pricing and Incentives

Accurately pricing the rental is essential for attracting quality tenants. Property managers should conduct a market analysis to determine competitive pricing based on the location, size, and features of the home. Offering move-in incentives, such as discounted rent for the first month or waiving certain fees, can make the property more attractive to potential tenants, especially in a competitive market.

2.8.5 Screening and Acquiring Quality Tenants

Once marketing efforts have generated interest, screening prospective tenants is a critical part of the tenant acquisition process. For single-family homes, property managers should prioritize tenant reliability and the ability to care for the property. This means conducting the following:

Background Checks: Conducting background checks helps verify the tenant's rental history, criminal record, and credit score. This information can provide insights into the tenant's reliability and ability to pay rent on time.

Reference Checks: Contacting previous landlords and employers can provide valuable information about the tenant's behavior and reliability.

Income Verification: Ensuring that the tenant has a stable income that is sufficient to cover the rent is essential. This can be done by requesting pay stubs, tax returns, or employment verification letters.

Given the more personalized nature of single-family rentals, choosing tenants who align with the property owner's expectations and will maintain the home well is especially important.

2.8.6 Lease Agreements

Drafting clear and comprehensive lease agreements helps protect both the property owner and the tenant. Lease agreements should outline the terms of tenancy, rent payment procedures, maintenance responsibilities, and rules for property use.

2.8.7 State Requirements

Most states require that lease agreements be in writing to be enforceable. A written lease agreement clearly delineates the rights and responsibilities of both the landlord and the tenant, providing legal protection in case of disputes. Written leases are crucial for ensuring transparency and preventing misunderstandings.

2.9 Managing Tenant Relations

Managing tenant relations in single-family homes requires a more personalized and attentive approach compared to multifamily or apartment settings. In single-family homes, tenants often have higher expectations for individualized service, given the nature of their living arrangements, which typically offer more privacy and space. Building strong tenant relations is crucial for ensuring tenant satisfaction, fostering long-term leases, and maintaining the property's value. Successful tenant relations in single-family homes revolve around effective communication, proactive problem-solving, and creating a positive living experience.

2.9.1 Personalized Communication

One of the key aspects of managing tenant relations in single-family homes is maintaining personalized communication. Since property managers are usually dealing with fewer tenants compared to an apartment complex, they can take a more hands-on approach when interacting with tenants. This means being responsive to tenant inquiries, addressing concerns quickly, and maintaining open lines of communication. Tenants in single-family homes tend to expect more frequent and direct communication from property managers, especially when it comes to maintenance issues, lease renewals, and updates about the property.

Effective tenant relations also involve clear and transparent communication about expectations. For instance, outlining responsibilities for lawn care, minor repairs, and other property upkeep tasks helps prevent misunderstandings. Clear communication regarding policies on rent payments, late fees, and property access for inspections or repairs helps establish a positive relationship based on mutual respect and understanding.

2.9.2 Proactive Problem-Solving

Tenants in single-family homes expect quick resolution of maintenance requests and other property-related issues. Property managers should be proactive in addressing potential problems, such as conducting regular inspections and ensuring preventive maintenance tasks are completed. When a tenant submits a maintenance request, prompt action is essential to maintain trust and satisfaction. Single-family home tenants often have a strong sense of ownership over their space, even though they are renters, and delays in addressing repairs or concerns can quickly sour the relationship.

Additionally, property managers should offer solutions that cater to the unique needs of single-family home tenants. For example, providing flexibility in lease terms, offering support for minor home customization (such as painting), or accommodating pet-friendly policies can improve tenant relations and increase tenant retention.

2.9.3 Encouraging Long-Term Tenancy

Long-term tenancy is a key goal for property managers overseeing single-family homes, as vacancies can be costly and difficult to fill. Fostering a positive relationship with tenants is crucial to encouraging lease renewals and long-term stays. Property managers can achieve this by regularly checking in with tenants, ensuring their needs are met, and addressing any potential issues before they escalate. Offering incentives for lease renewals, such as discounted rent or minor home upgrades, can also help encourage tenants to stay for longer periods.

2.9.4 Respecting Tenant Privacy

In single-family homes, tenants often expect a greater level of privacy compared to multifamily units. Property managers must respect this by minimizing unnecessary visits to the property and clearly communicating the reasons for any required access. Scheduling property inspections or maintenance at convenient times for tenants and providing adequate notice for entry is crucial to maintaining a good relationship. Respecting tenant privacy fosters trust and demonstrates professionalism, which can lead to higher tenant satisfaction and loyalty.

2.9.5 Conflict Resolution

When conflicts arise, such as disputes over maintenance responsibilities or noise complaints from neighbors, property managers must act swiftly and fairly to resolve the situation. Addressing conflicts in a timely and transparent manner helps prevent escalation and demonstrates a commitment to tenant well-being. By being an approachable and solution-oriented manager, tenants are more likely to feel supported and valued.

By understanding the rental market and focusing on tenant relations, property managers can make informed decisions, attract quality tenants, and maintain a positive living environment that encourages long-term occupancy and satisfaction.

2.9.6 Personalized Attention

Unlike multifamily residences, where issues can be addressed on a larger scale, single-family homes often require more personalized attention. Each home is unique, with its own layout, systems, and potential issues. Property managers must be proactive in conducting regular inspections and addressing maintenance needs promptly to keep the property in good condition and ensure tenant satisfaction.

2.10 Maintenance and Repairs

2.10.1 Routine and Emergency Maintenance

Regular maintenance and prompt repairs are critical for preserving the value of single-family rental properties and ensuring resident satisfaction. Effective property management involves both routine maintenance to prevent issues and emergency repairs to address unexpected problems that could compromise the property's safety, functionality, or habitability. Unlike multifamily properties, where maintenance responsibilities are often shared across teams or centralized systems, single-family property managers must coordinate individualized maintenance plans for each property, often with less on-site oversight.

Routine Maintenance

Routine maintenance is the foundation of proactive property management. A well-structured maintenance schedule helps identify potential issues early, reducing long-term costs and minimizing disruptions for residents. This proactive approach can prevent small, manageable issues from escalating into major, costly repairs. Routine maintenance responsibilities for single-family properties include:

- *Interior Inspections:* Regular inspections of the property's interior help identify early signs of wear and tear, plumbing leaks, electrical issues, pest infestations, and HVAC performance problems. Property managers should conduct these inspections at least once or twice a year, depending on the property's age and condition.
- *Exterior Inspections:* The exterior of the property should be regularly inspected for roofing damage, gutter blockages, siding deterioration, foundation cracks, and drainage issues. Ensuring proper grading around the home can prevent water intrusion, which is a common cause of structural damage.
- *Appliance Checks:* Routine checks of appliances such as water heaters, dishwashers, stoves, and washers/dryers help ensure they are functioning properly and efficiently. Preventative servicing can extend the life of these appliances and reduce repair costs over time.
- *Plumbing and Electrical Systems:* Regular inspections of plumbing and electrical systems are essential to prevent leaks, clogs, electrical shorts, or fire hazards. Look for signs of corrosion, water stains, or outdated wiring that may need upgrading.

Property managers should maintain detailed records of all inspections, including photos and notes, to track recurring issues and document the property's condition over time.

Seasonal Maintenance

Seasonal maintenance plays a key role in protecting single-family homes from weather-related damage and ensuring that systems operate efficiently throughout the year. Each season presents unique challenges that require specific maintenance tasks:

- *Spring:* Inspect the roof for winter damage, clean gutters and downspouts, service HVAC systems in preparation for summer, inspect irrigation systems, and address any landscaping needs.
- *Summer:* Focus on outdoor maintenance, such as lawn care, pest control, inspecting fences, sealing driveways, and checking for signs of water leaks or mold in humid conditions.
- *Fall:* Prepare for colder weather by cleaning gutters, checking for drafts around windows and doors, inspecting the furnace or heating system, servicing chimneys, and winterizing irrigation systems.
- *Winter:* Ensure that pipes are insulated to prevent freezing, check for ice dams on the roof, and confirm that heating systems are operating efficiently. Snow and ice removal may be necessary, depending on the region.

Proactive seasonal maintenance reduces the likelihood of costly emergency repairs, extends the lifespan of property components, and ensures that the home remains comfortable and safe for residents year-round

Emergency Repairs

No matter how thorough the routine maintenance plan is, emergency repairs are inevitable in property management. Emergencies can arise from natural disasters, mechanical failures, or sudden accidents that require immediate attention to prevent property damage, health hazards, or safety risks. Common emergency situations include:

- *Plumbing Emergencies:* Burst pipes, major leaks, or sewer backups can cause significant water damage if not addressed immediately.
- *Electrical Hazards:* Exposed wiring, electrical outages, or the smell of burning can signal dangerous electrical issues that pose fire risks.
- *HVAC Failures:* Loss of heating during extreme cold or air conditioning during severe heat can create unsafe living conditions, especially for vulnerable populations.
- *Structural Damage:* Roof collapses, broken windows, or falling trees during storms require urgent attention to secure the property.
- *Security Issues:* Broken doors, locks, or windows that compromise the property's security may also warrant emergency repairs.

Property managers should have an emergency response plan in place, including:

- A list of reliable, licensed contractors and service providers who can respond quickly to urgent situations.
- A 24/7 emergency contact number for residents to report issues promptly.

- Clear communication protocols to keep residents informed about the status of repairs and timelines for resolution.

It's also important to differentiate between what constitutes an emergency versus an urgent repair. For example, a dripping faucet may be inconvenient but doesn't pose the same immediate risk as a burst pipe flooding the home. Setting clear guidelines helps manage resident expectations and prioritize responses appropriately.

2.11 Legal Aspects of Single-Family Property Management

Managing single-family homes involves navigating a variety of legal obligations that ensure compliance with local, state, and federal laws. Two of the most critical legal areas property managers must address are landlord-tenant laws and fair housing laws. These regulations are designed to protect both property owners and tenants, while ensuring that property managers operate within legal frameworks. Understanding and adhering to these laws is essential for maintaining a successful, legally compliant property management practice.

2.11.1 Landlord-Tenant Laws for Single-Family Homes

Landlord-tenant laws govern the relationship between property owners (landlords) and tenants. These laws vary by state and locality, but they generally cover key issues such as rent collection, security deposits, maintenance responsibilities, tenant rights, and eviction procedures. For single-family homes, which are often managed with a more personalized approach than multifamily properties, adhering to landlord-tenant laws is critical to ensuring a fair and transparent rental process.

Rent Collection and Security Deposits: Landlord-tenant laws typically regulate the collection of rent and security deposits. Property managers of single-family homes must follow legal guidelines for setting rent, applying late fees, and managing security deposits. In most states, there are specific limits on the amount that can be collected for security deposits, and there are laws governing how and when these deposits must be returned after the lease ends. Failure to comply with these regulations can result in penalties or legal disputes.

Maintenance and Habitability: A key responsibility for property managers is ensuring that the single-family home meets local habitability standards. Landlord-tenant laws often outline the landlord's obligation to provide a safe, livable environment for tenants. This includes maintaining critical systems such as plumbing, heating, and electricity, and ensuring the home is free from hazards. Property managers must also respond to *repair requests* within a reasonable time frame, as failure to do so could result in tenant claims of negligence or violations of habitability laws.

Eviction Procedures: Evictions must be handled according to strict legal procedures, including proper notice and just cause for eviction. For example, tenants who fail to pay rent or violate the terms of the lease can be evicted, but property managers must follow state-specific eviction processes, such as providing written notice and giving the tenant a chance to remedy the situation before proceeding with legal action. Improper evictions can lead to costly legal disputes and damage the property's reputation.

Fair Housing Laws for Single-Family Homes

Fair housing laws, governed primarily by the federal Fair Housing Act, prohibit discrimination in housing practices based on protected classes, including race, color, religion, sex, national origin, disability, and familial status. These laws apply to all types of rental properties, including single-family homes, and it is crucial that property managers understand and adhere to them.

Nondiscrimination in Advertising and Tenant Selection: Property managers must ensure that all marketing and advertising for single-family homes complies with fair housing laws. For example, advertisements should not include language that discriminates against any protected class, such as excluding families with children or individuals with disabilities. Additionally, during the tenant screening process, property managers must apply the same criteria to all applicants. This includes conducting background checks, credit checks, and income verifications without bias.

Reasonable Accommodations for Disabled Tenants: Under the Fair Housing Act, property managers of single-family homes must make reasonable accommodations for tenants with disabilities. This could include allowing service animals in properties that otherwise have a no-pet policy, or permitting tenants to make reasonable modifications to the property (such as installing grab bars or ramps) to accommodate their disability. Property managers must ensure that they handle requests for accommodations fairly and comply with legal requirements.

Familial Status Protection: Single-family homes are often marketed to families, but property managers must be careful not to discriminate based on familial status. For instance, property managers cannot refuse to rent to families with children or impose different lease terms, such as higher security deposits, because the tenants have children. Doing so would be a violation of fair housing laws and could result in legal penalties.

2.11.2 Lease Agreements and Compliance

Basic Elements of a Single-Family Home Lease Agreement

A lease agreement for a single-family home is a legally binding contract that outlines the rights and responsibilities of both the property owner (landlord) and the tenant. Given the unique characteristics of single-family homes—such as increased space, privacy, and distinct property features—lease agreements for these properties often differ from those used for multifamily residences. Ensuring that the lease agreement is comprehensive and in compliance with local, state, and federal laws is critical to protecting both parties and ensuring a smooth rental experience.

Key Elements of a Single-Family Home Lease Agreement

Property Description: A single-family home lease agreement should include a detailed description of the property being rented. This includes the home's address, any additional structures (such as garages, sheds, or guest houses), and amenities (such as appliances, swimming pools, or outdoor features). For single-family homes, the lease should also clarify whether the tenant has exclusive use of certain areas, such as the yard, driveway, or parking spaces.

Rent and Payment Terms: The lease must specify the rent amount, due date, and acceptable payment methods. For single-family homes, rent is typically higher than for apartments, so the lease should be clear about any additional charges, such as fees for late payments or returned checks. The lease should also detail how utilities will be handled. In many cases, tenants in single-family homes are responsible for paying all utilities, including water, gas, electricity, and waste disposal. The lease should explicitly outline these responsibilities to avoid confusion.

Lease Term: Single-family home leases commonly range from 1 to 2 years, although month-to-month arrangements may also be possible. The lease should specify the start and end dates and any provisions for renewal or lease termination. In addition, it should explain how the lease will transition if it is not renewed, such as whether it will convert to a month-to-month agreement or require the tenant to vacate. Since single-family homes tend to attract long-term tenants, the lease should clearly define the procedures for lease renewal, including how and when both parties will notify each other of their intentions.

Security Deposit and Fees: The lease agreement must specify the amount of the security deposit and detail under what conditions it will be returned to the tenant. For single-family homes, where tenants are responsible for more extensive property upkeep, the lease should address how damages beyond normal wear and tear will be assessed. The lease should also mention any nonrefundable fees, such as pet fees or cleaning fees, that may apply.

Maintenance and Repair Responsibilities: Single-family home leases often place more responsibility on the tenant for general upkeep and maintenance. The lease should clearly outline which maintenance tasks are the tenant's responsibility (such as yard work, minor repairs, or snow removal) and which are the property owner's responsibility (such as major repairs or system replacements). For example, the tenant may be required to maintain the lawn, while the property owner must handle issues with the home's plumbing or heating system. The lease should also specify how and when the tenant should report maintenance issues and how quickly the property owner is expected to respond to repair requests.

Use of the Property: The lease agreement should define how the property is to be used. This typically includes provisions that restrict illegal activities, excessive noise, and property modifications without prior approval. Since single-family homes are often in residential neighborhoods, the lease should include guidelines for maintaining the home's exterior appearance, such as restrictions on storing large vehicles or debris in the yard. Additionally, rules about subleasing, home businesses, or the number of occupants allowed in the home should be clearly stated.

Compliance with Local, State, and Federal Laws: Single-family home leases must comply with all relevant local, state, and federal laws. This includes compliance with landlord-tenant laws, fair housing regulations, and any local ordinances governing rental properties. The lease should include clauses that ensure compliance with laws such as the Fair Housing Act, which prohibits discrimination in renting based on race, color, religion, sex, national origin, disability, or familial status. Additionally, compliance with habitability standards, safety regulations, and local property codes is critical for ensuring that the property is safe and legally habitable.

Entry and Access Rights: Since single-family home tenants generally expect a higher level of privacy, the lease should clearly outline the property owner's right to enter the home for inspections, repairs, or maintenance. The lease must include a clause specifying how much notice the property manager or owner must provide before entering the property, as well as any conditions under which entry is permitted (such as emergencies).

Eviction and Lease Termination: The lease agreement should outline the procedures for eviction and lease termination, including the notice periods required for each party. For single-family homes, where tenants may be more long-term, the lease should also address early termination provisions, such as conditions for breaking the lease and associated penalties. Property managers must ensure that any eviction or termination process complies with local and state laws, particularly regarding notice periods and grounds for eviction.

2.11.3 Sample Single-Family Home or Duplex Lease Agreement

Residential Lease for Single Family Home or Duplex
(FOR A TERM NOT TO EXCEED ONE YEAR)

A BOX (☐) OR A BLANK SPACE (____) INDICATES A PROVISION WHERE A CHOICE OR DECISION MUST BE MADE BY THE PARTIES.

THE LEASE IMPOSES IMPORTANT LEGAL OBLIGATIONS. MANY RIGHTS AND RESPONSIBILITIES OF THE PARTIES ARE GOVERNED BY CHAPTER 83, PART II, RESIDENTIAL LANDLORD AND TENANT ACT, FLORIDA STATUTES. A COPY OF THE RESIDENTIAL LANDLORD AND TENANT ACT IS ATTACHED TO THIS LEASE.

1. **PARTIES.** This is a lease ("the Lease") between ______________________________ (name & address of owner of the property) ______________________________ ("Landlord") and ______________________________ (name(s) of person(s) to whom the property is leased) ______________________________ ("Tenant.")

Landlord's E-mail address: ____________________
Landlord's Telephone Number: ____________________
Tenant's E-mail address: ____________________
Tenant's Telephone Number: ____________________

2. **PROPERTY RENTED.** Landlord leases to Tenant the land and buildings located at ______________________________ (street address) , Florida ____________ (zip code)

together with the following furniture and appliances [List all furniture and appliances. If none, write "none."] (In the Lease, the property leased, including furniture and appliances, if any, is called "the Premises"):

____
____
____

The Premises shall be occupied only by the Tenant and the following persons:
____
________________.

3. **TERM.** This is a lease for a term, not to exceed twelve months, beginning on ____________________ (month, day, year) and ending ____________________ (month, day, year) (the "Lease Term").

4. **RENT PAYMENTS, TAXES AND CHARGES.**

Tenant shall pay total rent in the amount of $ _________ (excluding taxes) for the Lease Term. The rent shall be payable by Tenant in advance in installments or in full as provided in the options below:

☐ in installments. If in installments, rent shall be payable

☐ monthly, on the ________ day of each month (if left blank, on the first day of each month) in the amount of $__________ per installment.

OR

☐ weekly, on the ___________ day of each week. (If left blank, on Monday of each week.) in the amount of $ ____________ per installment.

☐ in full on ____________________ (date) in the amount of $ ____________________.

Tenant shall also be obligated to pay taxes on the rent when applicable in the amount of $ ____________ ☐ with each rent installment ☐ with the rent for the full term of the Lease. Landlord will notify Tenant if the amount of the tax changes.

Payment Summary
☐ If rent is paid in installments, the total payment per installment including taxes shall be in the amount of $______________.
☐ If rent is paid in full, the total payment including taxes shall be in the amount of $_______________.

All rent payments shall be payable to ______________________________ (name) at ___________________________________(address). (If left blank, to Landlord at Landlord's address).

☐ If the tenancy starts on a day other than the first day of the month or week as designated above, the rent shall be prorated from _________ (date) through _____________(date)in the amount of $___________ and shall be due on___________ (date) (If rent paid monthly, prorate on a 30 day month.)

Tenant shall make rent payments required under the Lease by (choose all applicable) ☐ cash, ☐ personal check, ☐ money order, ☐ cashier's check, or ☐ other ___________________________(specify). If payment is accepted by any means other than cash, payment is not considered made until the other instrument is collected.

If Tenant makes a rent payment with a worthless check, Landlord can require Tenant ☐ to pay all future payments by ☐ money order, cashier's check or official bank check or ☐ cash or other (specify), and ☐ to pay bad check fees in the amount of $___________ (not to exceed the amount prescribed by Section 68.065, Florida Statutes.)

5. **MONEY DUE PRIOR TO OCCUPANCY.** Tenant shall pay the sum of $_________ in accordance with this paragraph prior to occupying the Premises. Tenant shall not be entitled to move in or to keys to the Premises until all money due prior to occupancy has been paid. If no date is specified below, then funds shall be due prior to Tenant occupancy. Any funds designated in this paragraph due after occupancy, shall be paid accordingly. Any funds due under this paragraph shall be payable to Landlord at Landlord's address or to

____
(name)

at
____
(address)

First ☐ month's ☐ week's rent plus applicable taxes	$	due	
Prorated rent plus applicable taxes	$	due	
Advance rent for ☐ month ☐ week of ____________ plus applicable taxes	$	due	
Last ☐ month's ☐ week's rent plus applicable taxes	$	due	
Security deposit	$	due	
Additional security deposit	$	due	
Security deposit for homeowner's association	$	due	
Pet Deposit	$	due	
Other ______________________________	$	due	
Other ______________________________	$	due	

6. LATE FEES. (Complete if applicable) In addition to rent, Tenant shall pay a late charge in the amount of $ ______________ (If left blank, 4% of the rent payment) for each rent payment made __________ days after the day it is due (if left blank, 5 days if rent is paid monthly, 1 day if rent is paid weekly).

7. PETS AND SMOKING. Unless this box ☐ is checked or a pet deposit is paid, Tenant may not keep pets or animals on the Premises. If Tenant may keep pets, the pets described in this paragraph are permitted on the Premises.

____
(Specify number of pets, type(s), breed, maximum adult weight of pets.)

Unless this box ☐ is checked, no smoking is permitted in the Premises.

8. NOTICES.

____ is Landlord's Agent. All notices must be sent to
☐ Landlord ____________________ at ________________________________
☐ Landlord's Agent ______________ at ________________________________

unless Landlord gives Tenant written notice of a change. All notices of such names and addresses or changes thereto shall be delivered to the Tenant's residence or, if specified in writing by the Tenant, to any other address. All notices to the Landlord or the Landlord's Agent (whichever is specified above) shall be given by U.S. mail or by hand delivery.

Any notice to Tenant shall be given by U.S. mail or delivered to Tenant at the Premises. If Tenant is absent from the Premises, a notice to Tenant may be given by leaving a copy of the notice at Premises.

9. UTILITIES. Tenant shall pay for all utilities services during the Lease Term and connection charges and deposits for activating existing utility connections to the Premises except for ______________________, that Landlord agrees to provide at Landlord's expense (If blank, then "NONE").

10. MAINTENANCE.

Landlord shall be responsible for compliance with Section 83.51, Florida Statutes, and shall be responsible for maintenance and repair of the Premises, unless otherwise stated below: (Fill in each blank space with "Landlord" for Landlord or "Tenant" for Tenant, if left blank, Landlord will be responsible for the item):

_____ roofs _____ windows _____ screens _____ steps
_____ doors _____ floors _____ porches _____ exterior walls
_____ foundations _____ plumbing _____ structural components
_____ heating _____ hot water _____ running water _____ locks and keys
_____ electrical system _____ cooling _____ smoke detection devices
_____ garbage removal/ outside receptacles
_____ extermination of rats, mice, roaches, ants and bedbugs
_____ extermination of wood-destroying organisms
_____ lawn/shrubbery _____ pool/spa/hot tub
_____ water treatment _____ filters (specify) ________________
_____ ceilings _____ interior walls
_____ Other (specify) ____

Tenant shall notify ______________________ (name) at ____________________ (address) (if left blank, Landlord at Landlord's address) and __________________________ (telephone number) of maintenance and repair requests.

11. ASSIGNMENT. Unless this box ☐ is checked, Tenant may not assign the Lease or sublease all or any part of the Premises without first obtaining the Landlord's written approval and consent to the assignment or sublease.

12. KEYS AND LOCKS. Landlord shall furnish Tenant

_________ # of sets of keys to the dwelling
_________ # of mail box keys
_________ # of garage door openers

If there is a homeowner's association, Tenant will be provided with the following to access the association's common areas/facilities:

_________ # of keys to ____
_________ # of remote controls to ____
_________ # of electronic cards to ____
______________ other (specify) to____

At end of Lease Term, all items specified in this paragraph shall be returned to ____________________________ (name) at ____ (address) (If left blank, Landlord at Landlord's address).

13. LEAD-BASED PAINT. ☐ Check and complete if the dwelling was built before January 1, 1978. **Lead Warning Statement** (when used in this article, the term Lessor refers to Landlord and the term Lessee refers to Tenant).

Housing built before 1978 may contain lead-based paint. Lead from paint, paint chips, and dust can pose health hazards if not managed properly. Lead exposure is especially harmful to young children and pregnant women. Before renting pre-1978 housing, Lessors must disclose the presence of known lead-based paint and/or lead-based paint hazards in the dwelling. Lessees must also receive a federally approved pamphlet on lead poisoning prevention.

Lessor's Disclosure (initial)

______ Presence of lead-based paint or lead-based paint hazards (check (i) or (ii) below):

_____ Known lead-based paint and/or lead-based paint hazards are present in the housing (explain).

____

____

(ii) _____ Lessor has no knowledge of lead-based paint and/or lead-based paint hazards in the housing

______ Records and reports available to the Lessor (check (i) or (ii) below):

______ Lessor has provided the lessee with all available records and reports pertaining to lead-based paint and/or lead-based paint hazards in the housing (list documents below).

____

____

______ Lessor has no reports or records pertaining to lead-based paint and/or lead-based paint hazards in the housing.

Lessee's Acknowledgment (initial)

______ Lessee has received copies of all information listed above.
______ Lessee has received the pamphlet Protect Your Family From Lead in Your Home.

Agent's Acknowledgment (initial)

_____ Agent has informed the Lessor of the Lessor's obligations under 42 U.S.C. 4852d and is aware of
_________ his/her responsibility to ensure compliance.

Certification of Accuracy

The following parties have reviewed the information above and certify, to the best of their knowledge, that the information provided by the signatory is true and accurate.

Lessor's signature	Date	Lessor's signature	Date
Lessee's signature	Date	Lessee's signature	Date
Agent's signature	Date	Agent's signature	Date

14. SERVICEMEMBER. If Tenant is a member of the United States Armed Forces on active duty or state active duty or a member of the Florida National Guard or United States Reserve Forces, the Tenant has rights to terminate the Lease as provided in Section 83.682, Florida Statutes, the provisions of which can be found in the attachment to this Lease.

15. LANDLORD'S ACCESS TO THE PREMISES. Landlord's Agent may enter the Premises in the following circumstances:

At any time for the protection or preservation of the Premises.

After reasonable notice to Tenant at reasonable times for the purpose of repairing the Premises.

To inspect the Premises; make necessary or agreed-upon repairs, decorations, alterations, or improvements; supply agreed services; or exhibit the Premises to prospective or actual purchasers, mortgagees, tenants, workers, or contractors under any of the following circumstances:

with Tenant's consent;

in case of emergency;

when Tenant unreasonably withholds consent; or

if Tenant is absent from the Premises for a period of at least one-half a rental installment period. (If the rent is current and Tenant notifies Landlord of an intended absence, then Landlord may enter only with Tenant's consent or for the protection or preservation of the Premises.)

16. HOMEOWNER'S ASSOCIATION. IF TENANT MUST BE APPROVED BY A HOMEOWNER'S ASSOCIATION ("ASSOCIATION"), LANDLORD AND TENANT AGREE THAT THE LEASE IS CONTINGENT UPON RECEIVING APPROVAL FROM THE ASSOCIATION. ANY APPLICATION FEE REQUIRED BY AN ASSOCIATION SHALL BE PAID BY ☐LANDLORD ☐ TENANT. IF SUCH APPROVAL IS NOT OBTAINED PRIOR TO COMMENCEMENT OF LEASE TERM, EITHER PARTY MAY TERMINATE THE LEASE BY WRITTEN NOTICE TO THE OTHER GIVEN AT ANY TIME PRIOR TO APPROVAL BY THE ASSOCIATION, AND IF THE LEASE IS TERMINATED, TENANT SHALL RECEIVE RETURN

OF DEPOSITS SPECIFIED IN ARTICLE 5, IF MADE. If the Lease is not terminated, rent shall abate until the approval is obtained from the association. Tenant agrees to use due diligence in applying for association approval and to comply with the requirements for obtaining approval ☐Landlord ☐Tenant shall pay the security deposit required by the association, if applicable.

17. USE OF THE PREMISES. Tenant shall use the Premises for residential purposes. Tenant shall have exclusive use and right of possession to the dwelling. The Premises shall be used so as to comply with all state, county, municipal laws and ordinances, and all covenants and restrictions affecting the Premises and all rules and regulations of homeowners' associations affecting the Premises. Tenant may not paint or make any alterations or improvements to the Premises without first obtaining the Landlord's written consent to the alteration or improvement. However, unless this box ☐ is checked, Tenant may hang pictures and install window treatments in the Premises without Landlord's consent, provided Tenant removes all such items before the end of the Lease Term and repairs all damage resulting from the removal. Any improvements or alterations to the Premises made by the Tenant shall become Landlord's property. Tenant agrees not to use, keep, or store on the Premises any dangerous, explosive, toxic material which would increase the probability of fire or which would increase the cost of insuring the Premises.

18. RISK OF LOSS/INSURANCE.

Landlord and Tenant shall each be responsible for loss, damage, or injury caused by its own negligence or willful conduct.

Tenant should carry insurance covering Tenant's personal property and Tenant's liability insurance.

19. PROHIBITED ACTS BY LANDLORD. Landlord is prohibited from taking certain actions as described in Section 83.67, Florida Statutes, the provisions of which can be found in the attachment to this Lease.

20. CASUALTY DAMAGE. If the Premises are damaged or destroyed other than by wrongful or negligent acts of Tenant or persons on the Premises with Tenant's consent, so that the use of the Premises is substantially impaired, Tenant may terminate the Lease within 30 days after the damage or destruction and Tenant will immediately vacate the Premises. If Tenant vacates, Tenant is not liable for rent that would have been due after the date of termination. Tenant may vacate the part of the Premises rendered unusable by the damage or destruction, in which case Tenant's liability for rent shall be reduced by the fair rental value of the part of the Premises that was damaged or destroyed.

21. DEFAULTS/REMEDIES. Should a party to the Lease fail to fulfill their responsibilities under the Lease or need to determine whether there has been a default of the Lease, refer to Part II, Chapter 83, entitled Florida Residential Landlord and Tenant Act which contains information on defaults and remedies. A copy of the current version of this Act is attached to the Lease.

22. SUBORDINATION. The Lease is automatically subordinate to the lien of any mortgage encumbering the fee title to the Premises from time to time.

23. LIENS. THE INTEREST OF THE LANDLORD SHALL NOT BE SUBJECT TO LIENS FOR IMPROVEMENTS MADE BY THE TENANT AS PROVIDED IN SECTION 713.10, FLORIDA STATUTES. Tenant shall notify all parties perfoming work on the Premises at Tenant's request that the Lease does not allow any liens to attach to Landlord's interest.

24. RENEWAL/EXTENSION. The Lease can be renewed or extended only by a written agreement signed by both Landlord and Tenant, but the term of a renewal or extension together with the original Lease Term may not exceed one year. A new lease is required for each year.

25. TENANT'S TELEPHONE NUMBER. Tenant shall, within 5 business days of obtaining telephone services at the Premises, send written notice to Landlord of Tenant's telephone numbers at the Premises.

26. ATTORNEYS' FEES. In any lawsuit brought to enforce the Lease or under applicable law, the party in whose favor a judgment or decree has been rendered may recover reasonable court costs, including attorneys' fees, from the non-prevailing party.

27. MISCELLANEOUS.

Time is of the essence of the performance of each party's obligations under the Lease.

The Lease shall be binding upon and for the benefit of the heirs, personal representatives, successors, and permitted assigns of Landlord and Tenant, subject to the requirements specifically mentioned in the Lease. Whenever used, the singular number shall include the plural or singular and the use of any gender shall include all appropriate genders.

The agreements contained in the Lease set forth the complete understanding of the parties and may not be changed or terminated orally.

No agreement to accept surrender of the Premises from Tenant will be valid unless in writing and signed by Landlord.

All questions concerning the meaning, execution, construction, effect, validity, and enforcement of the Lease shall be determined pursuant to the laws of Florida.

A facsimile copy of the Lease and any signatures hereon shall be considered for all purposes originals.

As required by law, Landlord makes the following disclosure: "RADON GAS." Radon is a naturally occurring radioactive gas that, when it has accumulated in a building in sufficient quantities, may present health risks to persons who are exposed to it over time. Levels of radon that exceed federal and state guidelines have been found in buildings in Florida. Additional information regarding radon and radon testing may be obtained from your county health department.

28. BROKERS' COMMISSION. ☐ Check and complete if applicable. The brokerage companies named below will be paid the commission set forth in this paragraph by ☐ Landlord ☐ Tenant for procuring a tenant for this transaction.

________________________	________________________
Real Estate Licensee	Real Estate Licensee
________________________	________________________
Real Estate Brokerage Company	Real Estate Brokerage Company
________________________	________________________
Commission	Commission

29. TENANT'S PERSONAL PROPERTY. TENANT MUST INITIAL IN THIS BOX ☐ FOR THE FOLLOWING PROVISION TO APPLY. BY SIGNING THIS RENTAL AGREEMENT, THE TENANT AGREES THAT UPON SURRENDER, ABANDONMENT, OR RECOVERY OF POSSESSION OF THE DWELLING UNIT DUE TO THE DEATH OF THE LAST REMAINING TENANT, AS PROVIDED BY CHAPTER 83, FLORIDA STATUTES, THE LANDLORD SHALL NOT BE LIABLE OR RESPONSIBLE FOR STORAGE OR DISPOSITION OF THE TENANT'S PERSONAL PROPERTY.

The Lease has been executed by the parties on the dates indicated below.

______________________________	______________________________
Landlord's Signature	Date
______________________________	______________________________
Landlord's Signature	Date
______________________________	______________________________
Landlord's Signature	Date
______________________________	______________________________
Tenant's Signature	Date
______________________________	______________________________
Tenant's Signature	Date

This form was completed with the assistance of:

Name of Individual: ______________________________
Name of Business: ______________________________
Address: ______________________________
Telephone Number: ______________________________

Copy of Current Version of Florida Residential Landlord and Tenant Act,

Part II, Chapter 83, Florida Statutes to Be Attached

EARLY TERMINATION FEE/LIQUIDATED DAMAGES ADDENDUM

[ ] I agree, as provided in the rental agreement, to pay $______ (an amount that does not exceed 2 months' rent) as liquidated damages or an early termination fee if I elect to terminate the rental agreement and the landlord waives the right to seek additional rent beyond the month in which the landlord retakes possession.

[ ] I do not agree to liquidated damages or an early termination fee, and I acknowledge that the landlord may seek damages as provided by law.

Landlord's Signature	Date
Landlord's Signature	Date
Landlord's Signature	Date
Tenant's Signature	Date
Tenant's Signature	Date

Credit and Disclaimer

Reprinted with permission from The Florida Bar.

This landlord-tenant form has been approved by the Florida Supreme Court. However, because the law is continually changing, there is no guarantee that these forms comport with current law. These forms are not a substitute for the advice of an attorney. It is always best to consult an attorney about your legal rights and responsibilities in your particular case.

Source: The Florida Bar—https://www-media.floridabar.org/uploads/2018/08/single-family-lease.pdf

2.11.4 Managing Risk and Liability

One of the primary responsibilities of property managers is managing the risks and liabilities associated with renting out single-family homes. Property managers must take proactive steps to minimize potential risks that could lead to tenant injury, property damage, or legal disputes. This includes ensuring the property meets all safety standards, conducting regular inspections to identify potential hazards, and responding to maintenance issues in a timely manner.

For instance, common areas of concern include defective wiring, malfunctioning heating or cooling systems, uneven walkways, and inadequate lighting. Any failure to address these issues could result in accidents, which may expose the property manager and owner to legal liability. Additionally, property managers should ensure the property complies with local building codes, zoning laws, and habitability standards. Failure to do so could lead to legal claims against the property owner or manager.

Moreover, property managers should be knowledgeable about liability concerns related to tenant behavior. For example, tenant-caused damages to neighboring properties or the misuse of the rental property for illegal activities could also expose the property owner and manager to legal action. Having clear lease agreements and enforcing tenant behavior policies can help mitigate these risks.

Understanding Insurance Requirements for Landlords, Tenants, and Property Managers

Adequate insurance coverage is essential in protecting all parties involved in the rental of single-family homes. Property managers must understand the insurance requirements for landlords, tenants, and themselves to ensure that all risks are properly covered.

Landlord Insurance

Landlord insurance typically includes coverage for property damage, liability, and loss of rental income due to events like fire, storm damage, or vandalism. Property managers should confirm that the property owner has a comprehensive landlord insurance policy in place. This coverage helps protect the landlord from financial losses due to unforeseen property damage or legal claims arising from tenant injuries on the property.

Tenant Renters Insurance

While not always required by law, many property managers require tenants to obtain renters insurance as part of the lease agreement. Renters insurance typically covers the tenant's personal belongings and provides liability protection in case the tenant causes damage to the property or injures someone while on the premises. Requiring renters insurance helps ensure that tenants are financially responsible for their own losses and reduces the likelihood of disputes over damages.

Property Manager Insurance

Property managers should also have their own insurance, typically in the form of general liability insurance and errors and omissions (E&O) insurance. *General liability insurance* protects property managers from claims related to bodily injury or property damage that may occur as a result of their management activities. E&O insurance covers professional mistakes, such as failing to properly screen a tenant or overlooking a critical maintenance issue that results in property damage or a legal claim.

Handling Security Deposits Legally

Security deposits are a common aspect of single-family home leasing, and property managers must handle them in accordance with local and state laws. Mishandling security deposits can lead to legal disputes and financial penalties for the property owner or manager.

Most states have strict regulations governing how security deposits should be collected, stored, and returned. Typically, property managers are required to:

- *Collect a reasonable deposit amount:* Many states set limits on how much a property manager can collect as a security deposit. For example, it may be capped at the equivalent of 1 or 2 months' rent.
- *Hold the deposit in a separate account:* In many states, security deposits must be kept in a separate, interest-bearing account. This ensures that the funds are protected and available for return to the tenant, minus any deductions for damages or unpaid rent.
- *Provide a detailed accounting:* When a tenant moves out, property managers must provide an itemized list of any deductions made from the security deposit for damages or repairs. Failing to do so can lead to penalties or the forfeiture of the right to make any deductions at all.
- *Return the deposit within a specific time frame:* Property managers must return the security deposit (or the remaining portion) within the time frame set by state law, usually 30 days after the tenant vacates the property.

By handling security deposits legally and transparently, property managers can avoid disputes and ensure compliance with state regulations.

2.12 Summary

Managing single-family homes presents a unique set of challenges and responsibilities that require property managers to adopt a more personalized approach compared to managing multifamily units. This chapter delves into the specific responsibilities of managing single-family homes, highlighting the critical components that contribute to successful property management, including tenant relations, maintenance, marketing, tenant acquisition, lease agreements, and legal compliance. Understanding these elements allows property managers to offer high-quality services to both tenants and property owners, while ensuring that the property is well-maintained, legally compliant, and financially viable.

A key responsibility in managing single-family homes is maintaining strong tenant relations. Given the individualized nature of single-family rentals, tenants often expect more personalized attention and quick responses to maintenance requests. Building a positive relationship with tenants involves clear communication, proactive problem-solving, and respecting tenants' privacy. Property managers must also be adept at resolving conflicts and addressing tenant concerns in a timely and transparent manner. These actions contribute to higher tenant satisfaction and long-term lease retention, which is particularly important in single-family homes, where turnover and vacancies can be more costly than in multifamily units.

Maintenance is another critical responsibility for property managers. Single-family homes require regular upkeep to preserve their value and meet tenants' expectations. Property managers must ensure that preventive maintenance is conducted, handle emergency repairs promptly, and manage tenant requests efficiently. The maintenance responsibilities are often more hands-on in single-family homes, where tenants expect the property to be in excellent condition, both inside and outside. Property managers must coordinate routine inspections and make sure that tenants are aware of their own responsibilities, such as lawn care or minor maintenance tasks. Effective maintenance practices not only keep tenants satisfied but also prevent costly repairs in the future.

Marketing and tenant acquisition for single-family homes require a targeted approach. Property managers must highlight the unique features of single-family homes, such as private yards, parking spaces, and family-friendly neighborhoods, to attract the right tenant demographics. By understanding the needs of families, young professionals, and retirees, property managers can create marketing strategies that appeal to these groups. Online listings, high-quality photographs, and virtual tours are essential tools in reaching prospective tenants. Once interested tenants are identified, property managers must conduct thorough screening processes to ensure that the selected tenants are reliable and responsible, thereby protecting the property owner's investment.

A well-drafted lease agreement is crucial to managing single-family homes effectively. The lease must clearly outline the terms of rent payment, maintenance responsibilities, security deposits, and other essential terms. For single-family homes, lease agreements may include additional clauses related to the use of outdoor spaces, garages, and amenities. Moreover, tenants in single-family homes are often responsible for more maintenance tasks compared to apartment dwellers, so the lease should clearly define what is expected of the tenant. Ensuring that the lease complies with local, state, and federal laws, including fair housing regulations, is essential to avoid legal disputes.

The legal aspects of single-family home management are particularly important in protecting both the property owner and the tenant. Property managers must comply with landlord-tenant laws, which govern critical aspects such as rent collection, security deposits, maintenance, and eviction procedures. These laws ensure that the tenant has a habitable living environment and that the property owner's rights are protected. Additionally, compliance with fair housing laws is crucial. Property managers must ensure that they are not discriminating against any protected classes when advertising, screening, or renting out single-family homes. Familiarity with these legal obligations helps property managers minimize liability and ensure that all transactions are conducted ethically and legally.

In summary, managing single-family homes involves a delicate balance of meeting tenant expectations, maintaining the property, adhering to legal requirements, and ensuring that the owner's investment remains profitable. Property managers who excel in these areas are well-equipped to handle the unique challenges of single-family home management, ensuring both tenant satisfaction and the long-term success of the property.

2.12.1 Looking Forward

The following chapters will explore the management of other residential property classifications, including manufactured home parks and multifamily residences. Each property type presents its own unique challenges and opportunities, and understanding these differences is key to becoming a successful property manager in the residential real estate industry.

2.13 Case Study: The Green Family's Investment Property

2.13.1 Background

The Green family owns a single-family rental home that serves as an important part of their investment portfolio. The property is a four-bedroom, three-bathroom house located in a desirable suburban neighborhood. The Greens rely on the rental income for their retirement fund and have asked you to manage all aspects of the property, from marketing and tenant acquisition to maintenance and legal compliance.

2.13.2 Scenario

The property has just become vacant, and you need to prepare it for new tenants. This involves marketing the property, screening potential tenants, drafting a lease agreement, and addressing any maintenance issues. Additionally, you need to ensure compliance with relevant landlord-tenant laws.

2.13.3 Tasks

1. *Marketing the Property*
   - Develop an attractive and detailed property listing.
   - Post the listing on multiple online rental platforms and local classifieds.
   - Arrange and conduct property viewings for prospective tenants.
2. *Tenant Screening*
   - Implement a comprehensive tenant screening process, including background checks, credit checks, reference checks, and income verification.
   - Ensure adherence to fair housing laws throughout the tenant selection process.
3. *Lease Agreement*
   - Draft a thorough lease agreement that includes all necessary terms, such as rent amount, payment due dates, security deposit requirements, maintenance responsibilities, and rules regarding property use.
   - Review the lease with the Green family to ensure it aligns with their expectations and complies with local laws.

4. *Maintenance and Repairs*
   - Conduct a detailed inspection of the property to identify any maintenance or repair needs.
   - Address minor repairs, such as repainting walls, fixing leaky faucets, and replacing worn-out carpeting.
   - Develop a routine maintenance schedule and plan for seasonal upkeep.
5. *Legal Compliance*
   - Review and ensure compliance with local, state, and federal landlord-tenant laws.
   - Include relevant clauses in the lease agreement to protect the interests of both the property owner and the tenant.

2.13.4 Challenges

1. *Marketing Challenge*
   - Despite listing the property on multiple platforms, you are not receiving enough inquiries. Consider alternative marketing strategies to attract more potential tenants.
2. *Tenant Screening Challenge*
   - You receive applications from two potential tenants: one with excellent credit but a shorter rental history, and another with average credit but a long-term stable rental history. Decide how to proceed with tenant selection.
3. *Maintenance Challenge*
   - During the property inspection, you discover that the water heater is at the end of its useful life. Determine how to handle this issue within the maintenance budget set by the Green family.
4. *Legal Compliance Challenge*
   - The Greens have requested a clause in the lease agreement that prohibits subleasing. Draft this clause and ensure it complies with local landlord-tenant laws.

2.13.5 Questions

1. *Marketing*
   - What additional marketing strategies could you implement to increase interest in the property?
   - How can you highlight the property's unique features to make it stand out in the rental market?
2. *Tenant Screening*
   - What factors should you consider when deciding between the two potential tenants?
   - How can you ensure that the tenant screening process is fair and compliant with fair housing laws?

3. *Maintenance*
   - How would you prioritize maintenance tasks to stay within the budget while ensuring the property is in good condition?
   - What steps can you take to address the aging water heater issue?
4. *Legal Compliance*
   - What key elements should be included in the lease agreement to protect both the property owner and the tenant?
   - How can you ensure that the lease agreement complies with local landlord-tenant laws, particularly regarding the prohibition of subleasing?

2.14 Review Questions

1. What is an effective marketing strategy for attracting tenants to a single-family home?
   (A) Posting blurry photos online
   (B) Creating detailed listings with high-quality photos
   (C) Ignoring online platforms
   (D) Hosting open houses without any prior advertising
2. *Which factor is important to consider during the tenant screening process?*
   (A) Tenant's favorite color
   (B) Credit history and references
   (C) Tenant's hobbies
   (D) Tenant's choice of furniture
3. *Why is understanding tenant demographics important in managing single-family homes?*
   (A) To reduce marketing efforts
   (B) To tailor management approaches to tenant needs and preferences
   (C) To avoid maintenance tasks
   (D) To increase rent indiscriminately
4. *Which of the following should be included in a lease agreement?*
   (A) Tenant's favorite activities
   (B) Clear terms and conditions, including rent amount and payment due dates
   (C) Arbitrary rent amounts
   (D) Undefined maintenance responsibilities
5. *What should a routine maintenance schedule for a single-family home include?*
   (A) Ignoring minor repairs
   (B) Regular inspections and seasonal maintenance tasks
   (C) Only emergency repairs
   (D) Random maintenance tasks
6. *Why is preventive maintenance important for single-family homes?*
   (A) To reduce tenant interactions
   (B) To prevent small issues from becoming major problems
   (C) To avoid routine inspections
   (D) To increase rent arbitrarily

7. *What is a crucial step when handling emergency repairs in single-family homes?*
   (A) Delaying the repairs
   (B) Having a list of reliable contractors
   (C) Ignoring tenant requests
   (D) Increasing rent immediately
8. *Why is it important to comply with local landlord-tenant laws?*
   (A) To avoid tenant interactions
   (B) To prevent legal disputes and ensure smooth operations
   (C) To increase rent arbitrarily
   (D) To reduce maintenance costs
9. *What is the purpose of a security deposit in a lease agreement?*
   (A) To cover the tenant's entertainment expenses
   (B) To ensure funds are available for any damages or unpaid rent
   (C) To increase the property's market value
   (D) To avoid tenant complaints
10. *Which law must property managers comply with to avoid discrimination in housing?*
   (A) Zoning laws
   (B) Fair Housing Act
   (C) Property tax regulations
   (D) Local noise ordinances

3 Introduction to Managing Timeshares

3.1 Learning Objectives

By the end of this chapter, students will be able to:

- Define the concept of timeshares and explain their unique legal and operational structures compared to other community associations.
- Analyze the advantages and disadvantages of timeshare ownership and management from both a consumer and property manager perspective.
- Understand the demographics and market trends of timeshares and apply this knowledge to effective marketing and operations strategies.
- Develop a comprehensive understanding of the operational, financial, and regulatory aspects of managing timeshare properties.

3.2 Key Terms

Timeshare
Right-to-Use Agreement
Deeded Ownership
Fractional Ownership
Maintenance Fees
Vacation Club
Exchange Program

D. A. Vaughn, *Essentials of Residential Property Management*, Springer Texts in Business and Economics, https://doi.org/10.1007/978-3-031-92329-6_3

3.3 Overview

Timeshares represent a unique segment of the residential property management landscape, combining elements of vacation homeownership, hospitality, and community association management. Unlike traditional community associations, timeshares are primarily geared toward vacation or short-term usage and often operate under specific legal and financial frameworks. This chapter explores the intricacies of managing timeshare properties, focusing on their legal structures, market characteristics, operational challenges, and compliance requirements. By understanding the unique aspects of timeshare management, property managers can navigate the complexities of this specialized field and maximize both operational efficiency and customer satisfaction.

3.3.1 Introduction to Timeshares

A *timeshare* is a form of property ownership in which multiple individuals share the right to use a vacation property for a designated period each year and can also be referred to as vacation ownership properties. They represent a unique sector of real estate that combines elements of hospitality and shared property management. They are structured to allow multiple owners to share usage rights to a property for specific periods each year, typically at vacation destinations. This introduction provides an in-depth explanation of what timeshares are, how they operate, and why they differ from traditional residential property management. Understanding the core principles of timeshares is essential for property managers entering this niche field.

3.3.2 History and Evolution of Timeshares

The concept of timeshares originated in Europe during the 1960s as a response to the rising costs of vacation accommodations. Developers sought to create a model where families could enjoy luxury properties at a fraction of the cost of full ownership by sharing expenses with others. This innovative approach quickly gained popularity and expanded to the United States by the 1970s.

Early timeshares were simple in structure, typically offering fixed-week ownership at a single property. Over time, the industry evolved to include flexible ownership options, global exchange networks, and a variety of property types, such as condominiums, villas, and cabins. By the 1990s, major hospitality brands like Marriott, Hilton, and Wyndham entered the market, lending credibility and professional management to the timeshare industry.

Today, timeshares represent a multibillion-dollar industry that continues to innovate with options like *fractional ownership*, destination clubs, and environmentally sustainable developments.

3.4 Legal Structure of Timeshares Compared to Other Community Associations

The legal structure of timeshares differs significantly from that of other community associations, such as homeowners' associations (HOAs) and condominium associations (COAs), primarily due to the shared and often temporary nature of ownership in timeshares. This section explores the key legal frameworks governing timeshares, comparing them to more traditional residential community associations to highlight how these differences impact governance, operations, and property management.

3.4.1 Types of Legal Structures

Timeshares are generally organized under two primary legal structures: *deeded ownership* and *right-to-use agreements*. Each structure defines the rights and responsibilities of owners differently and influences how the property is managed.

1. *Deeded Ownership:*
   - In deeded timeshares, owners hold a fractional interest in the property, similar to owning a share of real estate. Each owner receives a recorded deed that specifies their percentage of ownership and their allocated usage intervals.
   - This structure provides owners with tangible real estate rights, such as the ability to sell, transfer, or inherit their share. However, owners are also responsible for property taxes, maintenance fees, and potential special assessments.
   - Deeded timeshares are typically perpetual, with no expiration date unless otherwise specified in the agreement.

2. *Right-to-Use Agreements:*
   - In this model, owners do not hold real estate rights but instead acquire a long-term lease or license to use the property during specified intervals. These agreements typically last 10–50 years and expire at the end of the term.
   - Right-to-use timeshares are more flexible in certain jurisdictions, especially where foreign ownership of real estate is restricted. However, they lack the equity-building potential of deeded timeshares.

Both structures are designed to cater to different buyer preferences, with deeded ownership appealing to those seeking real estate investments and right-to-use agreements attracting those prioritizing flexibility and lower entry costs.

3.4.2 Governance of Timeshares Versus Other Community Associations

Like HOAs and COAs, timeshares are often governed by an association that oversees the property's operations and enforces rules. However, the governance structure of timeshares has distinct features tailored to their unique ownership model.

1. *Timeshare Governance:*
   - Timeshare properties are typically managed by a homeowners' association or resort management company, with oversight provided by an elected board of directors. The board represents the collective interests of owners, overseeing budgeting, maintenance, and rule enforcement.
   - Timeshare governance must address unique challenges, such as coordinating reservations, managing exchange programs, and handling high-volume maintenance needs. Additionally, the transient nature of occupants requires robust administrative systems to track ownership intervals and ensure compliance with rules.
2. *Governance in HOAs and COAs:*
   - In traditional HOAs and COAs, governance is focused on the long-term residential needs of full-time homeowners. Boards oversee common area maintenance, enforce community rules, and manage financial operations like collecting dues and funding reserves.
   - Unlike timeshares, where ownership is shared across multiple individuals for the same unit, HOAs and COAs typically involve individual ownership of specific properties or units, simplifying governance responsibilities.

Timeshare governance is inherently more complex due to the need to balance the interests of multiple stakeholders, including owners, renters, and exchange program participants. Effective governance requires clear policies, transparent communication, and professional management to ensure the property's success.

3.4.3 Regulatory Framework

Timeshares are subject to a unique set of legal requirements at the federal, state, and international levels. These regulations are designed to protect consumers and ensure fair practices in the timeshare industry:

1. *State Laws:*
   - Most U.S. states regulate timeshares through specific legislation that governs disclosures, rescission periods, and marketing practices. For example, timeshare developers must provide prospective buyers with a public offering statement detailing all financial obligations and property rights.
   - States may also require timeshare managers to hold specialized licenses or certifications to ensure competency and ethical conduct.
2. *Federal Oversight:*
   - At the federal level, the Federal Trade Commission (FTC) enforces consumer protection laws related to timeshare sales and advertising. Misleading claims, high-pressure sales tactics, and lack of transparency are areas of regulatory focus.
   - The Real Estate Settlement Procedures Act (RESPA) and the Truth in Lending Act (TILA) may also apply to timeshare transactions, particularly those involving financing.
3. *International Regulations:*
   - For timeshares located abroad, property managers must navigate the legal requirements of the host country. These may include restrictions on foreign ownership, tax implications, and compliance with local consumer protection laws.

3.4.4 Comparison of Legal Responsibilities

While timeshares share some legal responsibilities with traditional community associations, their unique ownership and usage structures create additional complexities:

Aspect	Timeshare Associations	HOAs/COAs
Ownership structure	Fractional or contractual; limited-time usage	Full ownership of units/homes and shared common areas
Governance	Elected board; transient occupants and high administrative needs	Elected board; stable ownership base
Financial management	Annual fees tied to fractional ownership; exchange program costs	Maintenance fees based on full ownership
Legal compliance	Subject to timeshare-specific disclosure and consumer laws	Subject to state real estate and community association laws

3.5 How Timeshares Differ from Traditional Residential Properties

Timeshares differ significantly from traditional residential properties in terms of their ownership structure, usage patterns, revenue models, and maintenance standards. These differences shape the unique operational and management challenges of timeshares, setting them apart from single-family homes, apartment buildings, and other forms of residential real estate. Understanding these distinctions is critical for property managers navigating the timeshare industry.

3.5.1 Usage Patterns

The usage patterns of timeshares stand in stark contrast to traditional residential properties. In a residential setting, tenants or homeowners typically occupy their units continuously, whether on a long-term lease or as full-time residents. Timeshares, however, operate on a time-based model, where owners have the right to use the property for a specific interval each year. These intervals can range from fixed weeks to flexible schedules, depending on the ownership agreement.

The short-term nature of timeshare occupancy creates a high turnover rate, similar to the hospitality industry. Units must be prepared for new occupants frequently, often within a single day. This requires efficient housekeeping, detailed inspections, and rapid resolution of maintenance issues. Additionally, the transient occupancy model necessitates robust reservation systems to coordinate usage among owners, renters, and exchange program participants.

3.5.2 Shared Ownership

Shared ownership is one of the defining characteristics of timeshares, setting them apart from traditional residential properties where ownership is typically singular and exclusive. In timeshares, multiple individuals hold rights to the same unit, dividing usage among themselves based on predefined intervals. This shared ownership can take two primary forms: deeded and right-to-use agreements.

In deeded timeshares, owners possess a fractional interest in the property, much like owning a partial stake in real estate. This type of ownership is perpetual and can be sold, transferred, or inherited. Conversely, right-to-use agreements function like long-term leases, granting owners the contractual right to occupy the property for a specific term without conveying real estate ownership. The shared nature of timeshares necessitates clear governance structures, as owners collectively contribute to property upkeep through maintenance fees and have a say in decision-making through associations or boards.

3.5.3 Revenue Streams

Revenue generation in timeshares differs significantly from traditional residential properties, which primarily rely on rental income. For timeshares, initial sales of ownership intervals constitute a substantial portion of revenue. These sales are often supported by aggressive marketing campaigns, sales tours, and promotional events.

Beyond sales, timeshares generate ongoing revenue through annual maintenance fees paid by owners. These fees cover operating expenses, reserve fund contributions, and amenities maintenance. Additionally, many timeshare properties offer rental programs to fill unused intervals, creating a secondary income stream. Properties affiliated with exchange networks, such as RCI or Interval International, may also generate revenue from exchange program fees. These diversified revenue streams require property managers to adopt a multifaceted approach to budgeting and financial planning.

3.5.4 Maintenance Standards

The maintenance standards for timeshares are higher and more frequent compared to traditional residential properties due to their short-term usage model and the high expectations of vacationers. Residential tenants or homeowners are often responsible for maintaining the interiors of their units, with property managers focusing on common areas and essential systems. In timeshares, however, the responsibility for unit maintenance falls entirely on the management team.

Timeshare managers must ensure that units are thoroughly cleaned and inspected between occupants. Preventative maintenance is essential to minimize disruptions, as timeshare properties cannot afford extended downtime for repairs. Additionally, timeshares must uphold high standards for amenities such as pools, fitness centers, and on-site dining facilities, as these features are integral to the vacation experience.

Renovations and updates are also more frequent in timeshares, as properties must remain competitive in the hospitality market. Reserve funds play a critical role in financing these updates, ensuring that timeshare properties can maintain their appeal over time.

3.5.5 Types of Timeshares

Timeshares offer various ownership models that cater to the diverse needs and preferences of vacationers. These models differ in terms of flexibility, usage rights, and ownership structures, providing prospective buyers with multiple options to suit their travel habits and financial goals. The primary types of timeshares include *Fixed Week*, *Floating Week*, *Points-Based Timeshares*, *Fractional Ownership*, and *Vacation Clubs*. Understanding these types is crucial for property managers as they influence the operational, marketing, and customer service strategies required to manage timeshare properties effectively.

Fixed Week

The *Fixed Week* model is one of the earliest and most straightforward types of timeshare ownership. In this arrangement, owners purchase the right to use a specific unit during the same week each year. For example, an owner may have rights to Unit 302 during Week 25 annually. This predictability appeals to buyers who prefer returning to the same destination at a consistent time each year, such as during holidays or specific vacation seasons.

While Fixed Week timeshares offer simplicity and ease of scheduling, their rigidity can be a drawback for owners who may want to travel at different times. Additionally, the marketability of Fixed Week timeshares depends heavily on the desirability of the unit's location and the specific week. For instance, prime vacation weeks in sought-after destinations may hold more value than off-peak intervals.

Floating Week

The *Floating Week* model introduces greater flexibility, allowing owners to reserve a week within a designated range, such as a specific season or even throughout the year. Owners must book their desired week in advance, often on a first-come, first-served basis. This flexibility appeals to buyers who value variety in their travel schedules and destinations.

However, Floating Week timeshares can present challenges in terms of availability, especially during high-demand periods. Property managers must implement efficient reservation systems to ensure fairness and transparency in scheduling. Effective communication is also essential to manage owner expectations and reduce conflicts over popular time slots.

Points-Based

Points-Based Timeshares have emerged as a highly flexible and modern alternative to traditional week-based systems. In this model, owners purchase points that can be used to book accommodations at various properties within a network. The number of points required depends on factors such as the property's location, the size of the unit, and the time of year.

This system offers unparalleled flexibility, allowing owners to tailor their vacations to their preferences. For example, an owner might use a large portion of their points for a luxury weeklong stay at a high-demand resort or spread their points across several shorter trips. Points-based systems also often include options to use points for non-accommodation purposes, such as airfare, cruises, or car rentals.

Despite its advantages, the complexity of points-based systems can be overwhelming for some owners. Property managers must provide clear guidance on how to maximize the value of points and ensure that reservation platforms are user-friendly and transparent.

Fractional Ownership

Fractional Ownership is a more premium form of timeshare ownership, offering a larger share of the property and extended usage rights. Unlike traditional timeshares, which divide ownership among 52 weeks, fractional ownership typically involves 4–13 owners per property, allowing for longer stays and a greater sense of exclusivity.

Fractional owners often hold deeded ownership, granting them a tangible real estate interest in the property. This model is particularly popular for high-end properties in luxury destinations, where buyers value the prestige and extended usage associated with fractional ownership. However, the higher cost of entry and ongoing expenses make it a less accessible option for budget-conscious buyers.

Vacation Clubs

Vacation Clubs represent a membership-based approach to timeshare ownership, offering unparalleled flexibility and access to a wide range of destinations and services. Members pay an upfront fee and annual dues to gain access to a portfolio of properties managed by the vacation club. Instead of owning a specific property or week, members enjoy the freedom to choose from various locations, accommodations, and amenities.

Vacation clubs often include additional perks, such as priority reservations, discounts on travel-related services, and access to exclusive events. This model appeals to younger, tech-savvy travelers who prioritize experiences and flexibility over traditional ownership structures. However, the lack of deeded ownership means members do not gain equity or real estate value, which may be a drawback for some buyers.

3.6 Understanding the Demographics

Understanding the demographics of timeshare owners and the broader market trends is critical for property managers to effectively target and serve this niche. This section explores the key characteristics of the timeshare consumer base, shifting market dynamics, and emerging trends that influence the management and marketing of timeshare properties. Timeshare owners represent a diverse range of consumers, though certain demographic patterns emerge based on income, age, and lifestyle preferences. These characteristics are crucial for property managers and marketers seeking to align their strategies with the needs and expectations of the target audience.

1. *Age Groups:*
   - Timeshare ownership historically skewed toward older buyers, particularly retirees seeking predictable vacation experiences. The average age of a timeshare owner today is in the mid-40s, reflecting a broadening appeal to middle-aged families.
   - Younger generations, such as Millennials and Gen Z, are becoming increasingly involved in the timeshare market, though they often prefer flexible, points-based systems over fixed-week ownership.

2. *Income Levels:*
   - Timeshare owners typically fall within middle- to upper-income brackets, with average household incomes exceeding $75,000. This reflects the affordability of timeshares compared to full ownership of vacation properties.
   - Buyers are often drawn to timeshares as a cost-effective way to enjoy high-quality accommodations without the financial burden of maintaining a second home.
3. *Geographic Trends:*
   - In the United States, timeshare ownership is particularly popular in states with desirable vacation destinations, such as Florida, California, Nevada, and Hawaii. Internationally, timeshares are prevalent in Europe, the Caribbean, and Southeast Asia.
   - Proximity to owners' primary residences can also influence demand, as many buyers prefer vacation destinations within driving distance.
4. *Lifestyle Preferences:*
   - Timeshare owners value predictability, quality accommodations, and access to resort-style amenities. Families often prioritize properties with kid-friendly features, while older couples may seek quiet, luxury-focused destinations.
   - Many owners participate in exchange programs, indicating a preference for flexibility and the ability to explore multiple destinations.

3.7 Management Operations of Timeshares

Managing timeshare properties presents unique challenges and opportunities that require a hybrid approach blending residential property management and hospitality operations. Timeshares, by nature, combine elements of long-term ownership with short-term usage, necessitating strategies that cater to both owners and temporary occupants. Effective management ensures operational efficiency, maximizes owner satisfaction, and enhances the guest experience. This section examines the core elements of timeshare management operations, focusing on staff management, guest services, and reservation systems.

3.7.1 Hybrid Approach: Residential Property and Hospitality Management

Timeshare management combines the long-term responsibilities of residential property management—such as maintenance, financial oversight, and owner relations—with the short-term demands of hospitality operations, including reservations, customer service, and high standards of cleanliness. This hybrid model demands flexibility, as timeshare properties must cater to both owners who view the property as an investment and guests who expect a premium vacation experience.

The residential aspect of timeshare management involves ensuring that the property is well-maintained, budgets are balanced, and owner associations are effectively governed. At the same time, the hospitality component focuses on creating a seamless and enjoyable experience for guests, who may include both timeshare owners and renters. Property managers must excel in both domains to meet these diverse needs.

3.7.2 Staff Management

A well-trained and motivated staff is the backbone of successful timeshare operations. Timeshare properties require personnel with diverse skill sets, combining expertise in property management, hospitality, and customer service.

1. *Roles and Responsibilities:*
   - *Property Managers:* Oversee daily operations, coordinate maintenance, and ensure compliance with regulations. Property managers act as the primary point of contact for owners and association boards.
   - *Front Desk Staff:* Handle check-ins, check-outs, and guest inquiries, ensuring a smooth arrival and departure experience.
   - *Housekeeping Teams:* Maintain cleanliness and prepare units for new occupants, often under tight turnaround times.
   - *Maintenance Personnel:* Address routine maintenance, emergency repairs, and preventative tasks to keep the property in top condition.
   - *Sales and Marketing Teams:* Promote timeshare ownership, rental programs, and exchange opportunities to attract new customers and retain existing ones.
2. *Staff Training:*
   - Cross-training staff in hospitality and property management practices is essential to ensure flexibility and efficiency. For example, front desk staff should be equipped to handle both owner inquiries and guest requests.
   - Specialized training programs, such as certifications from the American Resort Development Association (ARDA), can enhance staff expertise in timeshare-specific operations.
3. *Employee Retention:*
   - High staff turnover can disrupt operations and negatively impact owner and guest satisfaction. Offering competitive compensation, professional development opportunities, and a positive work environment helps retain skilled employees.

3.7.3 Guest Services

Providing exceptional guest services is a cornerstone of timeshare management. While owners may have a long-term relationship with the property, guests—whether through rental programs or exchange networks—evaluate their experience based on short-term interactions.

1. *Check-In and Check-Out Processes:*
   - Streamlined check-in and check-out procedures are critical for creating a positive first and last impression. Many timeshare properties use digital tools, such as mobile check-ins or keyless entry systems, to enhance convenience.
   - Front desk staff should be trained to handle common issues, such as early arrivals, late departures, and special requests.
2. *Concierge Services:*
   - Concierge services add value by assisting guests with local recommendations, activity bookings, and transportation arrangements. These services can enhance the overall vacation experience and encourage repeat visits.
3. *Conflict Resolution:*
   - Inevitably, issues such as double bookings, maintenance delays, or noise complaints may arise. Empowering staff with conflict resolution skills ensures that problems are addressed promptly and professionally.
4. *Guest Feedback:*
   - Soliciting and acting on guest feedback is essential for continuous improvement. Feedback can be collected through online reviews, surveys, or in-person interactions. Positive reviews contribute to the property's reputation, while constructive criticism identifies areas for enhancement.

3.7.4 Reservation Systems

Effective reservation systems are essential for managing timeshare usage and maximizing occupancy. Unlike traditional residential properties, timeshares must account for the complexities of shared ownership, exchange programs, and rental operations.

1. *Owner Scheduling:*
   - Owners typically reserve their usage intervals in advance, either for fixed weeks or through a flexible points-based system. Reservation systems must ensure fairness and transparency in allocating available dates.
   - Waitlist systems can be implemented to accommodate owner requests for popular weeks or seasons.
2. *Rental Programs:*
   - Many timeshare properties offer rental programs to fill unused intervals and generate additional revenue. These programs require integration with online travel agencies (OTAs) like Expedia or Airbnb to reach a wider audience.
   - Dynamic pricing models can be used to optimize rental rates based on demand, seasonality, and market trends.
3. *Exchange Programs:*
   - Properties affiliated with exchange networks, such as RCI or Interval International, must coordinate with these organizations to facilitate owner exchanges. This includes managing deposits, withdrawals, and availability for exchange intervals.

- Exchange-related reservations often involve additional fees, which must be communicated clearly to owners.

4. *Technology Integration:*
   - Modern reservation systems leverage cloud-based platforms to centralize scheduling, billing, and communication. These systems enable real-time updates and improve efficiency across departments.
   - Mobile apps and online portals provide owners and guests with self-service options for booking, payments, and inquiries.

3.7.5 Challenges and Best Practices in Timeshare Operations

Managing timeshare properties comes with unique challenges that require proactive strategies and attention to detail:

1. *High Turnover:*
   - Frequent turnover of occupants necessitates efficient housekeeping and maintenance procedures. Timeshare managers should establish clear protocols and schedules to minimize downtime between stays.
2. *Owner Expectations:*
   - Timeshare owners often have high expectations for property maintenance and customer service. Regular communication and transparent operations help build trust and loyalty.
3. *Compliance:*
   - Timeshare properties must adhere to a range of legal and regulatory requirements, including consumer protection laws, tax obligations, and safety standards. Ensuring compliance reduces liability risks and enhances operational integrity.
4. *Revenue Management:*
   - Balancing owner satisfaction with revenue generation requires careful planning. Rental programs, exchange fees, and ancillary services (e.g., spa treatments or dining) can supplement maintenance fee income.
5. *Sustainability Initiatives:*
   - Incorporating eco-friendly practices, such as energy-efficient appliances, waste reduction programs, and sustainable landscaping, aligns with evolving consumer preferences and reduces operational costs.

3.8 Amenities Management

Amenities are a defining feature of timeshare properties, significantly contributing to their appeal, value, and overall marketability. These facilities not only enhance the vacation experience for owners and guests but also differentiate timeshare properties from traditional residential or hotel accommodations. By offering a wide array of recreational, convenience, and luxury amenities, timeshare managers can attract prospective buyers, retain existing owners, and foster guest loyalty. However, managing amenities effectively requires a strategic approach, encompassing maintenance, programming, and operational excellence.

3.8.1 The Importance of Amenities in Timeshare Properties

Amenities are a primary draw for timeshare buyers and guests, often influencing purchasing decisions and satisfaction levels. High-quality amenities create a sense of luxury and exclusivity, aligning with the expectations of vacationers seeking memorable experiences. Features such as pools, fitness centers, spas, and on-site dining options enhance the property's value and can justify maintenance fees or premium pricing. Moreover, amenities serve as a key marketing tool, enabling timeshare properties to compete with hotels, resorts, and vacation rentals in an increasingly crowded market.

Amenities also play a critical role in owner retention and resale value. Properties with well-maintained and modern amenities are more likely to maintain their desirability, making it easier for owners to resell or exchange their timeshare intervals. Additionally, unique or innovative amenities, such as pet-friendly services or eco-friendly features, can appeal to niche markets and set a property apart from its competitors.

3.8.2 Managing Pools and Fitness Centers

Pools and fitness centers are among the most common and highly valued amenities in timeshare properties. Proper management of these facilities is essential for ensuring guest safety, maintaining functionality, and meeting health and regulatory standards.

Pools require regular cleaning, chemical balancing, and equipment inspections to provide a safe and enjoyable experience. Timeshare managers must comply with local health regulations, including lifeguard requirements, safety signage, and accessibility standards. Enhancements such as heated pools, poolside cabanas, or swim-up bars can elevate the guest experience and increase the property's marketability.

Fitness centers, meanwhile, cater to a wide range of guests seeking to maintain their exercise routines while on vacation. Equipment maintenance is crucial, as broken or outdated machines can lead to dissatisfaction or injuries. Managers should invest in a mix of cardio, strength, and flexibility equipment to accommodate diverse fitness needs. Additionally, offering fitness classes or personal training sessions can enhance the value of the fitness center and create additional revenue streams.

3.8.3 On-Site Restaurants and Dining Options

On-site dining options add convenience and luxury to timeshare properties, providing guests with easy access to quality meals without leaving the property. Managing a restaurant within a timeshare setting involves balancing operational efficiency with guest satisfaction. Menus should be diverse, catering to a range of dietary preferences and budgets, including vegetarian, vegan, and gluten-free options. Seasonal or local ingredients can also add a unique touch, reflecting the property's location and enhancing the culinary experience.

To maximize profitability, timeshare managers can implement themed dining nights, happy hour promotions, or cooking classes that engage guests and encourage repeat visits. Quality control is paramount, with consistent food quality and exceptional service as critical factors in maintaining a positive reputation.

3.8.4 Concierge Services and Guest Support

Concierge services are an integral part of the timeshare experience, offering personalized support to guests and owners. A knowledgeable concierge team can enhance the vacation experience by providing recommendations for local attractions, booking activities, or arranging transportation. This level of service fosters a sense of care and attentiveness, building guest loyalty and encouraging positive reviews.

To streamline operations, many timeshare properties are incorporating technology into their concierge services. Mobile apps and online portals allow guests to make requests, receive recommendations, and access property information at their convenience. This hybrid approach, combining human interaction with digital tools, ensures efficiency while maintaining a personal touch.

3.8.5 Recreational and Outdoor Spaces

Outdoor amenities, such as recreational areas, gardens, and event spaces, contribute to the ambiance and versatility of a timeshare property. Barbecue areas, fire pits, and playgrounds provide opportunities for families and groups to gather and socialize, while tranquil gardens or walking trails offer relaxation and connection with nature.

For properties with access to unique outdoor features, such as beaches or ski slopes, maximizing these assets is critical. Providing equipment rentals, guided tours, or private access to these areas can elevate the guest experience and increase the property's appeal.

3.8.6 Pet-Friendly Amenities

As more travelers choose to vacation with their pets, pet-friendly amenities are becoming an important consideration for timeshare properties. Designated pet areas, such as dog parks or relief stations, make it easier for guests to care for their animals. Additional services, such as grooming, pet-sitting, or pet welcome kits, create a welcoming environment for pet owners, broadening the property's appeal.

3.8.7 Sustainability and Eco-Friendly Amenities

Sustainability is an increasingly important factor for vacationers, and timeshare properties that prioritize eco-friendly practices can attract environmentally conscious buyers and guests. Amenities such as solar-heated pools, energy-efficient lighting, and recycling programs reduce the property's environmental impact while demonstrating a commitment to responsible management. Green certifications, such as LEED or Green Globe, can further enhance the property's reputation and marketability.

Timeshare managers should also consider incorporating educational components into their sustainability initiatives. For example, guided tours of eco-friendly features or informational signage about water conservation efforts can engage guests and reinforce the property's values.

3.8.8 Best Practices for Amenities Management

Managing amenities effectively requires a proactive approach that balances guest expectations with operational efficiency. Regular maintenance is critical, ensuring that facilities remain safe, functional, and visually appealing. Preventative maintenance schedules can reduce the likelihood of breakdowns or costly repairs, while guest feedback can identify areas for improvement or investment.

Collaboration between departments is also essential. For example, housekeeping and maintenance teams must coordinate closely to prepare facilities for guests, while marketing teams should highlight amenities in promotional materials. Staff training ensures that employees understand the importance of amenities to the overall guest experience and are equipped to provide exceptional service.

3.8.9 Challenges in Amenities Management

Despite their benefits, amenities can present challenges for timeshare managers. High operational costs, such as energy usage or staffing requirements, must be carefully managed to avoid budget overruns. Additionally, guest usage conflicts, such as overcrowded pools or limited availability of fitness equipment, require fair and transparent policies to address.

Adapting to changing trends and preferences is another challenge. Amenities that were once considered luxurious, such as basic fitness centers, may no longer meet guest expectations. Managers must stay informed about industry trends and invest in updates or innovations to maintain competitiveness.

3.9 Timeshare Budgeting

Budgeting is a critical component of managing timeshare properties, requiring careful planning and financial oversight to meet the unique cost structures inherent to this type of property management. Unlike traditional residential or hospitality properties, timeshares have distinct financial considerations, including marketing expenses, exchange program fees, and periodic renovations. A well-structured budget ensures financial sustainability, maintains owner satisfaction, and supports the operational efficiency of the property. This section explores the key elements of timeshare budgets and provides a comprehensive guide to creating and managing budgets tailored to the timeshare industry.

3.9.1 Understanding Unique Cost Structures in Timeshare Management

Timeshare properties operate with financial models that differ significantly from other types of real estate or hospitality properties. These unique cost structures arise from the shared ownership model, high turnover rates, and the emphasis on providing a premium vacation experience.

1. *Marketing Expenses:*
   - Timeshare properties often rely on aggressive marketing campaigns to attract new buyers and retain existing owners. This includes advertising costs, sales commissions, and promotional events such as tours or vacation previews.
   - Marketing budgets must account for the cost of lead generation, including partnerships with travel agencies or online platforms. Retargeting campaigns to encourage repeat buyers or renters are also essential components.
2. *Exchange Program Fees:*
   - Many timeshare properties participate in exchange networks, such as RCI (Resort Condominiums International) or Interval International, allowing owners to trade their usage intervals for stays at other properties. These affiliations come with membership fees, administrative costs, and sometimes additional marketing expenses to promote the program.
   - Exchange programs require financial coordination to ensure that associated fees are covered while providing value to owners.
3. *Periodic Renovations and Reserve Contributions:*
   - Maintaining the property's appeal and functionality requires regular renovations, such as updating furnishings, appliances, and amenities. Timeshare managers must plan for these costs through reserve funds.
   - Reserve contributions are often included in annual maintenance fees, calculated to cover both anticipated and unexpected capital expenses over time.
4. *High Turnover Costs:*
   - Timeshares experience frequent guest turnover, necessitating increased spending on housekeeping, unit preparation, and maintenance. These opera-

tional costs must be budgeted more precisely than for traditional residential properties.

3.9.2 Creating a Timeshare Budget: A Step-by-Step Guide

Developing a comprehensive timeshare budget involves balancing the property's revenue streams against its expenses to ensure financial sustainability. The following steps outline best practices for creating and managing an effective budget.

1. *Assess Revenue Streams:*
   - Identify and quantify all sources of income, including maintenance fees, rental income, and ancillary revenue from amenities such as restaurants, spas, or event hosting.
   - Consider the potential for additional revenue from exchange program participation or optional services, such as concierge or childcare programs.
   - Factor in seasonal variations in revenue, as timeshare occupancy rates often fluctuate based on demand and peak travel seasons.
2. *Categorize Expenses:*
   - *Fixed Expenses:* Include predictable costs such as salaries for staff, insurance premiums, and property taxes.
   - *Variable Expenses:* Account for costs that fluctuate based on occupancy or usage, such as utilities, housekeeping, and marketing efforts.
   - *Capital Expenses:* Plan for long-term investments, such as structural repairs, amenity upgrades, or major equipment replacements.
3. *Incorporate Reserve Contributions:*
   - Establish a reserve fund to cover future capital expenses and ensure the property remains in compliance with regulations. Contributions should be based on a reserve study that evaluates the property's long-term needs.
   - Reserve funds should be managed separately from operating accounts and invested conservatively to maintain liquidity.
4. *Allocate Marketing Budgets:*
   - Dedicate a portion of the budget to marketing campaigns, ensuring that funds are allocated to both acquisition and retention strategies. Track the return on investment (ROI) for different marketing channels to optimize spending.
   - Consider partnerships with online platforms or travel agencies to increase visibility and bookings.
5. *Plan for Renovations:*
   - Include line items for periodic renovations, such as refreshing interiors, updating technology, or enhancing amenities. Factor in the potential impact of renovations on revenue if units must be taken offline temporarily.
6. *Monitor Administrative Costs:*
   - Budget for administrative expenses, including accounting, legal services, and board meetings. These costs are critical for maintaining governance and compliance.

7. *Estimate Exchange Program Fees:*
    - Account for the costs of participating in exchange programs, including affiliation fees and administrative overhead. Ensure these fees are included in owner maintenance charges if applicable.

3.9.3 Managing Timeshare Budgets for Sustainability

Effective budget management requires ongoing oversight, communication, and adaptability to ensure that financial goals are met. The following strategies support sustainable financial management in timeshare operations.

1. *Regular Financial Reviews:*
    - Conduct monthly or quarterly reviews to compare actual expenses and revenue against budgeted amounts. Identify variances early and adjust spending or revenue strategies as needed.
    - Utilize property management software to automate financial tracking and generate detailed reports for the board and stakeholders.
2. *Transparent Communication with Owners:*
    - Provide owners with clear, detailed explanations of how maintenance fees are calculated and allocated. Transparency builds trust and reduces the likelihood of disputes over fees.
    - Share updates on reserve fund balances and planned renovations to keep owners informed about the property's long-term financial health.
3. *Cost Control Measures:*
    - Implement cost-saving measures, such as energy-efficient upgrades or bulk purchasing agreements for supplies. Regularly review vendor contracts to ensure competitive pricing.
    - Monitor staffing levels to ensure operational efficiency without compromising service quality.
4. *Adapting to Market Conditions:*
    - Adjust budgets to reflect changes in market demand, such as increased marketing during low-occupancy periods or scaling back discretionary expenses during economic downturns.
    - Stay informed about industry trends, such as shifts in travel preferences or emerging technologies, to identify new opportunities for revenue or cost optimization.
5. *Reserve Fund Management:*
    - Periodically review the adequacy of reserve contributions, particularly after major renovations or unexpected expenses. Ensure that the reserve study is updated regularly to reflect changes in property conditions or market conditions.
    - Avoid using reserve funds for operating expenses to maintain financial stability and compliance with regulations.

3.9.4 Challenges in Timeshare Budgeting

Timeshare budgeting presents unique challenges that require proactive solutions and meticulous planning.

1. *Balancing Owner Expectations with Financial Needs:*
   - Owners may resist increases in maintenance fees, even when necessary to cover rising costs or fund capital improvements. Property managers must communicate the rationale for fee adjustments effectively.
   - Striking a balance between affordability and the quality of services provided is essential for maintaining owner satisfaction.
2. *Managing Seasonal Revenue Variations:*
   - Seasonal fluctuations in occupancy can create cash flow challenges, particularly for properties relying heavily on rental income. Budgeting should account for these variations to avoid financial shortfalls.
3. *Navigating Regulatory Requirements:*
   - Compliance with tax laws, consumer protection regulations, and financial disclosure requirements adds complexity to timeshare budgeting. Managers must stay updated on regulatory changes to ensure compliance.

3.10 Summary

Timeshares represent a unique intersection of residential property management and hospitality operations, requiring a specialized approach to meet the needs of both owners and guests. This chapter explored the defining characteristics, operational requirements, and market dynamics of timeshares, providing students with a comprehensive understanding of this niche segment of property management. Timeshares are built on shared ownership models, including deeded and right-to-use agreements, allowing individuals to access high-quality vacation properties without the financial burden of sole ownership. Their hybrid nature introduces complexities in governance, legal compliance, and financial management, distinguishing them from traditional residential properties and hospitality operations.

A key focus of the chapter was the legal and operational frameworks that underpin timeshare management. Timeshares differ significantly from other community associations like HOAs and COAs due to their transient occupancy and unique cost structures. Effective management requires a clear understanding of governance practices, including managing owner expectations, enforcing policies, and coordinating high turnover rates. The chapter emphasized the importance of transparency and proactive communication in maintaining owner satisfaction while ensuring operational efficiency.

Understanding the demographics and market trends of timeshares is essential for managers aiming to align their properties with consumer preferences. The rise of points-based systems, branded hospitality programs, and sustainable practices reflects the evolving demands of timeshare buyers. These trends highlight the need for innovation and adaptability in timeshare management, particularly in marketing, amenities, and guest services.

Operational success in timeshare management depends on a holistic approach that integrates staff training, high-quality amenities, and advanced reservation systems. Amenities such as pools, fitness centers, and on-site dining play a critical role in enhancing guest experiences and increasing the property's marketability. Additionally, budgeting for timeshares requires careful consideration of marketing expenses, reserve contributions, and exchange program fees to ensure financial sustainability. The chapter concluded by emphasizing regulatory compliance as a cornerstone of ethical and effective timeshare management, ensuring long-term trust and value for owners and guests. Through these insights, students gain the knowledge and skills necessary to navigate the complexities of managing timeshare properties in today's dynamic market.

3.11 Case Study: Riviera Palm Resort

The Riviera Palm Resort is a luxury timeshare property located in Florida. The property operates under a points-based system, allowing owners to use their points for stays at Riviera Palm or other properties within its affiliated network. Recently, the resort has faced challenges, including disputes among owners over popular booking dates, increasing maintenance costs due to aging amenities, and complaints from guests about inconsistent housekeeping standards. Additionally, management is evaluating whether to expand its amenities to include a spa to remain competitive.

3.11.1 Discussion Questions

1. *Reservation Management:*
    - How can Riviera Palm Resort improve its reservation system to reduce conflicts over booking high-demand dates?
    - What strategies can the resort implement to communicate reservation policies more effectively to owners?
2. *Maintenance Challenges:*
    - What steps should the management take to address the increasing maintenance costs and aging amenities?
    - How can the resort ensure that maintenance issues do not negatively impact the guest experience?
3. *Guest Satisfaction:*
    - How can Riviera Palm Resort address the complaints about housekeeping inconsistencies?
    - What measures can the resort take to improve overall guest satisfaction?

4. *Amenities Expansion:*
   - What factors should the management consider before deciding to add a spa to the property?
   - How can the resort evaluate the potential return on investment (ROI) for this new amenity?

3.12 Review Questions

1. *What is the primary characteristic that distinguishes timeshares from traditional residential properties?*
   (A) Unlimited usage rights
   (B) Shared ownership and interval-based usage
   (C) Full real estate ownership for all participants
   (D) Long-term tenant occupancy
2. *In a deeded timeshare model, what do owners typically hold?*
   (A) A long-term lease agreement
   (B) A fractional ownership interest in real property
   (C) A right-to-use license with no real estate interest
   (D) Exclusive full-year usage rights
3. *Which of the following is an advantage of a points-based timeshare system?*
   (A) Guaranteed usage at the same time each year
   (B) Increased flexibility to book various locations and times
   (C) Lower maintenance fees than other timeshare types
   (D) Perpetual ownership without renewal fees
4. *What is the primary governance body typically responsible for managing timeshare properties?*
   (A) Homeowners' association board
   (B) Timeshare owner collective
   (C) Resort management company or board of directors
   (D) State real estate commission
5. *What is a common source of ongoing revenue for timeshare properties?*
   (A) Rental deposits
   (B) Annual maintenance fees
   (C) Exchange program membership fees
   (D) Real estate transaction taxes
6. *Which of the following is a key benefit of vacation clubs compared to traditional timeshare ownership?*
   (A) Deeded real estate ownership
   (B) Fixed annual fees with no additional costs
   (C) Access to a wide range of properties and services
   (D) Guaranteed usage at one specific location
7. *What is one of the primary challenges in managing timeshare reservations?*
   (A) Allocating specific rooms for full-time residents
   (B) Coordinating high-demand periods equitably among owners

(C) Increasing the frequency of usage among owners
(D) Tracking tax compliance for rental income

8. *Which of the following best describes fractional ownership in timeshares?*
   (A) Ownership based on a points-based system with no real estate interest
   (B) Shared ownership divided among a small number of owners with extended usage rights
   (C) A lease-based model that grants short-term occupancy rights
   (D) Membership in a vacation club with no specific property rights
9. *What is the primary purpose of a timeshare reserve fund?*
   (A) To cover day-to-day operational expenses
   (B) To provide refunds to dissatisfied owners
   (C) To fund long-term capital improvements and unexpected repairs
   (D) To finance marketing and sales activities
10. *Which regulatory body primarily oversees consumer protection for timeshare sales in the United States?*
   (A) Federal Trade Commission (FTC)
   (B) Real Estate Settlement Procedures Act (RESPA)
   (C) Federal Housing Administration (FHA)
   (D) Department of Housing and Urban Development (HUD)

Introduction to Manufactured Home Parks

4

4.1 Learning Objectives

By the end of this chapter, students will be able to:

- *Understand the Characteristics and Unique Aspects of Manufactured Home Parks*
  - Identify the defining features of manufactured home parks and distinguish them from other types of residential properties.
  - Explain the unique challenges and considerations involved in managing communities with individually owned manufactured homes on rented lots.
- *Evaluate the Advantages and Disadvantages of Manufactured Home Parks*
  - Analyze the benefits of manufactured home parks for both tenants and property owners, including affordability and potential for stable income.
  - Discuss the common disadvantages, such as community stigma, maintenance complexities, and regulatory challenges.
- *Implement Effective Operations Management for Manufactured Home Parks*
  - Outline best practices for managing daily operations in manufactured home parks, including maintaining common areas, providing utilities, and managing amenities.
  - Develop strategies for tenant management and community engagement to foster a positive living environment.
- *Ensure Regulatory Compliance for Manufactured Home Parks*
  - Identify the key regulations governing manufactured home parks at the local, state, and federal levels.
  - Understand the property manager's role in ensuring compliance with health, safety, zoning, and fair housing laws.
- *Draft Key Lease Terms to Include When Renting a Manufactured Home or Lot*
  - Understand the essential lease provisions that should be included in rental agreements for manufactured home parks.
  - Draft leases that address rent terms, park rules, severability clauses, and specific obligations for both landlords and tenants.

D. A. Vaughn, *Essentials of Residential Property Management*, Springer Texts in Business and Economics, https://doi.org/10.1007/978-3-031-92329-6_4

4.2 Key Terms

Manufactured Home
Manufactured Home Park
HUD Code
Lot Rent
Common Areas
Park Rules and Regulations
Rental Term
Severability Clause
Warranty of Habitability
Indemnification Clause

By mastering these learning objectives and understanding key terms, students will gain a thorough understanding of the complexities and unique aspects of managing manufactured home parks. This knowledge will prepare them to effectively handle the operational, legal, and managerial challenges associated with this type of residential property.

4.3 Overview

Manufactured home parks are a unique form of residential property that require specialized management strategies and an understanding of their distinct characteristics, market dynamics, and regulatory requirements. This chapter, *Introduction to Manufactured Home Parks*, provides a comprehensive guide to managing these communities, covering key topics such as the unique aspects of manufactured home parks, their advantages and disadvantages, effective operations management, tenant relations, and regulatory compliance. The goal of this chapter is to equip property managers with the knowledge and tools needed to effectively manage manufactured home parks, while ensuring resident satisfaction and compliance with legal standards.

One of the defining features of manufactured home parks is their ownership and rental structure. Unlike multifamily or single-family rentals, residents in manufactured home parks often own their homes but lease the land on which the home is situated. This arrangement creates a unique relationship between the property manager and residents, as the manager oversees the land and shared community areas rather than the physical homes. Consequently, this chapter explores the implications of this ownership model and how it affects lease agreements, tenant relations, and community management.

The chapter also highlights the benefits and challenges associated with managing manufactured home parks. On the positive side, manufactured home parks offer affordability, flexibility, and a strong sense of community for residents, while providing stable income for property owners. However, disadvantages such as property stigma, potential depreciation of manufactured homes, and complexities around land ownership and legal compliance are also discussed in detail. Understanding these dynamics allows property managers to develop strategies that leverage the parks' strengths and address potential drawbacks.

Effective operations management is another focal point of the chapter. Manufactured home parks often include shared amenities such as playgrounds, clubhouses, and utility infrastructure that must be maintained and managed efficiently. Property managers must handle a diverse range of responsibilities, including maintaining *common areas*, overseeing amenities, ensuring security, and managing resident relations. This chapter outlines best practices for maintaining these areas and creating a positive living environment.

In addition, regulatory compliance plays a vital role in managing manufactured home parks. Property managers must navigate a complex web of zoning laws, health and safety regulations, environmental standards, and tenant protections. The chapter provides guidance on understanding and adhering to these regulations to minimize legal risks and ensure the community operates within the bounds of the law.

Overall, this chapter provides a foundational understanding of the key aspects of managing manufactured home parks, equipping property managers to handle the unique challenges and opportunities presented by this type of residential property. By mastering these concepts, property managers can foster well-run communities that support resident satisfaction and long-term success for property owners.

4.4 Introduction to Manufactured Home Parks

4.4.1 Characteristics and Unique Aspects

Manufactured home parks are unique residential communities designed to accommodate manufactured homes, which are factory-built dwellings constructed according to federal *HUD Code* standards. Unlike traditional apartment complexes or single-family homes, these communities often blend aspects of both multifamily and single-family property management, requiring a specialized approach to oversight and operations. Managing manufactured home parks involves unique considerations, including resident ownership, leasing arrangements for lots, and the need to maintain shared community amenities.

Resident Ownership and Leasing Arrangements: One of the most distinct characteristics of manufactured home parks is the ownership and leasing structure. In many cases, residents own their homes but rent the lot space on which the home is situated. This creates a dual relationship where property managers oversee the land and common areas but have limited control over the homes themselves. This setup demands a different approach to lease agreements, focusing on *lot rent* and the use of community spaces, rather than traditional residential leases that encompass the dwelling itself. As a result, managers must balance enforcing park rules with respecting homeowners' rights to manage their private properties.

Community and Common Area Maintenance: Manufactured home parks often include a range of shared amenities, such as community centers, playgrounds, and recreational areas. Property managers are responsible for maintaining these common areas and ensuring that the entire park is kept in good condition. This includes overseeing landscaping, utility services (such as water, sewer, and electricity), and road maintenance within the community. Managing these services requires diligent planning and regular inspections to ensure the safety and satisfaction of residents. The quality of common area maintenance can significantly influence tenant retention and overall community appeal.

Unique Tenant Relations and Park Rules: Another characteristic that sets manufactured home parks apart is the emphasis on community engagement and adherence to park rules. Because residents often own their homes, they tend to have a greater sense of investment in the community. Property managers must foster positive relationships by being responsive to resident concerns, promoting a sense of community, and applying park rules fairly and consistently. Common rules may govern exterior home maintenance, noise levels, pet policies, and the use of shared amenities. Clear communication and transparency about these rules are essential to maintaining harmony within the park.

Regulatory Compliance and Zoning Challenges: Manufactured home parks are subject to a complex set of federal, state, and local regulations that govern everything from zoning to the construction and installation of homes. Zoning laws, in particular, can be challenging, as many municipalities have restrictions on where manufactured home parks can be located. Property managers must ensure compliance with these regulations, which often requires coordinating with local governments, understanding HUD Code requirements, and staying informed about changes in zoning and housing laws.

Overall, the unique characteristics of manufactured home parks require property managers to be well-versed in land lease management, community operations, and regulatory compliance. Successful management involves balancing the needs and rights of homeowners with maintaining the integrity and appeal of the park as a whole. By understanding these unique aspects, property managers can create a positive living environment that supports long-term community stability and satisfaction.

4.4.2 Advantages and Disadvantages

Manufactured home parks offer a distinct set of advantages and disadvantages that impact both property owners and residents. Understanding these benefits and challenges is essential for property managers to effectively promote the community's strengths and address any concerns that may arise. These factors can influence tenant satisfaction, community stability, and overall property management strategy.

Advantages of Manufactured Home Parks

1. *Affordability:* One of the most significant advantages of manufactured home parks is affordability. Manufactured homes typically cost less than traditional site-built homes, making them an attractive option for families, retirees, and individuals seeking cost-effective housing. For property owners, manufactured home parks can provide a steady income stream with relatively lower operating costs compared to multifamily or single-family rentals. Residents benefit from the lower overall cost of homeownership or renting, which includes the opportunity to own a home while paying reduced lot rent.
2. *Community Living:* Manufactured home parks often foster a strong sense of community among residents. The close-knit nature of these parks, combined with shared amenities such as community centers, playgrounds, and social events, creates a neighborhood atmosphere that encourages interaction and support among residents. This community living aspect appeals to families, seniors, and individuals who value the social opportunities and security of living in a park. Property managers can further enhance this environment by organizing community events, promoting resident engagement, and ensuring that common areas are well-maintained.

3. *Flexibility:* Manufactured home parks offer unique flexibility for both property owners and residents. Owners have the option to expand or reduce the number of home sites based on demand and available land, while residents can choose to rent a lot, rent both a home and lot, or even move their home to a different park if desired. This flexibility allows residents to adapt their living arrangements to changing needs, whether it's downsizing, upgrading, or relocating.

Disadvantages of Manufactured Home Parks

1. *Stigma and Perception:* Despite improvements in quality and design, manufactured home parks often suffer from negative stereotypes and stigmas. Some people perceive these communities as lower-quality housing options, which can deter potential residents. This stigma can affect property values and make it challenging to market the park to higher-income tenants or attract potential buyers. Property managers must work to combat this perception by emphasizing the quality, safety, and benefits of living in a well-managed park.
2. *Depreciation of Home Value:* Manufactured homes tend to depreciate in value over time, unlike traditional site-built homes, which typically appreciate. This depreciation can be a disadvantage for residents who own their homes but lease the lot space, as it reduces their home's resale value. Property managers should educate residents on maintenance strategies that can help slow depreciation and emphasize the long-term affordability of manufactured homes as a key benefit.
3. *Land Ownership and Control:* In most manufactured home parks, residents own their homes but not the land on which they are placed. This arrangement can create instability for homeowners, as they are subject to rent increases and park rule changes imposed by property owners. Additionally, if a park is sold or redeveloped, residents may be forced to move their homes, which can be costly and difficult. Property managers must navigate these complexities carefully, ensuring that park rules are fair and transparent and that any changes are communicated clearly and well in advance.

   Understanding the unique advantages and disadvantages of manufactured home parks allows property managers to better support residents, enhance community satisfaction, and position the park as a desirable and stable housing option.

4.5 Understanding the Market

Understanding the market dynamics of manufactured home parks is crucial for property managers and owners to position their communities effectively and attract the right residents. This process involves analyzing demographics, monitoring market trends, and conducting competitive analysis. By comprehensively understanding these factors, property managers can tailor their marketing and management strategies to meet the specific needs of potential residents, respond to market shifts, and ensure the long-term profitability and stability of the community.

4.5.1 Demographics

The demographics of manufactured home park residents are diverse, often including retirees, working-class families, and individuals seeking affordable housing options. The affordability of manufactured homes appeals to residents who desire homeownership without the high costs associated with traditional site-built homes. Many residents are seniors looking for a low-maintenance lifestyle, empty nesters who are downsizing, or families seeking more space at a lower cost compared to apartments. Property managers must consider these demographic factors when designing community amenities, establishing park rules, and setting rental rates.

Understanding resident demographics also involves identifying lifestyle preferences and income levels. For example, retirees may value amenities such as clubhouses, social activities, and fitness centers, while working families might prioritize proximity to schools, playgrounds, and safe streets. Tailoring amenities and services to the specific needs of these groups helps attract and retain residents. Additionally, the increasing demand for pet-friendly policies and flexible leasing options reflects broader demographic trends that property managers must address.

4.5.2 Market Trends

Manufactured home parks have experienced fluctuating market trends over the past few decades. Recently, these communities have seen a resurgence in popularity due to the growing need for affordable housing across the country. Rising home prices and a lack of affordable rental options in many urban and suburban areas have made manufactured home parks a more appealing choice for many demographics. This trend has driven increased investment in manufactured home communities, with large institutional investors entering the market, upgrading parks, and adding new amenities.

Property managers must stay attuned to trends such as rising rental demand, changing consumer preferences, and the impact of economic factors on tenant affordability. For example, recent market shifts show a greater emphasis on high-quality park amenities, eco-friendly infrastructure, and enhanced security measures to appeal to a broader range of potential residents. Recognizing and adapting to these trends is essential for maintaining a competitive edge.

4.5.3 Competitive Analysis

Conducting a competitive analysis helps property managers understand how their manufactured home park compares to others in the area. Key factors to consider include rental rates, amenities, park rules, and overall community reputation. Property managers should regularly analyze local competitors to identify strengths and weaknesses, determine which features are attracting tenants, and uncover opportunities for differentiation.

For example, if nearby parks offer more recreational amenities or superior maintenance services, property managers may consider upgrading their own offerings or emphasizing other unique advantages, such as larger lot sizes, lower lot rent, or a more family-oriented atmosphere. Understanding the competition also involves monitoring new developments and any changes in zoning laws that could impact the supply of manufactured home lots in the region.

Effective competitive analysis helps property managers position their parks strategically in the marketplace, create targeted marketing campaigns, and enhance their value proposition to meet the evolving expectations of potential residents. Ultimately, staying informed about local competition enables property managers to make data-driven decisions that attract and retain tenants, ensuring long-term success.

4.6 Operations Management for Manufactured Home Parks

Effective operations management is essential to the success and profitability of manufactured home parks. Unlike other residential property types, managing a manufactured home park involves overseeing not just individual rental lots, but also a range of shared spaces, amenities, and infrastructure. Property managers must ensure that common areas are well-maintained, amenities meet residents' needs, and security measures are in place to protect both the property and its residents. A proactive approach to managing these aspects enhances community satisfaction, attracts new tenants, and ensures long-term stability within the park.

4.6.1 Managing Common Areas and Facilities

Common areas in a manufactured home park typically include roads, sidewalks, green spaces, community centers, playgrounds, and parking lots. These shared spaces play a significant role in creating a welcoming environment for residents and maintaining the overall aesthetic appeal of the park. Property managers are responsible for regular upkeep and maintenance of these areas, which may involve landscaping, lighting, waste management, and road repairs. Ensuring these spaces are clean, safe, and well-maintained is crucial for resident satisfaction and retention.

Proper management of these areas requires routine inspections to identify potential hazards, such as uneven sidewalks, overgrown landscaping, or broken equipment. Addressing maintenance issues promptly not only helps avoid liability but also demonstrates the property manager's commitment to providing a high-quality living environment. During peak seasons, additional maintenance may be required, particularly for landscaping and recreational areas, to keep the property looking its best.

4.6.2 Amenities Management

Amenities play a critical role in differentiating manufactured home parks and adding value to the community. Common amenities in manufactured home parks may include swimming pools, clubhouses, fitness centers, laundry facilities, and recreational areas. Property managers must ensure that these amenities are accessible, well-maintained, and meet residents' needs. Regular cleaning, equipment servicing, and timely repairs are essential for maintaining the safety and usability of these facilities.

Managing amenities also involves setting clear policies and guidelines for their use. For example, property managers should establish rules for pool access, clubhouse reservations, and usage hours to prevent conflicts and ensure fair access for all residents. Offering a variety of amenities that cater to different demographics—such as creating senior-friendly spaces, children's play areas, and pet amenities—can enhance the community's appeal and help attract a diverse group of tenants.

4.6.3 Security Management

Security is a top concern for residents of manufactured home parks, as it directly impacts their sense of safety and well-being. Implementing effective security measures involves both physical security elements, such as gates, surveillance cameras, and lighting, and procedural strategies, such as resident screenings and clear visitor policies. For larger parks, hiring security personnel or employing a mobile patrol service can provide an added layer of protection.

Property managers should regularly evaluate the security needs of the park and adapt strategies based on feedback from residents and changes in the local environment. Installing proper lighting in parking areas and along walkways, maintaining secure entry points, and ensuring that emergency contact information is easily accessible can help create a safer environment. Additionally, fostering a sense of community can indirectly enhance security by encouraging residents to be vigilant and report suspicious activities.

4.6.4 Tenant Relations and Community Management

Tenant relations and community management are critical components in managing manufactured home parks successfully. Unlike traditional multifamily properties, manufactured home parks often cultivate a strong sense of community, given that many residents own their homes and reside in the park for extended periods. Property managers must foster positive tenant relationships, ensure smooth communication, and maintain a fair and structured management approach to create a harmonious living environment. Key areas of focus include communication, conflict resolution, resident services, rent collection, and legal compliance for land lease agreements.

Communication

Effective communication is the foundation of successful tenant relations in manufactured home parks. Property managers should establish clear and accessible lines of communication for residents to voice concerns, ask questions, and stay informed about community updates. Regularly distributing newsletters, posting announcements on community boards, and using digital platforms (such as resident portals or email updates) are effective ways to keep residents engaged and informed. Transparency is vital—residents should always be aware of any policy changes, upcoming maintenance work, or community events.

Property managers should also make themselves visible and approachable within the community by scheduling regular office hours or hosting meet-and-greet sessions. Establishing a rapport with residents helps build trust and promotes a sense of community ownership.

Conflict Resolution

Conflicts can arise in any community, and manufactured home parks are no exception. Common disputes may involve neighbor issues, property boundaries, noise complaints, or disagreements over community rules. Property managers must address conflicts swiftly and impartially, applying park rules consistently and fairly. Mediation may be required in some cases, especially when multiple residents are involved. Establishing a formal conflict resolution process helps ensure that issues are managed professionally and that all parties feel heard and respected.

Resident Services

Providing quality resident services is essential for tenant satisfaction and retention. These services may include facilitating home repairs, coordinating utility connections, organizing social events, or assisting with moving logistics. Managers should strive to offer a range of services that address the needs of diverse resident groups, such as families, retirees, and working professionals. A focus on exceptional resident services can set a park apart from others and contribute to a higher level of resident satisfaction.

Rent Collection and Financial Management

Rent collection in manufactured home parks can involve managing both lot rent and utility fees. Property managers must establish clear rent collection policies and provide convenient payment options, such as online portals or automatic deductions. Promptly addressing late payments and communicating consequences for nonpayment, such as late fees or potential eviction, is essential to maintaining financial stability. Keeping accurate financial records and providing regular statements to residents (if applicable) helps build transparency and trust.

Land Lease Agreements and Legal Compliance

Manufactured home parks often operate under unique land lease agreements, where residents own their homes but rent the land on which the home is situated. Property managers must ensure these agreements are legally compliant and include specific terms such as rent amounts, lot maintenance responsibilities, and park rules. It is also crucial to understand state-specific regulations governing manufactured home parks, such as the rights of residents during park sales, eviction procedures, and the terms under which the land lease can be renewed or terminated. Regular reviews of lease agreements and legal requirements help prevent disputes and protect both the park owner's and residents' rights.

4.7 Regulatory Compliance for Manufactured Home Parks

Regulatory compliance is a crucial aspect of managing manufactured home parks, given the complex web of local, state, and federal regulations that govern their operation. Property managers must navigate zoning laws, health and safety standards, environmental regulations, tenant rights, and lease agreements to ensure that the park is legally compliant and operates smoothly. Compliance not only protects property owners from legal disputes but also safeguards residents' rights and promotes a safe and habitable living environment. Below are the key areas of regulatory compliance specific to managing manufactured home parks.

4.7.1 Zoning Laws and Regulations

Zoning laws are one of the most challenging regulatory aspects for manufactured home parks. Many municipalities have strict zoning ordinances that dictate where manufactured homes can be placed and how parks can be developed. Property managers must be thoroughly familiar with local zoning laws, including permissible land uses, density restrictions, and setback requirements. Any changes to the park layout, expansion of existing lots, or addition of amenities must align with these regulations. Failure to comply can result in penalties, denial of permits, or forced removal of noncompliant structures. Working closely with local planning and zoning departments is essential when making modifications to the park.

4.7.2 Health and Safety Standards

Health and safety standards are designed to ensure that manufactured home parks are safe, sanitary, and livable. Property managers are responsible for maintaining these standards by conducting regular inspections, promptly addressing safety concerns, and ensuring that the park infrastructure, such as roads, water systems, and electrical services, meets regulatory requirements. For example, homes must be properly spaced to allow emergency access, and utilities must be installed and maintained according to code. Health and safety compliance also involves adhering to fire safety regulations, including maintaining fire lanes, installing fire hydrants where required, and providing clear evacuation plans.

4.7.3 Environmental Regulations

Environmental regulations are particularly relevant to manufactured home parks, especially those situated near wetlands, flood zones, or protected areas. Property managers must ensure compliance with environmental laws governing waste disposal, water management, and stormwater drainage. Managing these aspects involves preventing pollution, mitigating erosion, and ensuring that septic systems are functioning correctly. Environmental compliance is not only a legal obligation but also a critical factor in protecting residents' health and the surrounding ecosystem.

Tenant Rights and Protections

Tenant rights in manufactured home parks are typically more complex than in traditional rental properties due to the unique ownership structure. Many states have specific laws that provide additional protections to residents who own their homes but rent the lot space. Property managers must be aware of these tenant rights, which may include regulations around rent increases, eviction procedures, and park closures. For instance, some states require a minimum notice period (often 60–90 days) before raising lot rent or making significant changes to park rules. Evictions in manufactured home parks must be handled delicately, following state laws that often differ from general landlord-tenant regulations.

4.8 Lease Agreements

4.8.1 Lot Lease Agreement

The lot lease agreement is a critical document in manufactured home parks, outlining the terms under which residents lease their lot space. This agreement should detail the rent amount, payment terms, maintenance responsibilities, and rules for using shared community spaces. It should also specify the rights and obligations of both the park owner and the tenant, including the process for lease renewal or termination. Property managers must ensure that lot lease agreements comply with state laws and include necessary disclosures, such as the legal requirements for park closures or the sale of the property.

4.8.2 Manufactured Home Lease Agreement

For residents who rent both the home and the lot, a manufactured home lease agreement is used. This agreement is more comprehensive, covering not only lot rent but also home maintenance, use of appliances, and general upkeep. Property managers must ensure that these agreements comply with state-specific landlord-tenant laws, similar to traditional residential leases. This agreement should clearly distinguish between what the tenant is responsible for (such as interior home maintenance) and what the property manager must handle (such as exterior home repairs or infrastructure maintenance).

Key Lease Terms to Include When Renting a Manufactured Home or Lot:

A well-drafted lease agreement is crucial for managing manufactured home parks effectively. Key lease terms ensure clarity, protect both parties' rights, and provide a framework for resolving disputes.

1. Rent:
   - *Details:* The lease agreement should clearly specify the amount of rent due, the due date, and acceptable payment methods. It should also outline any late fees and penalties for missed payments. Clear terms regarding rent help prevent disputes and ensure a steady income for the property owner.
2. *Rental Term:*
   - *Details:* The lease should define the duration of the rental agreement, including the start and end dates. It should also cover renewal options, notice requirements for termination, and conditions for early termination. Specifying the rental term provides stability for both parties.
3. *Severability Clause:*
   - *Details:* This clause ensures that if one part of the lease is found to be invalid or unenforceable, the remaining provisions will still be in effect. Including a severability clause protects the integrity of the lease agreement.
4. *Security Deposits and Refunds:*
   - *Details:* The lease should state the amount of the security deposit, the conditions under which it can be withheld, and the process for refunding it at the end of the lease term. Clear guidelines on security deposits help avoid misunderstandings and ensure fairness.
5. *Warranty of Habitability:*
   - *Details:* This clause guarantees that the property meets basic living standards and is safe and habitable. It outlines the landlord's responsibility to maintain the property and make necessary repairs. Ensuring habitability is essential for tenant satisfaction and legal compliance.
6. *Mobile Home Park Rules:*
   - *Details:* The lease should include or reference the park rules and regulations that tenants must follow. These rules typically cover areas such as noise levels, pet policies, parking, and use of common areas. Clear rules help maintain order and a pleasant living environment.
7. *Duties and Rights of Tenants and Landlords:*
   - *Details:* The lease should outline the specific duties and rights of both tenants and landlords. This includes responsibilities for maintenance, property upkeep, and adherence to park rules. Clearly defining these roles helps prevent conflicts and ensures mutual respect.
8. *Indemnification Clause:*
   - *Details:* This clause protects the landlord from liability for injuries or damages that occur on the property due to the tenant's negligence. It requires

tenants to indemnify the landlord against such claims. Including an indemnification clause mitigates risk for the property owner.

By including these key lease terms, property managers can ensure that lease agreements for manufactured homes are comprehensive, legally sound, and clearly define the responsibilities and rights of both parties. This helps to create a fair and transparent leasing process, reducing the potential for disputes and fostering a positive living environment within the manufactured home park.

4.8.3 Sample Lease Agreements

Manufactured Home Lot Lease

AGREEMENT FOR THE LEASE OF MOBILE HOME PARK LOT

This Agreement is made and entered into on this ___ day of ________, ***20***, by and between __________________, as Lessor (hereinafter "Lessor"), and __________________, as Lessee (hereinafter "Lessee"), for the lease of the following described mobile home park lot (hereinafter the "Lot") located at _____________ Park, Lot No. _______, in _________ County, State of _________:

(INSERT LEGAL OR OTHER DESCRIPTION OF LOT TO BE LEASED)

Lessor and Lessee, in exchange for mutual covenants and other good and valuable consideration, agree that this Agreement is subject to the following terms and conditions:

1. **Term and Termination**
   - The initial term of this Agreement shall be for a period of ______ (weeks, months, years), commencing on the ____ day of ___________, ***20***, and ending on the ____ day of ___________, ***20.***
   - Lessee shall have the option to renew this Agreement for successive terms of ______ (weeks, months, years) by providing written notice of such renewal to Lessor at least ______ days prior to the expiration of the current term.
   - Either party may terminate this Agreement by providing written notice to the other party at least ______ days in advance. Termination by either party for non-compliance with the terms of this Agreement requires prior written notice and an opportunity to cure the non-compliance within ______ days of such notice.
2. **Access and Parking**
   - Lessor shall provide Lessee with access to the Lot at all times, subject to reasonable rules and regulations necessary to maintain the health, safety, and security of the Park.
   - Lessor shall provide Lessee with a written copy of such rules and regulations at the time of this Agreement.
3. **Rent**
   - Lessee agrees to pay Lessor the sum of $______ per ______ (week/month) as rent for the lease of the Lot. Rent shall be payable on the _____ day of each _____ (week/month), beginning on the ___ day of ___________, ***20.***
4. **Late Charges**
   - If rent is not paid by the due date specified above, a late charge of $______ shall apply for each _____ day(s) that the payment is overdue.
5. **Use of Premises**
   - Lessee agrees to use the Lot solely for residential purposes and to maintain the Lot in a clean and orderly condition.
   - Lessee shall not permit the Lot to be used for any illegal activities or purposes that violate health codes, ordinances, or create a public or private nuisance.

6. **Maintenance and Repairs**
    - Lessee shall be responsible for maintaining the Lot and any improvements made to it in good condition. Any structural changes or significant modifications require prior written approval from Lessor.
    - Lessor shall be responsible for major repairs to the Lot, provided such repairs are not caused by Lessee's negligence or misuse.
7. **Utilities**
    - Lessee shall be responsible for arranging and paying for all utilities serving the Lot, including but not limited to water, electricity, and waste disposal, unless otherwise stated in this Agreement.
8. **Rules and Regulations**
    - Lessee agrees to abide by all rules and regulations of the Park, as outlined in the Park's policies and as amended from time to time. Lessor shall notify Lessee in writing of any amendments to the Park's rules.
9. **Indemnification and Liability**
    - Lessee agrees to indemnify, defend, and hold Lessor harmless from and against all claims, liabilities, and expenses arising from Lessee's use or occupancy of the Lot, except where such claims result from Lessor's negligence.
10. **Default and Remedies**
    - If Lessee defaults on any terms of this Agreement, Lessor may terminate this Agreement and seek legal remedies, including eviction and collection of any unpaid rent or damages.
11. **Severability**
    - If any provision of this Agreement is found to be invalid or unenforceable, the remaining provisions shall remain in full force and effect.
12. **Entire Agreement**
    - This Agreement constitutes the entire agreement between the parties and supersedes any prior understandings or agreements. Modifications to this Agreement must be in writing and signed by both parties.

IN WITNESS WHEREOF, the parties have executed this Agreement as of the date first written above.

Lessor: ______________________

Signature: ______________________

Date: ___________________________

Lessee: ______________________

Signature: ______________________

Date: ___________________________

Manufactured Home Leas

Lease of Mobile (Manufactured) Home with Option to Purchase

This Agreement is made on the ___ day of __________, *20*, between __________________ (Name of Lessee), of __________________ (street address, city, county, state, zip code), referred to herein as "Lessee," and __________________ (Name of Lessor), of __________________ (street address, city, county, state, zip code), referred to herein as "Lessor."

For and in consideration of the mutual covenants contained in this Agreement, and other good and valuable consideration, the receipt and sufficiency of which are hereby acknowledged, the parties agree as follows:

1. **Description of Mobile (Manufactured) Home and Lot**
   - Lessor hereby leases to Lessee, and Lessee hereby leases from Lessor, the following described mobile (manufactured) home (hereinafter referred to as "Home"):
     - Serial Number: __________________
     - Description: (provide specific description of Home here, e.g., make, model, year)
   - The Home is located on the following described Lot: __________________________ (specific address or description of Lot).
2. **Term of Agreement**
   - The term of this Lease shall be for a period of ______ (number) months, beginning on the ___ day of __________, *20*, and ending on the ___ day of __________, *20*.
   - Lessee may renew this Lease for additional terms by providing written notice to Lessor at least ______ days prior to the expiration of the current term.
3. **Rental**
   - Lessee agrees to pay as rent for the use of the Home the sum of $________ (Dollars) per month.
   - The first payment is due on the ___ day of __________, *20*, with each subsequent payment due in advance on the ___ day of each month.
4. **Use of Home**
   - Lessee agrees to use the Home solely for residential purposes and shall not use the Home in any manner that violates applicable laws, ordinances, or regulations.
   - Lessee agrees not to engage in activities that may increase the insurance rate or cause the cancellation of insurance on the Home.
5. **Assignment and Subletting**
   - Lessee shall not assign this Lease or sublet the Home or any part thereof without prior written consent from Lessor.
6. **Deposit**
   - Lessee agrees to deposit the sum of $________ (Dollars) with Lessor as security for Lessee's compliance with the terms of this Lease.
   - The deposit shall be refunded to Lessee upon the termination of this Lease, provided the Home is returned in the same clean and undamaged condition as at the commencement of this Lease.

7. **Option to Purchase**
   - Lessor grants Lessee the exclusive option to purchase the Home during the term of this Lease for the sum of $________ (Dollars), subject to the following terms:
     - Lessee must provide written notice to Lessor of their intent to exercise the option at least ______ days prior to the desired purchase date.
     - If Lessee exercises this option, the security deposit shall be applied toward the purchase price.
8. **Maintenance and Repairs**
   - Lessee shall be responsible for maintaining the Home in a clean and habitable condition and for making minor repairs as needed.
   - Lessor shall be responsible for major structural repairs, unless such repairs are necessitated by the negligence or misuse of the Lessee.
9. **Utilities**
   - Lessee shall be responsible for arranging and paying for all utilities serving the Home, including electricity, water, sewer, and trash removal.
10. **Default and Termination**
    - If Lessee defaults on any terms of this Lease, Lessor may terminate the Lease and recover possession of the Home in accordance with applicable laws.
11. **Entire Agreement**
    - This Agreement constitutes the entire agreement between the parties and may not be modified except in writing, signed by both parties.

IN WITNESS WHEREOF, the parties have executed this Agreement as of the date first written above.

Lessor: ______________________

Signature: ______________________

Date: ______________________

Lessee: ______________________

Signature: ______________________

Date: ______________________

4.9 Summary

Managing manufactured home park communities presents unique challenges and opportunities that require specialized knowledge and skills. These communities are distinct from other residential property types due to their hybrid nature, where residents often own their manufactured homes but lease the land on which the homes sit. This dual arrangement creates a dynamic environment requiring property managers to balance the needs of individual homeowners with the responsibilities of maintaining common areas and community infrastructure.

A comprehensive understanding of the characteristics and unique aspects of manufactured home parks is essential for effective management. These parks are often designed with affordability and accessibility in mind, making them an attractive housing option for diverse demographics, including retirees, young families, and those seeking budget-friendly alternatives. Managers must recognize the advantages of these communities, such as their affordability, community-oriented living, and flexibility, while also addressing challenges like stigma, potential depreciation of homes, and the complexities of land ownership.

Tenant relations and community management play a crucial role in creating a harmonious living environment. Property managers must maintain open lines of communication with residents, resolve conflicts promptly, and provide services that enhance the quality of life within the community. This includes addressing resident concerns, ensuring compliance with park rules, and fostering a sense of community through organized events or programs.

Finally, regulatory compliance is a critical component of managing manufactured home parks. Property managers must navigate zoning laws, health and safety standards, environmental regulations, and tenant rights to ensure the community operates within legal boundaries. By staying informed about legal requirements and maintaining transparent communication with residents, managers can build trust and avoid potential legal issues.

In summary, managing manufactured home park communities requires a balanced approach that combines operational efficiency, financial oversight, and a commitment to resident satisfaction. By addressing these core elements, property managers can ensure the success and sustainability of these unique residential communities

4.9.1 Looking Forward

The following chapters will delve into the management of multifamily residences, including apartments, condominium associations, cooperatives, and homeowner associations. Each type of multifamily property presents its own unique challenges and opportunities, and understanding these differences is key to becoming a successful property manager in the residential real estate industry.

4.10 Case Study: Evergreen Manufactured Home Park

4.10.1 Background

Evergreen Manufactured Home Park is a well-established community with 100 homesites. The park features common amenities such as a playground, a community center, and a shared laundry facility. The park owner has hired you as the property manager to oversee daily operations, maintain the property, and ensure compliance with local regulations.

4.10.2 Scenario

Evergreen Manufactured Home Park has recently faced several challenges, including an increase in maintenance issues, conflicts between residents, and a need to update the park's infrastructure to comply with new zoning regulations. Your tasks include addressing these challenges, improving resident relations, and ensuring the park operates smoothly and legally.

4.10.3 Tasks

1. *Maintenance and Repairs*
   - Conduct a thorough inspection of the park to identify maintenance issues.
   - Develop a maintenance schedule for routine tasks and seasonal upkeep.
   - Coordinate with contractors to address immediate repairs, such as fixing playground equipment and repairing potholes in the roads.
2. *Community Management*
   - Organize a community meeting to address resident concerns and improve communication.
   - Develop a plan to foster a sense of community, including organizing social events and promoting resident involvement.
   - Implement conflict resolution strategies to address disputes between residents.
3. *Regulatory Compliance*
   - Review the park's compliance with local zoning laws and health and safety regulations.
   - Develop a plan to upgrade the park's infrastructure to meet new zoning requirements, including improving drainage systems and updating electrical wiring.
   - Ensure that lease agreements are clear, fair, and compliant with local laws.

4.10.4 Challenges

1. *Maintenance Challenge*
   - During your inspection, you discover that the community center's roof is leaking, and several homesites have drainage issues causing water to pool after rain. Determine how to prioritize these repairs within the budget provided by the park owner.
2. *Community Challenge*
   - Residents have been complaining about noise and disturbances from a few households. Develop a strategy to address these complaints and improve overall resident relations.

3. *Regulatory Compliance Challenge*
   - New zoning regulations require the park to install additional fire hydrants and improve road access for emergency vehicles. Plan how to implement these changes while minimizing disruption to residents.

4.10.5 Questions

1. *Maintenance*
   - How would you prioritize the maintenance tasks identified during your inspection?
   - What steps can you take to prevent future maintenance issues and ensure the park remains in good condition?
2. *Community Management*
   - What strategies can you use to improve communication and foster a sense of community among residents?
   - How would you handle the complaints about noise and disturbances to ensure a peaceful living environment for all residents?
3. *Regulatory Compliance*
   - What steps would you take to ensure the park complies with the new zoning regulations?
   - How can you communicate these changes to residents and involve them in the process to minimize disruption?

4.11 Review Questions

1. *What is a primary characteristic of manufactured home parks?*
   (A) Single-family homes on large plots of land
   (B) Manufactured homes on leased land with shared amenities
   (C) High-rise apartment buildings
   (D) Condominiums with individual ownership
2. *What is one of the main advantages of living in a manufactured home park?*
   (A) High property taxes
   (B) Affordability and community living
   (C) Expensive maintenance fees
   (D) Long commute times
3. *Which demographic is commonly attracted to manufactured home parks?*
   (A) Only young professionals
   (B) Families, retirees, and individuals seeking affordable housing
   (C) Exclusively retirees
   (D) Only high-income earners
4. *What is a common disadvantage of manufactured home parks?*
   (A) High appreciation in value
   (B) Stigma and potential depreciation

(C) Excessive land ownership by residents
(D) Overabundance of amenities

5. *What is a critical aspect of managing common areas in manufactured home parks?*
   (A) Ignoring resident concerns
   (B) Regular maintenance and ensuring safety
   (C) Reducing amenities
   (D) Increasing rent without improvements
6. *Why is effective communication important in managing manufactured home parks?*
   (A) To reduce the number of tenants
   (B) To build trust and address resident concerns promptly
   (C) To increase rent without notice
   (D) To avoid maintenance responsibilities
7. *What financial management practice is essential for managing manufactured home parks?*
   (A) Arbitrarily setting rental rates
   (B) Efficient rent collection and regular financial reporting
   (C) Ignoring expense management
   (D) Providing irregular financial reports
8. *Why is understanding zoning laws crucial for managing manufactured home parks?*
   (A) To increase property taxes
   (B) To ensure legal compliance and avoid penalties
   (C) To reduce tenant turnover
   (D) To eliminate the need for maintenance
9. *What should be included in a reserve study for a manufactured home park?*
   (A) List of resident complaints
   (B) Assessment of major components and estimation of future repair costs
   (C) Current rental rates
   (D) History of tenant evictions
10. *Which of the following is required to ensure fair housing compliance in manufactured home parks?*
    (A) Enforcing arbitrary rules
    (B) Adhering to the Fair Housing Act
    (C) Increasing rent based on race or religion
    (D) Ignoring tenant complaints

Managing Multifamily Residences 5

5.1 Learning Objectives

By the end of this unit, students will be able to:

- *Understand the Different Types of Multifamily Properties*
  - Identify and distinguish between various multifamily property types, including apartments, condominium associations, cooperatives, and homeowner associations.
  - Recognize the unique characteristics of each property type and how these characteristics impact management practices.
- *Analyze Key Differences in the Management of Multifamily Residences*
  - Explain the differences in ownership structures, governance, and management approaches across apartments, condominiums, cooperatives, and homeowner associations.
  - Understand the responsibilities of property managers in each setting, particularly how maintenance, repairs, and resident relations vary by property type.
- *Develop Effective Strategies for Property Management of Apartments*
  - Understand the core functions of apartment management, including leasing, rent collection, tenant relations, and maintenance coordination.
  - Apply best practices for maximizing income, minimizing expenses, and maintaining tenant satisfaction in apartment properties.
- *Master the Roles and Responsibilities in Managing Condominium Associations*
  - Explain the governance structure of condominium associations and the relationship between the property manager, the board of directors, and unit owners.
  - Implement strategies for managing common areas, enforcing rules, and ensuring compliance with the association's governing documents.
- *Address the Unique Management Challenges of Cooperatives*
  - Describe the cooperative ownership model and the role of property managers in supporting the cooperative board and shareholders.

D. A. Vaughn, *Essentials of Residential Property Management*, Springer Texts in Business and Economics, https://doi.org/10.1007/978-3-031-92329-6_5

  - Understand the specific challenges of managing shareholder relationships, maintaining transparency, and adhering to cooperative rules and regulations.
- *Implement Best Practices for Managing Homeowner Associations (HOAs)*
  - Outline the duties of HOA boards and the property manager's role in supporting effective governance and community management.
  - Develop strategies for enforcing community rules, managing maintenance tasks, collecting fees, and fostering resident engagement within HOA communities.
- *Apply Comprehensive Financial and Community Management Techniques*
  - Understand financial responsibilities, including budgeting, reserve fund management, and financial reporting, across different types of multifamily properties.
  - Utilize strategies to create a positive living environment, maintain open communication with residents or owners, and address conflicts effectively.

5.2 Key Terms

Apartments
Common Area Maintenance
Condominium Association
Cooperative (Co-op)
Homeowner Association (HOA)
Reserve Fund
Board of Directors
Proprietary Lease
Tenant-Landlord Law
Fiduciary Duty
Governing Documents
Rules and Regulations
Enforcement of Rules and Regulations
Maintenance Fee
Financial Statement
Property Management Agreement

By mastering these learning objectives and understanding the key terms, students will gain a thorough understanding of the complexities involved in managing various types of multifamily residences, equipping them with the knowledge to handle the distinct operational, legal, and financial challenges associated with each property type.

5.3 Overview

The chapter explores the multifaceted nature of managing various types of multifamily properties, including apartments, condominium associations, cooperatives, and homeowner associations (HOAs). Each of these property types requires unique management strategies, largely due to differences in ownership structure, governance, and operational responsibilities. Apartments, typically owned by a single entity or individual, focus on maximizing rental income, maintaining tenant satisfaction, and ensuring efficient building operations. The management team's primary role involves lease management, tenant relations, maintenance, and financial oversight, all while adhering to local housing regulations.

In contrast, condominium associations, cooperatives, and HOAs operate under a governance structure, where residents own their individual units or shares and collectively manage common areas. Property managers working in these settings must navigate complex legal frameworks and ensure compliance with governing documents, such as bylaws, declarations, and rules set by the board of directors. While condominium management involves overseeing common areas and enforcing community rules, cooperative management focuses on maintaining the building's financial health and coordinating shareholder participation in decision-making. HOA management deals with managing planned communities, including enforcing community rules, maintaining shared amenities, and collecting maintenance fees from homeowners.

A critical theme across these chapters is the understanding that each type of multifamily property requires tailored management approaches due to variations in ownership structures, governance models, and legal responsibilities. Property managers must adopt different strategies depending on whether they are dealing with tenant-occupied apartments or resident-owned communities such as condominiums, cooperatives, or HOAs. Moreover, the ability to communicate effectively, maintain strong relationships with owners or tenants, and ensure that the property operates in compliance with regulations are core responsibilities of successful multifamily property managers across all these types. These chapters collectively highlight the complexities of managing multifamily residences, emphasizing the need for property managers to adapt to each unique environment while maintaining operational efficiency and legal compliance.

5.3.1 Types of Multifamily Properties

Multifamily properties include various types of residential buildings where multiple separate housing units are contained within one building or several buildings within a complex. The primary types of multifamily residences are apartments, condominium associations, cooperatives, and homeowner associations (HOAs). Each type presents unique management challenges and opportunities.

Apartments

Apartments are rental units within a larger building or complex, owned by a single entity or individual. Tenants lease these units, and the property manager oversees the entire building's operations, maintenance, and tenant relations.

Condominium Associations

Condominiums (condos) are individually owned units within a larger building or complex. Owners pay fees to a condominium association, which manages common areas and amenities. Property managers work with the condo association's board to maintain the property and enforce community rules.

Cooperatives

Cooperatives (co-ops) are buildings owned by a corporation. Residents buy shares in the corporation, which entitles them to occupy a specific unit. Co-op boards govern these buildings, and property managers assist in maintaining the property and implementing board decisions.

Homeowner Associations (HOAs)

HOAs manage planned communities, including townhouses, single-family homes, and condos. Residents are members of the HOA, which enforces rules and maintains common areas. Property managers help the HOA board with administration, maintenance, and community engagement.

5.3.2 Key Differences in Management

Managing multifamily residences involves distinct approaches depending on the type of property, primarily due to differences in ownership structure, governance, maintenance responsibilities, and tenant or owner relations. Understanding these key differences is essential for property managers to effectively oversee operations and address the unique challenges each type presents. The four primary types of multifamily residences—apartments, condominium associations, cooperatives, and homeowner associations (HOAs)—each require tailored management strategies that reflect their specific characteristics.

Ownership Structure

The ownership structure is a fundamental differentiator between multifamily property types. In apartment complexes, a single entity, such as an individual owner or corporation, owns the entire property and leases individual units to tenants. In contrast, condominium associations and cooperatives are owned by multiple individual owners. Condominium owners hold title to their specific units and share ownership of common areas, such as hallways, parking lots, and recreational facilities. Cooperative shareholders, on the other hand, own shares in a corporation that holds the building title, and these shares grant them a *proprietary lease* to occupy a specific unit. In HOAs, residents typically own their homes outright, while the association governs shared spaces within the community.

Governance

Governance structures also vary significantly. In apartment properties, the property manager makes decisions on behalf of the owner, often without direct input from tenants. In condominium associations, cooperatives, and HOAs, however, governance is handled by a board of directors elected by the owners. These boards are responsible for setting policies, enforcing rules, and managing the community's financial health. Property managers in these settings must work closely with the board to implement decisions and navigate the complexities of community politics and owner expectations.

Maintenance and Repairs

Maintenance and repair responsibilities depend on the type of multifamily residence. In apartments, the property owner or manager handles all interior and exterior maintenance. In condominium associations, owners are responsible for maintaining the interior of their units, while the association handles the exterior and common areas. Cooperatives follow a similar model, but the cooperative board may also influence interior unit decisions depending on the proprietary lease terms. In HOAs, individual homeowners manage the maintenance of their own properties, while the association is responsible for common areas such as landscaping, community amenities, and streets.

Tenant and Owner Relations

Tenant and owner relations differ greatly based on the type of multifamily residence. In apartments, the focus is on tenant relations—ensuring tenant satisfaction, addressing complaints, and minimizing turnover. For condominium associations, cooperatives, and HOAs, the emphasis shifts to owner relations, which involve addressing owners' concerns, facilitating communication between the board and owners, and maintaining transparency in community operations. Property managers must be adept at balancing the diverse interests of individual owners, mediating conflicts, and ensuring that all parties feel engaged and informed.

5.3.3 Property Management of Apartments

Introduction

Property management for apartments is a dynamic and multifaceted discipline that requires a comprehensive understanding of both the physical and operational aspects of residential buildings. Apartments, unlike other multifamily property types, are typically owned by a single entity—either an individual or a corporate owner—who rents out units to tenants. This setup introduces a distinct set of responsibilities for the property manager, who is tasked with maintaining the property, managing tenant relationships, and ensuring financial viability.

A successful apartment property manager must balance day-to-day operations with long-term planning, addressing everything from leasing and rent collection to maintenance, legal compliance, and tenant retention. Apartments often have higher tenant turnover rates compared to other property types, requiring property managers to stay vigilant in marketing vacant units, screening prospective tenants, and overseeing move-in and move-out processes. Additionally, maintaining a well-kept, safe, and secure environment is essential for tenant satisfaction and minimizing vacancy rates.

Property management for apartments also involves close financial oversight, with managers responsible for developing budgets, controlling operating expenses, and maximizing rental income. Effective property managers must use software tools to handle rent rolls, track expenses, and generate reports, ensuring that they can make informed decisions quickly. In sum, managing apartments requires a blend of operational efficiency, financial acumen, and strong communication skills to meet the expectations of both property owners and tenants, while complying with local housing laws and regulations.

5.3.4 Types of Apartment Buildings

Understanding the different types of apartment buildings is crucial for effective property management. Each type presents unique challenges and opportunities, influencing everything from marketing strategies to maintenance practices.

Duplex

Description: A duplex is a residential building divided into two separate units, typically side-by-side or stacked one above the other. Each unit has its own entrance, and the units may share common walls.

Management Considerations: Duplexes often attract residents seeking more privacy, larger living spaces, and fewer shared amenities compared to traditional apartment buildings. Property managers should focus on maintaining clear boundaries between the units, addressing any shared maintenance issues promptly (such as roofing, exterior walls, or shared utilities), and managing potential conflicts between residents. Additionally, marketing strategies may emphasize the "home-like" feel, which appeals to small families or long-term renters.

Triplex

Description: Similar to a duplex, a triplex consists of three separate units within a single building. These units can be arranged side-by-side, in a row, or stacked vertically.

Management Considerations: Managing a triplex requires more coordination than a duplex, particularly when it comes to shared spaces and utilities. Property managers should implement clear policies for common area maintenance and ensure that tenants understand their responsibilities regarding noise, parking, and shared amenities. Additionally, routine inspections and proactive communication help prevent conflicts and maintain positive resident relations. Triplexes often appeal to small families, roommates, or individuals seeking affordable housing with a community feel.

Quadruplex (Fourplex)

Description: A quadruplex, also known as a fourplex, is a residential building divided into four separate units. These units can be arranged in various configurations, such as two units on the ground floor and two above or side-by-side layouts. Each unit generally has its own entrance, kitchen, bathroom, and living space, though some may share common outdoor areas or hallways.

Management Considerations: Quadruplexes introduce an additional layer of complexity compared to duplexes and triplexes due to the larger number of residents. Property managers must effectively coordinate maintenance schedules, manage common areas, and address potential disputes between residents sharing walls or outdoor spaces. Additionally, utilities may be separately metered or shared, requiring clear agreements on billing responsibilities. Quadruplexes appeal to a diverse tenant base, including small families, young professionals, and retirees looking for affordable, low-maintenance living options. Efficient property management can enhance tenant satisfaction, reduce turnover, and maintain property value over time.

Garden-Style Apartments

Description: Garden-style apartments are typically low-rise buildings, often two or three stories high, surrounded by landscaped grounds. They usually have outdoor walkways and may offer amenities like swimming pools and playgrounds.

Management Considerations: Garden-style apartments require significant attention to landscaping and outdoor maintenance. Property managers should focus on curb appeal and outdoor amenities to attract and retain tenants.

Townhouse

Description: Townhouses are multi-level residential units that share one or more walls with neighboring units but have separate, private entrances. They are typically designed as vertical living spaces with multiple floors, often featuring private garages, small yards, patios, or balconies. Townhouses may be individually owned, rented out, or part of a larger community managed under a homeowner association (HOA) or condominium association.

Management Considerations: Townhouses offer greater privacy and more living space compared to traditional apartments, making them appealing to families and long-term residents seeking a home-like environment. Property managers should focus on regular exterior maintenance, including landscaping, roofing, and siding, especially in communities where the HOA or property owner is responsible for common areas. In cases where townhouses are part of an HOA, managers must ensure compliance with community rules and coordinate with the board regarding shared spaces. Additionally, managers should address issues related to shared walls, such as soundproofing concerns and potential structural impacts from neighboring units. Clear communication with residents about their maintenance responsibilities versus those of the association or landlord is also critical.

Low-Rise Apartments

Description: Low-rise apartment buildings are typically one to three stories tall and may or may not include elevators, depending on the building's design. These buildings can range from small complexes with just a few units to larger communities with multiple buildings. Low-rise apartments often feature outdoor staircases, walk-up access, and fewer shared amenities compared to mid- or high-rise properties.

Management Considerations: Low-rise buildings are generally easier to manage due to their smaller scale, simpler building systems, and fewer common areas. Property managers can benefit from more direct tenant interactions and reduced maintenance complexity, especially in walk-up buildings without elevators. However, managers should pay close attention to security measures for ground-floor units, such as ensuring proper lighting, secure entry points, and surveillance systems if needed. Additionally, outdoor areas like parking lots, pathways, and green spaces require regular maintenance to maintain curb appeal and resident satisfaction.

Mid-Rise Apartments

Description: Mid-rise apartment buildings typically range from four to eight stories and often include elevators to accommodate residents on higher floors. These buildings are commonly found in urban and suburban areas and may offer a range of amenities, such as fitness centers, lounges, rooftop terraces, and concierge services. Mid-rise apartments often feature both indoor and outdoor common areas for residents to enjoy.

Management Considerations: Managing mid-rise buildings requires greater attention to building systems and operations, particularly regarding elevator maintenance, HVAC systems, and fire safety protocols. Property managers should prioritize common area upkeep, ensuring that lobbies, hallways, fitness centers, and other shared spaces are clean, functional, and visually appealing. Security is another key consideration, as controlled access points, surveillance cameras, and secure entry systems are often expected in mid-rise communities. Additionally, mid-rise properties may involve more complex leasing operations and higher resident turnover compared to smaller buildings, necessitating strong marketing and tenant retention strategies.

High-Rise Apartments

Description: High-rise apartment buildings are typically nine stories or taller and are common in densely populated urban areas. These buildings almost always feature elevators, advanced security systems, and a wide range of high-end amenities, such as swimming pools, rooftop decks, gyms, business centers, and sometimes on-site retail spaces. High-rise apartments can be luxury rentals, condominiums, or mixed-use developments with residential and commercial spaces.

Management Considerations: Managing a high-rise building presents significant operational challenges due to the building's scale, complexity, and the diverse needs of a large resident population. Property managers must oversee sophisticated building systems, including HVAC, plumbing risers, fire suppression systems, and elevator banks, all of which require regular maintenance and compliance with stringent safety regulations. Security is a top priority in high-rise management, often involving 24/7 concierge services, surveillance systems, and controlled access to various parts of the building. Additionally, high-rise properties often require a dedicated management team, including on-site maintenance staff, leasing agents, and security personnel. Effective communication, strong leadership, and excellent customer service skills are essential for managing resident expectations, coordinating with vendors, and ensuring the smooth operation of building amenities.

5.3.5 Understanding the Owner's Objectives

In apartment property management, understanding the owner's objectives is crucial to aligning management strategies with their goals and ensuring the long-term success of the investment. Apartment owners typically have a clear set of priorities that revolve around generating income, minimizing operating costs, maintaining property value, and ensuring tenant satisfaction. By addressing these objectives through clear communication and effective management practices, property managers can create a profitable and well-maintained community that meets both the owner's and the tenants' expectations.

Clear Communication

Effective property management begins with establishing clear communication channels between the property manager and the owner. Property managers must have a thorough understanding of the owner's short- and long-term goals, including their financial expectations, desired property improvements, and tenant relations philosophy. Regular meetings, detailed reporting, and transparency in all operations are essential to keeping the owner informed and engaged. Whether the owner is focused on maximizing cash flow or enhancing the property's marketability, open communication ensures that management strategies are tailored to meet these specific objectives. Providing consistent updates on occupancy rates, market trends, and any potential issues helps build trust and allows for proactive decision-making.

Maximizing Income

One of the primary objectives for apartment owners is maximizing rental income. Property managers must develop strategies to achieve high occupancy rates, optimize rent levels based on market conditions, and minimize vacancy periods. This involves effective marketing, tenant retention strategies, and competitive pricing. Additionally, property managers can explore ancillary revenue opportunities, such as leasing parking spaces, storage units, or offering premium services like furnished units, to increase overall income. Keeping abreast of local market trends and adjusting rent levels accordingly ensures that the property remains profitable and competitive.

Minimizing Expenses

While maximizing income is critical, controlling operating expenses is equally important. Property managers should implement cost-effective maintenance practices, negotiate favorable vendor contracts, and reduce utility expenses through energy-efficient upgrades. Monitoring and analyzing the property's budget regularly helps identify areas for cost savings without compromising service quality. For example, adopting preventive maintenance strategies can help avoid costly emergency repairs, ultimately reducing the property's long-term expenses.

Property Value Appreciation

Owners often view apartment properties as long-term investments that should appreciate in value over time. Property managers play a key role in enhancing property value by maintaining high standards for maintenance, making strategic capital improvements, and ensuring strong curb appeal. Regularly upgrading amenities, renovating units, and improving common areas can significantly boost property value and rental income potential. Additionally, property managers should prioritize compliance with local regulations to protect the property from devaluation due to legal issues or code violations.

Tenant Satisfaction

Tenant satisfaction is a crucial factor in achieving the owner's objectives, as satisfied tenants are more likely to renew their leases and refer others to the property. Property managers should focus on providing excellent customer service, addressing tenant concerns promptly, and creating a positive living environment. Implementing tenant engagement strategies, such as organizing community events and maintaining a responsive maintenance team, helps foster a sense of community and reduces turnover rates. High tenant satisfaction leads to stable occupancy, fewer vacancies, and a positive reputation in the rental market, all of which contribute to the owner's financial goals.

5.3.6 Apartment Management Contracts

Apartment management contracts are formal agreements that establish the terms and conditions under which a property manager will oversee the operations of an apartment complex on behalf of the property owner. These contracts are foundational documents that outline the responsibilities, expectations, and compensation of the property manager, ensuring that both parties have a clear understanding of their roles and obligations. An effective apartment management contract is critical to the smooth operation of the property, as it delineates the scope of services, financial arrangements, and legal considerations specific to the management of apartment communities.

Key Elements of an Apartment Management Contract

1. *Scope of Services*

   The scope of services section defines the specific tasks the property manager will perform. In apartment management, this typically includes advertising and leasing vacant units, collecting rent, handling maintenance requests, conducting tenant screenings, enforcing lease agreements, and managing tenant relations. It may also encompass financial services such as preparing budgets, managing bank accounts, and providing financial reports to the owner. The scope should be detailed enough to clarify which duties fall under the manager's purview and which responsibilities remain with the owner.
2. *Management Fees and Compensation*

   Apartment management contracts usually specify a management fee, which is typically calculated as a percentage of the total monthly rent collected. This percentage varies depending on the size of the apartment complex, location, and the complexity of services provided. Additional fees, such as leasing fees (for securing new tenants), renewal fees (for lease renewals), and maintenance oversight fees, should also be clearly defined. For large apartment communities, the contract may include performance-based incentives, such as bonuses for maintaining high occupancy rates or reducing operational expenses.

3. *Owner's Objectives and Manager's Authority*

   The contract should reflect the owner's objectives and provide the property manager with the necessary authority to achieve these goals. For example, if the owner prioritizes increasing rental income, the contract should grant the manager the authority to adjust rent levels according to market conditions. Similarly, if the owner is focused on maintaining high tenant satisfaction, the manager may be empowered to make minor improvements or offer tenant incentives. The contract should specify the manager's authority to enter into leases, hire contractors, and make repairs within a certain budgetary limit without prior owner approval.

4. *Maintenance and Repair Provisions*

   For apartment properties, maintenance is a significant aspect of daily operations. The management contract should define who is responsible for routine and emergency maintenance, including handling vendor relationships and ensuring that the property complies with safety and habitability standards. The contract should outline spending limits for repairs, specifying when the manager needs to obtain owner approval for major expenditures.

5. *Insurance and Liability*

   Liability and insurance clauses are essential in apartment management contracts to protect both the property owner and the manager. The contract should state that the property owner is responsible for maintaining adequate insurance coverage for the property itself, including liability, property damage, and business interruption insurance. The manager, in turn, should carry their own general liability and professional liability (errors and omissions) insurance to cover any claims arising from their management activities.

6. *Termination Clauses*

   The contract should include provisions for termination, specifying the notice period required by either party to end the agreement and the conditions under which the contract can be terminated early, such as for breach of contract, poor performance, or changes in ownership. This ensures that both the owner and the property manager can exit the agreement without unnecessary complications if the relationship is no longer beneficial.

5.3.7 Maintaining Owner-Manager Relationship

A strong relationship between the apartment owner and property manager is essential for the effective management and profitability of an apartment complex. Since property managers act as the owner's representative in daily operations, building a foundation of trust, mutual respect, and clear expectations is critical to achieving the owner's goals. Maintaining a positive and productive owner-manager relationship involves regular communication, transparency, feedback and adjustments, proactive problem-solving, and professionalism. By focusing on these key areas, property managers can ensure alignment with the owner's objectives, promote long-term success, and foster a cooperative working relationship.

Regular Communication

Establishing consistent and structured communication is a cornerstone of maintaining a strong owner-manager relationship. Property managers should schedule regular meetings or check-ins to provide updates on key operational metrics, such as occupancy rates, rent collection, maintenance issues, and any ongoing projects. Whether these communications are weekly, biweekly, or monthly depends on the complexity of the property and the owner's preferences. Additionally, property managers should remain accessible and responsive to the owner's inquiries, demonstrating attentiveness and a commitment to keeping the owner informed about property developments.

Transparency

Transparency is essential for building trust between the apartment owner and property manager. Providing detailed financial reports, maintenance logs, and documentation of any significant decisions ensures that the owner has a clear understanding of the property's performance. Transparency also involves openly discussing challenges and potential risks, such as market fluctuations, unexpected repair costs, or legal issues. By sharing both successes and setbacks, property managers establish credibility and help the owner make well-informed decisions.

Feedback and Adjustments

An effective owner-manager relationship is a two-way dialogue. Property managers should actively seek feedback from owners to understand their evolving priorities and preferences. Similarly, they should be open to providing their own insights and recommendations based on their expertise and on-the-ground experience. If an owner's goals change—such as shifting from maximizing cash flow to focusing on long-term property appreciation—the property manager should be willing to adjust their management approach accordingly. Regular feedback sessions allow both parties to reassess strategies and make necessary adjustments to remain aligned.

Proactive Problem-Solving

Being proactive in identifying and addressing issues before they escalate is crucial in apartment management. Property managers should adopt a forward-thinking approach to potential challenges, such as anticipating maintenance needs, preparing for market changes, and mitigating tenant disputes. When problems do arise, providing the owner with actionable solutions—rather than just reporting the issue—demonstrates the manager's commitment to safeguarding the property and its profitability. Proactive problem-solving not only prevents minor issues from becoming costly problems but also shows that the manager is actively working to protect the owner's investment.

Professionalism

Maintaining a high level of professionalism is fundamental to any owner-manager relationship. Property managers must uphold ethical standards, demonstrate integrity in all communications, and consistently act in the owner's best interest. This includes respecting confidentiality, adhering to contractual agreements, and maintaining the property in a manner that reflects positively on both the owner and the manager. Professionalism also extends to interactions with tenants, vendors, and contractors, as these relationships indirectly impact the owner's perception of the property manager's competence and effectiveness.

5.3.8 Rental Market Analysis

Conducting a comprehensive apartment rental market analysis is a vital step for property managers to ensure that their rental rates are competitive, their marketing strategies are effective, and their management decisions are data-driven. An apartment rental market analysis provides insights into local rental trends, tenant demand, and the competitive landscape, enabling property managers to maximize rental income and maintain high occupancy rates. Key elements of an effective market analysis include understanding local market conditions, analyzing tenant demographics, conducting a detailed competitor analysis, and utilizing technology to streamline the process.

Key Elements of an Apartment Rental Market Analysis

1. *Understanding Local Market Conditions*

   Local market conditions significantly influence rental pricing and demand for apartment units. Property managers must consider factors such as the overall economic climate, employment rates, and population growth in the area. For example, if a city is experiencing strong job growth and an influx of new residents, rental demand is likely to be higher, allowing for more aggressive rent increases. Conversely, if there is an economic downturn or a high vacancy rate in the area, property managers may need to offer incentives or adjust rent levels to attract tenants. Analyzing the supply of new apartment developments and vacancy rates in the surrounding neighborhood is also critical, as it provides insight into market saturation and potential shifts in demand.
2. *Tenant Demographics and Target Market*

   Understanding the demographics of the target market helps property managers tailor their marketing strategies and amenity offerings to meet tenant expectations. Key demographic factors include age, income levels, household size, and lifestyle preferences. For example, a property located near a university may attract more students, while an apartment complex in a suburban neighborhood might appeal to families and professionals. By identifying the target tenant profile, property managers can refine their marketing campaigns and prioritize upgrades or amenities that align with tenant preferences, such as pet-friendly policies, fitness centers, or work-from-home spaces.

3. *Competitor Analysis*

   A thorough competitor analysis involves comparing the property's features, rental rates, and amenities with similar properties in the area. This helps property managers understand how their units stack up against local competitors and identify areas for improvement. For example, if competing properties are offering incentives such as free first-month rent or have upgraded amenities like smart home technology, the property manager can assess whether implementing similar strategies would enhance their property's competitiveness.

   Modern property management technology, such as software platforms like Yardi, RealPage, and CoStar, can significantly streamline the competitor analysis process. These tools provide real-time market data, detailed reports on comparable properties, and insight into current rental rates, occupancy trends, and tenant feedback. Using these platforms allows property managers to quickly identify changes in the market, adjust pricing strategies, and make informed decisions that optimize the property's performance.
4. *Setting Rental Rates and Identifying Market Gaps*

   The final step in an apartment rental market analysis is setting appropriate rental rates. Property managers must establish rental rates that reflect the property's value while remaining competitive within the local market. Analyzing market data helps identify market gaps, such as underserved segments, which can inform decisions on unit renovations or new amenities. This data-driven approach ensures that rental rates are aligned with market conditions, helping to attract quality tenants and maximize revenue.

   By leveraging a thorough market analysis, property managers can position their apartments to succeed in a competitive rental landscape, set optimal rental rates, and make strategic decisions that drive long-term profitability. Incorporating technology into the analysis process enhances efficiency and accuracy, allowing managers to stay ahead of market trends and deliver superior results for property owners.

5.3.9 The RealPage Antitrust Lawsuit

In 2024, the United States Department of Justice (DOJ) filed a high-profile antitrust lawsuit against the real estate software company RealPage, Inc., accusing it of using its pricing tools and artificial intelligence (AI) technology to unlawfully influence rental markets and undermine competition among landlords. The lawsuit alleges that RealPage's algorithmic pricing tools were designed to manipulate rental prices in a way that prevented competitive pricing in the market, leading to artificially inflated rents. The case has drawn significant attention from property managers, landlords, and policymakers, as it highlights the potential risks associated with using advanced pricing technology in the multifamily housing sector.

Overview of the Allegations

The DOJ's complaint centers on RealPage's use of its proprietary YieldStar and AI Revenue Management (AIRM) software, which were marketed to multifamily property owners and managers as tools to maximize rental revenue. According to the lawsuit, RealPage used its pricing algorithms to analyze vast amounts of rental data from participating properties, including competitors, and then provided recommended rental rates that, when adopted by multiple landlords in the same market, reduced price competition. The DOJ contends that this practice violated federal antitrust laws by creating a shared pricing system among otherwise independent landlords, effectively allowing them to collude without direct communication.

The DOJ argues that RealPage's software used AI to recommend rent increases in markets with low vacancy rates, even when local economic conditions did not justify such changes. Additionally, when market conditions shifted and supply exceeded demand, the algorithm prevented landlords from lowering rents to attract new tenants. This strategy, according to the DOJ, artificially propped up rental prices, harming consumers by reducing their ability to negotiate rents in a competitive marketplace. The lawsuit also alleges that RealPage's software helped landlords avoid undercutting each other, which would have naturally occurred in a competitive market, thereby depriving renters of lower rental options.

Potential Implications for the Industry

The RealPage antitrust lawsuit has significant implications for the property management industry, particularly for owners and managers of large apartment complexes that rely on algorithmic pricing tools to set rental rates. If the DOJ's claims are substantiated, it could lead to stricter regulations on how such software can be used in the rental market. Property managers might be required to reevaluate their reliance on automated pricing tools and consider adopting more transparent pricing strategies that ensure compliance with antitrust laws.

The lawsuit also raises questions about data sharing and transparency in the multifamily sector. RealPage's software operated by aggregating and analyzing data from numerous landlords, allowing it to produce highly specific rental recommendations. The DOJ asserts that this data-sharing arrangement essentially created a cartel-like system where landlords' independent pricing decisions were influenced by shared information, stifling competition.

If the lawsuit results in a ruling against RealPage, property managers who have used similar software may face legal scrutiny and could be required to revise their pricing strategies. This could lead to a broader reevaluation of how technology and AI are used in real estate markets, emphasizing the need for property managers to adopt compliant practices that balance revenue optimization with ethical and legal considerations.

Moving Forward

Property managers should closely monitor the developments in the RealPage case and stay informed about any legal precedents that may arise. To mitigate potential risks, managers using algorithmic pricing tools should review their practices and ensure that their use of such technology does not inadvertently contribute to anti-competitive behavior. Additionally, implementing internal checks and involving legal counsel when using complex pricing software can help property managers navigate the evolving regulatory landscape.

As the case unfolds, the outcome of the RealPage lawsuit will likely shape future regulations and best practices in the multifamily industry, making it a critical issue for property managers and owners to watch.

5.3.10 Marketing Strategies and Tenant Screening

Effective marketing and tenant screening are critical components of successful apartment management. Property managers must implement targeted marketing strategies to attract quality tenants and ensure that those tenants are thoroughly vetted through a robust screening process. By combining strong marketing efforts with diligent screening procedures, property managers can maintain high occupancy rates, minimize turnover, and reduce the risk of problematic tenants. This section outlines the essential marketing strategies and tenant screening techniques specific to apartment management.

Marketing Strategies

Online Listings

Online listings are one of the most powerful tools for marketing apartment units. Property managers should leverage popular rental platforms like Zillow, Apartments.com, and Rent.com, as well as local listing websites, to maximize exposure. An effective listing should include a compelling description that highlights the unit's key features and amenities, such as in-unit laundry, updated appliances, or proximity to public transportation. Additionally, providing information about community amenities, such as fitness centers or pools, can help attract prospective tenants who are looking for more than just a living space.

Professional Photography

High-quality photography is essential to making a strong first impression in online listings. Professional photographs showcase the apartment's layout, lighting, and unique features, making the property stand out in a crowded market. Managers should ensure that each photo accurately represents the unit, with well-lit, clutter-free images that emphasize spaciousness and key areas like the kitchen, living room, and bedroom. For larger apartment complexes, consider investing in virtual tours or video walkthroughs, which allow potential tenants to explore the space remotely before scheduling an in-person viewing.

Incentives

Offering incentives is an effective way to generate interest and attract tenants, especially in competitive markets. Common incentives include discounts on the first month's rent, waived application fees, or offering free amenities such as reserved parking or gym access. Property managers can also offer move-in bonuses like gift cards or small home improvement items. These incentives can make a rental listing more appealing and encourage potential tenants to choose one property over another.

Tenant Screening Strategies

Credit Checks

Credit checks provide insight into a tenant's financial responsibility and help property managers assess their ability to pay rent on time. A good credit score generally indicates that the applicant has a history of managing debt responsibly. Managers should set clear criteria for acceptable credit scores and look for patterns of missed payments or significant debts that could indicate financial instability.

Background Checks

Background checks are crucial for ensuring the safety and security of the apartment community. Property managers should screen for any criminal history that could pose a risk to other residents. While it's important to avoid violating fair housing laws, property managers can establish reasonable screening criteria that balance safety with fairness. Background checks can include criminal records, eviction history, and previous legal disputes with landlords.

References

References from previous landlords or employers provide additional information about an applicant's behavior and reliability. Property managers should contact these references to verify the applicant's rental history, behavior as a tenant, and adherence to lease terms. This step can reveal important details that might not be captured in a credit or background check, such as whether the tenant consistently followed community rules or was involved in disputes.

Income Verification

Income verification ensures that the prospective tenant has sufficient income to cover the monthly rent. The general standard is that tenants should earn at least three times the monthly rent. Property managers can request recent pay stubs, employment verification letters, or tax returns to confirm income. This step is essential to reducing the risk of late or missed rent payments.

5.3.11 HUD Guidance on Application of the Fair Housing Act to the Screening of Applicants for Rental Housing

The U.S. Department of Housing and Urban Development (HUD) has issued specific guidance on how landlords and property managers can ensure that their tenant screening practices, particularly the use of credit history, comply with the Fair Housing Act (FHA). While credit history is a common tool used to assess a prospective tenant's financial responsibility, it can sometimes lead to unintended discriminatory effects, particularly against minority groups and low-income individuals. Understanding and applying HUD's guidance is critical to maintaining fair and nondiscriminatory screening practices in apartment management.

Discriminatory Effects and the Fair Housing Act

The FHA prohibits discrimination in housing based on race, color, national origin, religion, sex, familial status, and disability. When property managers use credit history as a screening criterion, they may inadvertently create a disparate impact—a situation where a neutral policy disproportionately affects a protected class, even without discriminatory intent. Minority groups and low-income individuals are statistically more likely to have lower credit scores or limited credit history, due to systemic inequalities and fewer financial resources. As a result, strict reliance on credit scores can exclude these groups from housing opportunities, raising potential compliance issues under the FHA.

For example, if a property manager sets a high minimum credit score requirement without considering alternative indicators of financial reliability, it could disproportionately eliminate applicants from minority communities, even if they have no history of rental delinquency or sufficient income to pay the rent. This practice could be deemed discriminatory if challenged under the FHA, even if it was not intended to discriminate.

HUD Guidance on Compliant Credit Screening Practices

HUD's guidance emphasizes that property managers must ensure their screening practices are both necessary and tailored to achieve a legitimate, nondiscriminatory purpose. To comply with the FHA, HUD suggests that landlords and property managers consider the following practices:

- *Evaluate the Necessity of Credit Screening:* Property managers should critically assess whether a strict credit score requirement is essential for evaluating a tenant's ability to pay rent. If less discriminatory alternatives, such as assessing recent rent payment history or verifying income, can achieve the same goal, these should be prioritized over rigid credit score thresholds.
- *Consider Alternative Indicators of Financial Responsibility:* Instead of solely relying on credit scores, property managers should review other financial indicators such as rent payment history, employment status, and overall debt-to-income ratio. This broader approach provides a more comprehensive view of an applicant's financial responsibility and can reduce the likelihood of inadvertently excluding qualified applicants.
- *Conduct an Individualized Assessment:* When credit history is used, property managers should conduct individualized assessments that take into account the context of negative credit items. For example, an applicant may have a low credit score due to medical debt or a temporary job loss but still have a stable income and good rental history. HUD advises considering these factors to avoid blanket exclusions based solely on credit scores.

- *Document the Screening Criteria:* To ensure compliance, property managers should document their screening policies and the rationale behind them. This documentation helps demonstrate that the criteria are applied consistently and serve a legitimate business purpose.

By implementing these practices, property managers can help ensure that their credit screening procedures align with HUD's guidance and the Fair Housing Act. Taking a balanced approach to credit screening not only reduces the risk of discrimination but also creates more equitable housing opportunities, supporting diversity and inclusion in the apartment community.

5.3.12 Lease Agreements

Drafting a clear and comprehensive lease agreement is essential for successful apartment rental management. An effective lease agreement serves as a legally binding document that establishes the rights and responsibilities of both the landlord and the tenant, ensuring smooth operations and reducing the potential for disputes. In apartment management, lease agreements should address specific elements that reflect the unique aspects of multifamily properties, such as shared amenities, community rules, and maintenance responsibilities. Below are the essential elements that should be included in a well-structured apartment lease agreement, along with a comparison to single-family home leases.

Essential Elements of an Apartment Lease Agreement

1. *Lease Term and Renewal Options:* The lease should clearly state the start and end dates, as well as any provisions for renewing or extending the lease. Apartment lease agreements often have fixed terms (typically 1 year) with options for month-to-month extensions or automatic renewals. Including renewal terms helps clarify the tenant's obligations and the procedures for lease continuation or termination.
2. *Use of the Property:* The lease should specify that the unit is to be used exclusively as a residential dwelling. It should prohibit unauthorized business use, subletting, or additional occupants not listed in the agreement. This clause helps maintain compliance with zoning regulations and ensures that the property is used appropriately.
3. *Rent Payment and Late Fees:* Clearly outline the amount of rent, due date, and acceptable payment methods. Additionally, include information on late fees and penalties for bounced checks. Apartment lease agreements often incorporate electronic payment options or specific rent collection policies that differ from single-family rentals, which may be less formal.
4. *Security Deposits and Move-In Fees:* Specify the security deposit amount, conditions for deductions, and the process for returning the deposit at the end of the lease. For apartments, additional move-in fees may be required for elevator use,

security deposits for shared amenities, or administrative fees. Single-family home leases typically focus more on property damage deposits.

5. *Maintenance and Repairs:* In apartment management, the landlord is usually responsible for maintaining the building's structure, common areas, and major systems (HVAC, plumbing, electrical). The lease should outline which maintenance tasks fall under the landlord's purview and which are the tenant's responsibility, such as minor repairs or notifying management of maintenance needs. Single-family home leases, in contrast, may place more responsibility on the tenant for yard care, snow removal, or minor upkeep.
6. *Use of Common Areas and Amenities:* Include a clause specifying the rules and policies for using shared amenities, such as fitness centers, laundry rooms, or parking areas. This section should detail any restrictions, hours of use, and expectations for maintaining shared spaces. Unlike single-family home leases, which typically lack shared facilities, apartment leases must be comprehensive in covering communal area usage.
7. *Community Rules and Regulations:* The lease should incorporate the property's community rules and regulations, covering issues like noise restrictions, pet policies, and visitor guidelines. Apartments, which have higher tenant density, often enforce stricter rules to ensure a safe and harmonious living environment. Single-family homes may have fewer community-specific regulations.
8. *Termination and Eviction Policies:* Clearly define the grounds for lease termination and the procedures for eviction. For apartments, this section should address issues such as nonpayment of rent, violations of community rules, or illegal activity. Single-family home leases may include more flexibility for early termination if the property owner decides to sell or move back into the home.

Key Differences Between Apartment and Single-Family Home Lease Agreements

- *Maintenance and Repairs:* In single-family homes, tenants are typically responsible for more maintenance tasks, such as lawn care or minor interior repairs, while in apartments, the landlord handles most maintenance issues.
- *Use of Common Areas:* Apartment leases must address the use of shared amenities and common areas, which are not a concern for single-family homes.
- *Community Rules and Regulations:* Apartment leases enforce stricter community rules to manage tenant behavior in a shared living environment, whereas single-family leases focus more on property-specific guidelines.
- *Lease Termination Flexibility:* Single-family home leases may include more flexible termination clauses, such as allowing the landlord to reclaim the property for personal use.

By tailoring these elements to reflect the unique characteristics of apartment properties, property managers can create lease agreements that set clear expectations, protect the owner's interests, and foster a positive living environment for tenants.

5.3.13 Sample Apartment Lease Contract

RESIDENTIAL LEASE FOR APARTMENT OR UNIT IN MULTI-FAMILY RENTAL HOUSING (OTHER THAN A DUPLEX) INCLUDING A MOBILE HOME, CONDOMINIUM, OR COOPERATIVE (FOR A TERM NOT TO EXCEED ONE YEAR)

(Not To Be Used For Commercial, Agricultural, or Other Residential Property)

WARNING: IT IS VERY IMPORTANT TO READ ALL OF THE LEASE CAREFULLY. THE LEASE IMPOSES IMPORTANT LEGAL OBLIGATIONS.

AN ASTERISK (*) OR A BLANK SPACE (_________) INDICATES A PROVISION WHERE A CHOICE OR A DECISION MUST BE MADE BY THE PARTIES.

NO CHANGES OR ADDITIONS TO THIS FORM MAY BE MADE UNLESS A LAWYER IS CONSULTED.

I. TERM AND PARTIES. This is a lease (the "Lease") for a period of _________ [number] months (the "Lease Term"), beginning ______________________________ [month, day, year] and ending ________________________ [month, day, year], between ______________________________ [name of owner of the property] and ______________________________ [name(s) of person(s) to whom the property is leased] (In the Lease, the owner, whether one or more, of the property is called "Landlord." All persons to whom the property is leased are called "Tenant.")

Landlord's E-mail address: ____________________
Landlord's Telephone Number: ____________________
Tenant's E-mail address: ____________________
Tenant's Telephone Number: ____________________

II. PROPERTY RENTED. Landlord leases to Tenant apartment or unit no. __________ in the building located at __________________________________ [street address] known as ________________________ [name of apartment or condominium], ______________ [city], Florida ____________ [zip code] together with the following furniture and appliances:

____
____
____

[List all furniture and appliances. If none, write "none."] (In the Lease the property leased, including furniture and appliances, if any, is called "the Premises.")

III. COMMON AREAS. Landlord grants to Tenant permission to use, during the Lease Term, along with others, the common areas of the building and the development of which the Premises are a part.

IV. RENT PAYMENTS AND CHARGES. Tenant shall pay rent for the Premises in installments of $________ each on the _______ day of each ____________________________ [month, week] (a "Rental Installment Period," as used in the Lease, shall be a month if rent is paid monthly, and a week if rent is paid weekly.) Tenant shall pay with each rent payment all taxes imposed on the rent by taxing authorities. The amount of taxes payable on the beginning date of the Lease is $_________ for each installment. The amount of each installment of rent plus taxes ("the Lease Payment"), as of the date the Lease begins, is $____________. Landlord will notify Tenant if the amount of the tax changes. Tenant shall pay the rent and all other charges required to be paid under the Lease by cash, valid check, or money order. Landlord may appoint an agent to collect the Lease Payment and to perform Landlord's obligations.

Unless this box ☐ is checked, the Lease Payments must be paid in advance beginning ____________________ [date].

If the tenancy starts on a day other than the first day of the month or week as designated above, the rent shall be prorated from ________________ (date) through ____________________ (date) in the amount of $________________ and shall be due on ____________________ (date) (If rent paid monthly, prorate on a 30 day month.)

V. DEPOSITS, ADVANCE RENT, AND LATE CHARGES. In addition to the Lease Payments described above, Tenant shall pay the following: (check only those items that apply)

________ a security deposit of $ __________ to be paid upon signing the Lease.

________ advance rent in the amount of $__________for the Rental Installment Periods of to be paid upon signing the Lease.

________ a pet deposit in the amount of $____________to be paid upon signing the Lease.

________ a late charge in the amount of $__________________ for each Lease Payment made more than____ number of days after the date it is due.

a bad check fee in the amount of $____________ (not to exceed $20.00, or 5% of the Lease Payment, whichever is greater) if Tenant makes any Lease Payment with a bad check. If Tenant makes any Lease Payment with a bad check, Landlord can require Tenant to pay all future Lease Payments in cash or by money order.

Other: ____.

Other: ____.

VI. SECURITY DEPOSITS AND ADVANCE RENT. If Tenant has paid a security deposit or advance rent the following provisions apply:

Landlord shall hold the money in a separate interest-bearing or non-interest-bearing account in a Florida banking institution for the benefit of Tenant. If Landlord deposits the money in an interest-bearing account, Landlord must pay Tenant interest of at least 75% of the annualized average interest paid by the bank or 5% per year simple interest, whichever Landlord chooses. Landlord cannot mix such money with any other funds of Landlord or pledge, mortgage, or make any other use of such money until the money is actually due to Landlord; or

Landlord must post a surety bond in the manner allowed by law. If Landlord posts the bond, Landlord shall pay Tenant 5% interest per year.

At the end of the Lease, Landlord will pay Tenant, or credit against rent, the interest due to Tenant. No interest will be due Tenant if Tenant wrongfully terminates the Lease before the end of the Lease Term.

If Landlord rents 5 or more dwelling units, then within 30 days of Tenant's payment of the advance rent or any security deposit, Landlord must notify Tenant in writing of the manner in which Landlord is holding such money, the interest rate, if any, that Tenant will receive, and when such payments will be made.

VII. NOTICES. ______________________________[name] is Landlord's Agent. All notices to Landlord and all Lease Payments must be sent to Landlord's Agent at ___________________________________[address], unless Landlord gives Tenant written notice of a change. Landlord's Agent may perform inspections on behalf of Landlord, subject to Article XII below. All notices to Landlord shall be given by certified mail, return receipt requested, or by hand delivery to Landlord or Landlord's Agent.

Any notice to Tenant shall be given by certified mail, return receipt requested, or delivered to Tenant at the Premises. If Tenant is absent from the Premises, a notice to Tenant may be given by leaving a copy of the notice at the Premises.

VIII. USE OF PREMISES. Tenant shall use the Premises only for residential purposes. Tenant also shall obey, and require anyone on the Premises to obey, all laws and any restrictions that apply to the Premises. Landlord will give Tenant notice of any restrictions that apply to the Premises.

If the Premises are located in a condominium or cooperative development, the Lease and Tenant's rights under it, including as to the common areas, are subject to all terms of the governing documents for the project, including, without limitation, any Declaration of Condominium or proprietary lease, and any restrictions, rules, and regulations now existing or hereafter adopted, amended, or repealed.

Unless this box ☐ is checked, Landlord may adopt, modify, or repeal rules and regulations for the use of common areas and conduct on the Premises during the Lease Term. All rules and regulations must be reasonable and in the best interest of the development in which the Premises are located.

Occasional overnight guests are permitted. An occasional overnight guest is one who does not stay more than _______ nights in any calendar month (If left blank, 7). Landlord's written approval is required to allow anyone else to occupy the Premises.

Unless this box ☐ is checked or a pet deposit has been paid, Tenant may not keep or allow pets or animals on the Premises without Landlord's approval of the pet or animal in writing.

Unless this box ☐ is checked, no smoking is permitted in the Premises.

Tenant shall not keep any dangerous or flammable items that might increase the danger of fire or damage on the Premises without Landlord's consent.

Tenant shall not create any environmental hazards on or about the Premises.

Tenant shall not destroy, deface, damage, impair, or remove any part of the Premises belonging to Landlord, nor permit any person to do so.

Tenant may not make any alterations or improvements to the Premises without first obtaining Landlord's written consent to the alteration or improvement. However, unless this box ☐ is checked, Tenant may hang pictures and install window treatments in the Premises without Landlord's consent, provided Tenant removes all such items before the end of the Lease Term and repairs all damage resulting from the removal.

Tenant must act, and require all other persons on the Premises to act, in a manner that does not unreasonably disturb any neighbors or constitute a breach of the peace.

IX. MAINTENANCE. Landlord and Tenant agree that the maintenance of the Premises must be performed by the person indicated below:

Landlord's Required Maintenance. Landlord will comply with applicable building, housing, and health codes relating to the Premises. If there are no applicable building, housing, or health codes, Landlord shall maintain and repair the roofs, porches, windows, exterior walls, screens, foundations, floors, structural components, and steps, and keep the plumbing in reasonable working order. If the Premises are located in a condominium, Landlord and Tenant acknowledge that the maintenance of the structural elements and common areas is performed by the condominium association as part of the common area maintenance. Landlord shall assure that the association complies with applicable building, housing, and health codes relating to the Premises. If there are no applicable building, housing, or health codes, Landlord shall assure that the association maintains and repairs roofs, porches, windows, exterior walls, screens, foundations, floors, structural components, and steps, and keeps the plumbing in reasonable working order. Landlord will be responsible for the maintenance of any items listed above for which the association is not responsible.

Elective Maintenance. Fill in each blank space in this section with Landlord or Tenant to show who will take care of the item noted. If a space is left blank, Landlord will be required to take care of that item (or assure that the association takes care of the items if the Premises are located in a condominium).

____________ Smoke detectors
____________ Extermination of rats, mice, roaches, ants, wood-destroying organisms, and bedbugs
____________ Locks and keys
____________ Clean and safe condition of outside areas
____________ Garbage removal and outside garbage receptacles
____________ Running water
____________ Hot Water
____________ Lawn
____________ Heat
____________ Air conditioning
____________ Furniture
____________ Appliances
____________ Fixtures
____________ Pool (including filters, machinery, and equipment)
____________ Heating and air conditioning filters
____________ Other: ____________________

Tenant's responsibility, if any, indicated above, shall not include major maintenance or major replacement of equipment.

Landlord shall be responsible for major maintenance or major replacement of equipment, except for equipment for which Tenant has accepted responsibility for major maintenance or major replacement in the previous paragraph.

Major maintenance or major replacement means a repair or replacement that costs more than $____________________.

Tenant shall be required to vacate the Premises on 7 days' written notice, if necessary, for extermination pursuant to this subparagraph. When vacation of the Premises is required for extermination, Landlord shall not be liable for damages but shall abate the rent.

Nothing in this section makes Landlord responsible for any condition created or caused by the negligent or wrongful act or omission of Tenant, any member of Tenant's family, or any other person on the Premises with Tenant's consent.

Tenant's Required Maintenance. At all times during the Lease Term, Tenant shall:

comply with all obligations imposed upon tenants by applicable provisions of building, housing, and health codes;

keep the Premises clean and sanitary;

remove all garbage from the dwelling unit in a clean and sanitary manner;

keep all plumbing fixtures in the dwelling unit clean, sanitary, and in repair; and use and operate in a reasonable manner all electrical, plumbing, sanitary, heating, ventilating, air conditioning, and other facilities and appliances, including elevators.

X. UTILITIES. Tenant shall pay all charges for hook-up, connection, and deposit for providing all utilities and utility services to the Premises during the Lease Term except________________________________, which Landlord agrees to provide at Landlord's expense. (Specify any utilities to be provided and paid for by Landlord such as water, sewer, oil, gas, electricity, telephone, garbage removal, etc.).

XI. SERVICEMEMBER.

If Tenant is a member of the United States Armed Forces on active duty or state active duty or a member of the Florida National Guard or United States Reserve Forces, the Tenant has rights to terminate the Lease as provided in Section 83.682, Florida Statutes, the provisions of which can be found in the attachment to this Lease.

XII. LANDLORD'S ACCESS TO PREMISES. Landlord or Landlord's Agent may enter the Premises in the following circumstances:

At any time for the protection or preservation of the Premises.

After reasonable notice to Tenant at reasonable times for the purpose of repairing the Premises.

To inspect the Premises; make necessary or agreed-upon repairs, decorations, alterations, or improvements; supply agreed services; or exhibit the Premises to prospective or actual purchasers, mortgagees, tenants, workers, or contractors under any of the following circumstances:

with Tenant's consent;

in case of emergency;

when Tenant unreasonably withholds consent; or

if Tenant is absent from the Premises for a period of at least one-half a Rental Installment Period. (If the rent is current and Tenant notifies Landlord of an intended absence, then Landlord may enter only with Tenant's consent or for the protection or preservation of the Premises.)

XIII. PROHIBITED ACTS BY LANDLORD. Landlord is prohibited from taking certain actions as described in Section 83.67, Florida Statutes, the provisions of which can be found in the attachment to this Lease.

XIV. CASUALTY DAMAGE. If the Premises are damaged or destroyed other than by wrongful or negligent acts of Tenant or persons on the Premises with Tenant's consent, so that the use of the Premises is substantially impaired, Tenant may terminate the Lease within 30 days after the damage or destruction and Tenant will immediately vacate the Premises. If Tenant vacates, Tenant is not liable for rent that would have been due after the date of termination. Tenant may vacate the part of the Premises rendered unusable by the damage or destruction, in which case Tenant's liability for rent shall be reduced by the fair rental value of the part of the Premises that was damaged or destroyed.

XV. DEFAULTS/REMEDIES. Should a party to the Lease fail to fulfill their responsibilities under the Lease or need to determine whether there has been a default of the Lease, refer to Part II, Chapter 83, entitled Florida Residential Landlord and Tenant Act which contains information on defaults and remedies. A copy of the current version of this Act is attached to the Lease.

XVI. ASSIGNMENT AND SUBLEASING. Unless this box ☐ is checked, Tenant may not assign the Lease or sublease all or any part of the Premises without first obtaining Landlord's written approval and consent to the assignment or sublease.

XVII. RISK OF LOSS. Subject to the next sentence, Landlord shall not be liable for any loss by reason of damage, theft, or otherwise to the contents, belongings, and personal effects of the Tenant, or Tenant's family, agents, employees, guests, or visitors. Landlord shall not be liable if such damage, theft, or loss is caused by Tenant, Tenant's family, agents, employees, guests, or visitors. Nothing contained in this provision shall relieve Landlord or Tenant from responsibility for loss, damage, or injury caused by its own negligence or willful conduct.

XVIII. SUBORDINATION. The Lease is automatically subordinate to the lien of any mortgage encumbering the fee title to the Premises from time to time.

XIX. LIENS. The interest of the Landlord shall not be subject to liens for improvements by the Tenant as provided in Section 713.10, Florida Statutes. Tenant shall notify all parties performing work on the Premises at Tenant's request that the Lease does not allow any liens to attach to Landlord's interest.

XX. APPROVAL CONTINGENCY. If applicable, the Lease is conditioned upon approval of Tenant by the association that governs the Premises. Any application fee required by an association shall be paid by ☐Landlord ☐ Tenant. If such approval is not obtained prior to commencement of Lease Term, either party may terminate the Lease by written notice to the other given at any time prior to approval by the association, and if the Lease is terminated, Tenant shall receive return of deposits specified in Article V, if made. If the Lease is not terminated, rent shall abate until the approval is obtained from the association. Tenant agrees to use due diligence in applying for association approval and to comply with the requirements for obtaining approval. ☐Landlord ☐Tenant shall pay the security deposit required by the association, if applicable.

XXI. RENEWAL/EXTENSION. The Lease can be renewed or extended only by a written agreement signed by both Landlord and Tenant, but in no event may the total Lease Term exceed one year. A new lease is required for each year.

XXII. LEAD-BASED PAINT. ☐ Check and complete if the dwelling was built before January 1, 1978. **Lead Warning Statement** (when used in this article, the term Lessor refers to Landlord and the term Lessee refers to Tenant)

Housing built before 1978 may contain lead-based paint. Lead from paint, paint chips, and dust can pose health hazards if not managed properly. Lead exposure is especially harmful to young children and pregnant women. Before renting pre-1978 housing, Lessors must disclose the presence of known lead-based paint and/or lead-based paint hazards in the dwelling. Lessees must also receive a federally approved pamphlet on lead poisoning prevention.

Lessor's Disclosure (initial)

______ (a) Presence of lead-based paint or lead-based paint hazards (check (i) or (ii) below):

(i) _____ Known lead-based paint and/or lead-based paint hazards are present in the housing (explain).

____

____

(ii) _____ Lessor has no knowledge of lead-based paint and/or lead-based paint hazards in the housing

______ (b) Records and reports available to the Lessor (check (i) or (ii) below):

(i) ______ Lessor has provided the lessee with all available records and reports pertaining to lead-based paint and/or lead-based paint hazards in the housing (list documents below).

____

____

(ii) ______ Lessor has no reports or records pertaining to lead-based paint and/or lead-based paint hazards in the housing.

Lessee's Acknowledgment (initial)

______ (a) Lessee has received copies of all information listed above.
______ (b) Lessee has received the pamphlet Protect Your Family From Lead in Your Home.

Agent's Acknowledgment (initial)

______ Agent has informed the Lessor of the Lessor's obligations under 42 U.S.C. 4852d and is aware of his/her responsibility to ensure compliance.

Certification of Accuracy

The following parties have reviewed the information above and certify, to the best of their knowledge, that the information provided by the signatory is true and accurate.

Lessor's signature	Date	Lessor's signature	Date
Lessee's signature	Date	Lessee's signature	Date
Agent's signature	Date	Agent's signature	Date

XXIII. ATTORNEYS' FEES. In any lawsuit brought to enforce the Lease or under applicable law, the party in whose favor a judgment or decree has been rendered may recover its reasonable court costs, including attorneys' fees, from the nonprevailing party.

XXIV. MISCELLANEOUS.

Time is of the essence of the performance of each party's obligations under the Lease.

The Lease shall be binding upon and for the benefit of the heirs, personal representatives, successors, and permitted assigns of Landlord and Tenant, subject to the requirements specifically mentioned in the Lease. Whenever used, the singular number shall include the plural or singular and the use of any gender shall include all appropriate genders.

The agreements contained in the Lease set forth the complete understanding of the parties and may not be changed or terminated orally.

No agreement to accept surrender of the Premises from Tenant will be valid unless in writing and signed by Landlord.

All questions concerning the meaning, execution, construction, effect, validity, and enforcement of the Lease shall be determined pursuant to the laws of Florida.

The place for filing any suits or other proceedings with respect to the Lease shall be the county in which the Premises is located.

Landlord and Tenant will use good faith in performing their obligations under the Lease.

As required by law, Landlord makes the following disclosure: "RADON GAS." Radon is a naturally occurring radioactive gas that, when it has accumulated in a building in sufficient quantities, may present health risks to persons who are exposed to it over time. Levels of radon that exceed federal and state guidelines have been found in buildings in Florida. Additional information regarding radon and radon testing may be obtained from your county health department.

XXV. TENANT'S PERSONAL PROPERTY. TENANT MUST INITIAL IN THIS BOX ☐ FOR THE FOLLOWING PROVISION TO APPLY. BY SIGNING THIS RENTAL AGREEMENT, THE TENANT AGREES THAT UPON SURRENDER, ABANDONMENT, OR RECOVERY OF POSSESSION OF THE DWELLING UNIT DUE TO THE DEATH OF THE LAST REMAINING TENANT, AS PROVIDED BY CHAPTER 83, FLORIDA STATUTES, THE LANDLORD SHALL NOT BE LIABLE OR RESPONSIBLE FOR STORAGE OR DISPOSITION OF THE TENANT'S PERSONAL PROPERTY.

The Lease has been executed by the parties on the dates indicated below:

______________________________	______________________________
Landlord's Signature	Date
______________________________	______________________________
Landlord's Signature	Date
______________________________	______________________________
Tenant's Signature	Date
______________________________	______________________________
Tenant's Signature	Date

This form was completed with the assistance of:

Name of
Individual:______________________
Name of
Business:______________________
Address:__________________________
Telephone
Number:______________________

Copy of Current Version of Florida Residential Landlord and Tenant Act,

Part II, Chapter 83, Florida Statutes to Be Attached

EARLY TERMINATION FEE/LIQUIDATED DAMAGES ADDENDUM

[ ] I agree, as provided in the rental agreement, to pay $______ (an amount that does not exceed 2 months' rent) as liquidated damages or an early termination fee if I elect to terminate the rental agreement and the landlord waives the right to seek additional rent beyond the month in which the landlord retakes possession.

[ ] I do not agree to liquidated damages or an early termination fee, and I acknowledge that the landlord may seek damages as provided by law.

______________________	______________________
Landlord's Signature	Date
______________________	______________________
Landlord's Signature	Date
______________________	______________________
Landlord's Signature	Date
______________________	______________________
Tenant's Signature	Date
______________________	______________________
Tenant's Signature	Date

Credit and Disclaimer

Reprinted with permission from The Florida Bar.

This landlord-tenant form has been approved by the Florida Supreme Court. However, because the law is continually changing, there is no guarantee that these forms comport with current law. These forms are not a substitute for the advice of an attorney. It is always best to consult an attorney about your legal rights and responsibilities in your particular case.

Source: The Florida Bar—https://www-media.floridabar.org/uploads/2018/08/multi-family-lease.pdf

5.3.14 Managing Tenant Relations

Maintaining strong tenant relations is critical for the successful management of apartment properties. Positive tenant relationships contribute to higher occupancy rates, better tenant retention, and a more harmonious living environment. Effective tenant management in apartments involves proactively building positive relationships, resolving disputes promptly and fairly, and implementing strategies to retain high-quality tenants. By focusing on these areas, property managers can create a welcoming community that attracts and keeps satisfied tenants for the long term.

Building Positive Relationships

The foundation of good tenant relations starts with building positive, professional relationships from the first point of contact. Property managers should prioritize excellent customer service by being responsive, approachable, and respectful in all interactions. This begins during the leasing process, where clear communication, prompt follow-ups, and transparency in policies set the tone for a positive relationship. Managers should strive to be visible and accessible, making regular visits to the property and holding office hours for tenants to discuss any issues or concerns.

A key aspect of relationship building is making tenants feel valued and appreciated. This can be achieved through small gestures such as welcome packages for new tenants, hosting community events, and sending personalized holiday or birthday greetings. Creating opportunities for residents to engage with each other—such as organizing social events or community activities—also fosters a sense of community, making tenants feel more connected to their neighbors and the property.

Handling Disputes

Disputes are inevitable in any rental community, but how they are handled can significantly impact tenant satisfaction. Property managers must approach conflict resolution with a fair and objective mindset. Listening to all parties involved, understanding the root of the problem, and finding mutually agreeable solutions are essential steps in resolving disputes effectively. Whether the issue is a noise complaint, maintenance concern, or disagreement over lease terms, addressing disputes promptly and professionally prevents small problems from escalating into larger issues.

It is also important for property managers to have clear policies and procedures for handling disputes, as this ensures consistency and fairness. Documenting complaints and following up on resolutions helps maintain transparency and builds trust with tenants, reinforcing that the property manager takes their concerns seriously.

Tenant Retention

Tenant retention is a key objective for any apartment property manager, as retaining good tenants is more cost-effective than constantly seeking new ones. Retention strategies should focus on keeping tenants satisfied with their living experience. Regularly soliciting tenant feedback through surveys or suggestion boxes can help managers identify areas for improvement. Additionally, offering lease renewal incentives, such as discounted rent for early renewal or upgrades to the unit, can encourage tenants to stay.

Providing exceptional maintenance services is another critical factor in tenant retention. Promptly addressing repair requests and keeping common areas in excellent condition demonstrate that the property manager values the tenant's comfort and satisfaction. A proactive approach, such as scheduling seasonal maintenance or offering preventative services, further contributes to tenant loyalty.

By building strong relationships, effectively managing disputes, and implementing targeted retention strategies, property managers can create a positive living environment that encourages long-term tenancy and enhances the overall success of the apartment community.

5.3.15 Rent Collection and Financial Management

Effective rent collection and financial management are essential to the success and profitability of apartment communities. In multifamily properties, where rent payments are the primary revenue source, establishing clear rent collection policies is critical to maintaining a steady cash flow. Additionally, robust financial management practices enable property managers to budget accurately, control expenses, and present detailed financial reports to owners. Implementing structured processes in both rent collection and financial management ensures operational efficiency and helps property managers meet the owner's financial objectives.

Rent Collection

Creating and enforcing a structured rent collection process is key to ensuring timely payments and minimizing delinquencies. A well-defined rent collection policy outlines expectations for tenants and provides consistency in handling payments. Property managers should consider the following strategies when managing rent collection for apartment communities:

- *Clear Rent Due Dates and Grace Periods:*
  - Establish a firm due date for rent payments, typically the first of each month.
  - Define a reasonable grace period (e.g., 3–5 days) before late fees are applied.
- *Acceptable Payment Methods:*
  - Offer multiple payment options such as online portals, ACH transfers, credit cards, and traditional methods like checks or money orders.
  - Implement online payment systems to streamline payments and automate tracking for large apartment communities.
- *Automated Payment Reminders:*
  - Send automated reminders via text or email before and after the rent due date to reduce late payments.
  - Use software solutions to generate payment reminders and track rent collection.
- *Late Payment Policies:*
  - Clearly state late fee amounts and when they apply to ensure tenants understand the consequences of late payments.
  - Consistently enforce late fees and communicate with tenants about any outstanding balances to avoid misunderstandings.
- *Handling Delinquencies:*
  - Implement a step-by-step process for managing delinquencies, starting with a written notice and followed by phone calls or meetings if necessary.

– Consider offering payment plans for tenants facing temporary financial hardships, depending on the owner's approval.

Financial Management

Sound financial management goes beyond rent collection and includes budgeting, expense control, and financial reporting. Property managers must monitor the financial health of the property and provide owners with accurate, detailed information to support strategic decision-making. Key financial management practices include:

- *Budgeting:*
  – Develop a comprehensive annual budget covering expected rental income, operating expenses, and capital improvements.
  – Review and update the budget periodically to reflect changing market conditions or unexpected expenses.
- *Expense Tracking:*
  – Track operating expenses in real-time to identify overspending or opportunities for cost savings.
  – Categorize expenses by type (e.g., maintenance, utilities, payroll) for clear financial analysis.
- *Cash Flow Management:*
  – Monitor cash flow regularly to ensure that the property remains financially solvent and can cover all operating costs.
  – Use software tools to forecast future cash flow needs based on rent collection and anticipated expenses.
- *Financial Reporting:*
  – Prepare regular financial reports, such as income statements, balance sheets, and cash flow statements, for the property owner.
  – Provide variance analyses comparing actual performance against the budget to identify discrepancies and areas for improvement.
- *Key Financial Metrics:*
  – Track key performance indicators (KPIs), such as net operating income (NOI), rent collection rate, and occupancy rate, to assess the property's financial health.
  – Use these metrics to support data-driven decision-making and optimize the property's profitability.

5.3.16 Maintenance and Repairs

In apartment management, maintenance and repairs are crucial to preserving the property's value, ensuring tenant satisfaction, and minimizing costly long-term damage. Maintenance responsibilities in apartment management differ significantly from those in condominiums and cooperatives, particularly regarding the scope of responsibilities and the level of oversight required. While apartment managers are responsible for nearly all aspects of property maintenance, condominium and cooperative managers share responsibilities with individual owners or shareholders, leading to distinct approaches in how maintenance is handled.

Differences in Maintenance Responsibility
In apartment management, the property manager or owner is responsible for maintaining both the individual units and common areas. This includes everything from routine repairs inside apartments—such as fixing plumbing issues, HVAC maintenance, and addressing structural repairs—to maintaining exterior areas like landscaping, parking lots, and building exteriors. All maintenance and repair costs fall on the property owner or management company, who must ensure that the building remains in good condition and complies with safety standards.

Routine Maintenance
In apartment management, routine maintenance includes regular tasks such as cleaning common areas, landscaping, ensuring proper lighting, and servicing HVAC systems. Property managers should establish a schedule for routine inspections of both individual units and shared areas to identify any maintenance needs before they become larger issues. Regular maintenance helps maintain tenant satisfaction by ensuring a comfortable and safe living environment.

Preventive Maintenance
Preventive maintenance involves proactive measures to avoid costly repairs and extend the lifespan of building systems. This includes regularly servicing HVAC systems, checking for plumbing leaks, inspecting roofing and building exteriors, and performing seasonal tasks such as winterizing the property. Preventive maintenance reduces the risk of major breakdowns and contributes to the long-term sustainability of the building.

Emergency Repairs
Emergency repairs in apartment management are critical to address immediately to ensure tenant safety and prevent further property damage. These emergencies may include burst pipes, electrical failures, or fire hazards. Property managers must have a clear protocol in place for handling emergencies, including an on-call maintenance team and a network of reliable contractors. Promptly addressing emergency repairs not only protects the property but also strengthens tenant relations by demonstrating a commitment to their safety and well-being.

For more details on creating a fully integrated maintenance plan, including proactive and emergency strategies, refer to the Sect. 6.3.3 in Chap. 6.

By understanding the different types of apartment buildings and their specific management needs, property managers can effectively address the unique challenges and opportunities presented by each type. This knowledge, combined with best practices in marketing, maintenance, financial management, and legal compliance, ensures the successful operation of apartment properties.

5.4 Case Study: Riverview Apartments

5.4.1 Background

Riverview Apartments is a 50-unit apartment complex located in a suburban area. The property features a mix of one-bedroom and two-bedroom units, a community pool, a small gym, and a shared laundry facility. The property owner has hired you as the property manager to oversee daily operations, maintain the property, and ensure tenant satisfaction.

5.4.2 Scenario

Riverview Apartments has recently faced several challenges, including a higher vacancy rate, maintenance issues with the community pool, and tenant complaints about noise disturbances. Your tasks include addressing these challenges, improving tenant relations, and implementing effective management strategies to enhance the property's performance.

5.4.3 Tasks

1. *Marketing and Tenant Acquisition*:
    - Develop a marketing strategy to attract new tenants and reduce the vacancy rate.
    - Create and post listings on multiple online rental platforms and local classifieds.
    - Organize open houses and property viewings for prospective tenants.
2. *Tenant Screening:*
    - Implement a comprehensive tenant screening process, including background checks, credit checks, reference checks, and income verification.
    - Ensure adherence to fair housing laws during the tenant selection process.
3. *Maintenance and Repairs:*
    - Conduct a detailed inspection of the community pool and other common areas to identify maintenance needs.
    - Coordinate with contractors to address immediate repairs, such as fixing the pool pump and resurfacing the pool deck.
    - Develop a routine maintenance schedule for common areas and individual units.
4. *Managing Tenant Relations:*
    - Address tenant complaints about noise disturbances and implement strategies to ensure a peaceful living environment.
    - Foster a sense of community by organizing social events and improving communication with tenants.

- Implement a system for collecting tenant feedback and addressing their concerns promptly.

5.4.4 Challenges

1. *Marketing Challenge:*
    - Despite advertising the property online, you are not receiving enough inquiries. Consider additional marketing strategies to increase interest in the property.
2. *Tenant Screening Challenge:*
    - During the tenant screening process, you receive applications from two potential tenants: one with excellent credit but a shorter rental history, and another with average credit but a long-term stable rental history. Decide how to proceed with tenant selection.
3. *Maintenance Challenge:*
    - During the inspection, you discover that the community pool pump is broken and needs immediate repair. Determine how to handle this issue within the maintenance budget provided by the property owner.
4. *Tenant Relations Challenge:*
    - Tenants have been complaining about noise disturbances from a few households. Develop a strategy to address these complaints and improve overall tenant relations.

5.4.5 Discussion Questions

1. *Marketing:*
    - What additional marketing strategies could you implement to increase interest in the property?
    - How can you highlight the property's unique features to make it stand out in the rental market?
2. *Tenant Screening:*
    - What factors should you consider when deciding between the two potential tenants?
    - How can you ensure that the tenant screening process is fair and compliant with fair housing laws?
3. *Maintenance:*
    - How would you prioritize the maintenance tasks identified during your inspection?
    - What steps can you take to prevent future maintenance issues and ensure the property remains in good condition?
4. *Managing Tenant Relations:*
    - What strategies can you use to improve communication and foster a sense of community among residents?

- How would you handle the complaints about noise and disturbances to ensure a peaceful living environment for all residents?

5.5 Management of Condominium Associations

5.5.1 Types of Residential Condominium Associations

Understanding the different types of residential condominium associations helps property managers and board members tailor their management strategies to the specific needs and characteristics of each type.

Condominiums and Townhomes

- *Description:* These are the most common types of residential condominium associations. Condominiums typically consist of individual units within a larger building, while townhomes that are established as condominiums are multi-level units sharing one or more walls with neighboring units but having separate entrances. Depending on their architectural design and layout, both types may share common areas such as lobbies, hallways, recreational facilities, and landscaped grounds.
- *Management Considerations:* Effective management of these properties involves maintaining common areas, enforcing community rules, and managing the association's finances. Regular communication with residents is essential to ensure compliance with rules and to address any maintenance issues promptly.

Condominium-Hotels (Condotels)

- *Description:* Condotels combine residential condominiums with hotel-like amenities and services. Units in a condotel can be rented out as hotel rooms when not occupied by their owners. These properties often include features like housekeeping, concierge services, and access to hotel amenities such as pools, fitness centers, and restaurants.
- *Management Considerations:* Managing a condotel requires balancing the needs of unit owners and hotel guests. Property managers must coordinate short-term rentals, ensure high-quality service, and maintain hotel amenities. Marketing and guest satisfaction are critical to the success of condotels, along with regular maintenance and adherence to hospitality standards.

Mixed-Use Condominiums

- *Description:* Mixed-use condominiums integrate residential units with commercial spaces, such as retail stores, offices, and restaurants. These properties are designed to provide a live-work-play environment, offering convenience and accessibility to residents.
- *Management Considerations:* Mixed-use properties require a comprehensive management approach that addresses both residential and commercial needs. Property managers must coordinate with commercial tenants, manage shared

amenities, and ensure that residential and commercial activities do not conflict. Effective communication and maintenance of both residential and commercial spaces are essential.

Short-Term Rentals

- *Description:* Short-term rental condominiums, often facilitated through platforms like Airbnb or VRBO, involve renting out units for short periods, typically less than 30 days. These properties can attract tourists and business travelers, offering a flexible and often more affordable alternative to traditional hotels.
- *Management Considerations:* Managing short-term rentals involves frequent tenant turnover, ensuring that units are cleaned and maintained between stays, and complying with local regulations regarding short-term rentals. Property managers must also address potential concerns from long-term residents, such as noise and security issues, and ensure that short-term rental activities align with the community's rules and regulations.

5.5.2 Governance and Board Management

The governance and board management of condominium associations are central to ensuring the community's smooth operation and long-term success. The board of directors, elected by the unit owners, serves as the governing body responsible for overseeing the condominium's financial and operational health. Property managers play an essential role in supporting the board by providing guidance, handling administrative tasks, and implementing board decisions. This section outlines aspects of governance, the roles and responsibilities of condominium board directors, the principles of effective meetings, board decision-making processes, and the role of committees in condominium governance.

Condominium Governing Documents

Condominium associations are governed by a set of foundational documents that outline the rights and responsibilities of unit owners, define the association's structure, and establish rules for managing the property. These governing documents include the Articles of Incorporation, the Declaration of Condominium, the Bylaws, and the Rules and Regulations. Each document serves a distinct purpose and plays a critical role in the effective governance and management of the association.

Articles of Incorporation

- *Purpose:* The Articles of Incorporation establish the legal entity of the condominium association as a nonprofit corporation. This document is filed with the state and provides the legal foundation for the association's existence.
- *Key Provisions:*
  - Name of the association.
  - Purpose and powers of the association.
  - Registered agent and office address.

  - Initial board of directors.
  - Membership structure, defining unit owners as members.
- *Importance:* The Articles give the association the legal authority to operate, enter into contracts, sue or be sued, and manage the property on behalf of its members.

Declaration of Condominium

- *Purpose:* Often referred to as the "Master Deed," the Declaration of Condominium defines the physical boundaries of the property, unit ownership rights, and the association's authority to manage common areas.
- *Key Provisions:*
  - Legal description of the property and individual units.
  - Definition of common elements and limited common elements.
  - Allocation of ownership interests, voting rights, and assessments.
  - Use restrictions and maintenance obligations for units and common areas.
  - Procedures for amending the Declaration.
- *Importance:* The Declaration is the most critical governing document as it establishes the rights and responsibilities of unit owners and the association, serving as the primary reference for resolving disputes.

Bylaws

- *Purpose:* The Bylaws provide the framework for the internal governance of the association, detailing how the board of directors operates and conducts association business.
- *Key Provisions:*
  - Procedures for electing and removing board members.
  - Board meeting rules, including frequency, quorum requirements, and voting procedures.
  - Powers and duties of the board and officers.
  - Budgeting and financial management policies.
  - Membership meetings, voting rights, and amendment procedures.
- *Importance:* The Bylaws guide the day-to-day governance of the association, ensuring that the board's operations are transparent and structured.

Rules and Regulations

- *Purpose:* The Rules and Regulations set specific guidelines for the behavior and activities of residents to promote a harmonious living environment and protect property values.
- *Key Provisions:*
  - Community conduct rules (e.g., noise restrictions, pet policies, parking regulations).
  - Architectural control guidelines (e.g., exterior modifications and landscaping).
  - Use of amenities and common areas.
  - Procedures for enforcing rules and assessing penalties for violations.

- *Importance:* The Rules and Regulations help maintain community standards and are typically more flexible than other governing documents, allowing the board to address specific issues as they arise.

Roles and Responsibilities of Condominium Board Directors

Condominium associations are typically governed by a board of directors that consists of volunteer unit owners who serve specific officer roles within the Board. Each officer position has distinct responsibilities that are essential for effective governance:

- *President:* Acts as the chief executive officer of the association. The president presides over meetings, sets agendas, and represents the board in official capacities. The president is responsible for ensuring that board decisions are carried out and that the association operates in accordance with the governing documents.
- *Vice President:* Supports the president and assumes their responsibilities in their absence. The vice president often oversees specific projects or committees as directed by the board.
- *Secretary:* Maintains accurate records of all board and membership meetings, handles official correspondence, and ensures that all association records are organized and accessible. The secretary's role is crucial for maintaining transparency and legal compliance.
- *Treasurer:* Oversees the financial management of the association, including budgeting, accounting, and reporting. The treasurer works closely with property managers to ensure that the association's finances are handled responsibly and that all financial reports are accurate and timely.

Effective Condominium Association Meetings

Condominium board meetings are a critical component of effective governance. Meetings should be well-organized, with a structured agenda that outlines key topics for discussion and decision-making. Open meetings, where unit owners can observe board deliberations, promote transparency and build trust within the community. Property managers support effective meetings by preparing materials, facilitating discussions, and ensuring that meetings stay focused on agenda items. They can also serve as moderators to guide discussions and provide professional insights on complex issues.

Board Decision-Making

The board's decision-making process should be transparent, fair, and aligned with the association's governing documents and the best interests of the community. Board members must review relevant information, consider input from unit owners, and vote on issues according to established procedures. Property managers assist by providing necessary background information, offering professional recommendations, and ensuring compliance with legal and procedural requirements. Good decision-making practices reduce the risk of conflicts and help maintain the community's stability and reputation.

The Role of Committees in Condominium Associations
Committees are invaluable to condominium associations, providing specialized support for specific areas such as finance, architectural review, landscaping, rules and regulation enforcement or social events. Committees are typically composed of volunteer unit owners who focus on researching issues, making recommendations to the board, and executing board-approved projects. Property managers often serve as liaisons to these committees, offering guidance, coordinating resources, and ensuring alignment with the board's strategic goals. Effective use of committees helps distribute the workload, encourages owner participation, and strengthens community engagement.

5.5.3 Managing Resident Relationships

Managing resident relationships is a fundamental aspect of condominium association management, as it directly influences community harmony, resident satisfaction, and overall property value. Unlike other property types, condominium associations have a complex governance structure that requires property managers to maintain strong relationships with a diverse group of owners, tenants, and board members. Building trust, fostering transparent communication, resolving conflicts, and encouraging resident participation are all essential elements for creating a thriving community. Below are key strategies specific to managing resident relationships in condominium associations.

Building Trust and Transparency
Trust is the foundation of any successful community, and condominium residents need to feel confident that the board and property managers act in the best interests of the community. Transparency is a critical component in building trust. Property managers should maintain an open line of communication about board decisions, budgetary matters, and upcoming projects. Providing access to financial reports, board meeting minutes, and maintenance schedules fosters an environment of openness. Regular updates on association activities, posted in newsletters or through digital platforms, can help reassure residents that management is transparent and accountable.

Effective Communication
Effective communication is vital to the smooth functioning of a condominium community. Property managers should establish multiple channels for communication, such as email, newsletters, social media groups, and resident portals, to ensure that all residents are informed and have a way to voice their concerns. Clear, concise, and timely communication about policies, rule changes, or ongoing maintenance projects helps prevent misunderstandings and reduces the likelihood of conflicts. For large associations, digital tools such as resident apps or automated notification systems can streamline communication efforts.

Conflict Resolution

Conflicts are inevitable in any residential community, but how they are managed can significantly impact the community's overall atmosphere. Property managers should approach disputes with empathy, impartiality, and a focus on finding mutually agreeable solutions. Establishing a formal conflict resolution process—such as mediation or involving a grievance committee—helps address issues fairly and consistently. Documenting complaints and resolutions can also aid in tracking recurring problems and identifying patterns that may require policy adjustments.

Involvement and Participation

Encouraging resident participation in community activities and decision-making processes fosters a sense of ownership and belonging. Property managers should create opportunities for residents to volunteer for committees, attend board meetings, and contribute to community projects. Promoting involvement strengthens the community's social fabric and ensures diverse perspectives are represented in decision-making.

Education and Training

Educating residents about the association's governance structure, rules, and financial obligations is essential for creating an informed community. Property managers can offer educational workshops, distribute informational guides, and provide training sessions on topics such as understanding the budget, board roles, and the implications of policy changes. An educated resident base is more likely to participate constructively in community affairs and less likely to challenge board decisions out of misunderstanding.

Feedback Mechanisms

Establishing formal feedback mechanisms, such as surveys, suggestion boxes, or online feedback forms, allows residents to express their opinions and concerns. Regularly seeking feedback on community management, amenities, and policies demonstrates that the board and property managers value residents' perspectives and are committed to continuous improvement. Implementing feedback in a transparent manner further builds trust and strengthens resident-manager relationships.

5.5.4 Maintenance Fee Collection and Financial Management

Effective maintenance fee collection and financial management are fundamental to the stability and success of any condominium association. Because condominium associations rely heavily on maintenance fees to fund their operations and capital reserves, property managers must implement sound financial practices to ensure that the community remains financially solvent and able to meet its obligations. This section outlines key strategies and best practices for accurate budgeting, timely fee collection, managing delinquencies, transparent financial reporting, and reserve fund management in condominium associations.

Accurate Budgeting

Accurate budgeting is the cornerstone of financial management for condominium associations. The annual budget should account for all anticipated operating expenses, such as utilities, maintenance, insurance, staffing, and administrative costs, as well as contributions to the reserve fund. Property managers should work closely with the board to project these expenses realistically and include a contingency fund to cover unexpected costs. Transparent communication of the budget to residents helps build understanding and support for the association's financial decisions, reducing resistance to potential fee increases. Chapter 5 covers the budgeting process in greater detail.

Timely Fee Collection

Timely collection of maintenance fees is crucial for maintaining a steady cash flow and ensuring that the association can meet its financial obligations. Property managers should establish clear procedures for collecting monthly or quarterly fees, including due dates, acceptable payment methods, and late fee policies. Offering online payment options and automated reminders can streamline the collection process and reduce late payments. It is essential to communicate fee schedules and collection policies clearly to residents to avoid confusion and ensure compliance.

Handling Delinquencies

Handling delinquent accounts promptly and consistently is critical to preserving the association's financial health. Property managers should implement a structured process for managing delinquencies, starting with reminder notices and escalating to legal actions if necessary. Establishing a firm yet fair approach to late payments, including offering payment plans where feasible, helps maintain a positive relationship with residents while safeguarding the association's financial interests.

Financial Reporting

Regular financial reporting provides the board and residents with a transparent view of the association's financial status. Property managers should prepare monthly and quarterly financial statements, including income and expense reports, cash flow summaries, and balance sheets. These reports should highlight any variances from the budget and provide explanations for significant changes.

5.5.5 Reserve Studies and Fund Management

Reserve funds are essential for covering long-term capital improvements and unexpected repairs, such as roof replacements or elevator upgrades. Property managers should work with the board to conduct regular reserve studies to assess the adequacy of the reserve fund and plan for future expenditure. This involves:

- *Reserve Studies*: Conduct regular reserve studies to assess the condition of major components and estimate future repair costs. Below are the common components typically found in a reserve study for condominium associations:
  1. *Building Structure*
     - *Roofing Systems*: Including the materials, condition, and expected life of roofing, such as flat roofs, shingle roofs, or tile roofs.
     - *Exterior Walls and Siding*: Assessment of walls, siding materials, or other external structural elements.
     - *Balconies and Decks*: Structural integrity and waterproofing of balconies and decks.
     - *Foundation*: Structural condition and any required repairs or maintenance.
  2. *Mechanical Systems*
     - *Heating, Ventilation, and Air Conditioning (HVAC)*: Central air systems, boilers, furnaces, and any common-area heating/cooling systems.
     - *Plumbing Systems*: Pipes, water mains, sewage lines, water heaters, and other essential plumbing components.
     - *Electrical Systems*: Including common-area electrical wiring, transformers, and backup generators.
     - *Elevator Systems*: Mechanical parts, cab interiors, and electrical control systems.
  3. *Common Area Amenities*
     - *Swimming Pools and Spas*: Pool shells, pumps, heaters, filtration systems, and decking around the pool.
     - *Fitness Centers*: Equipment, flooring, and HVAC for gyms or other exercise rooms.
     - *Clubhouses and Community Rooms*: General condition, furniture, and any installed AV or IT equipment.
  4. *Landscaping and Site Improvements*
     - *Landscaping*: Trees, shrubbery, irrigation systems, and general grounds maintenance.
     - *Sidewalks, Driveways, and Parking Lots*: Asphalt or concrete condition, striping, and necessary resurfacing or sealing.
     - *Retaining Walls and Fencing*: Structural integrity and condition of boundary walls or fencing.
     - *Stormwater Systems*: Drainage systems, retention ponds, and sewer systems.
  5. *Fire and Safety Systems*
     - *Fire Alarm Systems*: Condition and maintenance of fire alarms and detection systems.
     - *Fire Sprinkler Systems*: Inspections, testing, and lifespan of sprinkler systems.
     - *Security Systems*: Access control systems, surveillance cameras, and entry gate mechanisms.
  6. *Interior Common Areas*

    - *Lobbies and Hallways*: Flooring, wall finishes, lighting, and overall decor.
    - *Common-Area Furniture*: Replacement costs and lifespan of seating and tables in lounges or meeting rooms.
    - *Restrooms*: Plumbing, flooring, partitions, and fixtures in shared bathrooms.
7. *Exterior Maintenance Items*
    - *Windows and Doors*: Condition and replacement timeline for windows and exterior doors.
    - *Exterior Paint*: Estimated repainting schedule and cost for buildings and common structures.
    - *Gutters and Downspouts*: Assessment of drainage systems and maintenance schedule.
8. *Contingency and Miscellaneous Items*
    - *Insurance Deductibles*: Potential costs to cover deductibles in the event of a claim.
    - *Unforeseen Repairs*: A portion of reserves might be allocated for unexpected or emergency repairs.
9. *Replacement Reserves*
    - *Estimated Remaining Life*: Projection of how long before each component needs to be repaired or replaced.
    - *Replacement Cost Estimates*: Current and future costs for repair or replacement of each component.
    - *Funding Plan*: A strategy for accumulating the necessary funds over time to meet future repair needs without significant financial strain on the association or unit owners.

- *Structural Integrity Reserve Studies (SIRS)*: Condominiums in Florida that have buildings three stories or taller also need a special SIRS to assess the structural condition and future maintenance cost to repair or replace structural components only.
- *Budgeting*: Ensure adequate funding for reserves through careful budgeting and financial planning.
- *Transparency*: Provide owners with regular updates on reserve fund status and planned expenditures.

Audits and Reviews

Annual audits and financial reviews are critical for ensuring that the association's financial management practices are sound and compliant with applicable regulations. Property managers should facilitate independent audits by providing accurate records and supporting documentation. Regular audits help identify any discrepancies, reinforce financial transparency, and provide assurance to the board and residents that the association's finances are being managed responsibly.

By effectively managing resident relationships and maintaining robust financial practices, condominium associations can create a harmonious living environment and ensure long-term financial stability. These strategies help build a cohesive community and protect the value of the property for all residents.

5.5.6 Maintenance Responsibilities

Maintenance responsibilities in condominium associations are divided between the association and the individual unit owners, with specific obligations outlined in the governing documents such as the Declaration, Bylaws, and Rules and Regulations. The distinction between common area elements and unit elements determines which party is responsible for repairs, upkeep, and replacement. Understanding and clearly communicating these responsibilities is essential to prevent conflicts, ensure proper upkeep, and maintain property values. Below, the maintenance obligations for condominium common area elements and individual unit elements are outlined to provide clarity on the respective roles of the association and unit owners.

Maintenance of Condominium Common Area Elements

The condominium association is typically responsible for maintaining, repairing, and replacing all common area elements. Common areas are defined as parts of the property that are jointly owned and shared by all unit owners, and they often include:

- *Building Exteriors and Structural Components:* Roofs, exterior walls, foundations, and supporting structures fall under the association's purview. Regular inspections and maintenance of these elements are crucial to preserve the property's overall integrity.
- *Shared Amenities:* Facilities such as clubhouses, swimming pools, fitness centers, and recreation rooms are maintained by the association, ensuring they remain in good condition and safe for resident use.
- *Landscaping and Grounds:* The association is responsible for the maintenance of lawns, gardens, walkways, parking areas, and other exterior spaces.
- *Mechanical Systems:* HVAC systems (if shared), electrical wiring, plumbing systems, elevators, and fire safety equipment that service multiple units are managed and maintained by the association.
- *Common Area Interiors:* Lobbies, hallways, stairwells, and other interior common spaces are kept clean and well-maintained by the association, which includes managing lighting, flooring, and other fixtures.

The association's responsibility for common areas is funded through maintenance fees collected from unit owners, which are allocated to cover routine maintenance, emergency repairs, and long-term capital improvements.

For more details on creating a fully integrated maintenance plan, including proactive and emergency strategies, refer to the Sect. 6.3.3 in Chap. 6.

Maintenance of Condominium Unit Elements

Individual unit owners are generally responsible for maintaining everything within the interior boundaries of their own units. This includes:

- *Interior Walls and Finishes:* Painting, drywall, and other wall finishes inside the unit are typically the owner's responsibility.

- *Fixtures and Appliances:* Owners must maintain and replace items such as kitchen appliances, bathroom fixtures, water heaters, and HVAC units if they serve only their unit.
- *Interior Flooring and Carpeting:* Repair and upkeep of carpets, hardwood flooring, and other interior surfaces are handled by the unit owner.
- *Plumbing and Electrical Systems Within the Unit:* While the association handles shared systems, owners are responsible for plumbing and electrical lines that serve only their unit and are located within its interior walls.

Understanding these maintenance boundaries is essential for both the property manager and residents to ensure that repairs are handled by the appropriate party and that the community remains well-maintained. The property manager should routinely communicate these distinctions to residents, as unclear maintenance responsibilities can lead to disputes and misunderstandings, impacting the overall harmony of the community. By clearly defining maintenance roles, condominium associations can promote a proactive approach to upkeep and prevent unnecessary conflict over repair issues.

5.5.7 Management Contracts for Condominium Associations

Purpose of the Contract

A management contract formalizes the relationship between the condominium association and the property manager. It outlines the responsibilities, expectations, and compensation for managing the property, ensuring clarity and preventing disputes.

Key Elements of the Management Contract

1. *Scope of Services:*
   Clearly define the services the property manager will provide, such as managing common areas, collecting and accounting of assessments, handling maintenance and repairs, and enforcing rules.
2. *Compensation:*
   Detail the property manager's compensation, including management fees (typically a percentage of the monthly assessments), leasing fees for common area usage, and any additional charges for specific services.
3. *Authority:*
   Specify the property manager's authority to make decisions on behalf of the association, such as approving repairs up to a certain amount, negotiating service contracts, and handling resident disputes.
4. *Association's Responsibilities:*
   Outline the responsibilities of the condominium association, such as maintaining adequate insurance, providing funds for major repairs, and approving budgets.

5. *Duration and Termination:*
   State the duration of the contract and the terms for termination by either party, including notice periods and any termination fees.
6. *Dispute Resolution:*
   Include procedures for resolving disputes between the association and the property manager, such as mediation or arbitration.
7. *Legal Considerations:*
   Ensure that the contract complies with local, state, and federal laws and regulations. Consulting a legal professional can help draft a contract that protects the interests of both parties and minimizes potential legal issues.

5.5.8 Enforcement of Rules and Regulations in Condominium Associations

Importance of Rules and Regulations

Rules and regulations are essential for maintaining order, safety, and harmony within a condominium community. They help ensure that all residents adhere to community standards, contributing to a pleasant living environment and protecting property values. Effective enforcement of these rules is crucial to uphold the community's quality of life and to prevent conflicts among residents.

Creating Clear and Fair Rules

For rules to be effective, they must be clear, fair, and consistently enforced. The condominium board, often with input from residents and property managers, should develop comprehensive rules that address various aspects of community living, including noise levels, pet policies, parking regulations, use of common areas, and maintenance responsibilities. These rules should be documented in the condominium association's bylaws and made easily accessible to all residents.

Communication and Education

One of the first steps in enforcing rules is ensuring that all residents are aware of them. Distribute copies of the rules and regulations to new residents and provide regular reminders through newsletters, emails, or community meetings. Educating residents about the reasons behind the rules can foster greater understanding and compliance. It's also beneficial to have a dedicated section on the community's website where residents can easily access the rules and regulations.

Consistent Enforcement

Consistency is key to effective rule enforcement. The property manager, in collaboration with the condominium board, should establish a clear process for addressing rule violations. This process typically involves:

1. *Observation and Reporting*
   - Residents and property staff should be encouraged to report violations. This can be done through a formal reporting system where issues are documented and forwarded to the property manager or board for review.
2. *Initial Notice*
   - When a violation is reported, the property manager or board should issue a written notice to the offending resident. The notice should clearly describe the violation, reference the specific rule that was breached, and outline the expected corrective actions. A reasonable timeframe for compliance should also be provided.
3. *Follow-Up and Escalation*
   - If the resident fails to correct the violation within the given timeframe, a follow-up notice should be issued. This notice may include potential penalties, such as fines, suspension of community privileges, or, in severe cases, legal action. The enforcement process should escalate gradually, giving residents multiple opportunities to comply before more severe measures are taken.
4. *Documentation*
   - Maintain thorough records of all reported violations, notices issued, and actions taken. This documentation is crucial for transparency, accountability, and legal protection if disputes arise.
5. *Fairness and Impartiality*
   - It's important that rules are enforced fairly and impartially. All residents should be subject to the same standards, and personal biases should not influence enforcement actions. Consistent and fair enforcement helps build trust and respect within the community.

Resolving Disputes

Inevitably, some residents may dispute rule violations or the enforcement process. To handle these situations, the condominium association should establish a formal dispute resolution process. This may involve mediation, arbitration, or a hearing before the condominium board. Providing a structured and impartial process for resolving disputes helps ensure that all residents feel heard and treated fairly. It is best that the resolution process be developed and implemented with the guidance of the condominium association's legal counsel.

Periodic Review of Rules

Community needs and circumstances can change over time, so it's important to periodically review and update the rules and regulations. Solicit feedback from residents to identify any rules that may be outdated, overly restrictive, or difficult to enforce. Regular reviews ensure that the rules remain relevant and effective in maintaining the community's standards.

By establishing clear rules, educating residents, enforcing rules consistently, and resolving disputes fairly, condominium associations can maintain a harmonious and well-managed community. This proactive approach to rule enforcement helps protect property values, enhances the quality of life for residents, and fosters a cooperative living environment.

5.5.9 State and Federal Laws that Regulate Condominium Associations

Federal Laws

1. *Fair Housing Act (FHA)*
   Prohibits discrimination in housing based on race, color, religion, sex, national origin, familial status, and disability. Condominium associations must ensure their practices, including rules, marketing, and resident interactions, comply with the FHA.
2. *Americans with Disabilities Act (ADA)*
   Depending on the circumstances, The ADA may require condominium associations to provide reasonable accommodations for residents with disabilities, including modifications to common areas and ensuring accessibility.
3. *Fair Debt Collection Practices Act (FDCPA)*
   Regulates the collection of assessments and other fees, ensuring that associations use fair and legal methods for debt collection.

State Laws

1. *Condominium Acts*
   Most states have specific laws, often called Condominium Acts, that govern the creation, operation, and management of condominium associations. These laws outline the responsibilities of the association, the rights of unit owners, and the requirements for governance, financial management, and dispute resolution.
2. *Property Maintenance Codes*
   State and local property maintenance codes set standards for the upkeep of buildings and common areas. Condominium associations must comply with these codes to ensure the safety and habitability of the property.
3. *State Fair Housing Laws*
   In addition to the federal Fair Housing Act, many states have their own fair housing laws that may provide additional protections against discrimination. Condominium associations must comply with both federal and state fair housing laws.
4. *Disclosure Laws*
   State laws often require condominium associations to provide certain disclosures to prospective buyers, such as information about the association's financial status, rules and regulations, engineering reports and any pending litigation.
5. *Governance Requirements*
   State laws typically outline the governance requirements for condominium associations, including the election and duties of the board of directors, the conduct of meetings, and the process for amending bylaws and rules.

5.5.10 Compliance and Best Practices

Compliance and best practices are crucial for the effective management of condominium associations. With the complex legal environment surrounding condominium governance and the diverse interests of board members, property managers, and unit owners, adopting proactive compliance strategies is essential. A strong focus on training, legal guidance, policy management, and resident education helps ensure that the association operates within the bounds of the law and fosters a positive community environment. Below are the key components of a compliance-focused management approach specific to condominium associations.

Regular Training

Condominium board members and property managers must stay informed about the latest legal requirements, governance standards, and management best practices. Regular training sessions are critical to ensuring that both board members and property managers understand their roles and responsibilities. Training topics should include condominium law, fiduciary duties, ethical decision-making, financial management, and conflict resolution. Workshops and seminars provided by professional organizations, such as the Community Associations Institute (CAI), are valuable resources for keeping board members and managers updated on industry changes. Consistent training empowers the board to make informed decisions and reduces the likelihood of legal disputes arising from misunderstandings or noncompliance.

Legal Counsel

Condominium associations should maintain ongoing relationships with qualified legal counsel who specialize in community association law. Legal advisors play a key role in ensuring that the association's governing documents, policies, and actions comply with local, state, and federal laws. Legal counsel can provide guidance on complex issues such as amendments to the governing documents, enforcement of community rules, and compliance with fair housing regulations. Regular consultation with an attorney helps the association navigate legal challenges and minimizes the risk of costly lawsuits.

Policy Updates and Document Review

To stay compliant and reflect best practices, condominium associations should regularly review and update their policies and procedures. This includes reviewing governing documents, such as bylaws and the declaration, and ensuring they are in line with current laws. Policy updates should be made in consultation with legal counsel and, where necessary, voted on by the board or unit owners. Regularly updating policies ensures that the association's rules are enforceable and aligned with evolving legal standards and community needs.

Resident Education

Educating residents about their rights, responsibilities, and the association's rules is a crucial element of compliance management. A well-informed resident base helps reduce conflicts and fosters a cooperative community environment. Property managers can implement educational initiatives such as newsletters, workshops, or an online portal with resources and updates about the community's governance. Clear communication of the association's policies and any changes to rules helps residents understand why certain decisions are made and promotes adherence to community standards.

Ensure that board members and property managers receive regular training on federal and state laws that affect condominium associations.

Legal Counsel
Maintain ongoing relationships with legal counsel to ensure that the association's practices and documents comply with current laws and regulations.

Policy Updates
Regularly review and update the association's policies and procedures to reflect changes in laws and best practices.

Resident Education
Educate residents about their rights and responsibilities under federal and state laws to promote compliance and reduce conflicts.

By understanding and adhering to these legal requirements, condominium associations can operate effectively and protect the rights and interests of their residents.

5.5.11 Problems Frequently Encountered by Condominium Association Board of Directors

The role of a condominium association board of directors is pivotal in ensuring the smooth operation and governance of a condominium community. However, board members often face a myriad of challenges that can complicate their efforts to maintain a harmonious and well-managed environment. Understanding these common problems can help board members prepare and implement effective strategies to address them.

1. *Financial Management Issues*

   One of the most significant challenges for condominium boards is managing the association's finances effectively. This includes budgeting, collecting fees, and maintaining adequate reserve funds for future repairs and improvements. Boards often struggle with delinquent payments from unit owners, leading to cash flow problems. Additionally, balancing the budget while ensuring sufficient funds for unexpected expenses can be daunting, especially in older buildings that may require more maintenance.
2. *Compliance with Laws and Regulations*

   Keeping up with local, state, and federal laws that govern condominium associations is essential but challenging. Regulations such as the Fair Housing

Act, Americans with Disabilities Act, and various state condominium acts require constant attention and updates to policies and procedures. Noncompliance can result in legal issues and financial penalties, making it crucial for boards to stay informed and consult with legal experts regularly.

3. *Conflict Resolution*

   Board members often find themselves mediating disputes between residents or addressing complaints about rule violations. Handling these conflicts impartially and effectively is critical to maintaining a peaceful community. However, this task can be challenging, especially when residents have strong opposing views or when the board must enforce unpopular rules.

4. *Communication Breakdown*

   Effective communication between the board, property management, and residents is vital for transparency and trust. Boards frequently encounter issues with disseminating information or ensuring that residents feel informed and involved. Miscommunication or lack of communication can lead to misunderstandings, dissatisfaction, and reduced cooperation from residents.

5. *Maintenance and Repairs*

   Ensuring that the property is well-maintained is a perpetual challenge. Boards must prioritize maintenance tasks, schedule regular inspections, and handle emergency repairs. Balancing the desire to keep fees low with the need to fund necessary repairs and improvements requires careful planning and often involves difficult decisions that may not please all residents.

6. *Board Member Turnover and Burnout*

   Serving on a condominium board can be time-consuming and stressful, leading to high turnover rates among board members. Frequent changes in board composition can disrupt continuity and long-term planning. Additionally, burnout among board members can reduce their effectiveness and willingness to serve, further complicating governance and decision-making processes.

7. *Enforcing Rules and Regulations*

   Ensuring that all residents comply with community rules and regulations is essential but can be contentious. Boards often face resistance or noncompliance from residents, which can lead to conflicts and require formal enforcement actions. Striking a balance between being firm and fair while maintaining good relationships with residents is a delicate task.

8. *Managing Vendor Relationships*

   Boards must select and manage vendors for various services, such as maintenance, landscaping, and security. Ensuring that vendors perform their duties satisfactorily and managing contracts and negotiations can be complex. Issues with vendor performance or contract disputes can disrupt services and lead to additional costs.

9. *Strategic Planning*

   Long-term planning for the association's future needs, such as major capital improvements, technological upgrades, or changes in community demographics, is critical but often overlooked. Boards may struggle to focus on strategic planning while managing day-to-day operations, leading to a reactive rather than proactive approach.

10. *Resident Engagement*

    Encouraging resident participation in meetings, committees, and community activities can be challenging. Low engagement can make it difficult to achieve quorum for decisions, gather diverse input, and foster a sense of community. Boards need to find ways to motivate residents to take an active interest in their community.

    By recognizing and addressing these common challenges, condominium association boards can enhance their effectiveness, ensure better governance, and create a more harmonious and well-managed community. Implementing best practices, seeking professional advice when needed, and fostering open communication and engagement with residents are key strategies to overcome these obstacles.

5.6 Case Study: Harmony Condominium Association

5.6.1 Background

Harmony Condominium Association manages a 100-unit condominium complex with various amenities, including a fitness center, swimming pool, and community garden. The association is governed by a board of directors, and you have been hired as the property manager to oversee daily operations, maintenance, and resident relations.

5.6.2 Scenario

Harmony Condominium Association has recently faced several challenges, including disputes among residents, issues with the reserve fund, and compliance with new state regulations. Your tasks include resolving these disputes, ensuring the reserve fund is adequately managed, and updating policies to comply with state laws.

5.6.3 Tasks

1. *Dispute Resolution:*
   - Address ongoing disputes among residents regarding noise levels and use of common areas.
   - Implement a system for resolving future disputes in a fair and timely manner.
2. *Reserve Fund Management:*
   - Review the status of the reserve fund and identify any shortfalls.
   - Develop a plan to ensure the reserve fund is adequately funded for future repairs and improvements.

3. *Compliance with State Regulations:*
    - Review the new state regulations that affect condominium associations.
    - Update the association's policies and procedures to ensure compliance with these regulations.

5.6.4 Challenges

1. *Dispute Challenge:*
    - Residents have been complaining about noise from late-night parties in the common areas. Develop a strategy to address these complaints and enforce community rules.
2. *Reserve Fund Challenge:*
    - The reserve fund is underfunded, and there are major repairs needed for the swimming pool and roof. Determine how to manage the reserve fund effectively and prioritize these repairs.
3. *Regulatory Compliance Challenge:*
    - New state regulations require the installation of energy-efficient lighting in all common areas and regular safety inspections. Plan how to implement these changes within the association's budget.

5.6.5 Discussion Questions

1. *Dispute Resolution:*
    - What steps can you take to resolve the current disputes among residents regarding noise levels and use of common areas?
    - How can you implement a system to handle future disputes effectively?
2. *Reserve Fund Management:*
    - What strategies can you use to ensure the reserve fund is adequately funded?
    - How would you prioritize the repairs needed for the swimming pool and roof given the current financial constraints?
3. *Regulatory Compliance:*
    - What steps should you take to ensure compliance with the new state regulations regarding energy-efficient lighting and safety inspections?
    - How can you communicate these changes to residents and involve them in the process to minimize disruption?

5.7 Management of Cooperatives

5.7.1 Understanding the Legal Structure of Cooperatives

Cooperatives (or "co-ops") have a unique legal structure that significantly impacts their management and governance. Unlike traditional condominium associations, where individual owners hold title to their units, cooperative residents do not own real property in the conventional sense. Instead, they own shares in a corporation that holds the title to the entire building or property. These shares grant residents the right to occupy a specific unit under a proprietary lease or occupancy agreement. Managing cooperatives requires a thorough understanding of this structure, as it affects everything from decision-making and governance to maintenance responsibilities and resident relations.

Key Elements of Cooperative Management

1. *Ownership Structure:* In a cooperative, residents are shareholders in a corporation, not direct owners of real estate. This means that residents collectively own the entire property, and their rights to occupy their units are based on the number of shares they hold. Each shareholder is bound by the terms of a proprietary lease or occupancy agreement, which outlines their rights and responsibilities. Property managers must navigate this complex structure, managing the corporation's interests while balancing individual shareholders' needs.
2. *Governance:* Cooperatives are governed by a board of directors elected by the shareholders. The board has significant control over the cooperative's operations, including setting maintenance fees, approving renovations, and enforcing community rules. Property managers work closely with the board to implement decisions and ensure compliance with the governing documents. The board's power extends to approving new shareholders and overseeing the financial health of the cooperative, making property managers' support and expertise crucial in these areas.
3. *Financial Management:* Unlike condominium associations, where owners pay maintenance fees for shared expenses, cooperative shareholders pay monthly maintenance fees that cover not only operating costs but also the cooperative's mortgage (if applicable), property taxes, and reserves. Property managers must ensure that these fees are accurately calculated and collected, as any financial instability can impact the entire community.

Key Differences Between Cooperatives and Condominium Associations

- *Ownership and Shares:*
- In a cooperative, residents own shares in a corporation and hold proprietary leases, whereas in a condominium association, residents hold individual title to their units and a shared interest in common areas.
- *Approval of Buyers:*
- Cooperative boards have the authority to approve or reject prospective buyers based on specific criteria, making them gatekeepers to community membership. Condominium boards typically do not have this level of control and can only exercise a limited right of first refusal.
- *Financing and Mortgages:*
- Financing a cooperative unit often requires a special type of loan called a "share loan," which is different from a traditional mortgage used in condominiums. The

cooperative's overall financial health can impact an individual's ability to obtain financing, making financial transparency a critical management focus.

- *Governance Control:*
- Cooperative boards have more direct control over resident behavior and property use compared to condominium associations. This control can include restrictions on subletting, renovations, and the transfer of shares, all of which must be managed in accordance with the cooperative's bylaws.

Understanding these distinctions is crucial for property managers to effectively support cooperative boards and shareholders. Cooperative management requires a deeper involvement in governance and financial oversight, as the success of the cooperative depends on strong collaboration and alignment among residents, the board, and management.

5.7.2 Managing Shareholder Relationships

Managing shareholder relationships in cooperatives requires a distinct approach compared to other multifamily properties due to the unique ownership structure and governance model. Cooperative residents are not simply tenants—they are shareholders with vested interests in the building's financial and operational health. This means that property managers must engage with shareholders as partners, balancing their expectations while ensuring that the cooperative operates smoothly and within its budget. Fostering positive shareholder relationships involves focusing on effective communication, conflict resolution, participation, education, feedback mechanisms, and building transparency and trust.

Effective Communication

Clear and consistent communication is essential for maintaining strong relationships with shareholders. Property managers should establish multiple communication channels, such as newsletters, email updates, and community meetings, to keep shareholders informed about important issues, upcoming projects, and financial updates. Proactive communication helps prevent misunderstandings and demonstrates that the property manager values shareholder input and engagement. Additionally, open forums during meetings provide opportunities for shareholders to ask questions and voice concerns, creating a platform for constructive dialogue.

Conflict Resolution

Conflicts among shareholders, or between shareholders and the board, are common in cooperative communities. Property managers must approach these disputes impartially and strive to find solutions that balance individual interests with the collective good of the cooperative. Establishing a formal conflict resolution process, such as mediation or a grievance committee, can help resolve issues before they escalate. Effective conflict resolution requires patience, empathy, and a clear understanding of the cooperative's bylaws and rules.

Involvement and Participation

Encouraging shareholder participation in community decision-making fosters a sense of ownership and responsibility. Property managers should promote involvement by inviting shareholders to serve on committees, attend board meetings, and contribute to community projects. Providing clear information about how decisions are made and how shareholders can get involved helps increase engagement and support for board initiatives.

Education and Training

Educating shareholders about the cooperative's governance structure, financial obligations, and community rules is vital to ensuring informed participation. Property managers can organize training sessions and workshops on topics such as understanding financial statements, the role of the board, and the rights and responsibilities of shareholders. Educated shareholders are more likely to engage constructively and contribute positively to the cooperative's success.

Feedback Mechanisms

Creating structured feedback mechanisms, such as surveys or suggestion boxes, allows shareholders to express their opinions and provide input on community matters. Regularly soliciting feedback and following up on suggestions shows that management values their perspectives and is committed to continuous improvement.

Transparency and Trust

Transparency is a cornerstone of effective cooperative management. Property managers should provide shareholders with clear, comprehensive information about the cooperative's financial health, governance decisions, and policy changes. This includes sharing financial statements, meeting minutes, and any updates on maintenance or capital improvement projects. Transparency builds trust and helps avoid the suspicion or confusion that can arise from opaque management practices.

5.7.3 Financial Management and Legal Compliance

Managing the financial and legal aspects of a cooperative community is a complex task that requires a deep understanding of the unique cooperative structure. Cooperative boards and property managers must ensure that the cooperative's financial health is strong and that its operations comply with local, state, and federal laws. Financial management focuses on maintaining a balanced budget, collecting fees, and providing transparent financial reporting to shareholders. Legal compliance involves staying updated on legal changes, implementing appropriate policies, and seeking legal advice when necessary. Below are the essential elements of financial management and legal compliance in cooperative property management.

Financial Management

Proper financial management is critical to maintaining the cooperative's stability and ensuring that the board can meet its financial obligations. Effective budgeting, fee collection, and detailed financial reporting are essential components of managing a cooperative's finances.

- *Budgeting:*
  - Develop an annual budget that covers operating expenses, reserve contributions, debt servicing (if applicable), and planned capital improvements.
  - Include a contingency fund for unexpected expenses to prevent budget shortfalls.
  - Engage shareholders in the budgeting process by presenting proposed budgets at annual meetings and soliciting feedback.
- *Fee Collection:*
  - Collect monthly maintenance fees that cover the cooperative's operating costs, mortgage payments, property taxes, and reserve fund contributions.
  - Implement clear procedures for handling late payments, including reminders, late fees, and potential legal action if necessary.
  - Offer multiple payment options, such as online payments or direct deposit, to facilitate timely fee collection.
- *Financial Reporting:*
  - Prepare detailed financial reports, including income statements, balance sheets, and cash flow statements, for the board and shareholders.
  - Present quarterly and annual financial summaries at shareholder meetings to maintain transparency.
  - Highlight variances between actual expenses and the budget to identify areas for cost management.

Legal Compliance

Legal compliance in cooperatives involves adhering to regulations that govern cooperative housing and ensuring that all policies and procedures are legally sound. Staying compliant minimizes the risk of legal disputes and protects the cooperative's interests.

- *Legal Updates:*
  - Monitor changes in local, state, and federal laws that impact cooperative housing, such as landlord-tenant regulations, fair housing laws, and tax codes.
  - Update governing documents, including bylaws, occupancy agreements, and proprietary leases, to reflect new legal requirements.
- *Policy Implementation:*
  - Develop and implement policies that align with current laws and cooperative best practices.
  - Ensure that all policies are documented, communicated to shareholders, and consistently enforced.
- *Legal Advice:*

- Maintain a relationship with an attorney specializing in cooperative housing to provide legal guidance on complex issues, such as shareholder disputes, contract negotiations, and regulatory compliance.
- Consult legal counsel before making significant policy changes or undertaking major projects, such as building renovations or refinancing.

5.7.4 Management Contracts for Cooperatives

Management contracts for cooperatives are specialized agreements that outline the terms under which a property manager or management company will oversee the daily operations of the cooperative community. Given the unique ownership structure and governance model of cooperatives—where shareholders collectively own the building and make decisions through a board of directors—the management contract must address specific elements that reflect the cooperative's operational and financial needs. The contract not only defines the manager's duties and compensation but also delineates the authority and decision-making boundaries between the board, shareholders, and management. Understanding the distinctive requirements of cooperative management is crucial for drafting a contract that ensures smooth operations and aligns with the cooperative's objectives.

Key Elements of a Cooperative Management Contract

1. *Scope of Services:* The management contract should detail the specific services the manager will provide, such as financial management, maintenance oversight, shareholder communications, and administrative support. In cooperatives, managing the collection of monthly maintenance fees, maintaining the property's financial records, and coordinating shareholder meetings are critical responsibilities. The contract must clarify which tasks are handled by the manager and which remain under the purview of the board.
2. *Authority and Decision-Making:* Since the cooperative board has significant control over the community's governance, the contract must clearly outline the manager's authority to act on behalf of the board. This includes the manager's ability to enter into contracts for routine services, approve expenditures within specified limits, and make operational decisions without board approval. For example, the contract should specify if the manager has the authority to hire contractors for minor repairs or if board approval is needed for every service engagement.
3. *Financial Management Responsibilities:* Financial management is particularly complex in cooperatives, where the manager may be responsible for budgeting, managing the reserve fund, and ensuring timely payment of property taxes and insurance premiums. The contract should specify the manager's role in preparing financial reports, maintaining accurate records, and assisting the board in conducting audits. Any limitations on spending or financial decisions should be explicitly stated.

4. *Communication and Reporting Requirements:* Effective communication with both the board and shareholders is essential in cooperative management. The contract should specify the frequency and format of reports, such as monthly financial statements, maintenance updates, and shareholder correspondence. It should also establish protocols for regular board meetings and emergency communications.
5. *Compensation and Fee Structure:* Management contracts typically include a base management fee, which may be calculated as a fixed amount or a percentage of the cooperative's operating expenses. Additional fees for services such as capital project management or legal compliance support should be clearly defined. The contract should also outline the terms of payment and any conditions for adjusting fees based on the cooperative's needs.
6. *Contract Duration and Termination Clauses:* The duration of the management contract and the conditions under which either party can terminate the agreement must be clearly articulated. Termination clauses should specify notice periods, causes for early termination (such as poor performance or breach of contract), and the process for transitioning management responsibilities.

By understanding the legal structure of cooperatives, effectively managing shareholder relationships, and implementing comprehensive management contracts, property managers can navigate the unique challenges of cooperative housing and ensure the smooth operation and financial stability of the cooperative.

5.8 Case Study: Greenview Cooperative

5.8.1 Background

Greenview Cooperative is a 60-unit residential cooperative located in an urban area. The cooperative is managed by a board of directors elected by the shareholders, who own shares in the corporation that holds the property title. You have recently been hired as the property manager to oversee the cooperative's daily operations, manage shareholder relations, and ensure compliance with legal and financial requirements.

5.8.2 Scenario

Greenview Cooperative has recently faced several challenges, including conflicts among shareholders, issues with fee collection, and the need to update its bylaws to comply with new state regulations. Your tasks include resolving these conflicts, improving fee collection practices, and ensuring the cooperative's legal compliance.

5.8.3 Tasks

1. *Managing Shareholder Relationships:*
   - Address ongoing conflicts among shareholders regarding common area usage and noise complaints.
   - Implement strategies to foster better communication and community engagement among shareholders.
2. *Fee Collection and Financial Management:*
   - Review the current fee collection process and identify any shortfalls or issues.
   - Develop a plan to ensure timely and efficient collection of maintenance fees and manage the cooperative's finances effectively.
3. *Legal Compliance:*
   - Review the cooperative's bylaws and identify necessary updates to comply with new state regulations.
   - Develop a plan to update the bylaws and communicate these changes to the shareholders.

5.8.4 Challenges

1. *Conflict Challenge:*
   - Shareholders have been complaining about noise from common areas during late hours. Develop a strategy to address these complaints and enforce community rules.
2. *Fee Collection Challenge:*
   - The cooperative has experienced a decline in timely maintenance fee payments, leading to financial strain. Determine how to improve the fee collection process and address delinquent accounts.
3. *Regulatory Compliance Challenge:*
   - New state regulations require updates to the cooperative's bylaws to include provisions for electronic voting and meeting notices. Plan how to implement these changes and ensure shareholder approval.

5.8.5 Discussion Questions

1. *Managing Shareholder Relationships:*
   - What steps can you take to resolve the current conflicts among shareholders regarding common area usage and noise complaints?
   - How can you improve communication and foster a sense of community among shareholders?
2. *Fee Collection and Financial Management:*
   - What strategies can you use to ensure the timely and efficient collection of maintenance fees?

- How would you address delinquent accounts and improve overall financial management for the cooperative?

3. *Legal Compliance:*
   - What steps should you take to update the cooperative's bylaws to comply with new state regulations?
   - How can you effectively communicate these changes to shareholders and ensure their approval?

5.9 Management of Homeowner Associations (HOAs)

Homeowner Associations (HOAs) play a vital role in managing the operations and upkeep of planned communities, which may include townhouses, single-family homes, and even some condominium associations. Unlike other multifamily residential properties, HOAs are primarily responsible for maintaining the shared common areas, enforcing community rules, and preserving the aesthetic and financial value of the neighborhood. Their purpose is to promote a cohesive community environment by regulating property use, managing common amenities, and ensuring compliance with community standards. As a result, effective HOA management requires a unique approach that combines governance, financial management, and resident relations.

HOAs typically govern communities based on a set of governing documents that include the Declaration of Covenants, Conditions, and Restrictions (CC&Rs), Bylaws, and Rules and Regulations. These documents outline the rights and responsibilities of homeowners, the scope of the HOA's authority, and the rules that all residents must follow. The HOA is governed by a board of directors, which is often made up of volunteer homeowners elected by their peers. Property managers play an essential role in supporting the board by handling day-to-day operations, executing board decisions, and ensuring compliance with the association's rules.

The types of properties managed by HOAs vary widely. Single-family home communities often include extensive common areas such as parks, clubhouses, and recreational facilities, while townhouse and condominium-style HOAs might focus more on building maintenance and shared infrastructure. Regardless of the property type, the HOA's goal is to enhance the quality of life for residents and protect property values by maintaining high standards for community upkeep and governance. Successful HOA management balances the interests of individual homeowners with the collective needs of the community, fostering a well-maintained and harmonious living environment.

5.9.1 Governance and Board Management

Similar to condominium associations, the governance and management of a Homeowner Association (HOA) are centered around the board of directors, which serves as the governing body responsible for making key decisions and ensuring the smooth operation of the community. Property managers play a vital supporting role by implementing the board's policies, advising on best practices, and handling the administrative tasks necessary to maintain compliance and efficiency. Understanding the HOA governance, roles and responsibilities of the board, conducting effective meetings, facilitating sound decision-making, and utilizing committees effectively are all essential elements of successful HOA governance.

HOA Governing Documents

HOA governing documents provide the legal and operational framework for the community. Each document serves a specific purpose and collectively defines the association's structure, powers, and rules. Key governing documents include:

- *Articles of Incorporation:*
  - Purpose: Establishes the HOA as a legal entity, typically a nonprofit corporation.
  - Key Provisions:
    - Association's official name and location.
    - Statement of purpose and powers.
    - Identification of initial board members.
    - Membership structure and voting rights.
  - Importance: The Articles of Incorporation legally authorize the HOA to operate, enforce rules, collect fees, and enter into contracts.

- *Declaration of Covenants, Conditions, and Restrictions (CC&Rs):*
  - Purpose: The Declaration is the foundational document that establishes the association's authority over the community and defines the responsibilities of property owners.
  - Key Provisions:
    - Property boundaries and description.
    - Owner rights and obligations.
    - Rules governing the use of lots and common areas.
    - Architectural control and maintenance standards.
    - Assessment and fee obligations.
  - Importance: The CC&Rs are binding on all property owners and dictate how the property can be used, maintained, and modified.
- *Bylaws:*
  - Purpose: The Bylaws outline the HOA's internal governance structure, providing rules for how the board operates and conducts business.
  - Key Provisions:
    - Board member election and removal procedures.
    - Roles and responsibilities of board members and officers.
    - Meeting requirements (e.g., frequency, notice, quorum).
    - Voting rights and decision-making processes.
    - Financial management guidelines.
  - Importance: The Bylaws serve as the operational manual for the board, ensuring that meetings and governance activities are conducted in an orderly and consistent manner.
- *Rules and Regulations:*
  - Purpose: The Rules and Regulations set forth specific guidelines for resident behavior and property use.
  - Key Provisions:
    - Guidelines for community conduct (e.g., noise restrictions, parking rules, and pet policies).
    - Standards for architectural modifications.
    - Use of common areas and amenities.
    - Penalties for rule violations.
  - Importance: These rules are intended to maintain community standards and quality of life. They are typically more flexible than other governing documents and can be updated more easily to address emerging issues.

Roles and Responsibilities of HOA Board Directors

The board of directors is typically composed of elected homeowners who volunteer to oversee the association's operations. Each board member has specific roles and responsibilities, which may include:

- *President:* Oversees board meetings, sets the agenda, and acts as the primary spokesperson for the association. The president leads decision-making and ensures the board operates in accordance with the governing documents.

- *Vice President:* Assists the president and assumes their duties in the president's absence. Often involved in special projects and committee oversight.
- *Secretary:* Maintains accurate records of meetings, votes, and official correspondence. The secretary ensures that all board activities are properly documented.
- *Treasurer:* Manages the association's finances, including budgeting, accounting, and financial reporting. The treasurer is responsible for ensuring transparency and accuracy in the association's financial activities.

Each director should understand their *fiduciary duty* to act in the best interest of the community, maintaining ethical standards and prioritizing the collective well-being of residents.

Effective HOA Meetings

Effective meetings are crucial for good governance and transparent communication. Board meetings should have a structured agenda, clear objectives, and well-defined procedures for discussing and voting on issues. Property managers should support the board by preparing meeting materials, coordinating attendance, and ensuring that all discussions remain focused and respectful. Open meetings, where homeowners are invited to observe and participate in designated sections, foster transparency and encourage community engagement.

Board Decision-Making

Board decision-making should be a collaborative and transparent process. The board must consider the interests of the community, review relevant data, and consult governing documents before making decisions. Voting procedures should be consistent, and board members must avoid conflicts of interest. Property managers can assist by providing context, offering professional recommendations, and ensuring that decisions comply with legal requirements and association policies.

Role of Committees in HOAs

Committees play a significant role in supporting the board by focusing on specific areas such as finance, architectural review, landscaping, and social activities. Committees are typically composed of volunteer homeowners and are tasked with conducting research, making recommendations, and implementing board-approved projects. Property managers often serve as liaisons to these committees, providing guidance and ensuring alignment with the board's objectives. Committees not only help distribute the workload but also increase homeowner involvement and enhance the community's sense of ownership.

5.9.2 Managing Resident Relationships

Effective management of resident relationships is a cornerstone of successful Homeowner Association (HOA) management. Because HOAs often encompass diverse communities, from single-family homes to townhouses, maintaining positive relationships with homeowners requires a strategic and proactive approach. Unlike rental properties, HOA residents are homeowners who have a vested interest in the community's governance and maintenance. As such, building trust, fostering transparent communication, resolving conflicts fairly, encouraging involvement, and providing education are all critical to cultivating a strong, engaged, and cooperative community.

Building Trust and Transparency
Trust is fundamental in any HOA community, as homeowners rely on the board and management to act in the best interest of the community. Transparency in decision-making and financial management is crucial for building and maintaining that trust. Property managers should provide homeowners with access to association records, meeting minutes, and financial reports to promote an atmosphere of openness. Communicating the rationale behind board decisions, especially those affecting fees or community policies, helps residents understand and support the association's actions.

Effective Communication
Effective communication is vital for keeping residents informed, addressing their concerns, and promoting community engagement. Property managers should establish multiple channels for communication, such as email updates, newsletters, resident portals, and social media platforms, to ensure that all residents are kept up-to-date on important issues. Additionally, open forums and regular town hall meetings provide homeowners with opportunities to ask questions, share feedback, and voice their opinions. Clear, consistent, and respectful communication prevents misunderstandings and fosters a sense of unity.

Conflict Resolution
Disputes are inevitable in any community, but they must be managed professionally and fairly. Property managers should approach conflicts impartially, listening to all sides before making decisions. Establishing a formal dispute resolution process, such as a grievance committee or mediation service, helps ensure that issues are handled consistently and transparently. This reduces tension and prevents minor issues from escalating into larger disputes.

Involvement and Participation
Encouraging homeowner involvement in the community's decision-making process fosters a sense of ownership and pride. Property managers can support involvement by promoting opportunities to serve on committees, volunteer for community events, or attend board meetings. Creating diverse committees, such as landscaping, finance, or social committees, gives residents a voice in shaping their community and strengthens their commitment to the HOA's success.

Education and Training

Educating residents about the HOA's rules, governance structure, and their rights and responsibilities is essential for building an informed and cooperative community. Property managers should offer workshops, distribute informational materials, and provide training sessions for new homeowners and board members. Educated residents are more likely to comply with policies and participate constructively in community governance.

Feedback Mechanisms

Establishing formal feedback mechanisms, such as surveys, suggestion boxes, or online feedback forms, allows residents to express their opinions and concerns. Regularly soliciting feedback on management practices, community amenities, and overall satisfaction demonstrates that the HOA values resident input and is committed to continuous improvement. Acting on feedback in a transparent manner helps build trust and reinforces the community's sense of unity.

5.9.3 Maintenance Fee Collection and Financial Management

Effective maintenance fee collection and financial management are critical to the stability and functionality of any Homeowner Association (HOA). Maintenance fees are the primary source of funding for community operations, covering essential expenses like landscaping, utilities, common area maintenance, and reserves for future repairs and improvements. To maintain the financial health of the HOA, property managers must implement best practices for accurate budgeting, timely fee collection, managing delinquencies, transparent financial reporting, and regular audits. Below are the core elements of HOA financial management.

Accurate Budgeting

Accurate budgeting is the foundation of financial management in an HOA. The annual budget should reflect all expected operating costs, such as routine maintenance, utilities, management fees, insurance, and community amenities. It should also include contributions to the reserve fund for long-term capital projects and unexpected expenses. Property managers should collaborate with the board to create a realistic budget, ensuring that it is communicated clearly to residents so they understand how their fees are being utilized. Regularly reviewing and adjusting the budget as needed helps the association adapt to changing financial conditions and avoid shortfalls.

Timely Fee Collection

Timely fee collection is essential to ensure that the HOA can meet its financial obligations. Property managers should establish a structured process for collecting maintenance fees, including due dates, acceptable payment methods, and late fee policies. Offering convenient payment options, such as online portals or direct debit, can help minimize late payments and make fee collection more efficient. Clear communication of the fee schedule and consequences of late payments is crucial to maintaining compliance.

Handling Delinquencies

Delinquent accounts can significantly impact the financial health of an HOA. Property managers should implement a consistent process for managing delinquencies, beginning with reminder notices and escalating to formal legal action if necessary. Establishing a fair and consistent approach, such as offering payment plans for homeowners facing temporary financial hardship, helps resolve delinquencies while maintaining positive resident relationships.

Financial Reporting

Transparent financial reporting keeps the board and residents informed about the HOA's financial health. Monthly and quarterly financial reports should include detailed income and expense statements, balance sheets, and cash flow summaries. Property managers should present these reports at board meetings and make them accessible to homeowners, ensuring accountability and transparency in the association's financial operations.

5.10 Case Study: The Hammocks Community Association Fraud Scheme

The Hammocks Community Association, located in Miami, Florida, is one of the largest homeowner associations in the state, encompassing over 40 communities with approximately 18,000 residents. In 2022, the association became the center of a significant fraud investigation that highlighted the critical importance of robust financial management and accounting controls within HOAs.

5.10.1 Background

For years, residents of The Hammocks Community Association voiced concerns about increasing maintenance fees and a lack of transparency regarding the association's financial practices. Despite the rising fees, many community amenities fell into disrepair, and essential services were neglected. Residents struggled to obtain financial records, and board meetings were often conducted without proper notice or were inaccessible to homeowners.

5.10.2 The Fraud Scheme

In November 2022, an investigation by the Miami-Dade State Attorney's Office led to the arrest of several board members, including the association's president. They were charged with orchestrating a fraud scheme that embezzled approximately

$2–6 million from the association over several years. The charges included grand theft, money laundering, and racketeering.

The investigation revealed that the board members had allegedly manipulated financial records, created shell companies, and issued fraudulent invoices for services never rendered. Funds collected from homeowners for maintenance fees were diverted into personal accounts and used for luxury purchases, including high-end vehicles, vacations, and real estate investments.

Key factors that enabled the fraud included:

- *Lack of Financial Transparency:* The board failed to provide detailed financial statements to homeowners and resisted independent financial audits.
- *Inadequate Oversight:* There were insufficient checks and balances within the association's governance structure, allowing board members to approve expenditures without proper scrutiny.
- *Manipulation of Records:* The accused board members had control over accounting records, which they allegedly falsified to conceal the misappropriation of funds.
- *Suppression of Dissent:* Homeowners who questioned the board's actions were reportedly intimidated or faced legal threats, discouraging further inquiries.

Impact on the Community

The fraud had severe consequences for the residents:

- *Financial Losses:* Homeowners faced increased fees to cover the shortfall caused by the embezzlement.
- *Deterioration of Property:* Essential maintenance and repairs were neglected, leading to a decline in property values.
- *Legal Expenses:* The association incurred substantial legal costs related to the investigation and subsequent lawsuits.
- *Erosion of Trust:* The scandal damaged the trust between homeowners and the association's leadership, leading to a fragmented community.

Lessons Learned

This case underscores the critical importance of implementing strong financial management practices in HOAs:

- *Regular Audits:* Engaging independent auditors to review financial statements can detect discrepancies early and deter fraudulent activities.
- *Transparent Financial Reporting:* Providing homeowners with detailed and accessible financial reports fosters accountability and trust.
- *Robust Internal Controls:* Establishing checks and balances, such as requiring multiple signatures for large expenditures, reduces the risk of misappropriation.
- *Active Homeowner Participation:* Encouraging homeowner involvement in meetings and decisions strengthens oversight and community engagement.

- *Legal Compliance:* Adhering to state laws governing HOAs, including open meeting requirements and access to records, ensures lawful operation and accountability.

Conclusion

The Hammocks Community Association case highlights how the absence of proper accounting controls and financial management can lead to significant fraud and damage to a community. It serves as a cautionary tale for property managers and HOA boards about the vital role of transparency, oversight, and adherence to best practices in financial management.

Question

- Considering the critical importance of financial transparency and accountability demonstrated in this case, what proactive steps can property managers and HOA boards take to prevent fraud and ensure the trust of the community they serve?

5.10.3 Reserve Study and Fund Management

Reserve studies and fund management for homeowner associations (HOAs) are similar to those for condominium associations. The reserve fund and reserve study are closely connected, as the reserve study provides a detailed analysis of the major components in a community that will eventually require repair or replacement, and the reserve fund is the financial account set aside to cover these future expenses. The reserve study helps determine how much money the association needs to collect and set aside in the reserve fund to ensure that the association can meet these long-term obligations without requiring special assessments or loans. Property managers should encourage the board of directors to contract with a reserve analyst to conduct regular reserve studies. Here are the common components typically found in a reserve study for HOAs:

1. *Site Infrastructure*
    - *Private Roads*: Asphalt or concrete streets within the HOA, including resurfacing and repair schedules.
    - *Sidewalks, Curbs, and Gutters*: Concrete walkways, curb conditions, and drainage systems.
    - *Stormwater Management*: Drainage systems, retention ponds, storm drains, and related infrastructure.
    - *Parking Lots*: Shared parking spaces, striping, and resurfacing for common areas.
2. *Community Amenities*
    - *Swimming Pools and Spas*: Pool structures, decking, pool equipment (pumps, filters, heaters), and pool furniture.
    - *Clubhouses and Recreation Centers*: Structural integrity, interior finishes, furniture, fixtures, and HVAC systems in community centers.

- *Fitness Facilities*: Gym equipment, flooring, lighting, and HVAC specific to exercise rooms.
- *Tennis Courts, Basketball Courts, and Playgrounds*: Surface repairs, nets, fences, playground equipment, and landscaping around these areas.

3. *Landscaping and Grounds*
   - *Landscaping and Irrigation Systems*: Maintenance of common area lawns, trees, shrubs, and flowerbeds, as well as irrigation systems.
   - *Fencing and Entry Monuments*: Maintenance of boundary fences, gates, entry monuments, and signage.
   - *Ponds, Lakes, and Fountains*: Pumps, water treatment systems, aerators, and shoreline management for ponds or lakes.
   - *Retaining Walls*: Condition and lifespan of any retaining walls for erosion control or aesthetic purposes.
4. *Utilities and Mechanical Systems*
   - *Lighting Systems*: Streetlights, path lights, and electrical systems powering common areas.
   - *Water and Sewer Lines*: Maintenance of water mains, sewer lines, and stormwater drains (if managed by the HOA).
   - *Electrical Systems*: Electrical wiring, generators, and other shared utility systems.
   - *HVAC Systems*: Heating, ventilation, and air conditioning for any shared or community structures.
5. *Common Area Structures*
   - *Roofing and Building Exteriors*: Roof replacements or repairs for clubhouses, community buildings, or shared structures.
   - *Exterior Paint*: Regular painting or weatherproofing for buildings or structures in common areas.
   - *Windows and Doors*: Repair or replacement of windows and doors in shared buildings.
   - *Decks and Patios*: Structural repairs, sealing, or replacements of decking or patio spaces in common areas.
6. *Recreational Facilities*
   - *Parks and Green Spaces*: Maintenance of park facilities, benches, picnic areas, and sports fields.
   - *Walking and Bike Trails*: Condition of paved or natural trails, bridges, and related amenities.
   - *Golf Courses*: For communities with golf courses, maintenance of greens, fairways, irrigation systems, and clubhouses.
7. *Security and Access Control Systems*
   - *Gates and Gatehouses*: Maintenance of *security* gates, mechanical systems, and any guardhouse structures.
   - *Surveillance Systems*: Cameras, monitoring equipment, and access control systems.
   - *Intercoms and Callboxes*: Communication systems for gate or building entry points.

8. *Fire and Safety Systems*
    - *Fire Alarm and Detection Systems*: Maintenance of fire alarms, smoke detectors, and sprinkler systems in shared buildings.
    - *Fire Suppression Equipment*: Fire extinguishers, sprinkler systems, and water sources for fire prevention.
    - *Emergency Exit Lighting*: Lighting systems in community buildings to ensure safe evacuation routes.
9. *Miscellaneous Components*
    - *Mailboxes and Postal Areas*: Shared mailboxes, parcel lockers, or postal centers in the community.
    - *Trash Collection Areas*: Dumpsters, recycling areas, and enclosures for trash collection services.
    - *Signage*: Maintenance of street signs, directional signage, and community announcements boards.
10. *Replacement Reserves*
    - *Remaining Useful Life*: The estimated time each component can remain functional before replacement or major repairs are needed.
    - *Replacement Cost Estimates*: Projected costs for repairing or replacing each component based on current and future costs.
    - *Funding Plan*: A strategy for accumulating reserve funds over time to meet future repair or replacement needs without placing undue financial burden on homeowners.
11. *Contingency and Unforeseen Repairs*
    - *Emergency Repairs*: A reserve allocation for unexpected or emergency repairs, such as storm damage or mechanical failures.
    - *Insurance Deductibles*: Potential out-of-pocket costs for the association in the event of an insurance claim.

Audits and Reviews

Annual audits and financial reviews provide an independent assessment of the HOA's financial practices. Property managers should facilitate these audits by maintaining accurate records and ensuring compliance with legal requirements. Audits help identify any discrepancies, reinforce best practices, and build homeowner confidence in the association's financial management.

By implementing these financial management practices, HOAs can maintain a stable financial foundation, ensure proper use of maintenance fees, and effectively plan for the community's future needs. This approach enhances the association's ability to fulfill its responsibilities and maintain the property's value over the long term.

Maintenance Responsibilities

Maintenance responsibilities in Homeowner Associations (HOAs) are divided between the association and individual homeowners, with specific obligations typically outlined in the governing documents, such as the Declaration of Covenants, Conditions, and Restrictions (CC&Rs) and Bylaws. These documents define what constitutes the HOA's common areas versus privately owned property and specify which party is responsible for the upkeep, repair, and replacement of each element. Understanding these distinctions is essential for both property managers and homeowners to ensure that maintenance issues are handled promptly and that the community is properly maintained. Below is a breakdown of the maintenance responsibilities for HOA common area elements and private homeowner property.

5.10.4 Common Area Maintenance Responsibilities

HOA common areas are defined as spaces or amenities that are collectively owned and shared by all members of the community. The HOA is responsible for maintaining these areas to ensure they remain safe, aesthetically pleasing, and in good working condition. Common area responsibilities typically include:

- *Landscaping and Grounds Maintenance:* The HOA is responsible for maintaining all shared landscaping, including lawns, trees, shrubs, flower beds, and irrigation systems in common areas. This includes maintaining green spaces, entryways, and community parks.
- *Roads, Sidewalks, and Pathways:* Maintenance of private roads, sidewalks, and pedestrian pathways that are not owned or maintained by the municipality is typically the HOA's responsibility. This includes snow removal, pothole repairs, and upkeep of curbs and gutters.
- *Community Amenities and Recreational Facilities:* Clubhouses, swimming pools, tennis courts, playgrounds, and fitness centers fall under the HOA's purview. The association must ensure these amenities are safe, clean, and in good repair.
- *Exterior Lighting and Security Systems:* The HOA manages lighting for streets, walkways, and parking lots, as well as security systems such as gates, cameras, and access control systems.
- *Exterior Building Maintenance (for Certain Types of HOAs):* In townhouse or attached condominium-style HOAs, the association may be responsible for exterior building maintenance, including roofs, siding, and exterior painting.

For more details on creating a fully integrated maintenance plan, including proactive and emergency strategies, refer to the Sect. 6.3.3 in Chap. 6.

Homeowner Maintenance Responsibilities

Individual homeowners are responsible for maintaining their privately owned property, which generally includes the interior and exterior of their homes as well as any designated yard areas. Homeowner responsibilities typically include:

- *Home Exteriors:* Owners must maintain the exterior of their homes, including walls, windows, doors, and roofs, unless these elements fall under the HOA's responsibility (such as in a townhouse HOA).

- *Yard Areas (If Applicable):* In single-family home HOAs, homeowners are often responsible for maintaining their own front and back yards, including mowing, pruning, and watering.
- *Interior Maintenance:* All interior maintenance, including plumbing, electrical systems, HVAC, and appliances, is the responsibility of the homeowner.
- *Private Driveways, Walkways, and Fencing:* Homeowners are typically responsible for maintaining private driveways, walkways, fencing and any other hardscaping within their lot boundaries.

Understanding and clearly communicating these maintenance responsibilities helps prevent disputes and ensures that both the HOA and homeowners are fulfilling their obligations. Property managers should routinely educate homeowners on these distinctions and provide guidance on how to handle maintenance issues, creating a well-maintained and cohesive community.

5.10.5 Management Contracts

Management contracts for Homeowner Associations (HOAs) are formal agreements between the HOA board and a professional property management company that outline the scope of services, roles, and responsibilities of the property manager in managing the community's day-to-day operations. These contracts are essential for ensuring that the HOA's governance and maintenance obligations are met efficiently and that there is a clear understanding between the board and the property manager regarding authority, financial oversight, and service expectations. Unlike other residential property management agreements, HOA management contracts must account for the unique aspects of managing a community where homeowners, rather than tenants, have a direct stake in the property's management and financial health.

Key Elements of an HOA Management Contract

1. *Scope of Services:* The contract should comprehensively define the services the management company will provide. Typical services include overseeing maintenance of common areas, coordinating vendor contracts, conducting property inspections, ensuring compliance with HOA rules and regulations, managing communications with homeowners, and assisting with board meetings. The scope should be specific to avoid misunderstandings and include any administrative duties, such as maintaining records and preparing budgets.
2. *Financial Management:* Financial management is a critical component of HOA management. The contract should outline the manager's role in budgeting, assessment collection, and financial reporting. This may include preparing annual budgets, managing reserve funds, collecting maintenance fees, handling delinquencies, and ensuring that the HOA remains financially compliant with local and state regulations. The contract should specify whether the management

company has authority to sign checks or make financial decisions on behalf of the association.

3. *Maintenance Oversight:* The contract should detail the manager's responsibilities in overseeing maintenance activities, including routine landscaping, repairs, and capital improvement projects. It should specify the manager's authority to hire contractors and vendors, approve minor expenses without board approval, and ensure compliance with service contracts.
4. *Communication and Reporting:* Clear communication expectations between the manager and the board are essential. The contract should outline the frequency and format of financial and operational reports, as well as how and when the manager will communicate important updates to both the board and homeowners. Regular meetings, monthly reports, and access to a digital portal for real-time updates are common requirements.
5. *Term and Termination Clauses:* The contract should specify the duration of the agreement, typically ranging from 1 to 3 years, and include termination clauses that outline the conditions under which either party can terminate the agreement. Common reasons for termination include nonperformance, changes in management needs, or a breach of contract terms. The termination process should include a notice period and a plan for transitioning management responsibilities.
6. *Compensation Structure:* The contract should clearly define the management company's compensation, which may include a fixed monthly fee, a percentage of collected fees, or additional charges for special projects. The contract should also specify any extra fees for services outside the scope of the standard agreement, such as overseeing major renovation projects or legal compliance support.

By addressing these key elements, a well-crafted HOA management contract helps establish a strong working relationship between the HOA board and the property management company, ensuring that both parties understand their roles and responsibilities. This clarity is crucial for maintaining the community's operations, preserving property values, and fostering a positive environment for all homeowners.

5.10.6 Enforcement of Rules and Regulations

Effective enforcement of rules and regulations is a critical function of Homeowner Associations (HOAs) to maintain community standards, protect property values, and ensure a harmonious living environment. A well-structured enforcement process helps build respect for community guidelines and promotes compliance. Property managers play a key role in implementing the HOA's enforcement policies fairly and consistently. The enforcement process should be transparent, clearly communicated, and focused on encouraging voluntary compliance before resorting to punitive measures. Below are essential components of effective rule enforcement specific to HOA management.

Clear Rules & Regulations

The foundation of effective rule enforcement is having a clear set of rules and regulations that are easy to understand and follow. These rules should be outlined in the governing documents, such as the Declaration of Covenants, Conditions, and Restrictions (CC&Rs) and the Bylaws. Property managers should ensure that all residents receive a copy of these documents upon moving in and that they are accessible through the HOA's website or a resident portal. Rules should cover essential aspects of community living, such as property use, parking, noise, landscaping, and maintenance standards, and should be reviewed periodically to ensure they remain relevant and legally compliant.

Consistent Enforcement

Consistency is crucial for maintaining fairness and community trust. Property managers must apply the rules uniformly to all residents without favoritism or bias. This means that similar violations should result in similar consequences, regardless of the homeowner involved. Inconsistent enforcement can lead to resentment, perceptions of unfair treatment, and potential legal challenges. Establishing a standardized procedure for handling violations ensures that the process is transparent and fair.

Communication

Effective communication is vital when enforcing rules. Property managers should communicate rules and any updates through newsletters, email, and community meetings to keep homeowners informed. Educating residents on the purpose of the rules—such as safety, property value preservation, or community harmony—helps them understand the importance of compliance. Clear communication also involves explaining the consequences of noncompliance before any issues arise.

Violation Notices

When a violation occurs, property managers should issue a formal violation notice. The notice should specify the nature of the violation, reference the relevant rule or regulation, and outline the corrective action required. It should also include a timeframe for resolving the issue and the potential penalties if the violation is not addressed. The tone of these notices should be respectful yet firm, focusing on achieving compliance rather than punishment.

Appeals Process

An effective enforcement policy should include a fair and accessible appeals process. Homeowners should have the opportunity to present their case and request a review of the violation notice by the board or a designated committee. Establishing a structured appeals process ensures that homeowners feel their voices are heard and that decisions are made impartially.

Legal Support

In some cases, legal action may be necessary to enforce compliance, especially for repeated or severe violations. Property managers should work closely with the

HOA's legal counsel to determine when to escalate an issue and how to proceed. Legal support may involve sending formal demand letters, filing a lawsuit, or pursuing alternative dispute resolution methods. It's crucial to follow all legal protocols and ensure that the HOA's enforcement actions are fully compliant with state laws and the association's governing documents.

5.10.7 Problems Frequently Encountered by HOA Board of Directors

Serving on a Homeowner Association (HOA) board involves a significant amount of responsibility and the need to address various challenges that can affect the community. HOA boards are tasked with maintaining property values, ensuring compliance with community rules, and fostering a harmonious living environment. Here are some of the common problems frequently encountered by HOA board directors:

1. *Financial Management:* Effective financial management is a critical aspect of HOA governance. Boards must create and adhere to budgets, manage reserve funds, and ensure timely collection of dues and assessments. Financial difficulties arise when homeowners fail to pay their dues, leading to cash flow issues and inadequate funds for maintenance and improvements. Boards also face the challenge of balancing the budget while planning for future expenses and unexpected repairs.
2. *Compliance with Laws and Regulations:* HOA boards must navigate a complex landscape of local, state, and federal regulations. These include fair housing laws, property maintenance codes, and specific HOA statutes. Ensuring compliance can be challenging, especially as laws change and evolve. Failure to comply with legal requirements can result in fines, legal disputes, and damage to the HOA's reputation.
3. *Enforcing Rules and Regulations:* Maintaining community standards requires consistent enforcement of rules and regulations. Boards often struggle with residents who violate rules, such as parking restrictions, noise ordinances, and property maintenance standards. Enforcing these rules fairly and consistently, while managing conflicts and objections from residents, is a delicate balance that can strain board-resident relationships.
4. *Conflict Resolution:* Disputes among residents or between residents and the board are common in HOAs. Whether it's disagreements over rule enforcement, property boundaries, or shared amenities, boards must act as mediators to resolve conflicts. Effective conflict resolution requires impartiality, strong communication skills, and often, a significant time commitment.
5. *Communication Breakdown:* Clear and transparent communication is essential for fostering trust and cooperation within the community. Boards frequently encounter challenges in effectively communicating with residents about rules, financial matters, maintenance schedules, and upcoming projects. Poor com-

munication can lead to misunderstandings, dissatisfaction, and reduced resident engagement.

6. *Maintenance and Repairs:* Ensuring that common areas and shared amenities are well-maintained is a primary responsibility of the HOA board. This involves scheduling regular maintenance, addressing repair requests promptly, and planning for long-term capital improvements. Boards often face challenges in prioritizing maintenance tasks and securing adequate funding, especially in older communities with aging infrastructure.
7. *Board Member Turnover and Burnout:* Serving on an HOA board is a volunteer position that can be demanding and time-consuming. High turnover rates among board members can disrupt continuity and impede long-term planning efforts. Burnout among board members can also reduce the effectiveness of the board, leading to lapses in governance and decision-making.
8. *Vendor Management:* HOAs rely on various vendors for services such as landscaping, security, and property maintenance. Managing vendor contracts, ensuring quality service, and addressing performance issues can be challenging. Boards must negotiate contracts, oversee vendor work, and handle any disputes that arise, which requires diligence and attention to detail.
9. *Resident Engagement and Participation:* Encouraging residents to participate in community meetings, serve on committees, and engage in HOA activities can be difficult. Low participation rates make it challenging to achieve a quorum for decision-making, gather diverse perspectives, and foster a strong sense of community. Boards must find ways to motivate and involve residents in the governance process.
10. *Strategic Planning:* Long-term planning is essential for the sustainable management of an HOA. Boards must anticipate future needs, such as major repairs, infrastructure upgrades, and changes in community demographics. Developing and implementing a strategic plan while managing day-to-day operations can be overwhelming, leading to reactive rather than proactive management.

By understanding and addressing these common challenges, HOA boards can enhance their governance practices, ensure financial stability, and maintain a cohesive and well-managed community. Effective communication, consistent rule enforcement, and strategic planning are key strategies for overcoming these obstacles and fostering a positive living environment for all residents.

5.10.8 Community Building and Engagement

Building a strong sense of community is essential for the success of any HOA. A well-connected and engaged community not only enhances the quality of life for residents but also promotes a cooperative atmosphere that makes managing the HOA more effective. Property managers play a crucial role in fostering this sense of community by implementing strategies that encourage social interaction, communication, and resident involvement. Effective community engagement can be achieved through a combination of social events, clear communication channels, volunteer opportunities, and initiatives that promote resident participation.

Social Events

Organizing social events is one of the most effective ways to build community spirit and encourage residents to get to know their neighbors. Property managers can plan events such as seasonal parties, neighborhood barbecues, movie nights, or holiday celebrations. Events tailored to different age groups and interests, such as children's activities or senior gatherings, help ensure that all residents feel included. These events create opportunities for residents to connect in a relaxed setting, fostering relationships and building a stronger community.

Communication

Clear and consistent communication is the foundation of community engagement. Property managers should use multiple communication channels, such as newsletters, social media, resident portals, and community message boards, to keep residents informed about upcoming events, board decisions, and community news. Regular updates help residents feel connected to the community and aware of what's happening in their neighborhood.

Volunteer Opportunities

Creating volunteer opportunities is another powerful way to engage residents. Property managers can establish committees focused on areas like landscaping, social events, or community safety. Inviting residents to participate in volunteer activities gives them a stake in the community's success and encourages a sense of pride and ownership.

Resident Involvement

Encouraging resident involvement in decision-making processes strengthens the community's sense of inclusiveness. Property managers should invite residents to attend board meetings, participate in surveys, and contribute ideas for improving the neighborhood. Providing platforms for residents to share their opinions helps them feel valued and invested in the HOA's success.

Ensuring Long-Term Success

By effectively managing HOA governance, resident relationships, financial management, maintenance, and rule enforcement, property managers can create a well-functioning and harmonious community. These practices help maintain property values, enhance resident satisfaction, and ensure the long-term success of the HOA.

5.11 Case Study: Lakeview HOA

5.11.1 Background

Lakeview HOA manages a 200-home community with amenities such as a clubhouse, swimming pool, and tennis courts. The HOA is governed by a board of directors elected by the homeowners, and you have been hired as the property manager to oversee daily operations, maintenance, and resident relations.

5.11.2 Scenario

Lakeview HOA has recently faced several challenges, including disputes among residents about drivers speeding in the community and use of common areas, issues with timely fee collection, and the need to update the reserve fund for major repairs. Your tasks include resolving these disputes, improving fee collection practices, ensuring adequate reserve funding, and updating community rules to comply with new local regulations.

5.11.3 Tasks

1. *Managing Resident Relationships:*
   - Address ongoing conflicts among residents regarding drivers speeding in the community and use of common areas.
   - Implement strategies to improve communication and foster a sense of community among residents.
2. *Maintenance Fee Collection and Financial Management:*
   - Review the current fee collection process and identify any shortfalls or issues.
   - Develop a plan to ensure timely and efficient collection of maintenance fees and manage the HOA's finances effectively.
3. *Maintenance and HOA Reserve Funds:*
   - Conduct a reserve study to assess the condition of major components and estimate the funds needed for future repairs.
   - Develop a plan to ensure the reserve fund is adequately funded and communicate this plan to residents.

5.11.4 Challenges

1. *Conflict Challenge*:
   - Residents have been complaining about noise from late-night gatherings at the clubhouse. Develop a strategy to address these complaints and enforce community rules.

2. *Fee Collection Challenge:*
   - The HOA has experienced a decline in timely maintenance fee payments, leading to financial strain. Determine how to improve the fee collection process and address delinquent accounts.
3. *Reserve Fund Challenge:*
   - The reserve fund is underfunded, and there are major repairs needed for the swimming pool and tennis courts. Determine how to manage the reserve fund effectively and prioritize these repairs.

5.11.5 Discussion Questions

1. *Managing Resident Relationships:*
   - What steps can you take to resolve the current conflicts among residents regarding drivers speeding in the community and use of common areas?
   - How can you improve communication and foster a sense of community among residents?
2. *Maintenance Fee Collection and Financial Management:*
   - What strategies can you use to ensure the timely and efficient collection of maintenance fees?
   - How would you address delinquent accounts and improve overall financial management for the HOA?
3. *Maintenance and HOA Reserve Funds:*
   - What steps should you take to ensure the reserve fund is adequately funded for future repairs?
   - How can you effectively communicate the reserve funding plan to residents and gain their support?

5.12 Summary

The management of multifamily residences encompasses a diverse range of property types, including apartments, condominium associations, cooperatives, and homeowner associations, each requiring a tailored approach due to their unique ownership structures, governance models, and resident expectations. Property managers overseeing multifamily communities must be adept at navigating complex regulatory environments, financial management, maintenance responsibilities, and resident relations to ensure the success and stability of these communities.

Apartments are typically owned by a single entity and managed as rental properties. Apartment management focuses on maximizing rental income, maintaining high occupancy rates, and ensuring tenant satisfaction. Key elements include setting competitive rental rates through market analysis, implementing effective marketing strategies, conducting thorough tenant screening, and maintaining positive tenant relationships. Managers must also handle lease agreements, manage rent collection, and coordinate routine and emergency maintenance to preserve the property's value and appeal.

Condominium Associations are governed by a board of directors elected by unit owners, who individually own their units and share ownership of common areas. Property managers support the board in maintaining common areas, enforcing community rules, and managing the association's finances. Key responsibilities include overseeing maintenance, budgeting, reserve fund management, and conducting annual audits. Effective governance and communication are essential to balance the interests of diverse owners and maintain community harmony.

Cooperatives are unique in that residents do not own their units but rather hold shares in a corporation that owns the property. Property managers work closely with the cooperative's board to manage the building's finances, approve new shareholders, and ensure compliance with cooperative policies. Financial management is complex due to shared ownership structures, requiring precise budgeting, fee collection, and reserve fund planning.

Homeowner Associations (HOAs) typically govern planned communities, which may include single-family homes, townhouses, and even mixed-use properties. HOAs are responsible for maintaining common areas, enforcing rules, and preserving property values. Property managers help enforce community standards, manage finances, coordinate maintenance, and facilitate resident engagement through events and communication.

Overall, managing multifamily residences requires a multifaceted skill set that includes financial acumen, maintenance oversight, legal knowledge, and strong communication skills. By adapting management strategies to each property type's distinct needs, property managers can create thriving, well-maintained communities that benefit owners and residents alike.

5.12.1 Looking Forward

The following chapters will explore general property management practices, including the use of technology, human resources management, insurance, and federal and state laws. Understanding these broader aspects of property management will further enhance your ability to manage residential properties effectively.

5.13 Review Questions

1. *What is a key responsibility of a property manager for multifamily residences?*
   (A) Ignoring tenant complaints
   (B) Enhancing property value through effective management
   (C) Increasing rent without improvements
   (D) Avoiding legal compliance
2. *Which type of multifamily residence involves individual ownership of units and shared ownership of common areas?*

(A) Apartments
(B) Condominium associations
(C) Cooperatives
(D) Single-family homesa

3. *What is a primary challenge in managing multifamily residences compared to single-family homes?*
   (A) Less maintenance required
   (B) More complex tenant interactions and community dynamics
   (C) Lower rent collection rates
   (D) Simplified legal compliance
4. *What is an effective marketing strategy for attracting tenants to an apartment complex?*
   (A) Posting blurry photos online
   (B) Creating detailed listings with high-quality photos
   (C) Ignoring online platforms
   (D) Hosting open houses without any prior advertising
5. *Why is tenant screening important in property management for apartments?*
   (A) To increase vacancy rates
   (B) To ensure reliable and responsible tenants
   (C) To avoid maintenance responsibilities
   (D) To set arbitrary rent amounts
6. *Which factor is crucial in developing a maintenance schedule for an apartment complex?*
   (A) Ignoring tenant complaints
   (B) Regular inspections and preventive maintenance
   (C) Delaying repairs to save money
   (D) Performing maintenance only during tenant turnovers
7. *What is the role of the board of directors in a condominium association?*
   (A) Making key decisions about property management and maintenance
   (B) Setting arbitrary rules without homeowner input
   (C) Avoiding communication with residents
   (D) Ignoring legal compliance
8. *Why is transparency important in the financial management of a condominium association?*
   (A) To increase confusion among residents
   (B) To build trust and accountability
   (C) To hide financial issues
   (D) To complicate the budgeting process
9. *What should be included in a reserve study for a condominium association?*
   (A) List of resident complaints
   (B) Assessment of major components and estimation of future repair costs
   (C) Current rental rates
   (D) History of tenant evictions
10. *What is a unique characteristic of cooperatives compared to other types of multifamily residences?*

(A) Individual ownership of units
(B) Collective ownership of the property through shares
(C) Less involvement from residents
(D) Simplified financial management

11. *How should conflicts between shareholders in a cooperative be handled?*
(A) Ignored to avoid confrontation
(B) Addressed through fair and transparent processes
(C) Decided by a single board member
(D) Resolved by expelling the shareholder

12. *What is a key element of a management contract for cooperatives?*
(A) Undefined responsibilities
(B) Clear scope of services and compensation
(C) Arbitrary decision-making authority
(D) Ignoring performance metric

13. *What is a primary role of the HOA board of directors?*
(A) Avoiding homeowner input
(B) Making decisions that reflect the interests of the community
(C) Increasing fees without explanation
(D) Ignoring maintenance needs

14. *Why is regular communication important in managing resident relationships within an HOA?*
(A) To reduce transparency
(B) To build trust and keep residents informed
(C) To complicate decision-making
(D) To avoid resident feedback

15. *How should maintenance fee collection be handled in an HOA?*
(A) Ignoring delinquent accounts
(B) Implementing a consistent and efficient collection process
(C) Arbitrarily setting payment deadlines
(D) Avoiding communication about fees

16. *What should a preventive maintenance program for an HOA include?*
(A) Ignoring minor repairs
(B) Regular inspections and addressing potential issues early
(C) Only performing major repairs
(D) Delaying maintenance to save money

17. *Why is it important to have a well-funded reserve fund in an HOA?*
(A) To avoid budgeting for repairs
(B) To ensure funds are available for future repairs and replacements
(C) To reduce monthly fees
(D) To increase financial strain on homeowners

18. *What is a key aspect of enforcing rules and regulations in an HOA?*
(A) Ignoring violations to avoid conflict
(B) Consistent and fair application of rules
(C) Arbitrarily enforcing rules
(D) Avoiding communication with residents

19. *How can the effectiveness of a property management company for an HOA be evaluated?*
    (A) Ignoring performance metrics
    (B) Using clear performance metrics and regular reviews
    (C) Avoiding feedback from residents
    (D) Allowing the management company to operate without oversight
20. *What is the purpose of a management contract for an HOA?*
    (A) To create ambiguity about roles and responsibilities
    (B) To formalize the relationship and outline expectations and compensation
    (C) To reduce transparency and accountability
    (D) To avoid legal compliance

General Property Management

6

6.1 Learning Objectives

By the end of this unit, students should be able to:

- *Fundamentals of Building Systems:*
  - Acquire a working knowledge of the building systems specific to single-family, duplex, triplex, and quadruplex buildings, including HVAC, plumbing, electrical, and septic systems, as well as the special considerations for maintaining pool mechanical systems.
  - Identify and explain the essential building systems and infrastructure found in large residential buildings, including HVAC, electrical, plumbing, fire protection, elevators, and trash chute systems.
- *Technology in Property Management:*
  - Identify how technology streamlines property management operations, enhances communication, and improves security within residential properties.
  - Evaluate the impact of modern property management software on financial management, tenant relations, and maintenance coordination.
- *Property Management Accounting and Financial Reporting:*
  - Understand key financial management principles, including budgeting, accounting terminology, fee collection, and financial reporting.
  - Analyze the role of financial statements, reserve funds, and audits in maintaining the financial health of residential properties.
- *Establishing and Managing a Property Management Office:*
  - Understand the fundamental components of a property management office including identifying the essential elements required for setting up a property management office, including location considerations, office design, organizational systems, and technological needs.
  - Implement effective staffing and licensing practices.

D. A. Vaughn, *Essentials of Residential Property Management*, Springer Texts in Business and Economics, https://doi.org/10.1007/978-3-031-92329-6_6

- *Human Resources Management:*
  - Define the components of effective human resources management, including recruitment, training, and performance evaluation.
  - Describe the importance of clear job descriptions and compliance with employment laws in managing property management staff.
- *Insurance for Different Types of Residential Properties:*
  - Recognize the various insurance types needed for different residential property classifications, such as apartments, condominium associations, cooperatives, and homeowner associations.
  - Explain the implications of risk management and the insurance claims process for property managers.
- *Future Trends in Residential Property Management:*
  - Assess the impact of emerging trends such as sustainable building practices, tenant demand for amenities like electric vehicle charging stations, and the shift toward remote work.
  - Predict how evolving tenant expectations and technology innovations will shape the future of property management.
- *Federal and State Laws:*
  - Understand the key federal and state laws affecting residential property management, such as Fair Housing Laws, Americans with Disabilities Act, and the Lead-Based Paint Hazard Reduction Act.
  - Apply legal knowledge to ensure compliance and avoid discriminatory practices in residential property management.
- *Managing Life Safety:*
  - Identify common life safety issues in residential properties, including fire safety, hazard control, and emergency preparedness.
  - Develop safety protocols and risk management strategies to protect residents and comply with health and safety regulations.

6.2 Key Terms

HVAC (Heating, Ventilation, and Air Conditioning)
Main Electrical Distribution
Plumbing System
Sewer System
Trash Chute System
Property Management Software
Financial Statements
Budgeting and Forecasting
Reserve Fund Management
Human Resources Management
Employee Handbook
Insurance Coverage

Risk Management
Federal Fair Housing Laws
Americans with Disabilities Act (ADA)
Lead-Based Paint Hazard Reduction Act
Antitrust Laws
Cybersecurity
Capital Improvement
Sustainable Building Practices
Life Safety
Fire Safety Plans
Access Control Systems
Hazard Control
Security Protocols
Emergency Preparedness
Technology-Driven Amenities
Remote Work Accommodations

6.3 Fundamentals of Building Systems

6.3.1 Single Family, Duplex and Triplex, Quadruplex Building Systems

Single-family homes, duplexes, triplexes, and quadruplexes share many of the same building systems, but the complexity can increase as the number of units grows. Understanding the infrastructure and mechanical systems that support these residential properties is crucial for property managers to ensure proper maintenance, efficient operation, and occupant satisfaction. This section provides a technical overview of the key building systems, including heating, ventilation, and air conditioning (HVAC); electrical; lighting; plumbing; sewer and septic systems; and pool mechanical systems.

Heating, Ventilation, and Air Conditioning (HVAC)

In single-family homes and multiunit residential properties like duplexes, triplexes, and quadruplexes, HVAC systems play a crucial role in providing thermal comfort and maintaining indoor air quality. The type of HVAC system depends on the property's size and design, and can range from centralized systems to individual unit-based solutions.

- *Heating: Most single-family and multiunit residential properties use either furnaces (which heat air and distribute it through ducts) or boilers (which heat water and provide radiant heat). Furnaces are commonly powered by natural gas, electricity, or oil. In duplexes and triplexes, each unit may have its own heating system or share a centralized system, depending on the property's layout.*

- *Ventilation:* Proper ventilation is essential in these properties to regulate indoor air quality, particularly in tightly sealed, energy-efficient homes. Modern ventilation systems may include exhaust fans, ductwork for fresh air intake, and heat recovery ventilators (HRVs) to balance energy efficiency with airflow. Maintaining good ventilation is critical for preventing issues like mold growth and maintaining a healthy living environment.
- *Air Conditioning:* In addition to heating, air conditioning is provided either through central air systems, which cool and distribute air through ductwork, or through individual unit air conditioners in smaller properties. Maintaining proper refrigerant levels, cleaning filters, and servicing condenser units are key tasks in keeping air conditioning systems running efficiently.

For duplexes, triplexes, and quadruplexes, the HVAC systems can either be centralized or separated by unit, depending on how the property is designed. Property managers need to ensure that each unit's system is properly maintained and serviced, and if a shared system is used, monitoring energy consumption and efficiency is key to cost control.

Electrical Systems

Electrical systems are responsible for distributing power to each unit, ensuring that residents have access to electricity for lighting, appliances, and other essentials.

- *Main Service Panels: For single-family homes, the electrical system is typically managed through a single main electrical panel that controls power distribution throughout the house. In duplexes and other multiunit buildings, each unit may have its own electrical panel to manage power individually. Alternatively, a shared panel may distribute power with separate metering for each unit to ensure tenants are billed appropriately.*
- *Wiring and Outlets:* Residential buildings must comply with local electrical codes, ensuring that wiring and outlets are properly installed and maintained. Faulty wiring or overloaded circuits are common issues in older buildings, so regular inspections are necessary to prevent hazards such as electrical fires. For multiunit properties, property managers must ensure that the wiring for shared systems, such as lighting for common areas or HVAC systems, is properly maintained and complies with electrical safety standards.
- *Backup Power Solutions:* In areas prone to power outages, installing backup generators or battery storage systems may be a viable option to ensure continuous power for critical systems like heating, cooling, or refrigeration. This is especially important for duplexes or larger properties where multiple households depend on uninterrupted power.

Regular maintenance of the electrical system, including testing circuit breakers and inspecting wiring, is essential for safety and efficiency.

Lighting Systems

Lighting systems are essential for both safety and convenience in residential properties. In single-family homes, lighting is typically controlled individually by the homeowner, while in multiunit properties like duplexes and triplexes, exterior and common area lighting may be managed by the property owner or manager.

- *Interior Lighting: Properly placed lighting fixtures in living areas, kitchens, bedrooms, and bathrooms enhance the functionality and aesthetics of the home. Energy-efficient lighting solutions, such as LED bulbs, can significantly reduce electricity consumption, especially in properties where tenants or homeowners leave lights on for extended periods.*
- *Exterior and Common Area Lighting:* For duplexes, triplexes, and quadruplexes, exterior lighting plays a key role in security. Well-lit pathways, parking areas, and entryways can deter criminal activity and ensure resident safety. Property managers should install motion-sensor lighting or timers to conserve energy while ensuring safety in shared spaces.
- *Emergency Lighting:* In multiunit buildings, emergency lighting is often required to provide visibility during power outages or emergencies. This includes exit signs and hallway lighting that may be connected to backup power sources.

By ensuring proper installation and maintenance of lighting systems, property managers can enhance both the safety and comfort of their properties.

Plumbing Systems

Plumbing systems are responsible for delivering clean water and managing wastewater. Property managers must understand the design and maintenance needs of these systems to avoid common issues such as leaks or water pressure problems.

- *Water Supply and Distribution: In single-family homes, the water supply system is often simpler, with one main water line supplying the house. In duplexes and other multiunit properties, each unit typically has its own water meter and separate plumbing lines to ensure accurate billing and independent water supply for each residence.*
- *Water Heaters:* Depending on the property type, each unit may have its own water heater, or a shared water heater may serve multiple units. Property managers should schedule regular maintenance of water heaters to ensure they operate efficiently, prevent breakdowns, and avoid costly repairs.

Proper plumbing maintenance is essential to prevent water damage, ensure tenant satisfaction, and reduce water usage costs.

Sewer and Septic Systems

Sewer and septic systems manage the disposal of wastewater in residential buildings. The type of system depends on the location and infrastructure of the property.

- *Municipal Sewer Systems: Most urban and suburban single-family homes and multiunit properties are connected to municipal sewer systems, which transport wastewater to a treatment facility. Property managers must ensure that the building's sewer connections are intact and that the plumbing leading to the municipal system is free of blockages or leaks.*
- *Septic Systems:* In rural areas where municipal sewers are unavailable, properties often rely on septic systems for wastewater management. Septic systems require regular maintenance, including pumping the septic tank every few years to prevent overflow or contamination of the leach field. Property managers must educate tenants on proper septic system usage, such as avoiding flushing nonbiodegradable items, to prevent costly repairs or environmental damage.

Maintaining sewer and septic systems is critical for preventing health hazards, environmental damage, and costly repairs.

Pool Mechanical Systems

For properties with swimming pools, pool mechanical systems are essential for maintaining water quality, safety, and overall enjoyment.

- *Filtration Systems: Pools are equipped with filtration systems to remove debris and contaminants from the water. These systems include pumps and filters that circulate and clean the water. Regular maintenance of the filtration system is necessary to prevent buildup of bacteria, algae, and other harmful substances.*
- *Chemical Balancing:* Maintaining the correct chemical balance in the pool is essential for ensuring the safety and comfort of swimmers. Property managers or pool service providers must regularly test and adjust pH levels, chlorine content, and other chemicals to keep the water clean and safe.
- *Heating and Circulation:* Some pools are equipped with heating systems to maintain a comfortable water temperature year-round. Property managers should ensure that pool heaters are regularly serviced and that circulation systems operate efficiently to avoid stagnant water and temperature inconsistencies.

Proper maintenance of pool systems not only enhances resident enjoyment but also reduces the risk of costly repairs and potential safety hazards.

By understanding the building systems and infrastructure commonly found in single-family, duplex, triplex, and quadruplex properties, property managers can ensure that these properties remain safe, efficient, and comfortable for residents. Regular inspections, preventive maintenance, and a proactive approach to resolving issues are key to maintaining these systems.

6.3.2 Large Residential Building Systems

Large residential buildings rely on various interconnected systems to ensure the safety, comfort, and functionality of the living environment. Property managers must have a foundational understanding of these systems to manage maintenance, address issues, and work effectively with contractors and service providers. This chapter provides a working knowledge of key building systems commonly found in large residential properties, including heating, ventilation and air conditioning (HVAC); electrical; lighting; plumbing; fire alarm; fire protection; elevators; and trash chute systems.

Heating, Ventilation, and Air Conditioning (HVAC)

The HVAC system is a crucial component of any large residential building, providing heating, ventilation, and cooling to maintain comfortable indoor temperatures and air quality. HVAC systems in large buildings typically consist of centralized units that serve multiple floors or units, including boilers, chillers, air handling units, and ductwork.

- *Heating: In most large residential buildings, heating is provided by either boilers or furnaces that generate hot water or steam, distributed via radiators or forced air systems. Boilers can be fueled by gas, oil, or electricity, and regular maintenance is essential to ensure energy efficiency and safety.*
- *Ventilation:* Proper ventilation is critical to maintaining indoor air quality, especially in tightly sealed buildings designed for energy efficiency. Ventilation systems bring in fresh outdoor air, filter contaminants, and remove stale air. Inadequate ventilation can lead to issues such as mold growth and poor air quality, which can affect residents' health.
- *Air Conditioning:* Cooling is typically provided by chillers, which produce cold water that circulates through air handling units and cools the air distributed throughout the building. Maintaining refrigerant levels and cleaning coils and filters are essential tasks to keep air conditioning systems functioning properly.

Regular inspections and preventive maintenance of HVAC components are crucial to ensure system longevity and reduce energy consumption. Property managers must be knowledgeable about the HVAC system to address tenant complaints about temperature and air quality promptly.

Electrical Systems

Electrical systems in large residential buildings provide the power needed for lighting, appliances, elevators, HVAC systems, and other equipment. Understanding the structure and operation of the electrical system is critical for ensuring safety, managing energy use, and addressing power-related issues.

- *Main Electrical Distribution: Electrical power enters the building through a transformer, which reduces the high-voltage electricity supplied by the utility company to a usable level. The power is then distributed throughout the building via a main electrical panel and sub-panels, which regulate the flow of electricity to individual circuits.*

- *Wiring and Circuits:* Residential buildings typically have dedicated circuits for essential systems, such as HVAC, lighting, and elevators. Wiring in large buildings must comply with local building codes, and regular inspections should be conducted to identify any potential safety hazards, such as faulty wiring or overloaded circuits.
- *Backup Systems:* Large residential buildings often have emergency backup systems, such as generators or battery storage, to provide power in case of an outage. These systems ensure that essential services, such as elevators and emergency lighting, remain operational during power failures.

Property managers need to understand the electrical system's layout and components to effectively manage maintenance, schedule inspections, and quickly address power-related issues or emergencies.

Lighting Systems

Lighting systems in large residential buildings are essential for both functionality and safety. Lighting affects common areas, hallways, parking lots, and emergency exits, and plays a key role in both energy management and resident satisfaction.

- *Types of Lighting: Lighting systems typically include a mix of overhead lighting, wall sconces, and emergency lighting. Advances in energy-efficient technologies, such as LED lighting, have made it possible to significantly reduce electricity consumption while maintaining bright, reliable lighting for common areas.*
- *Emergency Lighting:* Emergency lighting is required in most large buildings to guide residents safely to exits in the event of power failure. These systems are often connected to backup generators to ensure they function during emergencies. Emergency lights must be regularly inspected and tested to ensure compliance with local building codes.
- *Lighting Control Systems:* Smart lighting control systems can be used to automate lighting schedules and optimize energy usage. Motion sensors, timers, and dimming systems are commonly used to reduce unnecessary lighting in unoccupied areas while still ensuring safety and security.

Effective management of lighting systems not only ensures resident comfort and safety but also helps reduce energy costs and improve sustainability.

Plumbing Systems

Plumbing systems are essential for delivering clean water, managing wastewater, and maintaining sanitary conditions in residential buildings. A well-maintained plumbing system is critical to tenant satisfaction and property value.

- *Water Supply and Distribution: Water enters the building through a main water supply line, which is distributed to individual units and common areas through a network of pipes. Property managers must ensure regular inspection and main-*

tenance of the water supply system, especially in older buildings where aging pipes can lead to leaks or water quality issues.
- *Wastewater and Drainage:* Plumbing systems also handle wastewater removal through a series of drain pipes that connect to the municipal sewage system. Clogs, leaks, and backups in the drainage system are common issues that property managers must address promptly to avoid property damage and health hazards.
- *Water Heaters:* Water heaters or boilers provide hot water for the building. Property managers must ensure regular maintenance of these systems to prevent breakdowns and ensure consistent water heating for residents.

Understanding the layout and function of the building's plumbing system allows property managers to identify and resolve issues such as leaks, clogs, or pressure problems before they escalate.

Fire Alarm Systems

A fire alarm system is a critical component of building safety, designed to alert residents and staff to the presence of smoke or fire. These systems include smoke detectors, alarms, and communication devices that can notify building occupants and emergency personnel.

- *Smoke and Heat Detectors: Detectors are installed throughout the building and are connected to the central alarm system. When smoke or excessive heat is detected, the alarm is triggered, prompting evacuation procedures.*
- *Manual Pull Stations:* Manual pull stations allow residents or staff to activate the fire alarm system in case of an emergency. These devices are typically located near exits and must be easy to access.
- *Alarm Monitoring and Communication:* In many cases, fire alarm systems are monitored by external services that notify the local fire department when an alarm is triggered. In larger buildings, communication systems within the fire alarm setup may also include intercoms or public address systems to provide instructions to residents during an evacuation.

Maintaining and regularly testing the fire alarm system ensures it functions properly and complies with fire safety regulations. Property managers must be familiar with these systems to coordinate regular inspections and communicate effectively with fire safety professionals.

Fire Protection Systems

Fire protection systems go beyond alarms to actively suppress and control fires. These systems can include sprinklers, fire extinguishers, and other emergency response tools designed to minimize the spread of fire and reduce property damage.

- *Sprinkler Systems: Most large residential buildings are equipped with sprinkler systems that activate when heat or flames are detected. These systems are con-*

nected to the building's water supply and distribute water to control or extinguish a fire before it spreads.

- *Fire Extinguishers:* Fire extinguishers are placed throughout the building to provide a first line of defense in case of a small fire. Property managers must ensure that extinguishers are easily accessible and regularly inspected.
- *Standpipes and Hose Connections:* Standpipes are vertical pipes connected to the building's water supply, allowing firefighters to quickly access water on each floor of the building. Hose connections are typically located in stairwells and/or hallways and must be maintained for quick response.

Property managers must ensure that fire protection systems are regularly inspected, tested, and maintained to comply with fire codes and provide maximum protection for residents.

Elevators

Elevators are essential in large residential buildings, providing accessibility and convenience for residents. Proper maintenance of elevators is crucial for ensuring safety, reducing breakdowns, and complying with regulatory requirements.

- *Types of Elevators: Residential buildings may have hydraulic or traction elevators. Hydraulic elevators are powered by a piston that moves the car up and down, while traction elevators use cables and counterweights. Each type requires specific maintenance procedures.*
- *Safety Features:* Modern elevators are equipped with multiple safety features, including emergency stop buttons, communication systems, and backup power systems. These safety features ensure that residents can safely exit the elevator in case of an emergency or power outage.
- *Inspection and Maintenance:* Regular inspections and preventive maintenance are required to keep elevators in compliance with safety regulations and to ensure proper operation. Property managers should schedule regular inspections by certified elevator technicians and quickly address any identified issues to minimize downtime and safety risks.

Trash Chute Systems

Trash chute systems provide residents with a convenient way to dispose of waste without having to leave their floors. These systems are common in high-rise residential buildings and must be maintained to ensure sanitary conditions.

- *Design and Functionality: A trash chute system typically consists of a vertical shaft with openings on each floor, leading to a collection bin or compactor at the base. Residents can deposit trash into the chute, which then falls to the collection area. In some buildings, separate chutes for recyclables are also provided.*
- *Maintenance:* Regular cleaning and inspection of the trash chute system are critical to prevent blockages, odors, and pest infestations. Property managers must

schedule routine maintenance to keep the system functioning efficiently and ensure the collection area is regularly cleaned and emptied.

- *Fire Safety Considerations:* Trash chutes can pose a fire hazard if not properly maintained. Chutes should be equipped with fire-rated doors and automatic closing mechanisms to prevent the spread of fire through the system.

By understanding the functionality and maintenance requirements of these building systems, property managers can ensure the safe, efficient, and reliable operation of large residential properties, contributing to tenant satisfaction and compliance with regulatory standards.

6.3.3 Development and Implementation of Building Maintenance Plans

Managing the maintenance of large residential buildings, such as apartments, condominiums, and cooperatives, requires a strategic and systematic approach to ensure that all building systems and infrastructure operate efficiently. A preventive maintenance plan is essential for prolonging the lifespan of building components, minimizing unexpected repairs, and enhancing tenant satisfaction. This section outlines a step-by-step approach to developing and implementing a preventive building maintenance plan that prioritizes goals, maintains assets, schedules work, and monitors progress.

Step 1: Assess Building Assets and Inventory

The first step in developing a maintenance plan is to assess all building assets. This includes identifying and cataloging the key components and systems of the building that require maintenance, such as HVAC systems, electrical systems, elevators, plumbing, lighting, fire safety systems, and more.

- *Create an Asset Inventory: Develop a detailed list of all assets in the building, including equipment, fixtures, and mechanical systems. Each item should have a description, installation date, expected lifespan, manufacturer details, and warranty information.*
- *Evaluate the Condition of Assets:* Assess the current condition of each asset to identify any issues or potential failures. This evaluation helps determine which components need immediate attention and which can be addressed through routine maintenance.
- *Prioritize Critical Assets:* Some assets are more critical than others for building operations and tenant safety (e.g., elevators, HVAC, fire alarms). These assets should be prioritized in the maintenance plan to ensure they remain functional at all times.

Step 2: Establish Maintenance Goals and Objectives

Once the building assets are assessed, the next step is to set clear maintenance goals and objectives. This includes defining what the maintenance plan aims to achieve, such as improving asset longevity, reducing emergency repairs, and maintaining safety standards.

- *Define Key Objectives: For example, an objective might be to reduce HVAC system breakdowns by 20% over the next year, or to ensure that all fire safety equipment is compliant with local regulations by the end of the quarter.*
- *Set Performance Benchmarks:* Establish measurable benchmarks for each objective to track progress. For instance, benchmarks could include reducing tenant complaints about heating and cooling issues, ensuring all elevators pass safety inspections, or minimizing unplanned maintenance costs by a certain percentage.
- *Align with Building and Tenant Needs:* Maintenance goals should align with both the operational needs of the building and the comfort and safety of the residents. Maintaining common areas, elevators, lighting, and essential systems like plumbing and HVAC must always be top priorities.

Step 3: Develop a Preventive Maintenance Schedule

A preventive maintenance schedule outlines the specific tasks required to maintain building systems and ensures that these tasks are performed regularly. Creating a well-organized schedule helps prevent breakdowns, extend the lifespan of equipment, and reduce unplanned repair costs.

- *Create Maintenance Checklists: For each asset or system, create a detailed checklist of the preventive maintenance tasks required. This might include changing HVAC filters every 3 months, lubricating elevator machinery, testing fire alarms, or inspecting plumbing for leaks.*
- *Establish Frequency of Tasks:* Determine how often each maintenance task should be performed. Some tasks, such as checking fire alarms, need to be done monthly, while others, such as cleaning ducts or inspecting roofs, may only be required annually.
- *Assign Responsibilities:* Assign responsibility for each task to specific team members, such as maintenance staff, contractors, or third-party vendors. Ensure that all personnel are adequately trained to perform the tasks assigned to them.
- *Utilize Maintenance Software:* Many property management firms use property management software to automate maintenance scheduling, track task completion, and monitor asset conditions. These systems send reminders when tasks are due, streamline work orders, and store maintenance history for easy reference.

Step 4: Schedule and Execute Maintenance Work

Once the preventive maintenance schedule is developed, the next step is to schedule and execute the work. A key aspect of this step is ensuring that all maintenance activities are carried out in a timely and efficient manner.

- *Plan Around Resident Convenience: Schedule maintenance work during times that minimize disruption to residents. For example, HVAC maintenance may be less disruptive during midday hours when many residents are at work, while plumbing inspections could be planned for off-peak water usage hours.*
- *Coordinate with Contractors and Vendors:* For specialized maintenance tasks, such as elevator inspections or HVAC repairs, coordinate with licensed contractors. Ensure that contracts are in place, outlining the frequency and scope of the work required.
- *Communicate with Residents:* Effective communication with residents is crucial for maintaining positive relationships and minimizing inconvenience. Provide advance notice of any planned maintenance work that may affect their access to services or living spaces, such as plumbing work or electrical inspections.

Step 5: Monitor Progress and Adjust the Plan

Monitoring the progress of the maintenance plan is essential for ensuring its success. By continuously tracking completed tasks and evaluating the performance of building systems, property managers can adjust the plan to address new issues and improve efficiency.

- *Track Task Completion: Use maintenance management software or manual tracking systems to ensure all scheduled maintenance tasks are completed on time. Any missed or delayed tasks should be flagged and rescheduled as soon as possible.*
- *Evaluate System Performance:* Periodically evaluate how building systems are performing based on the maintenance efforts. For example, track the number of breakdowns in HVAC systems, tenant complaints about plumbing, or emergency elevator repairs. If certain systems are still experiencing frequent issues, additional maintenance may be required.
- *Conduct Regular Inspections:* Perform regular building inspections to assess the effectiveness of the maintenance plan. This helps identify any new issues that may have arisen since the last assessment and ensures that the building remains in compliance with safety and regulatory standards.
- *Adjust and Update the Plan:* Based on the monitoring results, the maintenance plan should be adjusted to reflect changing needs, new goals, or lessons learned from previous activities. For example, if certain systems are requiring more frequent repairs than expected, it may be necessary to increase the frequency of preventive tasks or allocate additional resources.

A well-developed and implemented preventive maintenance plan is critical for managing large residential buildings. By assessing building assets, setting clear maintenance goals, scheduling preventive work, executing tasks effectively, and continuously monitoring progress, property managers can ensure that all building systems function properly, enhance tenant satisfaction, and reduce costly emergency repairs. Such a structured approach not only prolongs the life of building infrastructure but also ensures that the property complies with safety regulations and operates efficiently.

6.3.4 Sample Maintenance Plan

A comprehensive maintenance plan is essential for ensuring the long-term success of any residential building. Regular and systematic maintenance not only helps preserve the property's value but also ensures the safety, comfort, and satisfaction of residents. This sample maintenance plan is designed to cover routine, preventive, and emergency tasks, organized by frequency: monthly, quarterly, semiannual, and annual tasks. Property managers can use this plan as a guide to develop customized maintenance schedules based on the specific needs of their property.

Monthly Tasks

Monthly maintenance tasks are vital to the day-to-day operation of the building. These tasks ensure that basic systems are functioning properly and that the property is clean, safe, and well-maintained. Property managers should schedule these tasks regularly to avoid disruption to residents and prevent minor issues from escalating into major repairs.

- *Inspect HVAC Systems: Check for proper operation, clean air filters, and inspect for any visible issues. This ensures the building's heating and cooling systems are functioning efficiently.*
- *Inspect Common Areas:* Walk through lobbies, hallways, and recreational areas to ensure they are clean and free from hazards. Address any cleanliness issues immediately.
- *Check Lighting Systems:* Replace any burned-out bulbs in common areas such as stairwells, hallways, and parking lots. Ensure emergency lighting systems are operational.
- *Check Fire Alarms and Extinguishers:* Test fire alarm systems and ensure fire extinguishers are properly located and fully charged. This is crucial for maintaining safety standards.
- *Clean Common Area Floors and Carpets:* Schedule regular cleaning of floors and carpets in high-traffic areas to maintain aesthetics and hygiene.
- *Inspect Landscaping:* Ensure that outdoor areas are properly maintained. Trim shrubs, mow lawns, and remove any debris from the property.
- *Trash Removal and Recycling:* Ensure that trash and recycling areas are kept clean and emptied regularly to prevent odors and pest infestations.

Quarterly Tasks

Quarterly tasks are slightly more intensive than monthly tasks and often involve checking systems that require more thorough inspections. Completing these tasks every 3 months helps catch potential issues early before they lead to costly repairs or system failures.

- *Test and Service Elevators: Ensure that elevators are in safe operating condition by performing regular tests and inspections. Engage certified technicians for servicing and safety checks.*
- *Inspect Plumbing Systems:* Check for any leaks in pipes, faucets, and water heaters. Test water pressure and check for any signs of water damage, mold, or corrosion.
- *Check Building Security Systems:* Test surveillance cameras, intercom systems, and access control systems to ensure they are working properly and providing adequate security for the building.
- *Inspect Roof and Gutters:* Inspect the roof for any signs of damage, such as loose shingles or leaks. Clean gutters and downspouts to prevent water damage and blockages.
- *Check Water Drainage Systems:* Ensure that all storm drains and water drainage systems are clear and functioning properly to avoid flooding.
- *Check Exterior Lighting:* Walk the property after dark to inspect exterior lighting and ensure that walkways, parking lots, and entrances are properly illuminated.
- *Inspect Parking Facilities:* Look for any signs of cracks, potholes, or damage in parking structures or lots. Repair as needed and ensure proper signage is in place.

Semiannual Tasks

Semiannual tasks are generally more in-depth and may involve seasonal preparations for changes in weather. Completing these tasks twice a year helps keep the property in top condition and ensures that major systems continue to run efficiently.

- *HVAC System Servicing: Schedule a full service for heating and cooling systems in the spring and fall to prepare for seasonal changes. Replace air filters, clean coils, and check for any issues that may affect performance.*
- *Fire System Inspection:* Schedule a professional inspection of fire alarm systems, sprinkler systems, and fire extinguishers to ensure compliance with local fire safety regulations.
- *Pest Control:* Engage pest control professionals to conduct a preventive pest control treatment throughout the building, focusing on common areas and units where pests may be more prevalent.
- *Window and Door Inspections:* Check all windows and doors for proper operation, weather stripping, and seals. Address any drafts, leaks, or damage to ensure energy efficiency.
- *Deep Clean Common Areas:* Schedule a deep cleaning of common areas, including carpets, windows, and upholstery in lobbies, gyms, and recreation rooms.
- *Inspect and Service Generators:* Ensure backup generators are in good working order by performing a full inspection and test run. This is critical in the event of a power outage.
- *Exterior Power Washing:* Conduct a power wash of the building's exterior to remove dirt, mold, and grime that may have accumulated over time.

Annual Tasks

Annual tasks typically involve more extensive inspections, servicing, and preventive maintenance. These tasks are often performed by certified technicians and specialists to ensure compliance with local laws and to prolong the life of the building's major systems.

- *Conduct a Full Property Inspection: Engage professionals to conduct a thorough inspection of the building's structure, including foundations, roofs, walls, windows, and exterior facades. Address any structural concerns immediately.*
- *Electrical System Inspection:* Schedule a professional inspection of the building's electrical systems, including wiring, panels, and outlets, to ensure safety and compliance with electrical codes.
- *Inspect Plumbing Systems:* Conduct a comprehensive review of the entire plumbing system, including sewer lines, water heaters, and drainage systems. Identify any potential leaks, blockages, or system inefficiencies.
- *Repaint Exterior and Interior Common Areas:* Depending on wear and tear, repaint high-traffic areas and refresh exterior paint to maintain the building's curb appeal.
- *Test and Service Fire Systems:* Schedule a certified technician to conduct a full inspection and test of the fire sprinkler system, fire alarms, and emergency exit signs to ensure compliance with safety codes.
- *Review Security Systems:* Perform a detailed review of security systems, including camera systems, door locks, and keyless entry systems. Upgrade or replace outdated equipment if necessary.
- *Inspect and Repair Parking Areas:* Conduct a detailed inspection of parking lots or structures for cracks, drainage issues, or structural concerns. Repair or repave areas as needed.
- *Review Building Insurance Policies:* Work with the property owner to review and update building insurance policies to ensure adequate coverage for potential risks such as natural disasters, liability, or fire.
- *Update Emergency Preparedness Plans:* Review and update the building's emergency preparedness plans, including evacuation procedures, shelter locations, and communication protocols in the event of a disaster.

A comprehensive maintenance plan is key to ensuring that a building operates smoothly and retains its value over time. By adhering to a structured schedule of monthly, quarterly, semiannual, and annual tasks, property managers can proactively address maintenance issues, reduce operating costs, and create a safe and comfortable environment for residents.

6.4 Technology in Property Management

6.4.1 The Role of Technology in Modern Property Management

The integration of technology in residential property management has transformed the industry by improving efficiency, enhancing communication, and providing better security for properties and residents. Property managers now leverage a variety of digital tools and platforms to streamline daily operations, connect more effectively with tenants and owners, and implement advanced security solutions. Embracing these technologies is essential for modern property managers to stay competitive and meet the growing expectations of residents in today's fast-paced, digital world.

Streamlining Operations

Technology has significantly streamlined operational processes in residential property management, reducing the time and effort needed to manage day-to-day tasks. Software solutions like property management platforms (e.g., Yardi, AppFolio, and Buildium) offer comprehensive features that automate rent collection, maintenance scheduling, and financial reporting. These systems allow property managers to centralize data, track key performance metrics, and manage multiple properties from a single interface. Automated rent collection and payment tracking, in particular, reduce the risk of errors and ensure a steady cash flow. Additionally, technology simplifies lease management by enabling digital lease signing and storage, reducing paperwork, and ensuring compliance with legal requirements.

Improving Communication

Effective communication is critical in residential property management, and technology has made it easier to stay connected with tenants, homeowners, and staff. Property management platforms and resident portals enable instant communication through email, text messaging, and push notifications. These platforms can be used to send important updates, announce community events, and share maintenance schedules, keeping residents informed and engaged. Social media platforms and community forums also provide informal channels for residents to connect, ask questions, and share feedback. This digital communication fosters transparency, builds trust, and strengthens the overall sense of community.

Enhancing Security

Security is a top concern in residential property management, and technology has introduced advanced solutions to enhance the safety of properties and residents. Modern security systems now include smart locks, video surveillance, and access control systems that can be monitored and managed remotely. These systems allow property managers to grant or revoke access for vendors and service providers, monitor common areas, and respond quickly to security incidents. Implementing digital visitor management systems and mobile-based entry solutions improves security while providing convenience to residents. By leveraging technology, property managers can create a safer living environment and reduce liability risks.

Overall, technology has become an indispensable tool for residential property managers, helping them deliver more efficient, secure, and resident-centric services that elevate the overall management experience.

6.4.2 Property Management Software

Property management software has become an essential tool for efficiently managing residential properties, whether for single-family homes, apartment complexes, or large multifamily communities. These software platforms offer a wide range of features specifically designed to meet the unique needs of residential property managers. By automating routine tasks, providing real-time data, and improving communication, property management software enhances operational efficiency and enables property managers to deliver superior service to tenants and owners. This section covers the key features and benefits of property management software and highlights some of the most popular platforms used in the residential sector.

Features and Benefits of Property Management Software

Property management software provides a suite of features that streamline daily operations, improve financial management, and enhance the tenant experience. Below are some of the core features and benefits:

- *Tenant and Lease Management:*
  - Software solutions offer centralized lease tracking and tenant management tools. Managers can easily view lease expiration dates, send automated reminders, and store digital copies of lease agreements, reducing paperwork and ensuring compliance.
  - Tenant portals enable residents to access their lease documents, pay rent, submit maintenance requests, and communicate with management, providing a seamless tenant experience.
- *Automated Rent Collection:*
  - Online rent collection is one of the most valued features, allowing tenants to pay electronically via bank transfer, credit card, or other digital payment methods. Automated reminders reduce the number of late payments and simplify rent tracking for managers.
- *Maintenance Management:*
  - Managers can receive, track, and prioritize maintenance requests through the platform. Maintenance schedules, work orders, and vendor management are all integrated into a single system, ensuring timely responses and reducing downtime for repairs.
- *Financial Reporting:*
  - Property management software provides detailed financial reports, including income statements, balance sheets, and cash flow analysis. These tools offer a

transparent view of financial performance, helping managers make data-driven decisions.

- *Communication Tools:*

  – Built-in communication features, such as email and SMS notifications, streamline interactions with tenants and owners, ensuring timely updates and responses to inquiries.

Popular Platforms for Residential Property Management

Several property management software platforms are widely used in the residential sector, each offering unique features tailored to specific property types and management needs:

- *AppFolio: Known for its user-friendly interface and robust features, AppFolio is ideal for managing single-family homes, condos, and multifamily properties. It offers automated rent collection, digital lease signing, and powerful reporting tools.*
- *Buildium:* Buildium is a comprehensive platform designed for residential property management. It includes features for tenant management, accounting, and document storage, making it popular among small to midsized property managers.
- *Yardi:* Yardi is a versatile platform that caters to larger portfolios, offering advanced financial management, tenant screening, and integrated marketing solutions. Its scalability makes it suitable for managing multiple property types and communities.
- *Propertyware:* Propertyware is specifically designed for managing single-family homes and smaller multifamily properties. It provides customizable workflows, maintenance tracking, and robust owner portals.

By leveraging the features and capabilities of these property management platforms, residential property managers can significantly improve efficiency, reduce administrative overhead, and deliver a better overall experience for tenants and owners alike.

6.4.3 Smart Home Technology

Integration with Property Management

Smart home technology, such as smart thermostats, lighting, and security systems, can be integrated into property management practices. These technologies offer convenience to tenants and can lead to cost savings for property owners through energy efficiency and reduced maintenance needs.

Benefits for Tenants and Managers
Smart home devices provide tenants with greater control over their living environment, improving comfort and satisfaction. For property managers, these technologies offer remote monitoring capabilities and data insights that help in proactive maintenance and management.

6.4.4 Cybersecurity Best Practices

Importance of Cybersecurity: As property management increasingly relies on technology, protecting IT systems against cyber threats becomes paramount. Property managers must implement robust cybersecurity measures to protect sensitive data, maintain tenant trust, and ensure operational continuity.

Cybersecurity Best Practices:

1. *Data Encryption:*
   - *Encrypt sensitive data both in transit and at rest to protect it from unauthorized access.*
   - Use strong encryption protocols for all communications and data storage.
2. *Regular Software Updates:*
   - *Ensure that all software, including property management systems and access control platforms, is regularly updated to patch vulnerabilities.*
   - Enable automatic updates where possible to minimize the risk of running outdated software.
3. *Access Controls:*
   - *Implement strict access control measures to limit who can access sensitive information and systems.*
   - Use multifactor authentication (MFA) for all administrative accounts to add an extra layer of security.
4. *Employee Training:*
   - *Train employees on cybersecurity best practices, including recognizing phishing attempts, using strong passwords, and reporting suspicious activities.*
   - Conduct regular training sessions to keep staff informed about the latest cyber threats and prevention techniques.
5. *Incident Response Plan:*
   - *Develop a comprehensive incident response plan that outlines steps to take in the event of a cyberattack.*
   - Regularly test and update the plan to ensure it is effective and that all employees are familiar with their roles.
6. *Regular Backups:*
   - *Perform regular backups of all critical data and systems.*
   - Ensure backups are stored securely and tested periodically to ensure they can be restored in case of an attack.

Budgeting for Technology System Maintenance and Improvements: Allocate a portion of the budget for ongoing technology system maintenance and improvements. This includes investing in updated software, cybersecurity tools, and hardware upgrades. Regularly reviewing and adjusting the budget ensures that the property management team has the resources needed to maintain a robust cybersecurity posture.

Operational Continuity Plan:

1. *Alternative Communication Channels:*
   - *Establish alternative communication channels, such as emergency phone lines or backup email accounts, to ensure communication can continue during an IT outage.*
2. *Manual Processes:*
   - *Develop manual processes for critical operations, such as rent/maintenance fee collection and maintenance requests, to be used during technology outages.*
   - Train staff on these processes to ensure seamless transition if necessary.
3. *Regular Drills:*
   - *Conduct regular drills to practice the operational continuity plan and identify any areas for improvement.*

Action Plan for Cybersecurity Breach

Immediate Actions:

1. *Contain the Breach:*
   - *Disconnect affected systems from the network to prevent the spread of the attack.*
   - Disable user accounts that may have been compromised.
2. *Assess the Impact:*
   - *Determine the scope of the breach and identify what data or systems have been affected.*
   - Document all findings for further analysis and reporting.
3. *Notify Stakeholders:*
   - *Inform senior management, IT personnel, and, if necessary, law enforcement agencies about the breach.*
   - Communicate transparently with tenants and clients, providing them with information about the breach and steps being taken to address it.

Follow-Up Actions:

1. *Investigate the Breach:*
   - *Conduct a thorough investigation to identify the cause of the breach and how it occurred.*
   - Work with cybersecurity experts if necessary to analyze the attack.
2. *Implement Remediation Measures:*
   - *Fix vulnerabilities that were exploited during the attack.*

- Enhance security measures to prevent future breaches, such as updating software, changing passwords, and improving access controls.

3. *Review and Update Policies:*
   - *Review and update cybersecurity policies and procedures based on lessons learned from the breach.*
   - Conduct additional training for employees to reinforce best practices.

Examples of Cybersecurity Hacks in Property Management

Cybersecurity threats are a growing concern for residential communities, as property management companies and associations increasingly rely on digital systems to store sensitive information and manage day-to-day operations. Cyberattacks can compromise the personal data of residents, disrupt operations, and damage the reputation of the community. One of the most notable incidents occurred in 2021 with the Douglas Elliman Property Management data network breach, highlighting the critical need for robust cybersecurity measures in residential property management.

2021 Douglas Elliman Property Management Data Breach

In 2021, Douglas Elliman Property Management, one of the largest property management firms in New York City, suffered a significant data breach that exposed sensitive information for residents and employees of co-op and condominium buildings. The breach involved unauthorized access to the company's data network, resulting in the theft of highly sensitive personal data, including Social Security numbers, dates of birth, mailing addresses, driver's license numbers, passport numbers, and financial information. This incident put thousands of residents at risk of identity theft and financial fraud, raising serious concerns about the security practices of property management firms.

The breach affected not only the residents of the properties under management but also the staff members employed by the company. The stolen information could potentially be used for a wide range of fraudulent activities, from creating fake identities to accessing financial accounts. Following the breach, Douglas Elliman faced significant backlash from residents and board members demanding enhanced security measures and better communication about the incident.

This example underscores the importance of implementing strong cybersecurity protocols, such as encryption of sensitive data, regular network security assessments, and employee training on identifying phishing attempts. Property management firms must also establish a comprehensive incident response plan to manage data breaches effectively and minimize damage.

Other Notable Cybersecurity Incidents

- *2020 Wolfe & Associates Data Breach Cyberattack: In a significant cybersecurity incident, Wolfe & Associates, a property management firm, experienced a data breach when their online database was compromised by a group of cybercriminals. The attackers gained unauthorized access to sensitive information, including tenant personal data, payment records, and internal communications.*

The breach raised concerns about the firm's cybersecurity protocols, particularly regarding the security of their online portals and data storage systems.

- *2019 Property Management Company Ransomware Attack:* A property management company in Florida fell victim to a ransomware attack that locked its access to financial records and tenant information. The hackers demanded a ransom to restore access, disrupting operations for weeks and delaying rent collection.
- *2018 Community Association Management Data Leak:* A data leak at a community association management firm exposed confidential board documents and financial information, compromising sensitive project details and resident personal data. This incident highlighted the risk of using unsecured cloud storage services.

These incidents illustrate the vulnerability of residential property management systems to cyber threats and the potential consequences of lax security practices. Property managers must prioritize cybersecurity to protect resident data, maintain trust, and ensure the continuity of their operations. Implementing multifactor authentication, data encryption, regular software updates, and employee training are key steps in safeguarding residential communities against cyber threats.

6.5 Property Management Accounting and Financial Reporting

Property management accounting and financial reporting are critical elements in the management of residential properties, directly influencing their financial health, transparency, and long-term success. Property managers often oversee multimillion-dollar enterprises, whether managing income-generating properties or not-for-profit community associations. Understanding the financial nuances of these entities is essential to making informed decisions, maintaining fiscal stability, and enhancing property value. This section explores key topics such as accounting terminology, financial reports, collections, liens, foreclosures and bankruptcy, audits, and taxes, providing property managers with the tools they need to excel in this vital aspect of their role.

6.5.1 Managing Financially Significant Assets

Residential property management involves the oversight of financially significant assets. Properties such as apartment complexes, high-rise condominiums, and large homeowners' associations (HOAs) often have budgets that rival or exceed those of small businesses. Managing these substantial financial operations requires a deep understanding of budgeting, financial reporting, and cash flow management. Property managers play a pivotal role in allocating resources, forecasting expenses, and ensuring that funds are available for maintenance, capital improvements, and other essential activities.

A comprehensive grasp of financial accounting enables property managers to balance competing priorities effectively. For example, they must ensure that maintenance projects are adequately funded while preserving reserve accounts for long-term needs. Property managers who excel in financial management can position their properties for sustained growth and stability, ensuring that their operations remain resilient in the face of economic challenges.

6.5.2 Income-Generating Properties Versus Not-for-Profit Properties

A key distinction in property management accounting lies in understanding the difference between income-generating properties and not-for-profit properties.

Income-Generating Properties: These include rental properties such as single family homes, duplex, triplex, apartment complexes or vacation rentals, where the primary objective is to maximize revenue and profitability. Property managers for these properties must focus on increasing rental income, minimizing vacancy rates, and controlling expenses to improve net operating income (NOI). Strong financial performance enhances the property's market value and appeal to investors.

Not-for-Profit Properties: These include community associations such as HOAs, condominiums, cooperatives, and owner-controlled timeshare associations. The primary goal is not to generate profit but to maintain the property, provide services to residents, and ensure the community's financial health. Property managers must focus on collecting dues, balancing budgets, and managing reserve funds to meet the community's needs. While not-for-profit, financial transparency and prudent management are essential to building trust among residents and maintaining property value.

Recognizing the unique financial goals of these two types of properties allows property managers to tailor their strategies effectively.

6.5.3 Enhancing Property Value Through Financial Expertise

A property manager's ability to enhance property value is directly tied to their understanding of financial principles. Managers who excel in budgeting and financial reporting can identify opportunities for cost savings, revenue generation, and strategic investments. For example, a manager who monitors utility expenses closely may identify areas for energy efficiency improvements, reducing operating costs while increasing the property's appeal to environmentally conscious tenants or buyers.

Additionally, well-maintained financial records and transparent reporting instill confidence in stakeholders, including property owners, boards of directors, and residents. This confidence can lead to higher owner satisfaction, improved tenant retention, and increased willingness to invest in property improvements. Property managers who understand financials also play a crucial role in negotiating service contracts, securing favorable loan terms, and navigating complex tax regulations, all of which contribute to the property's financial success.

6.5.4 Accounting Terminology

Basic Terms: Understanding basic accounting terminology is crucial for effective property management. Key terms include:

- *Assets: Resources owned by the property that have economic value, such as buildings, equipment, and cash.*
- *Liabilities:* Obligations the property owes to others, including loans, accounts payable, and mortgages.
- *Equity:* The owner's interest in the property after liabilities are deducted from assets, representing the residual value.
- *Revenue:* Income generated from property operations, such as rent, parking fees, and laundry income.
- *Expenses:* Costs incurred in the operation and maintenance of the property, including utilities, repairs, and management fees.

Accounts Payable and Receivable:

- *Accounts Payable (A/P):* Money the property owes to vendors and service providers for goods and services received.
- *Accounts Receivable (A/R):* Money owed to the property by tenants or other entities for rent, services, or other charges.

General Ledger: The general ledger is the central repository for all financial transactions. It contains accounts for assets, liabilities, equity, revenue, and expenses, providing a comprehensive record of the property's financial activities. The general ledger is essential for preparing financial statements and ensuring accuracy in financial reporting.

Chart of Accounts: The chart of accounts is a structured list of all accounts used in the general ledger, categorized by type (assets, liabilities, equity, revenue, expenses). This organization facilitates accurate tracking of financial transactions and preparation of financial reports.

Financial Ratios: Financial ratios are tools used to evaluate the property's financial health and performance. Key ratios include:

- *Current Ratio: Measures liquidity by comparing current assets to current liabilities.*

- *Debt-to-Equity Ratio:* Assesses financial leverage by comparing total liabilities to equity.
- *Net Operating Income (NOI):* Measures profitability by subtracting operating expenses from gross income.
- *Capitalization Rate (Cap Rate):* Evaluates the property's return on investment by dividing NOI by the property's market value.

6.5.5 Budgeting

Effective budgeting is a cornerstone of successful property management, ensuring that both single-family and multifamily properties are financially sustainable while maintaining or enhancing property value. Developing and managing budgets for these properties requires an understanding of various accounting principles and practices that guide financial planning, monitoring, and decision-making. This section outlines how property managers can effectively develop and manage budgets using standard accounting principles, addressing key topics such as lease abstracts, rent rolls, financial statements, and more.

Ten Essential Steps to Effectively Develop and Manage Budgets for Residential Properties

1. *Understanding Revenue Projections*
    - *Lease Abstracts and Rent Rolls: For income generating properties, the first step in developing a budget is to understand the revenue generated by the property. This involves reviewing lease abstracts (summaries of individual leases) and the rent roll (a listing of all tenants, lease terms, and rents due). These documents help property managers project rental income and determine upcoming lease expirations that could affect revenue. Rent rolls also provide insights into current occupancy levels, which is critical for predicting potential vacancies and revenue changes.*
    - *Association Maintenance Revenue:* For multifamily properties like condominium associations or homeowner associations (HOAs), association maintenance revenue represents income generated from maintenance fees or dues paid by unit owners. These fees cover the maintenance and repair of common areas, as well as other operational costs. It is essential to accurately project this revenue based on the number of units and expected fee increases, ensuring that operating expenses are adequately funded.
2. *Estimate Vacancy and Loss Factors*

    Vacancy and collection loss is an unavoidable aspect of property management, and it's crucial to factor these potential losses into the budget. By analyzing historical data and market conditions, property managers can estimate realistic vacancy rates and loss factors that affect rental income. Including a buffer for vacancy and nonpayment ensures that the budget remains viable even when some units are unoccupied or when tenants are late on payments.

3. *Calculate Operating Expenses*

   Accurately calculating operating expenses is a critical component of effective budgeting for residential property management. Operating expenses include all the costs required to maintain the property's day-to-day operations, such as utilities, insurance, maintenance, and staff salaries. Implementing best practices in calculating these expenses ensures that the budget accurately reflects anticipated costs, reduces the risk of financial shortfalls, and helps property managers make informed decisions about resource allocation. Below are some key best practices for calculating operating expenses:

   Review Service Contractual Obligations

   One of the first steps in calculating operating expenses is to review all service contracts related to property management, including contracts for landscaping, janitorial services, waste disposal, security, and pest control. Property managers should examine each contract for details on pricing, payment schedules, and terms of service to ensure that projected costs align with contract stipulations. Reviewing contracts also allows property managers to identify any upcoming renewals or opportunities to renegotiate terms. Additionally, some contracts may include provisions for annual rate increases or additional fees for emergency services, which should be factored into the budget.

   Contact Utility Providers for Annual Rate Increases

   Utilities are often among the largest operating expenses for residential properties, encompassing electricity, gas, water, and waste services. To project accurate costs for the upcoming year, property managers should contact utility providers to inquire about any anticipated rate increases. Utility providers frequently adjust rates due to factors such as fuel costs, regulatory changes, and infrastructure upgrades, which can significantly impact the property's expenses. Property managers can also analyze historical utility usage data to identify seasonal trends or potential cost-saving measures. Understanding projected utility rates allows for more precise budgeting and helps avoid unexpected financial pressures.

   Work with Insurance Agents to Project Insurance Renewal Costs

   Insurance premiums are another major operating expense, and premium rates can vary each year based on market conditions, property claims history, and changes in coverage needs. Property managers should work closely with the property's insurance agent or broker to obtain cost projections for upcoming policy renewals. In some cases, property managers may also want to explore alternative policies or insurers to find the best coverage options at competitive rates. Additionally, if the property has undergone renovations, improvements, or changes in occupancy, it may be necessary to adjust coverage levels to reflect these updates accurately.

   Account for Maintenance and Repair Costs

   Maintenance and repairs are essential for property upkeep, and budgeting for these expenses involves understanding both routine and unexpected costs. Property managers should analyze historical maintenance data to identify recurring costs, such as HVAC servicing, plumbing repairs, and groundskeeping. Preventive maintenance programs can help reduce unexpected repair expenses, but it's essential to allocate a portion of the budget for emergencies. By tracking past maintenance costs and projecting routine expenses, property managers can estimate a realistic maintenance budget that covers both scheduled work and potential contingencies.

Include Staff Salaries and Benefits

If the property employs staff members, such as maintenance personnel, security, or administrative support, their salaries and benefits should be included in operating expenses. Property managers should review compensation agreements and consider any anticipated changes, such as salary increases or adjustments to benefits. Additionally, budgeting for professional development, certifications, and training can support staff performance and compliance with industry standards. Allocating funds for employee retention and development can improve service quality, enhance tenant satisfaction, and reduce turnover-related costs.

Allow for Inflation and Market Fluctuations

Inflation and market fluctuations can impact various aspects of operating expenses, from labor costs to materials for repairs. Property managers should factor a modest inflation rate (typically 2–3%) into the budget to account for these increases. Additionally, if there are known economic factors affecting the market, such as supply chain disruptions or material shortages, it may be wise to set aside contingency funds to cover unexpected price hikes in areas like building materials or contractor fees.

Review Capital Expenditures and Replacement Reserves

Operating expenses should be calculated separately from capital expenditures, which cover major upgrades, renovations, or replacements of property elements. However, property managers must ensure that enough reserve funds are allocated for capital expenses. Budgeting for replacement reserves helps manage operating cash flow by reserving funds specifically for future capital projects, such as replacing roofs, elevators, or HVAC systems. Proper reserve planning can prevent operating budgets from being strained by unanticipated large expenses.

Analyze Expense Variances from Prior Years

Reviewing and analyzing expense variances from previous budgets can provide valuable insights into cost patterns and help refine future expense projections. If certain expenses have consistently exceeded budgeted amounts, property managers should adjust the current budget accordingly. Understanding the reasons for past variances—whether due to increased utility usage, rising contractor costs, or higher-than-expected maintenance needs—can improve accuracy in future expense calculations.

4. *Forecast Capital Expenditures, Replacement Reserves, and Depreciation*

   For multifamily properties, significant repairs or replacements are inevitable. Property managers must account for *capital expenditures*, such as roof replacements or major system upgrades, by forecasting these costs over time.

- *Replacement reserves are funds set aside for major repairs or replacements of property components, such as elevators, pools, tennis courts, roofs, plumbing systems, concrete repairs and waterproofing. For multifamily properties, maintaining adequate replacement reserves is essential for avoiding unexpected expenses and ensuring that the property remains in good condition. Property managers should conduct regular assessments to determine reserve adequacy and adjust reserve contributions as necessary.*
- *Depreciation* accounts for the gradual wear and tear of property assets over time. In budgeting, depreciation is used to allocate the cost of capital assets over their useful life. While it is a noncash expense, it must be accounted for in financial statements to provide an accurate picture of the property's value.

This sample budget outlines standard income sources, such as rent and amenities, alongside common operating expenses for a large residential community. The *Net Income* reflects the difference between total income and total operating expenses, which can be allocated to reserves or reinvested in the property. This format ensures clarity and aligns with standard property management financial reporting (Fig. 6.1).

This sample budget reflects typical income sources, such as HOA dues and clubhouse rentals, and common operating expenses for a large community association. *Net Income* shows a minimal surplus, often intentional for community associations, as they operate to maintain community resources rather than generate profit. This structure aligns with HOA and condominium financial best practices, ensuring that reserve funds are adequately funded and operating expenses are fully covered (Figs. 6.2 and 6.3).

5. *Incorporate Increases or Adjustments*

   When developing a budget, it's important to plan for *rent increases* or adjustments based on market trends, inflation, and property improvements. Property managers should analyze the local rental market to determine competitive pricing for the property's units while considering any legal restrictions on rent control. Association property managers should plan for *maintenance assessment increases* or adjustments based on contractual obligations, inflation and property improvements. Predicting these increases helps maintain positive cash flow and ensures that the property remains financially viable over time.
6. *Prepare Cash Flow Statements*

   A *cash flow statement* provides an overview of the inflows and outflows of money for the property over a specific period. This statement tracks revenue from rents, fees, and other income sources, as well as expenses such as payroll, utilities, and repairs. Property managers should ensure that the cash flow projection reflects realistic expectations, accounting for seasonal variations in expenses and rental income. Monitoring cash flow allows managers to address potential cash shortages proactively.
7. *Choose Between Accrual and Cash Accounting*

   Accurate *record-keeping* is essential for managing property finances, ensuring that all transactions are documented and accounted for. Deciding whether to use *accrual* or *cash accounting* is a key decision in managing property budgets.

Category	Item	Projected Annual Amount ($)
Income		
	Rental Income	$1,300,000
	Parking Fees	$50,000
	Amenity Rental (e.g., Party Rooms)	$15,000
	Late Fees	$5,000
	Other Income (e.g., vending, laundry)	$10,000
		$1,380,000
Total Income		
Expenses		
Administrative	Management Fees	$60,000
	Office Supplies	$50,000
	Legal and Professional Services	$10,000
	Insurance	$80,000
	Bad Debt Allowance	$5,000
Utilities	Electricity	$100,000
	Water and Sewer	$75,000
	Gas	$50,000
	Trash Removal	$30,000
	Internet and Cable (Common Areas)	$15,000
Maintenance & Repairs	Routine Maintenance	$120,000
	HVAC Repairs	$20,000
	Elevator Maintenance	$40,000
	Plumbing Repairs	$25,000
	Landscaping	$30,000
	Pool Maintenance	$15,000
	Painting and Exterior Maintenance	$50,000
	Pest Control	$10,000
	Maintenance Personnel	$150,000
Reserves and Capital Projects	Reserve Fund Contribution	$100,000
Amenity Operations	Gym Equipment Repairs	$10,000
	Concierge Services	$40,000
	Security Personnel	$150,000
	Event Hosting	$5,000
Total Expenses		**$1,240,000**
Net Income		**$140,000**

Fig. 6.1 Sample budget for Sunrise Apartment rentals tower

Category	Item	Projected Annual Amount ($)
Income		
	HOA Dues	$1,174,000
	Special Assessments	$50,000
	Clubhouse Rentals	$10,000
	Late Fees	$5,000
	Interest Income	$3,000
		$1,242,000
Total Income		
Expenses		
Administrative	Management Fees	$50,000
	Office Supplies	$50,000
	Legal and Professional Services	$10,000
	Insurance	$80,000
	Bad Debt Allowance	$5,000
	Audit and Tax Prep	$10,000
Utilities	Electricity	$100,000
	Water and Sewer	$75,000
	Gas	$50,000
	Trash Removal	$30,000
	Internet and Cable (Clubhouse)	$15,000
Maintenance & Repairs	Routine Maintenance	$120,000
	HVAC Repairs	$20,000
	Elevator Maintenance	$40,000
	Plumbing Repairs	$25,000
	Landscaping	$30,000
	Pool Maintenance	$15,000
	Painting and Exterior Maintenance	$50,000
	Pest Control	$10,000
	Maintenance Personnel	$150,000
Reserves & Capital Projects	Reserve Fund Contribution	$100,000
Amenity Operations	Gym Equipment Repairs	$10,000
	Concierge Services	$40,000
	Security Personnel	$150,000
	Community Events	$5,000
Total Expenses		**$1,240,000**
Net Income		**$2,000**

Fig. 6.2 Sample budget for Sunrise HOA

1. Reserve Fund Status

As of the end of the fiscal year, the Harmony Condominium has a total of $1,250,000 in reserve funds. Based on the current condition of building components, the projected expenses for the next 30 years, and the estimated costs of future replacements, the reserve fund is currently 75% funded. This indicates a moderately healthy reserve balance but suggests that additional contributions will be necessary to avoid future shortfalls.

Recommended annual contribution increases are detailed in the Reserve Funding Plan Summary to ensure that future repairs and replacements can be funded without significant financial strain on the building's budget.

2. Reserve Component List

The following components have been evaluated based on their estimated useful life, remaining life expectancy, and estimated replacement cost:

Component	Useful Life (Years)	Remaining Life (Years)	Estimated Replacement Cost
Roof Replacement	20	10	$500,000
HVAC System Replacement	25	15	$300,000
Elevator Modernization	30	12	$450,000
Fire Alarm System Upgrade	15	7	$150,000
Exterior Painting	10	5	$100,000
Parking Lot Resurfacing	15	8	$75,000
Pool Mechanical System	12	6	$60,000

3. Reserve Funding Plan Summary

To ensure the Harmony Condominium maintains its reserve fund at an adequate level to cover future repairs and replacements, the following reserve funding plan is recommended:

- **Current Annual Contribution**: $125,000
- **Recommended Increase for Year 1:** 5% increase ($6,250)
- **Recommended Future Increases:** 3% annual increase for the following years

Year	Annual Contribution	Projected Expenses	Reserve Fund Balance
2025	$131,250	$75,000	$1,306,250
2026	$135,188	$0	$1,441,438
2027	$139,244	$100,000	$1,480,682
2028	$143,421	$60,000	$1,564,103
2029	$147,724	$450,000	$1,261,827
2030	$156,622	$0	$1,496,434

Fig. 6.3 Sample reserve study report for the Harmony Condominium

- *Accrual accounting records income and expenses when they are earned or incurred, regardless of when the cash is actually received or paid. This method provides a more comprehensive view of the property's financial position, especially for larger multifamily properties, as it captures outstanding invoices, accrued expenses, and future income.*
- *Cash accounting*, on the other hand, records transactions only when cash changes hands. This method is simpler and often used by smaller properties or individual landlords managing single-family homes. However, it may not provide as detailed a financial picture as accrual accounting.

8. *Monitor and Analyze Variances*

   Throughout the year, property managers should compare actual income and expenses against the budget in a process known as *variance analysis*. This step helps identify discrepancies between budgeted amounts and actual performance, allowing property managers to adjust spending, revise revenue forecasts, or identify inefficiencies. Regular variance analysis is essential for staying on top of financial trends and avoiding significant shortfalls at the end of the year.

9. *Plan for Taxes and Insurance*

   Property taxes and insurance premiums are significant fixed costs that must be incorporated into the budget. Property managers should estimate *property tax* liabilities based on the assessed value of the property and account for any changes due to reassessments or legislative changes. *Insurance costs*, including general liability and property insurance, must also be carefully projected and factored into the annual budget.

10. *Conduct Regular Financial Audits*

    Lastly, conducting *financial audits* ensures that the property's financial practices comply with legal standards and that the budget accurately reflects the property's financial health. Audits provide transparency to stakeholders, such as property owners or board members, and help identify any discrepancies or opportunities for improvement.

6.5.6 Financial Reports

Income Statement: The income statement, or profit and loss statement, summarizes revenue and expenses over a specific period, showing the property's financial health. Key components include:

- *Gross Income: Total income from all sources before expenses.*
- *Operating Expenses:* Costs associated with running the property, such as utilities, maintenance, insurance, and management fees.
- *Net Income:* Profit or loss after all expenses are deducted from gross income.

Balance Sheet: The balance sheet provides a snapshot of the property's financial position at a specific point in time. It lists assets, liabilities, and equity, showing the property's net worth. Key sections include:

- *Assets: Current assets (cash, receivables) and fixed assets (buildings, equipment).*
- *Liabilities:* Short-term liabilities (accounts payable, short-term loans) and long-term liabilities (mortgages, bonds).
- *Equity:* Owner's equity, retained earnings, and other equity accounts.

Cash Flow Statement: The cash flow statement tracks the flow of cash in and out of the property, highlighting operating, investing, and financing activities. It helps managers understand the property's liquidity and cash management. Sections include:

- *Operating Activities: Cash flows from daily operations, such as rent or maintenance assessment collection and payment of operating expenses.*

Account	2025 Actual	2025 Budget
Revenues		
Association Fees	$800,000	$795,000
Special Assessments	$50,000	$50,000
Parking Income	$25,000	$24,000
Rental Income (Clubhouse)	$10,000	$12,000
Late Fees	$5,000	$6,000
Interest Income	$3,000	$2,500
Total Revenues		
Expenses		
Maintenance & Repairs	$150,000	$145,000
Landscaping	$30,000	$32,000
Utilities	$80,000	$85,000
Security Services	$60,000	$60,000
Insurance	$100,000	$98,000
Property Management Fees	$90,000	$90,000
General Administration	$20,000	$18,000
Reserve Fund Contribution	$125,000	$120,000
Total Expenses	**$655,000**	**$648,000**
Net Income	**$238,000**	**$241,500**

Fig. 6.4 Sample financial report for the Harmony Condominium. (**a**) Income Statement (Year Ending December 31, 2025) (**b**) Balance Sheet (As of December 31, 2025) (**c** and **d**) Cash Flow Statement (Year Ending December 31, 2025)

- *Investing Activities:* Cash flows from the purchase or sale of long-term assets, such as buildings or equipment.
- *Financing Activities:* Cash flows from borrowing or repaying loans, issuing equity, or paying dividends.

Ending Cash Balances

Ending cash balances represent the funds remaining after all income and expenses have been accounted for. Maintaining a healthy ending cash balance ensures that the property has sufficient funds to cover upcoming expenses, manage emergencies, and avoid cash flow shortages.

By applying these budgeting principles and using standard accounting practices, property managers can effectively develop, manage, and monitor budgets, ensuring financial stability and long-term success for both single-family and multifamily properties (Fig. 6.4).

Assets	Amount
Current Assets	
Cash and Cash Equivalents	$150,000
Accounts Receivable	$25,000
Prepaid Expenses	$10,000
Total Current Assets	**$185,000**
Fixed Assets	
Building and Improvements (Net)	$1,200,000
Furniture and Equipment (Net)	$50,000
Total Fixed Assets	**$1,250,000**
Other Assets	
Reserve Fund	$500,000
Total Other Assets	**$500,000**
Total Assets	**$1,935,000**
Liabilities	
Accounts Payable	$20,000
Accrued Expenses	$15,000
Long-Term Loan (Capital Projects)	$150,000
Total Liabilities	**$185,000**
Equity	
Retained Earnings	$1,512,000
Current Year Net Income	$238,000
Total Equity	**$1,750,000**
Total Liabilities and Equity	**$1,935,000**

Fig. 6.4 (continued)

6.5.7 Collections

Rent or Maintenance Fee Collection: Effective rent and maintenance fee collection processes are essential for maintaining cash flow. Property managers should implement clear policies and procedures for collection, including due dates, late fees, and acceptable payment methods. Utilizing property management software can streamline the collection process and automate reminders. Key strategies include:

- *Automated Payments: Encourage tenants to set up automatic payments through bank transfers or credit cards to ensure timely collection.*
- *Online Portals:* Provide residents with an online portal to view their account balances, make payments, and access important documents.
- *Early Payment Discounts:* Offer discounts for early or on-time payments to incentivize timely collection.

Cash Flows from Operating Activities	**Amount**
Net Income	$238,000
Adj to Reconcile Net Income to Net Cash	
Depreciation	$30,000
Increase in Accounts Receivable	($5,000)
Decrease in Prepaid Expenses	$2,000
Increase in Accounts Payable	$3,000
Increase in Accrued Expenses	$1,000
Net Cash Provided by Operating Activities	**$269,000**
Cash Flows from Investing Activities	
Purchase of Furniture and Equipment	($15,000)
Contribution to Reserve Fund	($125,000)
Net Cash Used in Investing Activities	**($140,000)**
Cash Flows from Financing Activities	
Loan Repayment (Capital Projects)	($50,000)
Net Cash Used in Financing Activities	**($50,000)**
Net Increase in Cash and Cash Equivalents	**$79,000**
Cash and Cash Equivalents at Beginning of Year	$71,000
Cash and Cash Equivalents at End of Year	**$150,000**

Fig. 6.4 (continued)

Delinquency Management: Managing delinquent accounts involves consistent follow-up with tenants who have missed payments. Property managers should establish a process for sending late notices, negotiating payment plans, and taking further action if necessary. Key steps include:

- *Late Notices: Send timely reminders and late notices to tenants who miss payment deadlines, clearly outlining late fees and consequences.*
- *Payment Plans:* Work with tenants to create manageable payment plans that help them catch up on overdue rent while maintaining cash flow.
- *Legal Action:* When necessary, take legal action to recover unpaid rent, including eviction proceedings. Ensure compliance with local laws and regulations throughout the process.

Resident Communication: Clear and consistent communication with residents about collection policies, due dates, and consequences of late payments is essential. Providing multiple communication channels, such as email, phone, and in-person meetings, helps ensure residents are informed and can address any issues promptly.

6.5.8 Liens

Understanding Liens: A lien is a legal claim against a property for unpaid debts. Property managers should be aware of different types of liens, including:

- *Mechanic's Liens: Filed by contractors or suppliers for unpaid work or materials.*
- *Tax Liens:* Placed by government authorities for unpaid property taxes.
- *Judgment Liens:* Resulting from legal judgments against the property owner for unpaid debts.

Managing Liens: To manage liens, property managers must ensure that all debts are paid on time and keep accurate records of payments. In cases where a lien is placed on the property, prompt resolution is necessary to avoid legal complications and potential foreclosure. Key strategies include:

- *Regular Payments: Ensure timely payment of all bills, including property taxes, contractor invoices, and other obligations.*
- *Record Keeping:* Maintain detailed records of all financial transactions, payments, and communications related to liens.
- *Legal Assistance:* Consult with legal professionals to resolve lien issues, negotiate settlements, and ensure compliance with relevant laws and regulations.

Preventive Measures: Implementing preventive measures can help avoid liens and protect the property's financial health. These measures include:

- *Vendor Management: Establish clear contracts with vendors and contractors, outlining payment terms, work scope, and dispute resolution procedures.*
- *Insurance Coverage:* Maintain adequate insurance coverage to protect against potential liabilities, including property damage, legal claims, and unpaid debts.

Community Associations and Judgment Liens: Community associations, such as homeowners associations (HOAs) and condominium associations, often use judgment liens as a collections enforcement mechanism against delinquent property owners. When property owners fail to pay their dues, assessments, or fines, the association may file a lawsuit to obtain a judgment. If successful, the judgment can be used to place a lien on the property. Here's how the process works and its implications:

1. *Assessment of Dues:*
    - *Community associations typically levy dues and assessments to cover the cost of maintaining common areas, amenities, and other shared services. These fees are crucial for the association's financial health and the overall upkeep of the community.*

2. *Initial Collection Efforts:*
   - *When property owners fail to pay their dues, the association will usually begin with initial collection efforts, such as sending late notices and reminders. These communications should outline the outstanding balance, late fees, and potential consequences of nonpayment.*
3. *Legal Action and Obtaining a Judgment:*
   - *If initial collection efforts are unsuccessful, the association may file a lawsuit against the delinquent property owner in small claims court or another appropriate legal venue. The goal is to obtain a judgment for the unpaid amount, including dues, assessments, late fees, interest, and legal costs.*
   - Once the association obtains a judgment, it has the legal right to place a lien on the property. The lien must be recorded with the local county recorder or land records office to be enforceable.
4. *Impact of Judgment Liens:*
   - *Judgment liens can significantly impact the delinquent property owner's ability to sell or refinance the property, as the lien must be satisfied before the title can be transferred. This often motivates property owners to settle their debts.*
   - Additionally, judgment liens accrue interest, increasing the total amount owed over time. This can further incentivize property owners to pay off the debt promptly.
5. *Foreclosure Proceedings:*
   - *In some cases, if the debt remains unpaid, the community association may pursue foreclosure proceedings to recover the owed amount. This is typically a last resort due to the complexity and costs involved. However, it can be an effective method for ensuring compliance and maintaining the association's financial stability.*
   - Foreclosure laws vary by state, and associations must follow specific legal procedures to initiate and complete the foreclosure process. Consulting with legal professionals is essential to navigate these proceedings correctly.
6. *Protecting the Association's Interests:*
   - *To protect its financial interests and maintain the community, the association should adopt clear policies for handling delinquencies. This includes setting due dates, outlining late fees, and detailing the steps for collection and legal action.*
   - Transparent communication with all property owners about these policies and the importance of timely payments can help prevent delinquencies and ensure smooth operations.
7. *Legal and Ethical Considerations:*
   - *While judgment liens are a powerful tool for community associations, they must be used judiciously and ethically. Associations should ensure that all actions comply with state laws, governing documents, and fair debt collection practices.*

- Providing delinquent property owners with opportunities to negotiate payment plans or dispute the debt can help maintain goodwill and foster a cooperative community environment.

Effective Communication and Record Keeping:

- *Clear communication with property owners about dues, assessments, and the consequences of nonpayment is crucial. Associations should provide regular statements and updates, making it easy for owners to understand their financial obligations.*
- Keeping meticulous records of all communications, payments, and legal actions ensures transparency and supports the association's position in any legal disputes.

Working with Legal Professionals:

- *Community associations should work closely with legal professionals to navigate the complexities of judgment liens and foreclosure proceedings. Legal counsel can provide guidance on state laws, procedural requirements, and best practices for enforcing liens while minimizing legal risks.*

Judgment liens are a vital tool for community associations to enforce collections and maintain financial health. By understanding the process, implementing clear policies, and working with legal professionals, associations can effectively manage delinquent accounts and ensure the stability and well-being of the community.

6.5.9 Foreclosures and Bankruptcy

Foreclosures: Foreclosure is the legal process by which a lender takes control of a property due to unpaid mortgage debt. Property managers need to understand the foreclosure process and the implications for property management. Working closely with legal professionals is crucial in these situations. Key steps include:

- *Understanding the Process: Familiarize yourself with the foreclosure laws and procedures in your jurisdiction, including timelines, notices, and rights of the property owner and tenants.*
- *Communication with Lenders:* Maintain open communication with lenders to stay informed about the property's financial status and any potential foreclosure actions.
- *Tenant Rights:* Educate tenants about their rights during foreclosure, including their right to remain in the property until the foreclosure process is complete.

Bankruptcy: Bankruptcy can affect property management in various ways, depending on whether it's the tenant or the property owner filing. Understanding the different types of bankruptcy (Chaps. 7, 11, and 13) and their impact on lease agreements and rent collection is essential for property managers. Key considerations include:

- *Automatic Stay: Understand the automatic stay provision, which temporarily halts collection efforts, evictions, and legal actions once bankruptcy is filed.*
- *Proof of Claim:* File a proof of claim in bankruptcy court to secure the property's rights to unpaid rent or other debts.
- *Lease Termination:* Evaluate the impact of bankruptcy on existing lease agreements and determine whether leases can be terminated or modified.

Mitigation Strategies: Implementing mitigation strategies can help manage the financial impact of foreclosures and bankruptcies. These strategies include:

- *Diversifying Revenue Streams: Explore additional revenue sources, such as short-term rentals, parking fees, or ancillary services, to reduce dependence on a single income stream.*
- *Risk Assessment:* Conduct regular risk assessments to identify potential financial risks and develop contingency plans to address them.

6.5.10 Audits and Taxes

Conducting Audits: Regular financial audits ensure the accuracy and integrity of the property's financial records. Audits can be internal, conducted by the property management team, or external, conducted by an independent auditor. If hiring an independent auditor, property managers should make sure they are hiring one that has prior experience in auditing their type of property. Audits help identify discrepancies, improve financial practices, and maintain compliance with regulations. Key steps include:

- *Internal Controls: Establish robust internal controls to prevent fraud, errors, and mismanagement. This includes segregation of duties, approval processes, and regular reconciliations.*
- *Documentation:* Maintain comprehensive documentation of all financial transactions, contracts, and communications to support audit activities.
- *Audit Process:* Follow a structured audit process, including planning, fieldwork, reporting, and follow-up on audit findings and recommendations.

Types of Audits: There are different types of audits that property managers may encounter, including:

- *Financial Audits: Focus on the accuracy and completeness of financial statements, ensuring they fairly represent the property's financial position.*
- *Compliance Audits:* Assess compliance with laws, regulations, and internal policies, identifying areas of noncompliance and recommending corrective actions.
- *Operational Audits:* Evaluate the efficiency and effectiveness of property management operations, identifying opportunities for improvement and cost savings.

Tax Compliance: Property managers must ensure compliance with local, state, and federal tax regulations. This includes filing property taxes, income taxes on rental income, and other applicable taxes. Keeping detailed financial records and working with tax professionals can help property managers navigate complex tax requirements and avoid penalties. Key considerations include:

- *Property Taxes: Ensure timely payment of property taxes to avoid liens, penalties, and interest charges. Keep track of assessment schedules and appeal any incorrect valuations.*
- *Income Taxes:* Accurately report rental income and deductible expenses on income tax returns. Understand tax implications of different types of income, such as short-term rentals or commercial leases.
- *Sales and Use Taxes:* Comply with sales and use tax regulations for goods and services purchased for the property, including materials, equipment, and maintenance services.

Tax Planning: Effective tax planning can help property managers minimize tax liabilities and optimize financial performance. Key strategies include:

- *Depreciation Deductions: Take advantage of depreciation deductions for buildings, equipment, and other assets to reduce taxable income.*
- *Tax Credits:* Explore available tax credits, such as energy efficiency credits, historic preservation credits, or low-income housing credits.
- *Entity Structure:* Evaluate the benefits of different legal entities, such as partnerships, LLCs, or corporations, to optimize tax treatment and liability protection.

Record Keeping: Maintaining accurate and organized financial records is essential for tax compliance and audit readiness. Key practices include:

- *Document Retention: Retain financial records, tax returns, and supporting documents for the required retention period, typically 7 years.*
- *Digital Records:* Use digital record-keeping systems to store and organize financial documents, making it easier to retrieve and review records during audits or tax preparation.

- *Reconciliation:* Regularly reconcile bank accounts, credit card statements, and other financial records to ensure accuracy and identify discrepancies promptly.

By understanding these key aspects of property management accounting and financial reporting, property managers can effectively oversee the financial health of their properties, ensure compliance with legal requirements, and make informed decisions that enhance property performance and profitability. Regular financial monitoring, accurate record-keeping, and proactive management strategies are essential components of a successful property management operation.

6.6 Establishing and Managing a Property Management Office

Establishing and managing a property management office is a cornerstone of an efficient and successful property management operation. Whether for an on-site office serving a single property or a corporate office overseeing multiple properties, a well-organized and properly staffed office ensures smooth day-to-day operations, effective communication, and compliance with regulatory requirements. This chapter explores the elements and staffing needs of a property management office, addressing considerations for office location, design, organization, equipment, and licensing requirements. It also distinguishes between the unique requirements of on-site property management offices and main corporate offices.

6.6.1 Office Location

The location of a property management office plays a crucial role in its functionality and accessibility. The choice of location depends largely on the scope of the property management operation:

- *On-Site Property Management Office: Typically located within the property itself, such as in a clubhouse, lobby, or dedicated office space, on-site offices are convenient for residents and staff. These offices are ideal for handling daily property operations, tenant concerns, and maintenance coordination. Accessibility to tenants and visibility within the community are primary considerations when choosing the location for an on-site office.*
- *Corporate Property Management Office:* Corporate offices serve as the central hub for overseeing multiple properties and managing broader administrative tasks, such as marketing, accounting, and compliance. These offices are usually located in commercial office spaces within city centers or business districts to facilitate professional networking and client meetings.

For both types of offices, ample parking, accessibility for individuals with disabilities, and proximity to key services (e.g., courthouses, banks, or contractors) should be factored into the location decision.

6.6.2 Office Design

Office design directly impacts workflow, employee productivity, and resident engagement. A well-designed property management office should balance functionality, aesthetics, and comfort while addressing the specific needs of its operations.

- *Layout: The layout should include dedicated spaces for administrative work, private meetings, and public interactions. For example, an on-site office might require a reception area for residents and a private office for lease signings or sensitive discussions, while a corporate office might need multiple conference rooms for staff meetings and client presentations.*
- *Ergonomics:* Providing ergonomic office furniture, such as adjustable chairs and desks, enhances employee comfort and productivity. Proper lighting and ventilation are also critical to maintaining a comfortable working environment.
- *Security:* Offices should be equipped with secure entry systems, including keycards or coded access, to protect sensitive information and property. For on-site offices, secure storage for resident records, lease agreements, and financial documents is essential.

Organization and Filing Systems

Proper organization is key to running an efficient property management office. Effective filing systems, both physical and digital, ensure that records are easily accessible and securely stored.

- *Physical Filing Systems: Physical files should be categorized and labeled systematically, with separate sections for leases, maintenance records, vendor contracts, and financial documents. Fireproof filing cabinets and locked storage are recommended to protect sensitive information.*
- *Digital Filing Systems:* In the digital age, most property management offices rely on cloud-based filing systems that allow for easy access and secure storage. Digital systems should include backups to prevent data loss, and permissions-based access should be implemented to protect confidential information.
- *Compliance with Record-Keeping Requirements:* Property management offices must comply with local, state, and federal regulations regarding document retention. For example, financial records and tenant applications may need to be retained for several years, depending on jurisdiction.

Computers and Software

Technology plays a central role in modern property management. The choice of hardware and software should align with the office's operational needs.

- *Hardware: Offices should be equipped with reliable computers, printers, and scanners. For larger operations, servers or high-capacity storage devices may be necessary. On-site offices might also require tablets or mobile devices for maintenance staff to access work orders remotely.*
- *Property Management Software:* Specialized property management software, such as AppFolio, Yardi, or Buildium, streamlines operations by integrating lease management, accounting, maintenance tracking, and communication into a single platform. Software selection should consider the size of the portfolio, the complexity of operations, and budget constraints.
- *Customer Relationship Management (CRM) Tools:* CRM tools help property managers maintain detailed records of tenant interactions, track inquiries, and manage leads for vacancies. This is particularly useful in corporate offices overseeing multiple properties.

6.6.3 Staffing Requirements

The staffing needs of a property management office depend on the size of the operation and the scope of responsibilities.

- *On-Site Property Management Office Staffing:*
  - *Property Manager:* Oversees daily operations, handles resident concerns, and coordinates maintenance.
  - *Leasing Agent:* Manages the leasing process, including marketing, showings, and resident/tenant screening.
  - *Maintenance Supervisor:* Handles work orders and schedules maintenance staff or vendors.
  - *Receptionist or Administrative Assistant:* Provides front-desk support, answers inquiries, and handles documentation.
- *Corporate Property Management Office Staffing:*
  - *Regional Property Manager:* Supervises on-site managers and ensures consistency across properties.
  - *Accountant or Bookkeeper:* Manages financial reporting, accounts receivable/payable, and budgeting.
  - *Marketing Specialist:* Develops marketing campaigns and oversees advertising for vacancies.
  - *Human Resources Manager:* Handles hiring, training, and compliance with labor laws.

6.6.4 Licensing Requirements

Licensing requirements play a critical role in ensuring that property managers and their offices operate legally and professionally. State real estate regulatory agencies often mandate that individuals performing specific property management activities hold a real estate or community association manager license. These requirements are designed to protect clients and residents by ensuring that property managers possess the necessary knowledge and skills to handle their responsibilities effectively.

Real Estate Licensing Requirements

For general property management activities, a real estate license is typically required when individuals are performing tasks related to leasing or property transactions. Tasks that may require real estate licensing include:

- *Drafting and Negotiating Leases: Individuals involved in preparing or negotiating lease agreements for tenants and landlords often need a real estate license.*
- *Collecting Rents and Security Deposits:* Accepting and processing payments on behalf of property owners typically falls under activities requiring licensure.
- *Marketing Rental Properties:* Advertising vacancies, conducting property showings, and interacting with potential tenants may require a license.
- *Facilitating Tenant and Landlord Agreements:* Acting as an intermediary to resolve lease-related disputes or finalize agreements often requires a licensed professional.

Community Association Manager Licensing Requirements

For offices managing condominiums, cooperatives, HOAs, timeshares, or mobile home communities, a community association manager (CAM) license may be required. This licensing ensures that individuals managing the operational and financial aspects of these communities are adequately trained. Tasks that may require CAM licensing include:

- *Controlling or Disbursing Funds: Managers who handle the association's financial transactions must often hold a CAM license.*
- *Preparing Budgets or Financial Documents:* Drafting financial reports, reserve studies, or annual budgets requires licensure.
- *Assisting with Meetings:* Helping to notice or conduct board or community association meetings may necessitate a CAM license.
- *Coordinating Maintenance:* Overseeing contractors or scheduling repairs for community association facilities is typically regulated.

6.7 Human Resources Management

6.7.1 Components of Human Resource Management

Human resource management in the property management industry requires a strategic approach to address the unique demands of managing a diverse workforce, including office staff, maintenance personnel, leasing agents, and on-site managers. Effective human resource management not only helps in attracting and retaining skilled employees but also ensures compliance with labor laws and creates a safe, productive work environment. Below are the core components of human resource management in the property management industry.

Recruitment and Hiring

Recruitment in the property management industry involves attracting qualified candidates for various roles, from administrative positions to maintenance technicians. Given the diverse skill sets needed, property managers must use targeted recruitment strategies such as specialized job boards, industry associations, and networking events to identify talent. During the hiring process, it is crucial to conduct thorough background checks, reference verifications, and skill assessments to ensure candidates meet the professional and safety standards required for the role. Effective recruitment reduces turnover and ensures that the property has capable staff to handle day-to-day operations.

Training and Development

Training and development are vital for equipping employees with the skills they need to excel in their roles. This includes onboarding new hires with orientation programs that cover company policies, property management software, and safety protocols. Ongoing training should address industry-specific topics such as fair housing compliance, customer service, hospitality training and conflict resolution. Development programs for management-level staff might include leadership training, project management, and strategic planning. Investing in employee development improves job satisfaction and prepares staff for advancement within the organization.

Employee Safety Training

Employee safety training is a top priority, particularly for maintenance staff and on-site property managers who may face physical risks. Safety training should include topics such as proper use of equipment, hazard communication, emergency procedures, and personal protective equipment (PPE) usage. Regular safety audits and refresher courses ensure that safety protocols are followed and reduce the risk of workplace accidents.

Performance Management

Performance management involves setting clear expectations, regularly assessing employee performance, and providing constructive feedback. Property managers should implement formal evaluation processes that include performance reviews, goal-setting sessions, and progress tracking. Regular feedback helps employees understand their strengths and areas for improvement, ensuring alignment with organizational goals. In the property management industry, where staff often work independently, effective performance management is crucial for maintaining accountability and high standards of service.

Compensation and Benefits

Compensation and benefits must be competitive to attract and retain talent in the property management industry. Compensation packages should be aligned with industry standards and consider factors such as experience, certifications, and geographic location. In addition to base pay, property managers should offer benefits such as health insurance, retirement plans, and paid time off. Nonmonetary benefits, such as flexible work schedules, professional development opportunities, and performance bonuses, can also enhance job satisfaction.

Employee Relations

Maintaining positive employee relations is essential for fostering a collaborative and motivated workforce. Property managers should promote an inclusive and respectful work environment through open communication, conflict resolution, and employee engagement initiatives. Regular check-ins, team-building activities, and recognition programs contribute to a positive organizational culture and reduce the risk of turnover. In the property management context, strong employee relations translate into better resident/owner interactions and improved property performance.

Compliance with Labor Laws

Compliance with labor laws is critical to minimizing legal risks and maintaining a fair workplace. Property managers must be knowledgeable about federal and state employment regulations, such as the Fair Labor Standards Act (FLSA), Occupational Safety and Health Administration (OSHA) requirements, and antidiscrimination laws. Staying up-to-date with changes in labor regulations and incorporating them into HR policies and procedures is essential for preventing costly legal issues.

By focusing on these core components, property managers can create an effective human resource management strategy that enhances employee performance, ensures legal compliance, and supports the overall success of the property management organization.

Employee Handbook

An employee handbook in the property management industry serves as a comprehensive guide for staff, outlining company policies, workplace expectations, and procedures specific to the industry. Given the diverse roles involved—ranging from leasing agents and property managers to maintenance personnel—the handbook must provide clear guidance on operational standards, legal compliance, and safety protocols. Below is an outline tailored to the unique needs of property management companies, covering essential sections for effective employee orientation and ongoing management.

1. *Introduction and Welcome Statement*
   - *Purpose: This section introduces the company's mission, values, and culture. It sets the tone for what employees can expect and how they contribute to the organization's success.*
   - *Content:*
     - Brief company history and overview.
     - Statement of the company's commitment to providing quality property management services.
     - Welcome message from senior leadership.
2. *Employment Policies*
   - *Purpose: Defines the employment relationship, including the organization's policies on hiring, classification, and equal opportunity employment.*
   - *Content:*
     - Employment classification (full-time, part-time, temporary).
     - Equal Employment Opportunity (EEO) statement.
     - Anti-discrimination and harassment policies.
     - Job descriptions and expectations.
3. *Workplace Conduct*
   - *Purpose: Outlines expected behaviors, professional conduct, and ethics to ensure a respectful and productive work environment.*
   - *Content:*
     - Dress code and grooming standards, especially for roles involving resident interactions.
     - Code of conduct and anti-harassment policies.
     - Social media and confidentiality guidelines.
4. *Compliance with Industry Regulations*
   - *Purpose: Provides an overview of compliance requirements specific to the property management industry.*
   - *Content:*
     - Fair Housing Laws and regulations.
     - Americans with Disabilities Act (ADA) compliance.
     - OSHA standards for safety and hazard communication.
5. *Compensation and Benefits*
   - *Purpose: Details how employees are compensated and what benefits are available.*
   - *Content:*

   - Payroll policies, including pay periods and deductions.
   - Overtime rules and holiday pay.
   - Health insurance, retirement plans, and other benefits.
6. *Leave Policies*
   - *Purpose: Defines the company's policies on time off and leaves of absence.*
   - *Content:*
     - Vacation, personal, and sick leave policies.
     - Family and Medical Leave Act (FMLA) provisions.
     - Bereavement and jury duty leave.
7. *Performance and Development*
   - *Purpose: Explains the processes for performance evaluation, career development, and training.*
   - *Content:*
     - Annual performance review procedures.
     - Professional development opportunities.
     - Skill-building programs specific to property management, such as resident relations and conflict resolution.
8. *Workplace Safety*
   - *Purpose: Ensures that all employees are aware of safety protocols to prevent accidents and injuries.*
   - *Content:*
     - Emergency procedures (e.g., fire, natural disaster).
     - Personal Protective Equipment (PPE) requirements.
     - Reporting safety concerns and incidents.
9. *Disciplinary Actions*
   - *Purpose: Outlines the steps taken when an employee violates company policies or fails to meet performance standards.*
   - *Content:*
     - Progressive discipline process (verbal warnings, written warnings, suspension).
     - Grounds for immediate termination.
     - Appeal and grievance procedures.
10. *Termination and Exit Procedures*
    - *Purpose: Provides clear guidelines for voluntary and involuntary terminations.*
    - *Content:*
      - Notice period for resignation.
      - Final pay and benefits handling.
      - Exit interviews and return of company property.
11. *Employee Acknowledgment*
    - *Purpose: Confirms that the employee has read, understood, and agreed to comply with the handbook.*
    - *Content:*
      - Signature page for employee acknowledgment.
      - Space for questions and clarifications.

By incorporating these elements, the employee handbook serves as a key resource for setting expectations, promoting a positive work culture, and ensuring compliance with industry-specific regulations. A well-structured handbook enhances organizational efficiency and helps minimize risks associated with employment practices in property management.

6.7.2 Importance of a Job Description

A well-defined job description is a crucial tool in the property management industry, serving multiple purposes that go beyond simply listing duties and responsibilities. Property management encompasses a diverse range of roles, from on-site managers and leasing agents to maintenance personnel and administrative staff. Each position requires specific skills, competencies, and expectations that must be clearly communicated to ensure operational efficiency. A comprehensive job description not only helps clarify expectations for employees but also supports effective recruitment, selection, and performance management. Below are the key benefits of a detailed job description specific to property management.

Clarifying Expectations

A job description is fundamental in setting clear expectations for each role within a property management organization. It outlines the scope of responsibilities, reporting relationships, and essential duties required for successful job performance. For example, a property manager's job description should specify tasks such as budget management, resident relations, and oversight of maintenance activities, while a leasing agent's description might focus on marketing vacant units and conducting property tours. By defining these roles precisely, job descriptions minimize ambiguity, reduce the risk of role overlap, and ensure that each team member understands their individual contributions to the organization's overall success.

Recruitment and Selection

Job descriptions are indispensable during the recruitment and selection process, as they provide a clear picture of what the organization is looking for in a candidate. A well-crafted job description should include key qualifications, such as required certifications (e.g., CAM or CPM designations), relevant experience in property management, and specific skills like conflict resolution or knowledge of property management software. This information helps attract qualified candidates and allows hiring managers to assess applicants based on predetermined criteria. For instance, a job description for a maintenance technician might specify HVAC certification or experience in multifamily property maintenance, ensuring that only suitable candidates apply.

Performance Evaluation

Job descriptions play an essential role in performance evaluations by serving as a benchmark against which employee performance can be measured. During evaluations, property managers can refer to the job description to assess whether employees are meeting the outlined expectations and responsibilities. If a leasing agent is expected to maintain a certain occupancy rate or a property manager is responsible for staying within budgetary limits, these criteria can be used to set performance goals and provide constructive feedback. When used effectively, job descriptions help identify areas for improvement, support employee development, and facilitate fair and objective performance appraisals.

By clearly defining roles, supporting effective hiring, and providing a framework for performance management, job descriptions in the property management industry are indispensable tools for building a skilled and efficient workforce. A well-defined job description contributes to the overall success of the organization by aligning employee performance with business objectives and industry standards.

6.7.3 Government Agencies & Laws Related to Human Resources

In the United States, labor regulations governing employees, contractors, and volunteers are enforced by a variety of federal, state, and local agencies. These agencies are responsible for upholding laws designed to protect workers' rights, ensure fair pay, promote workplace safety, and prevent discrimination. Property management organizations must be familiar with these agencies and the laws they enforce to ensure compliance, avoid legal penalties, and maintain ethical labor practices. Below is an overview of the primary federal, state, and local agencies and laws that affect human resource management in the property management industry.

Federal Agencies and Laws

1. *U.S. Department of Labor (DOL):* (http://www.dol.gov)
   - *The Department of Labor enforces a wide range of laws governing workplace practices. It is responsible for ensuring that workers receive fair wages, work under safe conditions, and are treated equitably.*
   - Key laws enforced by the DOL include:
     - *Fair Labor Standards Act (FLSA):* This law establishes minimum wage, overtime pay, record-keeping, and child labor standards for employees in both the private and public sectors.
     - *Family and Medical Leave Act (FMLA):* This law provides eligible employees with up to 12 weeks of unpaid, job-protected leave per year for specific family and medical reasons.

2. *Equal Employment Opportunity Commission (EEOC):* (http://www.eeoc.gov)
   - *The EEOC enforces laws prohibiting workplace discrimination based on race, color, religion, sex, national origin, age, disability, or genetic information.*
   - Key laws enforced by the EEOC include:
     - *Title VII of the Civil Rights Act of 1964:* This law prohibits employment discrimination based on race, color, religion, sex, or national origin.
     - *Americans with Disabilities Act (ADA):* This law prohibits discrimination against individuals with disabilities and requires employers to provide reasonable accommodations.
     - *Age Discrimination in Employment Act (ADEA):* This law protects employees and job applicants who are 40 years of age or older from discrimination based on age.
3. *Occupational Safety and Health Administration (OSHA):* (http://www.osha.gov)
   - *OSHA, a branch of the DOL, is responsible for ensuring safe and healthy working conditions by setting and enforcing safety standards and providing workplace safety training.*
   - Property management organizations must comply with OSHA standards, particularly in roles involving maintenance and construction, where physical risks are higher.

4. *Internal Revenue Service (IRS):* (http://www.irs.gov)
   - *The IRS oversees tax compliance, including the classification of workers as employees or independent contractors.*
   - Employers must follow IRS guidelines to ensure proper tax withholding, reporting, and compliance with benefits-related regulations.

State and Local Agencies and Laws

1. *State Departments of Labor:*
   - *Most states have their own Department of Labor that enforces additional labor laws, such as state minimum wage laws, overtime regulations, and unemployment insurance.*
   - States may also enforce labor laws that offer greater protections than federal standards. For instance, California and New York have stricter wage and hour laws, providing higher minimum wages and greater protections for workers.
2. *State Occupational Safety and Health Agencies:*
   - *Some states, like California (Cal/OSHA), have their own occupational safety and health programs that operate alongside federal OSHA. These state programs may impose stricter safety regulations, especially in high-risk industries such as construction and property maintenance.*
3. *State and Local Human Rights Commissions:*
   - *Many states and cities have human rights or civil rights commissions that enforce local anti-discrimination laws in employment. These commissions*

often provide additional protections beyond federal laws, such as protections based on sexual orientation or gender identity.
- Local laws may also regulate paid sick leave, family leave, and other benefits not covered under federal law.

6.7.4 Understanding the Difference Between Contract, Salaried, and Hourly Employees

In the property management industry, understanding the distinction between contract, salaried, and hourly employees is crucial for compliance with labor laws, proper employee classification, and effective workforce management. Each type of employment comes with unique responsibilities, compensation structures, and legal obligations, which property management organizations must navigate to ensure a productive and compliant work environment. Below is a breakdown of the differences between these employee types as they pertain to the property management sector.

Contract Employees

Contract employees, also known as independent contractors, are typically hired for specific tasks or projects, such as building maintenance, landscaping, or specialized repairs like plumbing or electrical work. They are not considered employees of the property management firm, which means the company does not withhold taxes, provide benefits, or guarantee ongoing work.

- *Key Characteristics:*
  - Contractors usually work on a project basis and are paid according to the terms outlined in their contracts.
  - They operate independently, often using their own equipment, setting their own schedules, and working for multiple clients.
  - Common roles for contract employees in property management include third-party maintenance providers, construction specialists, and security personnel.
- *Benefits and Challenges:*
  - *Benefits:* Flexibility and reduced administrative burden, as the company is not responsible for employee benefits, taxes, or long-term commitments.
  - *Challenges:* Misclassifying a contractor as an employee can lead to legal penalties. Clear contracts must outline the scope of work, compensation, and timelines.

Salaried Employees

Salaried employees in property management are typically full-time staff with consistent pay, regardless of the number of hours worked each week. These employees are often exempt from overtime pay, meaning they receive a fixed annual salary for completing their duties. Property managers, leasing agents, and administrative staff are commonly salaried positions.

- *Key Characteristics:*
  - Salaried employees are generally responsible for core operational tasks, such as overseeing tenant relations, managing property budgets, or supervising maintenance teams.
  - They often hold managerial or administrative positions where they are expected to fulfill job responsibilities beyond a fixed schedule.
- *Benefits and Challenges:*
  - *Benefits:* Salaried employees provide stability and continuity, often holding leadership roles that drive long-term business objectives.
  - *Challenges:* Because they are exempt from overtime, employers must carefully manage workloads to prevent burnout.

Hourly Employees

Hourly employees in the property management industry are typically nonexempt workers who are paid based on the number of hours worked. They are entitled to overtime pay, usually at one-and-a-half times their regular rate, for any hours worked beyond the standard 40-hour workweek. Maintenance workers, janitorial staff, and part-time leasing agents often fall into this category.

- *Key Characteristics:*
  - Hourly employees are paid for each hour worked and are subject to time-tracking to ensure compliance with wage and hour laws.
  - Their roles often involve direct labor or customer service, such as handling repair requests or assisting residents during designated shifts.
- *Benefits and Challenges:*
  - *Benefits:* Flexibility in scheduling, particularly for part-time or seasonal workers, and cost savings if work demand fluctuates.
  - *Challenges:* Employers must adhere to wage and hour laws, including proper overtime compensation, and maintain accurate records of hours worked.

By understanding the specific distinctions between contract, salaried, and hourly employees, property management organizations can better manage their workforce, ensure compliance with labor regulations, and create clear expectations for each employee type. This knowledge also helps optimize labor costs while maintaining service quality.

6.7.5 Hiring, Training, Supervising, and Terminating Employees

Effective human resource management is crucial for ensuring that all staff, from maintenance personnel to leasing agents and property managers, are well-trained, compliant with industry standards, and capable of meeting the demands of managing residential properties. This section provides an overview of the critical components involved in hiring, recruiting, screening and selection, preventing discrimination and harassment, employee training, supervision, and the termination process.

Recruiting, Screening, & Selection

The hiring and recruitment process begins with identifying the skills and qualifications required for each position, from property managers and leasing agents to maintenance technicians. Recruiting can be done through industry job boards, networking events, and referrals from within the industry. When advertising job openings, property management companies must ensure job descriptions are clear and compliant with equal opportunity employment regulations.

- *Screening & Selection: During the screening process, background checks, reference verifications, and interviews are essential to ensure candidates meet the necessary qualifications and fit the company culture. For example, maintenance personnel may need specific certifications, such as HVAC or electrical skills, while property managers should be familiar with local and state landlord-tenant laws. The selection process must also follow federal and state regulations to prevent discrimination based on race, gender, religion, disability, or other protected classes.*

Discrimination & Harassment Prevention

The property management industry is subject to strict regulations related to discrimination and harassment, especially when dealing with diverse populations of residents and employees. Employers must establish a zero-tolerance policy toward harassment and discrimination in the workplace. This includes educating employees on their rights and responsibilities under the *Equal Employment Opportunity (EEO)* laws and the *Fair Housing Act*, which ensures that both employees and residents are treated fairly regardless of their background. Ensuring a safe and respectful working environment helps to avoid costly lawsuits and creates a positive work culture.

Training

Training is an ongoing process that is vital for both compliance and operational success in property management. Effective training programs should be tailored to the specific needs of the industry, including:

- *Fair Housing Laws: Employees, especially leasing agents and property managers, must be thoroughly trained on fair housing laws to avoid discriminatory practices in tenant/resident selection and interactions. This training should include real-world scenarios to help employees recognize and prevent unintentional discrimination.*
- *Maintenance Protocols:* Maintenance staff should be trained on industry-standard maintenance protocols, including equipment handling, repairs, and pre-

ventative maintenance procedures. Property management companies must also ensure that maintenance workers have the necessary certifications for tasks such as plumbing, electrical work, and HVAC systems.

- *Occupational Safety:* Training on occupational safety is essential, particularly for employees involved in physical tasks, such as maintenance staff and on-site managers. Compliance with *OSHA (Occupational Safety and Health Administration)* regulations is critical to maintaining a safe working environment. Employees should be trained in using personal protective equipment (PPE), identifying workplace hazards, and emergency response procedures.

Supervising Employees

Supervision involves not only overseeing daily tasks but also ensuring compliance with legal standards and company policies. Supervisors should maintain open communication with their teams, provide regular feedback, and hold employees accountable for their job performance. In addition, supervising employees requires understanding the specific needs of different roles. For example, maintenance staff need direction on managing work orders, while leasing agents and assistants may need supervision regarding tenant relations and lease compliance.

Terminating Employees

Terminating employees must be done carefully and in compliance with labor laws. Whether due to poor performance, misconduct, or business restructuring, the termination process must follow legal guidelines to avoid wrongful termination claims. A structured approach to termination involves documenting performance issues, offering opportunities for improvement, and providing severance packages when appropriate. When terminating employees, it is also critical to conduct exit interviews to gather feedback and ensure the return of any company property.

6.7.6 Employee Performance Evaluations and Disciplinary Processes

Performance evaluations and disciplinary processes are essential components of human resource management. These processes help ensure that employees meet the standards of their roles, contribute to the success of the property, and adhere to both legal and company policies. In the property management industry, where employees may handle resident relations, financial management, and maintenance duties, regular evaluations and a clear disciplinary process are critical for maintaining operational efficiency and ensuring high levels of service.

Employee Performance Evaluations

Performance evaluations provide a structured approach to assess an employee's job performance, set goals, and offer feedback. In the property management industry, evaluations must consider the wide range of roles employees may hold, from leasing agents and property managers to maintenance technicians and administrative staff.

- *Frequency and Structure: Regular performance evaluations, typically conducted annually or biannually, offer an opportunity to review the employee's contributions to the organization. In the fast-paced property management environment, midyear reviews or quarterly check-ins may be beneficial to address performance issues promptly.*
- *Key Metrics:* Property management performance evaluations focus on role-specific metrics. For property managers, this could include tenant retention rates, budget management, and compliance with legal regulations. For maintenance staff, key performance indicators (KPIs) may include the timeliness of repairs, adherence to safety protocols, and tenant satisfaction.
- *Goal Setting and Development:* Performance reviews should also focus on goal setting and professional development. For instance, a leasing agent may be encouraged to improve lead-to-lease conversion rates, while a maintenance technician might set goals to gain additional certifications. Regular evaluations help align employee performance with the broader goals of the property.

Disciplinary Process

The disciplinary process is essential to address performance deficiencies, misconduct, or noncompliance with company policies. In property management, where employees often work independently, a well-structured disciplinary process ensures accountability and consistent enforcement of rules.

- *Progressive Discipline: The disciplinary process typically follows a progressive approach, starting with verbal warnings and escalating to written warnings, suspension, or termination if the issue persists. This method allows employees the opportunity to improve while ensuring that serious infractions are addressed promptly.*
- *Documentation:* Proper documentation is critical in the disciplinary process. Every step, from verbal warnings to formal notices, should be documented and stored in the employee's file. This protects the organization from potential legal issues and provides a clear record of the employee's conduct and the steps taken to address problems.
- *Legal Compliance:* Property management companies must ensure that their disciplinary processes comply with federal and state employment laws, such as those enforced by the Equal Employment Opportunity Commission (EEOC). Disciplinary actions should be consistent and nondiscriminatory to avoid any claims of unfair treatment.

By implementing structured performance evaluations and clear disciplinary processes, property management organizations can ensure that employees remain productive, compliant, and aligned with company goals. This approach fosters a culture of accountability while providing employees with the support and feedback they need to succeed.

6.7.7 Managing Workplace Stress

The property management industry is uniquely demanding, with workplace stressors that can test even the most experienced professionals. The daily responsibilities of property managers include handling unexpected maintenance emergencies, meeting tight deadlines for rent and maintenance collections, and navigating complex legal regulations. Adding to these challenges are the need to balance resident satisfaction with the expectations of property owners or boards of directors and managing constant communication demands from residents, contractors, and stakeholders. These stressors are often compounded by long working hours due to the unpredictable nature of the job, leaving property managers vulnerable to burnout if stress is not managed effectively.

Workplace Stressors in Property Management

Property managers face a variety of stressors specific to their field. One common challenge is dealing with difficult residents who may have unrealistic expectations, emotional concerns, or conflicts with neighbors. Addressing these situations diplomatically while adhering to policies can be emotionally draining. Another stressor is the need to respond quickly to emergencies, such as water leaks, heating and cooling failures, or security breaches, which require immediate attention regardless of the time of day.

Tight deadlines, such as collecting rent or completing maintenance tasks, further contribute to the high-pressure environment. Property managers are also expected to maintain compliance with intricate and ever-changing legal and regulatory requirements, which demands both precision and vigilance. Balancing the interests of residents with those of property owners or boards of directors can create tension, especially when financial constraints or competing priorities arise. Finally, the need to remain available for constant communication, whether via phone, email, or in-person meetings, can lead to feelings of being perpetually on call.

Reducing Workplace Stress

To mitigate these stressors, property managers and their employers must adopt proactive strategies for managing workplace stress. Gathering employee feedback is imperative to understanding specific stressors within the workplace. Regular surveys, one-on-one meetings, and open forums allow employees to voice their concerns and suggest improvements. By incorporating this feedback, employers can implement targeted solutions that address the unique challenges faced by their workforce.

Time management is another effective tool for reducing stress, allowing property managers to prioritize tasks, set realistic deadlines, and delegate responsibilities when possible. Employers can support this by providing robust property management software to streamline workflows and automate repetitive tasks, reducing the cognitive load on employees.

Employers must also establish clear boundaries around work hours. While property management often requires after-hours availability, defining designated times for responding to nonemergency issues helps managers maintain a healthier work-life balance. Providing training in conflict resolution and communication skills empowers managers to handle difficult residents and disputes more effectively, reducing emotional strain.

Additionally, employers can leverage resources like the Occupational Safety and Health Administration (OSHA) guidance on workplace stress. According to OSHA's recommendations (https://www.osha.gov/workplace-stress/employer-guidance), stress management can improve morale, increase productivity, reduce workplace injuries, and lower turnover. Incorporating OSHA's best practices—such as ensuring employees have access to mental health support, creating flexible work policies, and offering stress management workshops—can significantly reduce workplace stress in property management.

Benefits of Reducing Workplace Stress

Reducing workplace stress offers numerous benefits for both employees and employers. For employees, lower stress levels can lead to improved physical health, including lower blood pressure, a stronger immune system, and reduced risk of chronic conditions. Employees who feel supported and less stressed are also less likely to experience burnout, leading to fewer sick days and reduced turnover.

For employers, the benefits of addressing workplace stress are equally significant. Employees with better morale are typically more productive and focused, which can directly impact the efficiency and profitability of operations. Additionally, a supportive work environment can lead to fewer workplace injuries, as employees are less likely to make errors when they are not overwhelmed. Retaining skilled property managers by fostering a less stressful workplace reduces recruitment and training costs, contributing to overall organizational stability.

6.8 Insurance for Different Types of Residential Properties

6.8.1 Understanding Property Insurance

Types of Insurance

Different types of residential properties require specific insurance coverages. Common types include property insurance, liability insurance, and renter's insurance. Property insurance covers physical damage to the property, while liability insurance protects against legal claims from third parties.

Coverage for Single-Family Homes

Insurance for single-family homes typically includes coverage for the structure, personal property, liability, and additional living expenses. Homeowners may also consider add-ons like flood insurance or earthquake insurance, depending on the location.

Insurance for Multifamily Residences

Comprehensive Coverage

Multifamily residences demand comprehensive insurance policies that account for the property's structural elements, common areas, and operational risks. For apartment complexes, this typically includes property insurance to cover damage to buildings, such as roofs, walls, and shared facilities like gyms or swimming pools. Liability insurance is equally important, offering protection against claims resulting from accidents or injuries occurring on the property. Additionally, loss of rental income insurance can safeguard property owners' revenue streams in the event that units become uninhabitable due to covered perils like fire or flooding.

In the case of condominiums, insurance coverage is more complex due to the division of ownership between the condominium association and individual unit owners. Condominium associations are generally required to maintain a master policy, which provides coverage for common areas, shared structural elements, and the building's exterior. The master policy may also extend to the interiors of units up to a specified point, often referred to as "walls-in" coverage. However, unit owners are responsible for obtaining separate individual condominium unit insurance policies (commonly referred to as HO-6 policies) to cover the contents of their units, personal belongings, and improvements made to the unit. Property managers should ensure that unit owners are aware of this distinction and understand their responsibilities to avoid coverage gaps.

Tenant Insurance

Encouraging or requiring tenants to obtain renter's insurance is a best practice that mitigates risks for property owners and enhances tenant accountability. Renter's insurance covers tenants' personal belongings against damage or loss due to events such as theft, fire, or water leaks. Additionally, it provides liability coverage, which can protect tenants if they are found responsible for damage to the unit or injuries to others within their rented space. For example, if a tenant accidentally starts a fire that damages neighboring units, their renter's insurance policy may cover the associated costs, reducing the financial burden on the property owner or association.

Property managers can streamline this process by partnering with insurance providers to offer renter's insurance options directly to tenants, simplifying enrollment and ensuring compliance. Educating tenants about the benefits of renter's insurance not only protects them but also minimizes potential disputes and liabilities for the property owner.

Insurance for Manufactured Home Parks

Unique Considerations

Unlike traditional multifamily properties, manufactured home parks primarily consist of tenant-owned units situated on rented land. This arrangement creates specific insurance challenges. The park owner is typically responsible for securing property insurance that covers the land, roads, utilities, and common areas such as playgrounds, clubhouses, or swimming pools. The infrastructure of the park, including water, sewer, and electrical systems, must also be included in the coverage to address potential damages or disruptions caused by storms, accidents, or aging systems.

Additionally, liability insurance is critical for protecting the park owner against claims arising from injuries or accidents occurring in common areas or on the park's infrastructure. For example, if a resident is injured while using a park-maintained amenity, such as a basketball court, liability insurance can help cover medical expenses and legal costs.

Tenant-Owned Units

A significant challenge in manufactured home parks is the insurance coverage of tenant-owned homes. While tenants are typically responsible for insuring their individual units, the property owner may face liability if park-related issues, such as falling tree branches or infrastructure failures, damage a tenant's home. Property managers should encourage tenants to obtain adequate homeowner's insurance for their manufactured homes to ensure that personal belongings and structural damages are covered. Clear communication about the boundaries of landlord versus tenant responsibilities can prevent disputes and ensure seamless claims processing in the event of an incident.

Specialized Policies

Given the specific risks associated with manufactured home parks, property managers should consider specialized insurance policies tailored to these communities. These policies can combine property, liability, and even business interruption insurance to address the financial impacts of extended vacancies or operational disruptions. Working with experienced insurance brokers who understand the manufactured housing industry is essential to crafting a comprehensive insurance plan.

6.8.2 Risk Management

Overview

Risk management is a crucial aspect of property management, involving the identification, assessment, and prioritization of risks followed by the application of resources to minimize and control the probability or impact of unforeseen events. There are four primary methods of risk management: risk avoidance, risk reduction, risk transfer, and risk retention.

Risk Avoidance

Implications: This involves eliminating a risk entirely by avoiding actions that could lead to potential loss. While it reduces exposure to certain risks, it may limit opportunities for growth or operational efficiency. For example, a property manager might choose not to allow certain high-risk amenities, such as swimming pools, to avoid the associated liability.

Risk Reduction

Implications: This method involves taking steps to reduce the likelihood or impact of risks. Implementing safety measures, regular maintenance, and staff training are ways to reduce risks. This approach often involves upfront costs but can prevent larger losses over time, such as installing security systems to deter theft.

Risk Transfer

Implications: Risk transfer involves shifting the risk to another party, typically through insurance or contractual agreements. Purchasing insurance policies is the most common way to transfer risk, ensuring that the financial burden of potential losses is borne by the insurer. Property managers can also transfer risk through tenant leases, making tenants responsible for certain types of damage.

Risk Retention

Implications: In some cases, it may be more cost-effective to retain the risk and cover any potential losses internally. This approach is used when the cost of transferring or reducing the risk is higher than the potential loss. An example is setting aside a reserve fund to cover minor property damage repairs.

6.8.3 Insurance Claims

Role of the Property Manager

Property managers play a critical role in the insurance claims process, acting as the intermediary between the property owner and the insurance company. Their responsibilities include:

- *Immediate Response: Upon noticing a loss, the property manager must ensure the safety of all occupants and take immediate steps to prevent further damage. This might include temporary repairs, securing the property, and notifying emergency services if necessary.*
- *Documentation*: Accurate and thorough documentation of the damage is essential. Property managers should take photos, record videos, and compile written descriptions of the damage. Keeping an inventory of damaged property can also be helpful.
- *Notifying the Insurer*: The property manager should promptly contact the insurance company to report the loss and initiate the claims process. Timely notification is crucial to comply with policy requirements and avoid claim denials.

- *Working with Adjusters*: Insurance adjusters will assess the damage to determine the claim's value. The property manager should provide them with all necessary documentation and facilitate access to the property for inspection.
- *Overseeing Repairs*: Once the claim is approved, the property manager or a project manager is usually tasked with coordinating the repair work. This includes hiring contractors, ensuring the work is completed to standard, and verifying that all repairs are consistent with the insurance claim.
- *Communication*: Throughout the claims process, the property manager must maintain clear communication with the property owner, insurance company, contractors, and tenants. Keeping all parties informed helps to ensure a smooth and efficient claims process.

Property Preservation:
In the event of a loss, property preservation is a critical responsibility of the property manager. This involves taking proactive measures to protect the property from further damage and ensuring that it remains habitable or safely secured. Key actions include:

- *Temporary Repairs: Implementing temporary fixes, such as boarding up broken windows or placing tarps over roof damage, to prevent additional damage from weather or vandalism.*
- *Security Measures:* Enhancing security to protect the property from theft or unauthorized access during the repair process. This may involve installing temporary fencing, additional lighting, or security patrols.
- *Maintenance of Utilities:* Ensuring that utilities are safely managed and maintained during the repair period. This includes shutting off water or gas lines if necessary to prevent further damage or hazards.
- *Tenant Communication:* Keeping tenants informed about the status of repairs and any necessary steps they need to take, such as relocating temporarily or avoiding certain areas of the property.

By understanding and implementing effective risk management strategies and actively participating in the insurance claims process, property managers can safeguard the properties under their care, minimize financial losses, and maintain the trust and satisfaction of property owners and tenants.

6.9 Federal and State Laws

6.9.1 Federal Fair Housing Laws

Federal Fair Housing Laws, established under the Fair Housing Act of 1968 and subsequent amendments, aim to eliminate discrimination in housing-related activities. These laws prohibit discrimination based on race, color, religion, sex, national origin, familial status, and disability. Property managers must ensure that their practices comply with these regulations, including advertising, tenant selection, and lease terms. Violations can result in severe penalties, including fines and legal action. To comply, property managers should implement fair housing training for staff, develop nondiscriminatory policies, and maintain detailed records of their housing practices. Understanding and adhering to these laws is essential to promote equal housing opportunities and avoid legal repercussions.

6.9.2 Americans with Disabilities Act (ADA)

The Americans with Disabilities Act (ADA) of 1990 ensures equal access and non-discrimination for individuals with disabilities in all public and commercial spaces, including residential properties with public access areas. Property managers must ensure that common areas, such as lobbies, parking lots, and pathways, are accessible to individuals with disabilities. This may involve installing ramps, widening doorways, and providing accessible parking spaces. The ADA also requires reasonable accommodations within rental units, such as allowing service animals or modifying units to be accessible. Property managers should be proactive in understanding these requirements, implementing necessary modifications, and fostering an inclusive environment for all residents.

6.9.3 Antitrust Laws

Antitrust laws, primarily governed by the Sherman Act, Clayton Act, and Federal Trade Commission Act, aim to promote fair competition and prevent monopolistic practices in various industries, including real estate. Property managers must avoid activities that could be construed as price-fixing, market allocation, or bid-rigging. This includes colluding with competitors to set rental rates or agree on market territories. Violations of antitrust laws can lead to severe penalties, including substantial fines and imprisonment. Property managers should ensure their practices are independent and competitive, maintain transparency in their dealings, and seek legal counsel if they are uncertain about the implications of specific actions on competition laws.

6.9.4 Fair Credit Reporting Act

The Fair Credit Reporting Act (FCRA) regulates the collection, dissemination, and use of consumer information, including credit information. Property managers often rely on credit reports to screen potential tenants, making compliance with FCRA critical. Under the FCRA, property managers must obtain written permission from applicants before accessing their credit reports. If a decision is made based on the credit report, such as denial of tenancy, the property manager must provide the applicant with an adverse action notice, including the reason for the decision and the contact information of the credit reporting agency. Adhering to these regulations helps ensure fair treatment of applicants and protects the property manager from legal liabilities.

6.9.5 Megan's Law

Megan's Law mandates that law enforcement authorities make information available to the public regarding registered sex offenders. This law was enacted in response to the tragic case of Megan Kanka, a 7-year-old girl who was sexually assaulted and murdered by a neighbor who was a convicted sex offender. The law aims to protect communities by providing access to information about potentially dangerous individuals living nearby. For property managers, it is essential to understand the requirements of Megan's Law and ensure that this information is accessible to tenants. This includes informing residents about how to access local sex offender registries and considering this information when screening potential tenants, balancing the need for community safety with legal compliance and fair housing regulations.

6.9.6 Lead-Based Paint Hazard Reduction Act

The Lead-Based Paint Hazard Reduction Act, enacted in 1992, aims to protect families from exposure to lead-based paint hazards in residential properties. This federal law requires landlords and property managers to disclose known lead-based paint hazards to tenants before leases are signed. Properties built before 1978 are most likely to contain lead-based paint, which can pose serious health risks, particularly to children and pregnant women. Compliance involves providing tenants with a lead hazard information pamphlet, including a lead warning statement in the lease, and maintaining records of compliance for at least 3 years. Property managers must also ensure that any maintenance or renovations in older properties are conducted safely to prevent lead contamination. Understanding and adhering to these requirements is crucial for protecting tenant health and avoiding substantial fines and legal liability.

6.9.7 Uniform Residential Landlord and Tenant Act

The Uniform Residential Landlord and Tenant Act (URLTA) was developed to standardize the legal relationship between landlords and tenants across different states. Enacted in 1972, the URLTA provides a framework for rental agreements, specifying the rights and responsibilities of both parties. Key provisions include regulations on security deposits, maintenance obligations, tenant privacy, and the handling of lease violations. The act aims to balance the interests of landlords and tenants, promoting fair treatment and reducing disputes. Property managers must familiarize themselves with the URLTA provisions as adopted in their state and ensure their lease agreements and practices comply with these standards. This includes maintaining the property in a habitable condition, respecting tenant privacy, and providing clear terms for lease termination and renewal.

6.9.8 Servicemembers Civil Relief Act

The Servicemembers Civil Relief Act (SCRA) offers various protections to active-duty military personnel, including provisions related to housing leases. Enacted in 2003, the SCRA allows servicemembers to terminate residential leases without penalty if they receive orders for a permanent change of station or deployment for a period of at least 90 days. This law ensures that military members are not financially burdened by their service obligations. Property managers must understand the procedures for verifying eligibility and processing lease terminations under the SCRA. This includes requiring a written notice from the servicemember and a copy of their military orders. Compliance with the SCRA not only supports military families but also helps property managers avoid legal repercussions and foster positive relationships with military tenants.

6.10 Federally Funded Housing Programs: HUD, LIHTC, and USDA 515

Federally funded housing programs play a critical role in addressing the housing needs of low- and moderate-income families, seniors, and individuals with disabilities in the United States. These programs, administered by government agencies or through public-private partnerships, aim to expand affordable housing options and stabilize communities. This section provides a high-level overview of three major federally funded housing programs: the U.S. Department of Housing and Urban Development (HUD), Low-Income Housing Tax Credits (LIHTC), and the USDA Section 515 Rural Rental Housing Program. While these programs offer essential resources for housing providers and residents, they are highly specialized and subject to frequent changes in requirements, funding levels, and regulatory oversight.

6.10.1 U.S. Department of Housing and Urban Development (HUD)

HUD is the primary federal agency responsible for overseeing affordable housing programs in the United States. Established in 1965, HUD administers a wide range of programs designed to increase housing affordability, combat homelessness, and promote inclusive community development. Key HUD programs relevant to property management include Public Housing, Section 8 Housing Choice Vouchers, and Project-Based Section 8.

Public Housing Program

Public housing is government-owned housing designed to provide safe and affordable rental options for low-income families, seniors, and individuals with disabilities. Property managers of public housing work under strict HUD guidelines and collaborate closely with local public housing authorities (PHAs). Responsibilities include managing tenant eligibility, ensuring compliance with HUD occupancy standards, and maintaining the physical condition of units in accordance with federal regulations.

Section 8 Housing Choice Vouchers

The Section 8 Housing Choice Voucher program allows eligible low-income families to secure rental housing in the private market. HUD provides funding to local PHAs, which administer vouchers to qualifying households. Property managers participating in this program must comply with HUD regulations for tenant selection, unit inspections, and rent pricing, which cannot exceed fair market rent (FMR) levels set by HUD. Additionally, annual recertifications are required to verify continued tenant eligibility.

Project-Based Section 8

Unlike Housing Choice Vouchers, which are tenant-based, Project-Based Section 8 ties rental assistance directly to specific units within a property. Property managers of project-based Section 8 properties are responsible for ensuring compliance with HUD's affordability and occupancy requirements. This includes managing waiting lists, conducting income certifications, and maintaining the property in compliance with HUD's housing quality standards.

6.10.2 Low-Income Housing Tax Credits (LIHTC)

The LIHTC program, created by the Tax Reform Act of 1986, is a federal initiative that incentivizes private investment in affordable housing development. LIHTC properties are financed through tax credits allocated to developers, who in turn agree to set aside a portion of units for low-income tenants at reduced rents for a specified compliance period, typically 15–30 years.

How LIHTC Works

LIHTC is administered at the federal level by the Internal Revenue Service (IRS) and distributed to states through state housing finance agencies (HFAs). Developers apply to these agencies for tax credit allocations, which are awarded based on criteria such as the project's affordability, location, and alignment with community housing needs.

Affordability Requirements

Property managers of LIHTC properties must adhere to strict affordability requirements. These include ensuring that a designated percentage of units remain affordable to households earning 60% or less of the area median income (AMI). Rent limits are calculated based on AMI and include allowances for utilities. Property managers must monitor tenant income annually and maintain detailed compliance records to meet reporting requirements for both the state HFA and IRS.

Compliance Challenges
LIHTC compliance is a specialized area of property management due to the complex regulations governing tenant eligibility, rent restrictions, and unit designations. Changes in tenant income or household composition can impact the property's compliance status, making ongoing training and meticulous record-keeping essential for property managers.

6.10.3 USDA Section 515 Rural Rental Housing Program

The USDA Section 515 program provides low-interest loans to developers for the construction or rehabilitation of affordable rental housing in rural areas. This program is critical for addressing the unique housing challenges faced by low-income families in rural communities, where affordable rental options are often scarce.

Program Overview
Section 515 loans are used to finance properties with reduced rental rates for low- and very low-income households. Eligible properties must be located in rural areas defined by the USDA, which include towns with populations under 35,000. While the program's funding for new developments has diminished in recent years, it continues to support existing properties through loan restructuring and rental assistance.

Rental Assistance
Many Section 515 properties also receive rental assistance through the USDA's Section 521 Rental Assistance Program. This subsidy ensures tenants pay no more than 30% of their income toward rent, similar to HUD programs. Property managers are responsible for verifying tenant income eligibility, maintaining rent schedules, and ensuring compliance with USDA regulations.

Maintenance and Preservation
Preserving the aging stock of Section 515 properties has become a major focus for the USDA. Property managers must work closely with the USDA to implement maintenance plans, complete inspections, and address issues such as deferred maintenance or structural deficiencies. Funding constraints and limited resources in rural areas can pose significant challenges for property managers overseeing Section 515 properties.

6.10.4 Challenges and Specialization in Federally Funded Housing Programs

Managing properties under HUD, LIHTC, or USDA 515 programs requires a specialized skill set due to the intricate regulatory frameworks and frequent changes in program requirements. Property managers must stay up-to-date with evolving rules, including shifts in funding allocations, reporting standards, and affordability thresholds. Some of the key challenges include:

- *Tenant Compliance: Ensuring that tenants meet income and occupancy requirements while navigating sensitive issues such as income fluctuations and family composition changes.*
- *Program Overlaps:* Properties may participate in multiple programs (e.g., a property receiving LIHTC funding might also accept Section 8 vouchers), requiring property managers to coordinate compliance across overlapping regulations.
- *Affordability Restrictions:* Federally funded properties often operate under long-term affordability restrictions that can impact revenue potential and operational flexibility.
- *Data and Reporting Requirements:* Extensive documentation and reporting are required to maintain compliance with federal and state agencies. This includes tenant income certifications, financial audits, and physical inspections.
- *Training and Expertise:* Property managers overseeing federally funded programs benefit from specialized training, such as certifications offered by organizations like the National Affordable Housing Management Association (NAHMA) or the Institute of Real Estate Management (IREM).

6.11 Managing Life Safety

6.11.1 Overview of Common Life Safety Issues

Identifying Risks

Life safety issues in residential properties encompass a wide range of potential hazards that can impact the health and well-being of tenants. These hazards include fire risks, structural deficiencies, environmental hazards, and security threats. Effective property management involves proactively identifying these risks through regular inspections, risk assessments, and ongoing monitoring. Utilizing professional services for thorough inspections and assessments ensures that no potential hazard is overlooked.

Regulatory Compliance

Ensuring compliance with local, state, and federal regulations is a cornerstone of managing life safety issues. Property managers must stay informed about the latest building codes, fire safety regulations, health standards, and environmental protection laws. Compliance not only helps in maintaining a safe living environment but also protects property owners and managers from legal liabilities and penalties. Regular training and certification for staff on safety regulations and emergency procedures are essential to maintain high safety standards.

6.11.2 Security Measures

Ensuring the security of residential properties is a critical responsibility for property managers, requiring a combination of physical security measures, proactive management strategies, and the integration of trained security personnel. Effective security not only protects residents, property, and assets but also fosters a sense of safety and trust within the community. By implementing comprehensive security protocols, property managers can address potential vulnerabilities and reduce the risk of criminal activity or unauthorized access.

Physical Security Measures
Physical security forms the foundation of any property's safety strategy. This includes installing access control systems, such as key fobs, PIN codes, or biometric systems, to regulate entry into the property and restrict access to authorized individuals. Surveillance cameras strategically placed in common areas, entry points, parking lots, and stairwells act as a deterrent to crime and provide valuable evidence in case of incidents. Proper lighting is equally essential, particularly in outdoor areas like walkways, parking lots, and entrances, to reduce the likelihood of criminal activity under the cover of darkness. Additionally, secure entry points, such as reinforced doors, deadbolt locks, and shatterproof windows, prevent unauthorized access and enhance the property's overall safety.

Proactive Management Strategies
While physical security measures are critical, proactive management strategies play an equally important role. Conducting background checks during the resident screening process ensures that individuals with a history of criminal behavior are not admitted into the community. Property managers can also foster a sense of collective responsibility among residents by encouraging participation in community watch programs. These programs empower residents to report suspicious activity and create a collaborative approach to safety. Building and maintaining strong relationships with local law enforcement agencies further strengthens security efforts. These partnerships provide property managers with access to valuable resources, such as crime prevention workshops and quicker emergency response times. Regular security audits and updates to security systems are essential to address emerging threats and incorporate new technologies.

The Role of Security Officers

Security officers play a crucial role in protecting life and property within residential communities. Their presence alone serves as a deterrent to criminal activity, reducing the likelihood of theft, vandalism, or unauthorized access. Security officers are trained to handle emergencies, such as medical crises, fires, or acts of violence, ensuring that residents receive immediate assistance when needed. They also monitor surveillance systems, patrol the premises, and enforce community rules to maintain order.

In addition to their visible duties, security officers often act as the first point of contact for residents and visitors. Their ability to communicate effectively and resolve conflicts diplomatically contributes to a safer and more harmonious living environment. For larger residential communities or high-risk areas, employing licensed and trained security officers is a best practice that enhances overall security measures.

Integrating Technology with Security Personnel

Modern residential security strategies increasingly combine technology with the expertise of security officers. For example, access control systems and surveillance cameras can be integrated into a centralized monitoring station managed by on-site or remote security personnel. This approach allows for real-time monitoring and swift responses to security breaches or emergencies. Security officers can also use mobile devices to receive alerts, track patrol routes, and document incidents, increasing their efficiency and effectiveness.

Ongoing Training and Professional Development

To ensure security officers perform their duties effectively, security firms should prioritize ongoing training and professional development. This training should cover topics such as conflict resolution, emergency response protocols, and the use of surveillance equipment. Regularly updated training ensures that security officers remain equipped to handle evolving threats and challenges within the residential property environment.

Benefits of Comprehensive Security Measures

Implementing robust security measures benefits both residents and property owners. Residents gain peace of mind knowing their safety is prioritized, which contributes to higher satisfaction and retention rates. Property owners benefit from reduced liability risks, fewer incidents of vandalism or theft, and enhanced property value. Moreover, a secure property attracts higher-quality residents, further strengthening the community.

6.11.3 Fire Safety

Fire hazards are a major concern in residential properties. Preventative measures such as installing smoke detectors, fire extinguishers, and sprinkler systems, combined with regular fire drills and tenant education on fire safety practices, can significantly reduce fire risks. Developing and maintaining an effective fire emergency plan, ensuring clear evacuation routes, and regular inspections of electrical systems and appliances are essential to prevent fire incidents and protect tenants.

By understanding and addressing these common life safety issues, property managers can create a safer environment for tenants, comply with regulations, and prevent potential disasters. Proactive risk management, continuous education, and robust emergency planning are key components of a comprehensive life safety strategy in residential property management.

Fire Safety Preventive Measures

Fire safety in residential properties is a multifaceted effort that requires a combination of preventive measures, regular maintenance, and tenant education. The installation and maintenance of fire safety equipment are fundamental. Every unit should be equipped with working smoke detectors and carbon monoxide detectors, which should be tested regularly. Fire extinguishers should be strategically placed in common areas and individual units, and tenants should be instructed on their proper use. Sprinkler systems are an additional protective measure that can significantly mitigate fire damage and should be inspected and tested regularly.

Electrical Safety

Electrical fires are a common cause of residential fires, often stemming from faulty wiring, overloaded circuits, or the misuse of electrical appliances. Regular inspections of the property's electrical systems by certified electricians are crucial. This includes checking for frayed wires, ensuring outlets are not overloaded, and verifying that all electrical installations comply with current safety codes. Encouraging tenants to report any electrical issues promptly and educating them on the dangers of using damaged electrical appliances can also prevent potential fire hazards.

Cooking Safety

Cooking is another leading cause of residential fires. Property managers should provide residents with guidelines on safe cooking practices, such as never leaving cooking food unattended, keeping flammable items away from the stove, and using timers as reminders. Installing stove alarms that detect excessive heat or smoke can add an extra layer of safety. Regularly cleaning kitchen appliances, particularly range hoods and vents, helps prevent grease buildup, which can easily ignite.

Heating Safety

During colder months, heating equipment, including space heaters, fireplaces, and central heating systems, can pose fire risks. Property managers should ensure that all heating equipment is regularly inspected and maintained. Space heaters should be used with caution, placed away from flammable materials, and never left unattended. Chimneys and fireplaces should be cleaned regularly to prevent the buildup of flammable creosote. Tenants should be educated about the importance of using heating equipment safely and the potential hazards of improper use.

Resident Education

Educating residents about fire safety is a proactive measure that can significantly reduce the risk of fire incidents. This includes providing information on safe cooking and heating practices, the proper use and maintenance of fire safety equipment, and the importance of reporting potential fire hazards. Regular communication through newsletters, emails, and community meetings can keep fire safety top of mind for residents.

Maintenance and Inspections

Regular maintenance and inspections are critical components of fire safety. Property managers should develop a schedule for inspecting fire safety equipment, electrical systems, and heating appliances. Any identified issues should be addressed promptly to prevent potential fire hazards. Documenting these inspections and maintenance activities is essential for tracking compliance and ensuring that all safety measures are up to date.

By implementing these comprehensive fire safety measures, property managers can create a safer living environment for tenants and significantly reduce the risk of fire-related incidents. Proactive prevention, regular maintenance, tenant education, and effective emergency planning are key elements of a robust fire safety strategy in residential property management.

6.11.4 Emergency Planning

Developing and implementing a comprehensive emergency response plan is a critical responsibility for property managers. Such plans ensure the safety and well-being of residents, staff, and visitors by addressing a wide range of potential threats, including fires, flooding, explosions, severe weather, and other emergencies. A well-prepared plan requires detailed protocols, clear communication strategies, and regular training and drills. Tailoring the emergency response plan to the property's specific risks and geographic location is essential for ensuring its effectiveness.

Fire Emergency Planning

Fire emergencies are among the most common threats faced by residential properties, making fire preparedness a cornerstone of any emergency plan. A fire emergency plan should include clearly marked evacuation routes that are free of obstructions and easily accessible to all residents, including those with mobility challenges. Assembly points at safe distances from the building should be designated, and all residents and staff should be made aware of these locations. Procedures for reporting fires, such as activating fire alarms or contacting emergency services, must also be clearly outlined and communicated. Conducting regular fire drills is essential to familiarize residents and staff with these procedures, ensuring a swift and organized evacuation in an actual emergency. Additionally, distributing written emergency plans and holding informational meetings can reinforce the importance of fire safety practices.

Flooding and Water Damage

Flooding, whether caused by heavy rainfall, plumbing failures, or sewer backups, poses a significant risk to residential properties. An effective flooding response plan should include monitoring local flood warnings and alerts to stay informed about potential risks. Evacuation plans must identify safe routes and shelter locations for residents if flooding necessitates leaving the property. Staff should be trained to locate and operate water shutoff valves to minimize water damage during plumbing-related flooding. Post-flood cleanup protocols are equally important, particularly for addressing mold growth and structural damage. In flood-prone areas, property managers should consider preventative measures such as installing sump pumps, waterproofing foundations, and maintaining proper drainage systems.

Explosion and Evacuation Procedures

Explosions, although less common, require specific preparedness measures due to their potential for widespread damage. Gas leaks are a frequent cause of explosions, making it essential for property managers to include gas shutoff training in their emergency response plans. Evacuation protocols should be established to ensure the safe removal of residents and staff from the affected area. Clear and immediate communication with residents is critical to provide instructions and minimize panic. Regular inspections and maintenance of gas lines and related equipment can help prevent such incidents from occurring in the first place.

Elevator Emergency Procedures

Elevator emergencies can pose serious risks, particularly in high-rise residential buildings. An elevator emergency plan should include equipping all elevators with functional emergency communication systems that connect directly to monitoring centers or emergency services. Residents should be educated on how to remain calm and use these systems if they become trapped in an elevator. Regular inspections and maintenance of elevators are essential to reduce the likelihood of malfunctions. Property managers should also establish protocols for responding to elevator incidents, including clear procedures for notifying residents and coordinating repair efforts.

Active Shooter Safety Planning

In recent years, the rise of active shooter incidents in both residential and commercial properties have highlighted the critical need for safety planning in property management. Preparing for such events involves specific training for both staff and residents. The widely recognized "Run, Hide, Fight" protocol provides clear guidance on how individuals should respond during an active shooter situation. Property management companies, especially those overseeing large residential communities or condominiums, must prioritize the safety of employees, residents, and visitors by implementing comprehensive active shooter safety plans.

A tragic reminder of the importance of such planning is the shooting incident at the 1280 West condominium in Atlanta, Georgia. In August 2023, two employees of Beacon Management Services were shot and killed by a disgruntled resident and former employee of the firm. This incident underscores the potential for violence in the workplace, even in residential settings, and the need for property management firms to be prepared for such emergencies by working with their local law enforcement to provide their staff active shooter response training.

Planning for Severe Weather

Severe weather events, such as wildfires, earthquakes, tornadoes, and hurricanes, demand tailored emergency plans that consider the unique risks associated with a property's geographic location. A well-structured procedures manual for management and residents is essential for navigating these potentially devastating scenarios. The manual should provide detailed guidance on preparation, response, and recovery for each type of severe weather event, ensuring the safety of all stakeholders and minimizing property damage. Below is an overview of recommended procedures for managing these emergencies.

Wildfires

Wildfires can spread rapidly and unpredictably, making preparedness critical for properties in fire-prone regions. The procedures manual should emphasize the importance of maintaining a defensible space around the property by removing flammable vegetation and debris within a 30-ft perimeter. Management should conduct regular inspections to ensure compliance with local fire safety regulations.

Resident Procedures:

Residents should be informed of evacuation routes and assembly points well in advance. The manual should include a checklist of items to take during evacuation, such as identification, medications, and important documents. Residents should also be educated on how to identify early signs of a wildfire and the importance of monitoring local alerts and warnings.

Management Procedures:

Property management must establish partnerships with local fire departments and emergency services to stay informed about wildfire risks. Management should ensure that fire suppression tools, such as hoses and extinguishers, are readily available and operational. During active wildfire threats, management should implement an evacuation protocol, notify residents, and assist individuals with mobility challenges.

Earthquakes

Earthquakes occur without warning, requiring proactive measures to mitigate risks and ensure swift response. The manual should outline procedures for ensuring structural safety by conducting regular seismic inspections and retrofitting buildings to meet safety standards.

Resident Procedures:

Residents should be educated on the "Drop, Cover, and Hold On" technique to protect themselves during an earthquake. The manual should include instructions for securing heavy furniture and appliances to prevent injuries. Residents should also be encouraged to create emergency supply kits with water, food, and first aid materials.

Management Procedures:

Management should identify safe areas within buildings, such as doorframes or reinforced stairwells, and communicate these locations to residents. Emergency drills should be conducted periodically to familiarize residents with earthquake safety protocols. After an earthquake, management should inspect the property for structural damage, gas leaks, and other hazards before allowing residents to re-enter.

Tornadoes

Tornadoes pose a significant threat due to their high winds and potential for destruction. The manual should designate safe areas within the property, such as basements or interior rooms without windows, as shelters during tornado warnings.

Resident Procedures:

Residents should be instructed to move to the nearest safe area immediately upon hearing a tornado siren or receiving a warning. The manual should provide guidance on using blankets, mattresses, or helmets to protect against flying debris. Residents should also be advised to stay updated on weather alerts via radio or smartphone apps.

Management Procedures:

Management should ensure that all designated safe areas are accessible and equipped with emergency supplies, including water, flashlights, and first aid kits. Regular tornado drills should be conducted to ensure residents know how to reach shelter quickly. After the tornado, management should assess the property for damage, prioritize repairs, and coordinate with emergency services for additional assistance.

Hurricanes

Hurricanes provide advance warning, giving property managers and residents time to prepare. The manual should include detailed storm preparation protocols, such as securing outdoor furniture, boarding up windows, and clearing drainage systems.

Resident Procedures:

Residents should be informed of evacuation orders and provided with a checklist of items to pack, including essential documents, medications, and emergency supplies. Those remaining on-site should be advised to stock up on food, water, and batteries. Residents should also be educated on safe practices during the storm, such as avoiding windows and staying in interior rooms.

Management Procedures:

Management must stay in close contact with local emergency services to monitor hurricane developments and evacuation orders. Before the storm, management should secure common areas, inspect and test backup power generators, and ensure that sump pumps and drainage systems are operational. During the storm, staff should maintain communication with residents and emergency responders.

Post-storm procedures include assessing property damage, coordinating cleanup efforts, and addressing immediate repair needs to ensure resident safety.

6.11.5 Health and Environmental Hazard Control

History of the Occupational Safety and Health Act of 1970

The Occupational Safety and Health Act (OSHA) of 1970 was a landmark legislation designed to ensure safe and healthy working conditions for employees by setting and enforcing standards. OSHA established guidelines to mitigate workplace hazards, including those related to environmental and chemical exposures. The act's primary goal is to reduce workplace injuries, illnesses, and fatalities through comprehensive safety regulations and education.

Hazardous Substances in Property Management

Property managers must address various hazardous substances to ensure the safety and health of tenants and staff. Key hazardous substances include asbestos, radon, mold, carbon monoxide, and lead-based paint.

Asbestos: Asbestos is a naturally occurring mineral fiber that was commonly used in building materials for its heat resistance and insulating properties. However, asbestos exposure can lead to serious health issues, including lung cancer, asbestosis, and mesothelioma. Property managers must be aware of the presence of asbestos in older buildings, particularly in insulation, roofing materials, and floor tiles. When asbestos-containing materials are in good condition, they may not pose a risk, but when damaged, they can release fibers into the air. Property managers should hire licensed professionals to conduct asbestos inspections and removal if necessary. Proper documentation and communication with tenants about asbestos management practices are essential to ensure safety.

Radon: Radon is a radioactive gas that forms naturally from the decay of uranium in soil and rock. It can seep into buildings through cracks in foundations, walls, and floors. Radon is odorless, colorless, and tasteless, making it undetectable without proper testing. Long-term exposure to high levels of radon increases the risk of lung cancer. Property managers should conduct radon testing, particularly in basements and ground-floor units, and implement mitigation measures if radon levels exceed the EPA's recommended action level of 4 picocuries per liter (pCi/L). Mitigation can involve sealing cracks, improving ventilation, and installing radon reduction systems.

Mold: Mold is a type of fungus that thrives in moist environments and can grow on various surfaces, including walls, ceilings, and floors. Mold exposure can cause respiratory issues, allergic reactions, and other health problems. Property managers must promptly address water leaks, humidity issues, and poor ventilation to prevent mold growth. Regular inspections and maintenance of plumbing, HVAC systems, and building exteriors can help identify and resolve moisture problems. When mold is detected, it is crucial to clean and remediate the affected areas using appropriate protective gear and cleaning agents. Communication with tenants about mold prevention and reporting procedures is vital for maintaining a healthy living environment.

Carbon Monoxide: Carbon monoxide (CO) is a colorless, odorless gas produced by burning fuels such as natural gas, propane, oil, and wood. Exposure to high levels of CO can cause headaches, dizziness, nausea, and even death. Property managers should ensure that all fuel-burning appliances, such as furnaces, water heaters, and stoves, are properly maintained and vented. Installing CO detectors in units and common areas is critical for early detection of CO leaks. Regular testing and replacement of CO detectors, along with tenant education on CO safety, can prevent CO poisoning incidents.

Lead-Based Paint: Lead-based paint was commonly used in residential buildings before it was banned in 1978 due to its health risks. Lead exposure can cause developmental delays, learning difficulties, and other severe health issues, particularly in children. Property managers must identify and manage lead-based paint hazards in older properties. This involves conducting lead inspections, encapsulating or removing deteriorating paint, and following safe work practices during renovations or repairs. Providing tenants with information about lead hazards and preventive measures is required under federal law and ensures tenant safety.

Air Quality Issues

Sick Building Syndrome (SBS)

Sick Building Syndrome refers to situations where building occupants experience acute health and comfort effects that appear to be linked to time spent in a building, but no specific illness or cause can be identified. Symptoms often include headaches, dizziness, nausea, eye, nose, or throat irritation, dry cough, dry or itchy skin, and difficulty concentrating. These symptoms typically resolve after leaving the building. Poor indoor air quality is a common cause of SBS, often resulting from inadequate ventilation, chemical contaminants from indoor sources (such as adhesives, carpeting, upholstery, manufactured wood products, copy machines, pesticides, and cleaning agents), biological contaminants (such as mold, pollen, and bacteria), and insufficient fresh air intake. Property managers can mitigate SBS by improving ventilation, using low-emission building materials and furnishings, and maintaining HVAC systems properly.

Building-Related Illness (BRI)

Building-related Illness refers to diagnosable illnesses that can be directly attributed to specific airborne building contaminants. These illnesses are often more severe than the symptoms of Sick Building Syndrome and can include conditions like Legionnaires' disease, hypersensitivity pneumonitis, and certain types of infections and allergies. Unlike SBS, where symptoms usually subside upon leaving the building, BRI symptoms persist and require medical treatment. Property managers must ensure regular inspections and maintenance of building systems that can harbor and spread contaminants, such as HVAC systems, humidifiers, and water systems.

Prompt remediation of identified contaminants and maintaining high standards of cleanliness and ventilation are critical in preventing BRI.

Air Quality and Energy Efficiency

The push for higher energy efficiency standards in buildings has, in some cases, contributed to air quality issues such as Sick Building Syndrome and Building-related Illness. Energy-efficient buildings are often sealed tightly to minimize energy loss, which can reduce the infiltration of outdoor air and increase the concentration of indoor pollutants. Poor ventilation in energy-efficient buildings can lead to the buildup of contaminants such as volatile organic compounds (VOCs), mold spores, and other allergens. To balance energy efficiency with indoor air quality, property managers should ensure that HVAC systems are properly designed and maintained to provide adequate ventilation. This may involve incorporating energy recovery ventilators (ERVs) or heat recovery ventilators (HRVs) that bring in fresh air while conserving energy. Additionally, using low-emission building materials and regular air quality monitoring can help maintain a healthy indoor environment without compromising energy efficiency.

Employer Obligations

Under OSHA, employers are required to provide employees with information and training on hazardous chemicals in the workplace. This includes:

Hazard Communication Standard

Employers must develop a written hazard communication program, maintain a list of hazardous chemicals, and ensure that all containers are properly labeled.

Safety Data Sheets (SDS)

Employers must provide access to Safety Data Sheets for all hazardous chemicals, detailing the properties, health hazards, protective measures, and safety precautions.

Employee Training

Employers must train employees on how to safely handle hazardous chemicals, understand labels and SDS, and respond to emergencies involving hazardous substances.

Best Practices for Managing Hazard Control

Identification and Assessment

The first step in hazard control is identifying potential hazards within the property. Conduct thorough assessments to identify substances such as asbestos, radon, mold, carbon monoxide, and lead-based paint. Use professional inspectors who are trained to recognize these hazards and assess their severity. Regular monitoring and re-evaluation are necessary, as conditions can change over time, introducing new risks or exacerbating existing ones.

Regulatory Compliance

Property managers must be familiar with and comply with local, state, and federal regulations regarding hazardous substances. This includes understanding the Occupational Safety and Health Administration (OSHA) guidelines, Environmental Protection Agency (EPA) regulations, and local health and safety codes. Ensuring compliance not only protects tenants but also shields property managers from legal liabilities and potential fines.

Asbestos Management: Asbestos-containing materials should be left undisturbed if they are in good condition. If the materials are damaged or renovation is planned, hire certified asbestos abatement professionals to safely remove or encapsulate the asbestos. Proper signage and tenant notification about asbestos-containing areas are crucial. Keep detailed records of all asbestos-related activities, including inspections and remediation efforts.

Radon Mitigation: Radon levels can be reduced through several mitigation techniques, such as improving ventilation, sealing cracks in floors and walls, and installing radon reduction systems. Regular radon testing is essential, especially in areas known for high radon levels. Educate tenants about the dangers of radon and the importance of testing and provide information on how they can conduct their own radon tests.

Mold Prevention and Remediation: Control moisture to prevent mold growth by promptly addressing leaks, maintaining proper humidity levels, and ensuring adequate ventilation in high-moisture areas like bathrooms and kitchens. Regular inspections should focus on areas prone to moisture accumulation. When mold is discovered, use appropriate protective equipment and cleaning agents to remediate the affected areas. Engage professional mold remediation services for extensive contamination and follow up with additional inspections to confirm the effectiveness of the remediation.

Carbon Monoxide Safety: Install carbon monoxide detectors in all residential units and common areas, particularly near sleeping areas and fuel-burning appliances. Regularly test and replace detectors according to the manufacturer's recommendations. Educate tenants on the symptoms of carbon monoxide poisoning and the importance of reporting any potential CO leaks immediately. Ensure that all fuel-burning appliances are regularly serviced and vented properly.

Lead-Based Paint Control: For properties built before 1978, conduct lead inspections to identify areas with lead-based paint. When lead paint is found, encapsulate or remove it using lead-safe work practices. This includes minimizing dust, containing the work area, and cleaning up thoroughly. Provide tenants with information about lead hazards and the steps taken to mitigate them. Keep records of all inspections, remediation efforts, and tenant notifications as required by law.

Communication and Education: Effective communication with tenants is essential in managing hazardous substances. Inform tenants about the presence of hazardous materials, the risks they pose, and the measures taken to mitigate these risks.

Provide guidelines on how tenants can contribute to maintaining a safe environment, such as reporting leaks or ventilation issues promptly. Educational materials, workshops, and regular updates can help tenants stay informed and engaged in maintaining a safe living environment.

Emergency Response Planning: Develop comprehensive emergency response plans for dealing with hazardous substance incidents. This includes clear procedures for evacuations, emergency contacts, and coordination with local health and safety authorities. Conduct regular drills and ensure that all staff and tenants are familiar with the emergency procedures.

By implementing these best practices for managing hazard control, property managers can effectively reduce risks associated with hazardous substances, ensure compliance with regulations, and create a safer living environment for tenants. Regular assessments, professional interventions, tenant education, and robust emergency planning are critical components of a comprehensive hazard control strategy.

6.11.6 Structural Deficiencies

Identifying Structural Deficiencies

Structural deficiencies in residential buildings are a different set of hazards that can lead to catastrophic life safety issues. These deficiencies may arise from poor design, substandard construction materials, inadequate maintenance, or natural wear and tear. Common signs of structural problems include cracks in walls or foundations, sagging floors or ceilings, water infiltration, and visible corrosion of structural components. Regular inspections by qualified engineering professionals are essential to identify and address these issues before they escalate.

6.11.7 Champlain Towers South Collapse

The tragic collapse of the Champlain Towers South Condominium in Surfside, Florida, in June 2021, underscores the critical importance of addressing structural deficiencies. The collapse resulted in the loss of 98 lives and significant property damage. Ongoing investigations into the cause of the collapse have highlighted several factors that contributed to the disaster, offering important lessons for property managers.

This photo shows part of the 12-story oceanfront Champlain Towers South Condo that collapsed June 24, 2021 in Surfside, Florida. (Credit: National Institute of Standards and Technology)

Lessons Learned:

1. *Importance of Regular Inspections:*
   - *The Champlain Towers South had undergone various inspections and assessments over the years. However, critical issues, such as significant concrete deterioration and water infiltration, were not adequately addressed. Regular, thorough inspections by structural engineers can identify potential risks and prevent catastrophic failures.*
2. *Timely Maintenance and Repairs:*
   - *Delayed maintenance and repairs contributed to the structural weaknesses in Champlain Towers South. Property managers must advise owners to prioritize timely repairs of identified issues, particularly those related to structural integrity. Implementing a proactive maintenance and repair plan can mitigate risks and extend the lifespan of the building.*
3. *Effective Communication:*
   - *Communication breakdowns between the condominium association, residents, and engineers played a role in the disaster. Transparent and effective communication about the condition of the building, necessary repairs, and associated costs is crucial. Keeping all stakeholders informed fosters cooperation and ensures that critical safety measures are implemented.*

4. *Adequate Funding for Repairs:*
   - *Funding challenges delayed essential repairs in Champlain Towers South. Property managers should work with owners to establish adequate reserve funds for major repairs and maintenance. Conducting regular reserve studies helps determine the appropriate funding levels needed to address long-term maintenance and repair needs.*
5. *Regulatory Oversight:*
   - *Enhanced regulatory oversight and stricter enforcement of building codes could have potentially prevented the collapse. Property managers must stay informed about local regulations and ensure that their properties comply with all building codes and safety standards. Collaboration with local authorities, professional engineers and adherence to regulatory requirements are vital for maintaining building safety.*

By understanding the risks associated with structural deficiencies and learning from past incidents like the Champlain Towers South collapse, property managers can take proactive steps to ensure the safety and structural integrity of the buildings they manage. Regular inspections, timely maintenance, effective communication, adequate funding, and compliance with regulations are essential components of a comprehensive approach to managing life safety.

6.11.8 Health and Safety Inspections

Best Practices for Conducting Inspections

Conducting health and safety inspections is a vital responsibility for property managers, ensuring that properties remain safe, compliant with regulations, and free from hazards. These inspections help identify potential risks to residents, staff, and visitors, providing a foundation for proactive maintenance and hazard mitigation. Below are best practices for conducting thorough and effective health and safety inspections, with a focus on using comprehensive checklists and actionable strategies.

Regular Scheduling

Establishing a consistent schedule for health and safety inspections is essential to maintaining property safety. Annual comprehensive inspections should be complemented by more frequent checks of high-risk areas, such as utility rooms, playgrounds, and swimming pools. High-traffic common areas like lobbies and hallways should also be included in periodic assessments. A regular inspection schedule helps ensure that potential issues are identified and addressed promptly, minimizing risks to residents and liability to property owners.

Comprehensive Checklist

Using a comprehensive checklist is critical for ensuring that no aspect of the property is overlooked during an inspection. A well-crafted checklist should be tailored to the specific property type, accounting for its unique features and risks. Examples of checklist categories include:

- *Fire Safety: Inspect fire alarms, smoke detectors, extinguishers, sprinkler systems, and evacuation routes. Verify that fire exits are unobstructed and that all equipment is in good working order.*
- *Trip, Slip, and Fall Hazards:* Identify uneven flooring, loose carpets, damaged stair railings, and slippery surfaces in common areas.
- *Unsafe Electrical Conditions:* Check for exposed wiring, overloaded circuits, and malfunctioning outlets or fixtures.
- *Distressed or Unstable Structural Elements:* Inspect foundations, walls, and ceilings for cracks, water damage, or other signs of instability.
- *Biohazards:* Look for asbestos, mold, mildew, pest infestations, or other conditions that could compromise indoor air quality or health.
- *Dangerous Debris:* Remove sharp objects, broken glass, or other hazardous materials from outdoor areas, such as parking lots or playgrounds.

Regularly update the checklist to reflect changes in building codes, safety standards, and property features. Including a section for tenant-reported issues ensures that concerns from residents are incorporated into the inspection process.

Qualified Inspectors

Health and safety inspections should be conducted by qualified personnel who understand building codes, safety standards, and potential hazards. For general inspections, in-house staff with appropriate training may suffice. However, specialized inspections—such as those involving asbestos, lead, or other environmental hazards—should be carried out by certified professionals. Engaging qualified inspectors not only ensures a thorough evaluation but also demonstrates due diligence in meeting legal and safety requirements.

Resident Communication

Informing residents about upcoming inspections fosters collaboration and helps identify issues that may not be immediately visible to inspectors. Encourage residents to report maintenance concerns or potential hazards through regular communication channels, such as newsletters, email updates, or tenant portals. This collaborative approach strengthens the property's overall safety culture and empowers residents to play an active role in maintaining their living environment.

Documentation and Record-Keeping

Maintaining detailed records of all inspections is critical for compliance, transparency, and effective property management. Records should include the inspection date, findings, actions taken, follow-up activities, and supporting documentation such as photographs or repair receipts. Proper record-keeping not only helps track recurring issues but also provides evidence of compliance with health and safety regulations during audits or legal proceedings.

Follow-Up and Maintenance

Identifying hazards during inspections is only the first step; addressing them promptly is equally important. Property managers should develop a system for prioritizing repairs based on the severity of the issue and its potential impact on resident safety. For example, repairing a broken fire alarm should take precedence over repainting a scuffed wall. Regular follow-up inspections ensure that corrective actions have been completed and are effective in resolving the issue.

Compliance with Regulations

Staying informed about local, state, and federal health and safety regulations is essential for conducting compliant inspections. Regulations often dictate the frequency and scope of inspections, as well as requirements for specific property elements such as elevators, HVAC systems, and fire safety equipment. Noncompliance can result in fines, lawsuits, or reputational damage, making regulatory knowledge a critical component of effective property management.

Emergency Preparedness

Incorporating emergency preparedness into health and safety inspections ensures that the property is ready to handle crises such as fires, floods, or structural failures. Inspectors should verify that emergency exits are accessible, fire extinguishers and alarms are functional, and emergency plans are in place. Additionally, ensure that these plans are communicated to tenants and updated regularly to reflect current conditions and best practices.

Fig. 6.5 Example of fire safety condition. Leaking fire sprinkler system

Fig. 6.6 Example of fire safety condition. Missing smoke detector

Fig. 6.7 Examples of trip and fall hazard. Uneven sidewalk surface due to raised concrete slab

Fig. 6.8 Example of trip and fall hazard. Uneven sidewalk surface due to cracked concrete slab

Fig. 6.9 Example of trip and fall hazard. Uneven pool deck walking surface and concrete cracks

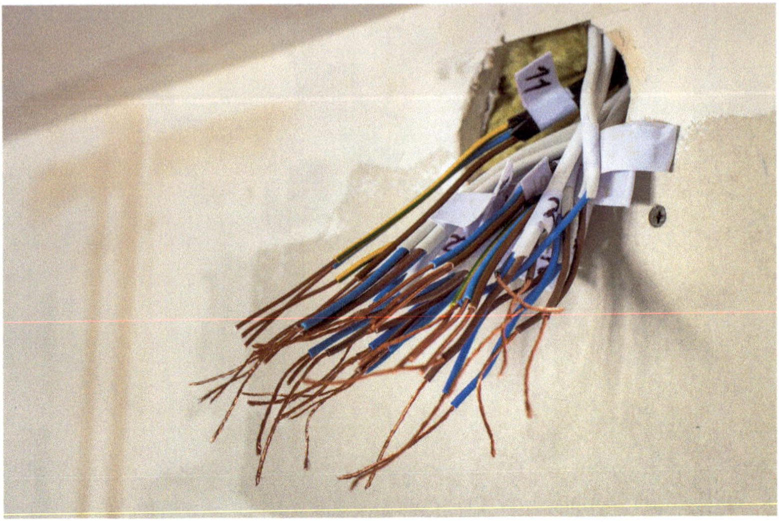

Fig. 6.10 Example of unsafe electrical condition. Exposed electrical wiring

Resident Education

Educating residents about recognizing and reporting hazards is a proactive step toward maintaining a safe property. Provide residents with information on identifying issues such as trip hazards, fire risks, or signs of mold growth. Emergency procedures, including evacuation routes and contact numbers, should also be shared and updated regularly. An informed resident base can act as an additional layer of oversight, contributing to the safety of the property (Figs. 6.5, 6.6, 6.7, 6.8, 6.9, 6.10, 6.11, 6.12, 6.13, and 6.14).

6.11.9 Security Access Control Systems

Introduction to Access Control Systems

Access control systems are critical for enhancing the security of residential properties. These systems regulate who can enter the building and specific areas within the property, thereby preventing unauthorized access and enhancing the safety of residents. Implementing effective access control measures can deter criminal activity, reduce the risk of vandalism, and provide peace of mind for both tenants and property managers.

Types of Access Control Systems

There are several types of access control systems, each offering varying levels of security and convenience:

Fig. 6.11 Examples of structural element deterioration. (**a** and **b**) Structural beam deterioration

- *Keycard Systems: These systems use cards encoded with digital information to grant access. They are easy to manage and can be quickly deactivated if lost or stolen.*

Fig. 6.12 Example of distressed structural element. Structural beam crack

- *Keypad Entry:* Residents enter a numeric code to gain access. This system eliminates the need for physical keys or cards but requires regular updates to codes for security.
- *Biometric Systems:* These systems use fingerprint, facial recognition, or retina scans to grant access. Biometric systems offer high security but can be expensive to install and maintain.
- *Smartphone-Based Access:* Modern systems allow access via smartphones using apps or Bluetooth technology. These systems provide convenience and can be integrated with other smart home technologies.

Fig. 6.13 Example of distressed structural element. Failing concrete at structural balcony slabs

Implementation and Management

When implementing an access control system, property managers should consider the specific needs of their property and residents. Factors such as the size of the property, the number of residents, and the desired level of security will influence the choice of system. It is essential to ensure that the system is user-friendly and reliable. Regular maintenance and updates are crucial to keep the system functioning correctly. This includes software updates, battery replacements for wireless components, and routine inspections.

Integrating with Other Security Measures

Access control systems should be integrated with other security measures for comprehensive protection. Surveillance cameras can monitor entry points and common

Fig. 6.14 Example of biohazard. Mold growth on ceiling

areas, providing a visual record of who enters and exits the property. Security lighting can enhance visibility and deter potential intruders. Alarm systems can alert property managers and law enforcement to unauthorized access attempts. Combining these measures creates a layered security approach that enhances overall safety.

Tenant Education and Communication

Educating tenants on how to use access control systems effectively is vital. Property managers should provide clear instructions on operating the system, reporting issues, and what to do if access credentials are lost or stolen. Regular communication about updates to the system or changes in security protocols helps keep residents informed and engaged. Hosting workshops or creating instructional videos can be effective ways to educate tenants.

Legal and Privacy Considerations

Implementing access control systems involves considering legal and privacy issues. Property managers must ensure that the systems comply with local laws and regulations regarding surveillance and data protection. It is important to establish clear policies on how data collected by access control systems, such as entry logs and biometric data, will be stored, used, and protected. Informing tenants about these policies and obtaining necessary consents is crucial to maintaining trust and compliance with legal requirements.

By implementing robust access control systems and integrating them with other security measures, property managers can significantly enhance the safety and security of residential properties. These systems not only protect tenants and property but also provide a sense of security that can improve tenant satisfaction and retention.

6.11.10 Managing Criminal Activity

Preventive Strategies

Preventing criminal activity in residential properties requires a multifaceted approach that includes environmental design, proactive management, and community involvement. Crime Prevention Through Environmental Design (CPTED) principles can be applied to create safer environments. This includes designing landscapes to eliminate hiding spots, using fencing to define property boundaries, ensuring adequate lighting in common areas, and maintaining clear sightlines around the property. Regularly trimming bushes and trees to reduce cover for potential intruders is also essential.

Tenant Screening

Conducting thorough tenant screening is a critical preventive measure. Background checks, credit checks, and reference verification help identify potential tenants with a history of criminal activity or financial instability. Consistent screening processes ensure that all applicants are evaluated fairly and help maintain a safe living environment. Property managers should also be aware of and comply with fair housing laws during the screening process to avoid discriminatory practices.

Community Engagement

Building a strong sense of community can deter criminal activity. Encouraging residents to get to know their neighbors and look out for each other can create an informal neighborhood watch. Hosting community events and meetings can foster relationships and build trust among residents. Providing residents with information on how to report suspicious activity and encouraging them to do so can also help prevent crime.

Collaboration with Law Enforcement

Developing a good relationship with local law enforcement can enhance security. Property managers can invite police officers to speak at community meetings, provide crime prevention tips, and conduct safety audits. Regular patrols by local police can serve as a deterrent to criminal activity. Property managers should also stay informed about local crime trends and collaborate with law enforcement to address specific concerns.

Security Personnel

Employing security personnel can provide an additional layer of protection. Security guards can monitor entry points, patrol the property, and respond to incidents. Property managers should ensure that security personnel are well-trained, licensed, and equipped to handle various situations. Clear protocols for communication and coordination between security personnel and property management are essential for effective operations.

Surveillance Systems

Installing surveillance cameras in strategic locations can help deter criminal activity and provide valuable evidence in case of incidents. Cameras should cover entry points, common areas, parking lots, and other vulnerable spots. High-quality cameras with night vision capabilities are recommended. Property managers should ensure that cameras are regularly maintained and that footage is stored securely. Informing residents about the presence of surveillance systems can also enhance their sense of security.

Response Plans

Having a clear and well-documented response plan for criminal incidents is crucial. This plan should outline procedures for reporting crimes, cooperating with law enforcement, and communicating with residents. Property managers should provide training for staff on how to handle emergencies and ensure that contact information for local police and emergency services is readily available. Regular drills and reviews of the response plan can help ensure preparedness.

Legal Considerations

Managing criminal activity involves understanding and adhering to legal requirements. Property managers must respect tenants' rights and ensure that any security measures do not infringe on their privacy. Clear policies regarding surveillance, data protection, and tenant interactions must be established and communicated to residents. Consulting with legal professionals to ensure compliance with local laws and regulations is advisable.

By implementing these comprehensive strategies, property managers can effectively manage and reduce criminal activity in residential properties. A proactive approach that combines environmental design, tenant screening, community engagement, collaboration with law enforcement, security personnel, surveillance systems, and well-defined response plans creates a safer and more secure living environment for all residents.

6.12 Case Study: Whispering Pines Apartment Gang Issues

The Whispering Pines Apartments in Aurora, Colorado, experienced a significant increase in criminal activity due to the presence of organized gangs. The issues reported included drug trafficking, violent crimes, vandalism, and intimidation of residents, creating a hostile living environment and leading to tenant turnover, property damage, and negative publicity for the property. The safety of the residents and staff was increasingly at risk, and law enforcement interventions were frequent.

Background of Criminal Activity: Whispering Pines Apartments became a hotspot for gang-related activity due to several factors, including deferred building maintenance, lack of robust security measures, and low tenant screening standards. Over time, gangs established a presence in the complex, leading to:

- *Drug Trafficking: Gangs used the property as a base for selling drugs, leading to an influx of nonresidents and illegal activities.*
- *Violence and Intimidation:* Rival gangs frequently engaged in violent altercations on the property, putting residents in danger. Residents also reported feeling unsafe due to gang members threatening and intimidating tenants, including using force to illegally collect and divert rent payment.
- *Vandalism:* Gang members vandalized the property, defacing walls with graffiti, damaging amenities, and destroying property. This contributed to a decline in the overall aesthetic and safety of the complex.
- *Tenant Flight:* Many residents, especially families and older tenants, moved out due to safety concerns, resulting in high vacancy rates and financial losses for the property management team.

What are some strategies that the property manager to implement to curb criminal activity at Whispering Pines?

6.13 Future Trends in Residential Property Management

Residential property management is evolving rapidly with the advancement of *technology-driven amenities*, changing tenant expectations, and shifts in societal trends. Staying ahead of these changes is crucial for property managers who wish to remain competitive and meet the needs of current and future tenants. This section explores some of the most significant trends shaping the future of residential property management, including the growing demand for amenities such as electric vehicle (EV) charging stations, pet grooming facilities, and expanded business center services to accommodate the increase in remote work.

6.13.1 Growing Tenant Demand for Leasing Options and Amenities

Flexible Leasing Options

The changing dynamics of the rental market have led to a growing demand for flexible leasing options. Tenants are seeking more adaptable lease terms that align with their lifestyles and circumstances.

Short-Term Leases:

- *Monthly Leases:* Offering month-to-month leases provides tenants with the flexibility to move without long-term commitments. This option can attract tenants who need temporary housing or are uncertain about their future plans.
- *Seasonal Leases:* Seasonal leases cater to tenants who need housing for a specific period, such as students, contract workers, or vacationers. Providing furnished units and flexible lease terms can enhance the property's appeal.

Co-Living Arrangements:

- *Shared Housing:* Co-living arrangements involve multiple tenants sharing common spaces while having their own private bedrooms. This model offers affordable housing options and fosters a sense of community. Property managers should establish clear guidelines for shared spaces and ensure compatibility among tenants.
- *Roommate Matching:* Implementing roommate matching services helps tenants find compatible roommates, enhancing their living experience. Online platforms and screening processes can facilitate the matching process.

Remote Work Accommodations:

- *Work-from-Home Packages:* Offering work-from-home packages that include high-speed Internet, ergonomic furniture, and access to business center amenities can attract remote workers. These packages provide tenants with the resources they need to be productive and comfortable.
- *Flexible Space Design:* Designing units with flexible spaces that can be easily converted into home offices or study areas caters to the needs of remote workers and students. Providing built-in desks, shelving, and ample electrical outlets enhances functionality.

Rent Payment Flexibility:

- *Flexible Payment Plans:* Offering flexible rent payment plans, such as biweekly or split payments, accommodates tenants' varying income schedules. These plans can reduce financial stress and improve tenant satisfaction.
- *Online Payment Options:* Providing multiple online payment options, including credit card payments, bank transfers, and digital wallets, enhances convenience for tenants and ensures timely rent collection.
- *Cryptocurrency Payment Option:* Accepting cryptocurrency as a rent payment method allows landlords to attract tech-savvy tenants and streamline transactions using blockchain technology. This modern option can provide transparency, faster payments, and potential revenue through cryptocurrency appreciation or staking, though landlords should carefully manage risks like market volatility and regulatory compliance. Implementing this option with trusted payment platforms and clear policies can enhance competitiveness in the rental market.

Health and Wellness Amenities

The emphasis on health and wellness has become a significant trend in residential property management. Tenants are increasingly prioritizing properties that offer amenities and services that promote physical and mental well-being.

Fitness and Recreational Facilities:

- *On-Site Gyms:* Well-equipped fitness centers with a variety of exercise machines, free weights, and fitness classes provide residents with convenient access to

physical activity. Regularly updating equipment and offering diverse fitness programs can enhance resident engagement.
- *Outdoor Spaces:* Creating well-maintained outdoor spaces, such as parks, walking trails, and rooftop gardens, encourages residents to spend time outdoors and engage in physical activities. These spaces can also serve as communal areas for socializing and relaxation.
- *Swimming Pools:* Swimming pools are popular amenities that offer both recreational and fitness benefits. Regular maintenance and safety measures are essential to ensure a positive resident experience.

Wellness Services:
- *Yoga and Meditation Classes:* Offering yoga and meditation classes promotes relaxation and mental well-being. Providing dedicated spaces for these activities can enhance the appeal of the property.
- *Spa Services:* On-site spa services, such as massages, facials, and wellness treatments, provide tenants with convenient access to relaxation and self-care. Partnering with local spa providers can offer a variety of services without significant upfront investment.
- *Mental Health Support:* Providing access to mental health resources, such as counseling services and wellness workshops, supports tenants' overall well-being. Creating a supportive and inclusive environment can improve tenant satisfaction and retention.

Community Building:
- *Social Events:* Organizing social events, such as fitness challenges, wellness workshops, and community gatherings, fosters a sense of community and encourages tenant interaction. These events can also promote healthy living and wellness practices.
- *Community Gardens:* Establishing community gardens allows tenants to grow their own fruits, vegetables, and herbs, promoting healthy eating and sustainability. These gardens can also serve as communal spaces for socializing and relaxation.

Electric Vehicle Charging Stations

As electric vehicles (EVs) become more prevalent, the demand for EV charging stations in residential properties is increasing. This trend is driven by several factors, including environmental concerns, government incentives, and advancements in EV technology.

Environmental and Regulatory Drivers:
- *Environmental Concerns:* With increasing awareness of climate change and environmental sustainability, many tenants are choosing EVs over traditional

gasoline-powered vehicles. Providing EV charging stations aligns with these values and attracts environmentally conscious tenants.
- *Government Incentives:* Many governments offer incentives for both EV buyers and property owners who install charging stations. These incentives can include tax credits, rebates, and grants, making it financially attractive for property managers to invest in this infrastructure.

Technological Advancements:
- *Improved Charging Technology:* Advances in EV charging technology have made it more efficient and accessible. Rapid chargers can now provide a significant charge in a short period, making them more convenient for tenants.
- *Smart Charging Solutions:* Smart charging stations can manage energy usage more effectively, reducing costs for property managers. These systems can optimize charging times based on electricity rates and demand, and integrate with renewable energy sources.

Implementation Strategies:
- *Assessing Demand:* Before installing EV charging stations, property managers should assess the current and projected demand among residents. Surveys and feedback can provide valuable insights into resident needs.
- *Choosing the Right Technology:* Selecting the appropriate type and number of charging stations is crucial. Options range from standard Level 2 chargers to faster DC fast chargers. Property managers should consider factors such as installation costs, maintenance, and compatibility with various EV models.
- *Installation and Maintenance:* Partnering with experienced contractors and service providers ensures proper installation and ongoing maintenance. Regular inspections and updates are necessary to keep the charging stations operational and safe.

Marketing and Resident Engagement:
- *Promoting Green Initiatives:* Highlighting the availability of EV charging stations in marketing materials can attract environmentally conscious residents and enhance the property's reputation.
- *Encouraging Usage:* Providing incentives for residents to use EV charging stations, such as discounted rates or priority access, can encourage adoption and usage.

Pet Grooming Amenities

The increasing number of pet owners among residents has led to a growing demand for pet-friendly amenities. Pet grooming facilities are becoming a popular addition to residential properties, catering to tenants who want convenient and high-quality services for their pets.

Market Demand:

- *Rising Pet Ownership:* Pet ownership has been on the rise, with more residents viewing their pets as family members. This trend has increased the demand for pet-friendly amenities, including grooming services.
- *Convenience Factor:* Residents appreciate the convenience of on-site pet grooming facilities, which save them time and effort. Providing these services can enhance resident satisfaction and retention.

Design and Implementation:

- *Facility Layout:* Designing a pet grooming facility requires careful planning. Key considerations include space for grooming stations, bathing areas, drying stations, and storage for grooming supplies. Safety and hygiene are paramount, with proper ventilation, nonslip flooring, and easy-to-clean surfaces.
- *Equipment and Supplies:* Investing in high-quality grooming equipment and supplies is essential. This includes grooming tables, tubs, dryers, clippers, and grooming products. Partnering with professional groomers can ensure the facility meets industry standards and provides excellent service.
- *Staffing and Training:* Hiring experienced groomers or partnering with local pet grooming businesses can provide professional services to tenants. Training staff on pet handling, grooming techniques, and customer service is crucial for maintaining high standards.

Operational Considerations:

- *Booking and Scheduling:* Implementing an efficient booking and scheduling system ensures smooth operations. Online booking platforms can provide tenants with convenient access to grooming services.
- *Pricing and Packages:* Offering competitive pricing and grooming packages can attract tenants and encourage repeat business. Special promotions and loyalty programs can further enhance tenant engagement.

Marketing and Community Building:

- *Promoting Pet-Friendly Features:* Highlighting pet grooming amenities in marketing materials can attract pet-owning tenants. Social media and community events can showcase these features and engage current and prospective tenants.
- *Community Events:* Hosting pet-related events, such as adoption drives, pet training sessions, and grooming demonstrations, can build a sense of community and strengthen tenant relationships.

Expanded Business Center Services

The shift towards remote work has significantly impacted tenant expectations for business center amenities. As more people work from home, there is a growing need for expanded and enhanced business center services in residential properties.

Trends in Remote Work:

- *Increased Remote Work:* The COVID-19 pandemic accelerated the trend of remote work, and many companies have adopted flexible or hybrid work models. Tenants now seek environments that support productivity and work-life balance.
- *Home Office Limitations:* While some tenants have home offices, others may lack the space or resources to create an effective work environment. Providing well-equipped business centers can meet this need and enhance tenant satisfaction.

Designing Effective Business Centers:

- *Flexible Workspaces:* Modern business centers should offer a variety of workspaces to accommodate different working styles. This includes private offices, shared workspaces, meeting rooms, and collaborative areas.
- *Ergonomic Furniture:* Investing in ergonomic furniture, such as adjustable desks and chairs, improves comfort and productivity for tenants. High-quality furniture can also enhance the overall aesthetic and appeal of the business center.
- *High-Speed Internet:* Reliable, high-speed Internet is essential for remote work. Business centers should provide robust Wi-Fi connectivity and wired Internet options to meet tenant needs.
- *Technology and Equipment:* Equipping business centers with essential technology, such as printers, scanners, videoconferencing equipment, and charging stations, ensures tenants have the tools they need to work efficiently.

Operational Considerations:

- *Access and Security:* Implementing access control systems, such as keycard entry, ensures that only authorized tenants can use the business center. Security measures, such as surveillance cameras and secure storage, protect tenant belongings and data.
- *Booking and Scheduling:* An efficient booking system allows tenants to reserve workspaces and meeting rooms easily. Online platforms and mobile apps can streamline the process and provide real-time availability.
- *Maintenance and Cleanliness:* Regular maintenance and cleaning of the business center are crucial for creating a professional and comfortable environment. Implementing strict cleanliness protocols, especially in shared spaces, ensures tenant safety and satisfaction.

Additional Amenities:

- *Coffee and Refreshments:* Providing complimentary coffee, tea, and refreshments can enhance the tenant experience and create a more welcoming environment.
- *Outdoor Workspaces:* Offering outdoor workspaces, such as patios or rooftop areas with Wi-Fi connectivity, provides tenants with alternative work environments and promotes well-being.

Marketing and Tenant Engagement:

- *Promoting Business Center Amenities:* Highlighting the availability and features of the business center in marketing materials can attract remote workers and professionals. Showcasing tenant testimonials and success stories can further enhance appeal.
- *Community Building:* Hosting networking events, workshops, and seminars in the business center can foster a sense of community and provide tenants with valuable opportunities for professional development and connection.

6.13.2 Adapting to Climate Change: Strategies to Enhance Resilience

As climate change continues to impact weather patterns, infrastructure, and ecosystems, property managers must adopt proactive strategies to enhance the resilience of residential real estate. By integrating sustainable and green building practices into the management of residential properties, property managers can mitigate the current and future risks associated with climate change. This section outlines key strategies such as energy efficiency, renewable energy integration, water conservation, waste management, and green building certifications, offering practical solutions to reduce environmental impact while maintaining long-term property value and tenant satisfaction.

Energy Efficiency and Renewable Energy Integration

Energy efficiency is one of the most effective strategies for adapting residential real estate to climate change. Property managers can implement energy-saving measures to reduce consumption, lower operating costs, and minimize carbon footprints. Examples of energy efficiency improvements include installing energy-efficient windows, upgrading to LED lighting, and retrofitting heating, ventilation, and air conditioning (HVAC) systems to more efficient models. Implementing smart thermostats and motion-activated lighting in common areas also contributes to reducing energy use.

In addition to energy efficiency, integrating renewable energy sources is essential for long-term sustainability. Property managers can explore options such as solar panel installations on rooftops or over parking areas, which can reduce reliance on grid electricity and lower greenhouse gas emissions. Wind energy and geothermal systems may also be viable solutions depending on the location of the property. By generating on-site renewable energy, properties can achieve greater resilience in the face of energy grid disruptions caused by climate-related events.

Water Conservation

Water conservation practices are becoming increasingly important as climate change leads to more frequent droughts and water shortages in many regions. Property managers can implement water-saving strategies by installing low-flow fixtures in residential units and common areas, such as faucets, showerheads, and toilets. Implementing irrigation systems that use rain sensors or drip irrigation can reduce water waste in landscaping, while xeriscaping (landscaping that requires minimal water) can further minimize outdoor water use.

Collecting rainwater through rainwater harvesting systems is another way to conserve water, particularly for non-potable uses such as irrigation. Property managers should also focus on educating residents about water-saving behaviors, such as reducing water usage in daily tasks, to foster a culture of conservation within the community.

Waste Management

Effective waste management is a critical component of sustainable building practices. Property managers can create or improve waste management systems that encourage recycling and composting while minimizing landfill waste. Providing clearly labeled recycling bins in common areas and educating residents about proper waste disposal practices can lead to higher participation in recycling programs.

Composting organic waste, such as food scraps and yard waste, is another way to reduce the volume of waste sent to landfills. Property managers can establish community composting programs or partner with local composting services to manage organic waste responsibly. Additionally, implementing e-waste disposal programs for electronics and batteries helps prevent hazardous materials from polluting the environment.

Green Building Certifications

Green building certifications, such as LEED (Leadership in Energy and Environmental Design), BREEAM (Building Research Establishment Environmental Assessment Method), and ENERGY STAR, provide a framework for adopting sustainable practices and ensuring that buildings meet specific environmental performance standards. Property managers can pursue these certifications to enhance the marketability of their properties while reducing environmental impact. Certified green buildings often attract eco-conscious tenants, increase property value, and provide long-term cost savings through reduced energy and water consumption.

Achieving green building certifications typically involves implementing energy-efficient building systems, improving indoor air quality, reducing water use, and using sustainable materials in construction and renovation. For property managers, this process requires ongoing assessment and collaboration with architects, contractors, and sustainability experts.

Adaptation Measures for Climate Resilience

In addition to sustainable building practices, property managers can implement specific adaptation measures to enhance resilience to climate change impacts. These measures can help properties withstand extreme weather events and minimize damage.

1. *Flood Mitigation:* For properties located in flood-prone areas, property managers should implement flood mitigation strategies such as installing flood barriers, elevating electrical systems, and using permeable pavement to improve water drainage. Installing sump pumps and backflow preventers can also protect properties from water damage during heavy rainfall.
2. *Stormwater Management:* Climate change is increasing the intensity of storms, leading to more stormwater runoff. Property managers can enhance stormwater management systems by using rain gardens, bioswales, and green roofs to absorb excess water and reduce runoff. These systems not only mitigate flood risks but also improve the property's environmental footprint.
3. *Heat Mitigation:* As global temperatures rise, property managers should consider implementing heat mitigation strategies. Planting shade trees and installing reflective roofing materials can help reduce the heat island effect in urban areas, keeping the building and surrounding areas cooler. Installing energy-efficient air conditioning systems and improving insulation can also help reduce indoor temperatures during heat waves.
4. *Wildfire Protection:* For properties located in wildfire-prone regions, property managers should implement defensible space strategies by creating buffer zones around buildings that are clear of flammable vegetation. Using fire-resistant building materials, such as metal roofing and concrete siding, can further protect structures from wildfires. Regularly clearing gutters and rooftops of debris can also reduce fire hazards.

Adapting residential real estate to climate change requires a multifaceted approach that incorporates sustainable and green building practices, as well as proactive adaptation measures to enhance resilience. By focusing on energy efficiency, renewable energy integration, water conservation, waste management, and green building certifications, property managers can reduce environmental impact and create a more sustainable living environment. Furthermore, implementing adaptation measures such as flood mitigation, stormwater management, heat mitigation, and wildfire protection ensures that residential properties remain resilient in the face of climate-related challenges. These strategies not only protect the long-term value of the property but also foster a healthier and more sustainable community for residents.

6.13.3 The Role of Proptech in Property Management

The integration of property technology (proptech) is revolutionizing the residential property management industry. Proptech solutions enhance efficiency, streamline operations, and improve tenant experience through innovative applications and platforms.

Automation and Efficiency:

- *Automated Rent Collection:* Proptech platforms automate rent collection, reducing administrative burden and ensuring timely payments. Tenants can set up automatic payments, view their payment history, and receive reminders.
- *Maintenance Management:* Automated maintenance management systems allow tenants to submit requests online, track progress, and receive updates. Property managers can prioritize tasks, assign work orders, and monitor completion.
- *Smart Building Systems:* Integrating smart building systems, such as HVAC control, lighting automation, and energy management, enhances operational efficiency and reduces costs. These systems can be managed remotely and provide real-time data for informed decision-making.

Enhanced Tenant Experience:
- *Tenant Portals:* Comprehensive tenant portals provide a one-stop platform for tenants to access important information, make payments, submit maintenance requests, and communicate with property management.
- *Virtual Tours and Leasing:* Virtual tour technology enables prospective tenants to explore properties remotely, enhancing the leasing process. Online leasing platforms streamline applications, approvals, and lease signings.
- *Community Engagement:* Proptech solutions facilitate community engagement through digital communication tools, event calendars, and social networking features. Tenants can connect with neighbors, participate in community activities, and stay informed about property updates.

Data-Driven Decision-Making:
- *Predictive Analytics:* Utilizing predictive analytics helps property managers anticipate trends, such as occupancy rates, maintenance needs, and tenant preferences. This data-driven approach enables proactive management and strategic planning.
- *Tenant Insights:* Analyzing tenant data provides valuable insights into demographics, behaviors, and satisfaction levels. Property managers can tailor services, amenities, and communication strategies to meet tenant needs.

Sustainability and Energy Management:
- *Energy Monitoring:* Proptech solutions for energy monitoring track consumption patterns and identify areas for improvement. Property managers can implement energy-saving measures and monitor their impact in real time.
- *Renewable Energy Integration:* Integrating renewable energy sources, such as solar panels and wind turbines, with smart energy management systems enhances sustainability and reduces operational costs.
- *Environmental Impact Reporting:* Proptech platforms provide tools for tracking and reporting environmental impact metrics, such as carbon footprint and water usage. These reports demonstrate the property's commitment to sustainability and attract eco-conscious tenants.

Security and Access Control:

- *Smart Security Systems:* Proptech-enabled security systems, including surveillance cameras, access control, and alarm systems, enhance property security. These systems can be monitored remotely and provide real-time alerts.
- *Keyless Entry:* Implementing keyless entry systems, such as smart locks and biometric access, improves convenience and security for tenants. Property managers can easily manage access permissions and monitor entry logs.

Challenges and Considerations:

- *Privacy and Data Security:* Ensuring the privacy and security of tenant data is a critical consideration when implementing proptech solutions. Property managers must adhere to data protection regulations and employ robust security measures.
- *Technology Adoption:* Encouraging tenants and staff to adopt new technologies may require training and support. Providing clear instructions and demonstrating the benefits of proptech solutions can facilitate adoption.
- *Cost and ROI:* Evaluating the cost and return on investment (ROI) of proptech solutions is essential. Property managers should consider the long-term benefits, such as increased efficiency, tenant satisfaction, and reduced operational costs, when making investment decisions.

6.13.4 Embracing Diversity and Inclusion

Promoting diversity and inclusion in residential properties is not only a social responsibility but also a key factor in creating vibrant and welcoming communities. Property managers should adopt inclusive practices that reflect the diverse backgrounds and needs of their tenants.

Inclusive Marketing and Leasing Practices:

- *Fair Housing Compliance:* Adhering to fair housing laws and ensuring nondiscriminatory marketing and leasing practices is essential. Training staff on fair housing regulations and fostering an inclusive culture can prevent discriminatory behaviors.
- *Multilingual Services:* Providing leasing and property information in multiple languages accommodates tenants with diverse linguistic backgrounds. Hiring multilingual staff or using translation services can enhance communication and tenant satisfaction.

Cultural Sensitivity:

- *Celebrating Diversity:* Organizing cultural events and celebrations that reflect the diverse backgrounds of tenants fosters a sense of community and belonging. Recognizing cultural holidays and traditions can create an inclusive environment.

- *Inclusive Amenities:* Offering amenities that cater to diverse tenant needs, such as religious prayer rooms, community kitchens for cultural cooking, and inclusive fitness classes, enhances tenant experience.

Accessible Housing:

- *ADA Compliance:* Ensuring that properties meet the requirements of the Americans with Disabilities Act (ADA) is crucial for providing accessible housing. This includes accessible entrances, elevators, restrooms, and common areas.
- *Universal Design:* Implementing universal design principles creates inclusive living environments for tenants of all abilities. Features such as wider doorways, grab bars, and adjustable countertops enhance accessibility.

Tenant Engagement and Feedback:

- *Tenant Surveys:* Conducting regular tenant surveys to gather feedback on diversity and inclusion efforts helps identify areas for improvement. Engaging with tenants through focus groups and community meetings fosters open communication.
- *Inclusive Policies:* Developing and implementing policies that promote diversity and inclusion, such as anti-discrimination policies and diversity training for staff, creates a supportive and respectful community.

6.13.5 Staying Informed on Legal Changes

The laws governing rental properties and property management practices are constantly evolving, and property managers must stay informed about any changes that could affect how they operate. New regulations or court rulings can impact everything from eviction procedures and tenant screening to fair housing laws and property maintenance requirements.

To stay informed, property managers should:

- *Regularly Attend Legal and Industry Training: Attending workshops, seminars, and webinars on property management laws can help managers stay up to date on the latest legal developments.*
- *Join Professional Organizations:* Membership in property management organizations discussed in Chap. 1. These organizations can provide access to legal resources, educational materials, and updates on legal changes.
- *Consult with Legal Counsel:* Establishing a relationship with an attorney who specializes in real estate or property management law can provide property managers with expert advice when dealing with complex legal issues.
- *Subscribe to Industry Newsletters:* Many industry publications offer regular updates on legal changes that affect property management. Subscribing to these resources can help property managers stay informed without dedicating significant time to legal research.

6.14 Case Study: Inverwood Heights Apartment Complex

Inverwood Heights is a large apartment complex consisting of three 10-story buildings, each with 50 units. The complex is equipped with HVAC systems, elevators, centralized plumbing, lighting, and trash chute systems. Over the past year, the property management team has encountered several issues, including inconsistent heating in multiple units during the winter, frequent elevator breakdowns, and tenant complaints about poor lighting in common areas and an unresponsive trash chute system. Additionally, Inverwood Heights has a large outdoor pool with mechanical systems that have required multiple costly repairs. The management team is preparing a comprehensive maintenance and budgeting plan to address these issues while planning for future upgrades to meet resident demands, such as installing electric vehicle (EV) charging stations.

Discussion Questions

1. *HVAC System Issues:*
   - *What steps should the management team take to resolve the inconsistent heating issues in the affected units?*
   - How can the team ensure regular maintenance of the HVAC system to prevent future problems?
2. *Elevator Maintenance:*
   - *What actions should the property management take to address frequent elevator breakdowns and ensure tenant safety?*
   - How can regular elevator inspections help in maintaining elevator functionality and compliance with safety regulations?
3. *Lighting and Trash Chute Systems:*
   - *What improvements can be made to the common area lighting to address tenant complaints and improve energy efficiency?*
   - What strategies can the property management implement to ensure the trash chute system remains functional and sanitary?
4. *Pool Mechanical System:*
   - *How should the management approach ongoing issues with the pool's mechanical systems to reduce costly repairs?*
   - What steps should be taken to maintain the pool system in compliance with health and safety standards?
5. *Future Planning and Budgeting:*
   - *How can the property management team incorporate replacement reserves into the budgeting process for long-term repairs and upgrades?*
   - What should be considered when planning for the installation of EV charging stations to meet growing tenant demands?

6.15 Review Questions

1. *Which of the following is a primary benefit of using property management software in residential property management?*
   (A) Increasing property value
   (B) Streamlining operations and communication
   (C) Reducing the need for maintenance staff
   (D) Eliminating tenant turnover
2. *What is one way technology improves security in residential property management?*
   (A) Offering virtual property tours
   (B) Using automated rent collection systems
   (C) Installing access control systems and smart locks
   (D) Reducing the need for in-person interactions
3. *Which of the following is a popular property management platform used in residential property management?*
   (A) Salesforce
   (B) AppFolio
   (C) Trello
   (D) Google Sheets
4. *What is the primary purpose of financial reporting in property management?*
   (A) To set rental rates
   (B) To evaluate employee performance
   (C) To track income, expenses, and overall financial health
   (D) To communicate directly with tenants
5. *Which of the following is typically included in a property management financial report?*
   (A) Renters' credit scores
   (B) Occupancy rates
   (C) Income statements and cash flow analysis
   (D) Landscaping schedules
6. *Reserve fund management is important for which of the following reasons?*
   (A) To allocate funds for unexpected property repairs
   (B) To increase tenant turnover
   (C) To reduce employee compensation
   (D) To manage security protocols
7. *In the property management industry, which of the following is essential for employee safety training?*
   (A) Conflict resolution strategies
   (B) Fair housing law updates
   (C) Personal Protective Equipment (PPE) protocols
   (D) Marketing strategies
8. *Which of the following is a key aspect of effective recruitment and hiring in property management?*
   (A) Offering a flexible work schedule

(B) Conducting skills assessments and background checks
(C) Relying on employee referrals only
(D) Avoiding job descriptions

9. *Progressive discipline in disciplinary process typically starts with which action?*
(A) Written warning
(B) Verbal warning
(C) Suspension without pay
(D) Termination

10. *Which of the following insurance types is crucial for protecting property managers and owners from legal claims?*
(A) Property insurance
(B) General liability insurance
(C) Life insurance
(D) Health insurance

11. *Which type of insurance to cover damages caused by fires or natural disasters?*
(A) Vehicle insurance
(B) Property insurance
(C) Liability insurance
(D) Business interruption insurance

12. *Which of the following is not typically covered by general liability insurance for residential properties?*
(A) Slip and fall accidents in common areas
(B) Damage to the tenant's personal property
(C) Third-party bodily injury claims
(D) Legal fees related to liability lawsuits

13. *Which of the following is a common life safety issue property managers need to address?*
(A) Lease renewals
(B) Fire safety and hazard control
(C) Software integration
(D) Social event planning

14. *Which law regulates the use of lead-based paint in residential properties?*
(A) Fair Housing Act
(B) Clean Air Act
(C) Lead-Based Paint Hazard Reduction Act
(D) Uniform Residential Landlord and Tenant Act

15. *Which of the following is NOT a common life safety issue property managers must address?*
(A) Fire safety
(B) Hazard control
(C) Resident marketing
(D) Security systems

16. *Which federal law prohibits discrimination in housing based on race, color, religion, sex, national origin, familial status, or disability?*
(A) Americans with Disabilities Act

   (B) Fair Labor Standards Act
   (C) Fair Housing Act
   (D) Antitrust Law
17. *The Lead-Based Paint Hazard Reduction Act requires property managers to:*
   (A) Remove all lead-based paint from buildings
   (B) Provide disclosures to tenants about potential lead hazards
   (C) Test every property for lead paint every 5 years
   (D) Ban the use of paint on property exteriors
18. *The Americans with Disabilities Act (ADA) requires property managers to:*
   (A) Provide equal access to amenities for disabled residents
   (B) Install additional lighting in parking lots
   (C) Reduce rental rates for disabled tenants
   (D) Offer additional insurance coverage for residents
19. *Which amenity is increasingly demanded by tenants due to the rise in remote work?*
   (A) Playgrounds
   (B) Expanded business centers with office space
   (C) Pet grooming stations
   (D) Fitness centers
20. *How are property managers adjusting to the increased demand for work-from-home accommodations?*
   (A) By reducing the availability of Internet services
   (B) By offering expanded business centers, high-speed Internet, and private office spaces
   (C) By reducing rent in work-from-home units
   (D) By removing common spaces

Answer Key

Answer Key for Unit 1 Review Questions

1. B) Ensuring the optimal performance of the property
2. B) To prevent legal disputes and ensure smooth operations
3. B) Post-World War II
4. B) Educational programs and certifications
5. C) Through management fees and leasing commissions
6. B) They offer essential resources, certifications, and networking opportunities
7. B) To set competitive rental rates and develop effective marketing strategies
8. B) Representing single-family residential property managers
9. B) Minimizing expenses while ensuring property upkeep
10. B) It increases the complexity and professionalism required to manage properties effectively
11. C) Increased consumer confidence and rising property values
12. D) Contraction
13. B) Offer rental concessions and focus on resident retention
14. B) Employment rates improve, consumer confidence returns, and housing demand increases
15. B) Declining property values and reduced construction activity

Answer Key for Unit 2 Case Study

Case Study Exercise: The Green Family's Investment Property
Exercise Answer Key:

1. **Marketing the Property:**
   - Detailed listing should highlight key features such as proximity to schools, parks, and local amenities.
   - Use professional photos and virtual tours to enhance online listings.
   - Schedule open houses and private viewings to accommodate potential tenants.

D. A. Vaughn, *Essentials of Residential Property Management*, Springer Texts in Business and Economics, https://doi.org/10.1007/978-3-031-92329-6

2. **Tenant Screening:**
   – Conduct thorough background checks, credit checks, reference checks, and income verification.
   – Ensure all screening processes comply with fair housing laws to avoid discrimination.
3. **Lease Agreement:**
   – Include essential terms such as rent amount, payment due dates, security deposits, maintenance responsibilities, and property use rules.
   – Ensure the lease agreement is legally compliant and reviewed by a legal professional.
4. **Maintenance and Repairs:**
   – Conduct a detailed inspection and prioritize repairs based on urgency.
   – Develop a routine maintenance schedule and plan for seasonal tasks to prevent future issues.
5. **Legal Compliance:**
   – Review local, state, and federal landlord-tenant laws to ensure compliance.
   – Include necessary legal clauses in the lease agreement to protect both the owner and the tenant.

Challenges Answer Key:

1. **Maintenance Challenge:**
   – Prioritize the leaking roof repair immediately. Plan a phased approach for drainage issues, starting with the most critical areas.
   – Balance repairs within the provided budget while addressing the most urgent needs first.
2. **Community Challenge:**
   – Address noise complaints by verifying the issues, communicating with involved residents, and implementing quiet hours.
   – Encourage community participation through meetings and social events to build better relationships among residents.
3. **Regulatory Compliance Challenge:**
   – Plan and implement the installation of fire hydrants and road improvements in compliance with new regulations.
   – Communicate the planned changes and benefits to residents to gain their cooperation and minimize disruption.

Answer Key for Unit 2 Review Questions

1. B) Creating detailed listings with high-quality photos
2. B) Credit history and references
3. B) To tailor management approaches to tenant needs and preferences
4. B) Clear terms and conditions, including rent amount and payment due dates
5. B) Regular inspections and seasonal maintenance tasks
6. B) To prevent small issues from becoming major problems

7. B) Having a list of reliable contractors
8. B) To prevent legal disputes and ensure smooth operations
9. B) To ensure funds are available for any damages or unpaid rent
10. B) Fair Housing Act

Answer Key for Unit 3 Case Study

Case Study: Riviera Palm Resort

1. **Reservation Management:**
   - Riviera Palm Resort can improve its reservation system by implementing a tiered priority system based on ownership levels or a lottery for high-demand dates. Investing in advanced scheduling software can also streamline the process and reduce conflicts.
   - To communicate reservation policies effectively, the resort should use multiple channels such as email, a mobile app, and in-person owner meetings, ensuring clarity about booking timelines and alternative options during peak periods.
2. **Maintenance Challenges:**
   - Management should conduct a comprehensive assessment of the property's infrastructure to prioritize urgent repairs and create a phased plan for renovations. Allocating reserve funds and exploring bulk purchasing agreements for materials can help control costs.
   - To maintain guest satisfaction, proactive maintenance schedules should be implemented, and clear communication with guests about ongoing work can help set expectations.
3. **Guest Satisfaction:**
   - Addressing housekeeping complaints requires regular staff training, consistent quality checks, and possibly increasing staffing levels during peak seasons. Introducing a feedback mechanism for guests to report issues in real time can help resolve problems promptly.
   - Measures to improve guest satisfaction include enhancing customer service training, maintaining well-kept amenities, and ensuring a smooth check-in/check-out process.
4. **Amenities Expansion:**
   - Before adding a spa, management should evaluate owner demand, analyze competitor offerings, and assess the initial investment and operational costs. A survey of owners and guests can help gauge interest and willingness to pay for spa services.
   - To evaluate ROI, the resort should project revenue from spa services, factor in potential increases in maintenance fees, and consider how the amenity might improve the property's marketability and owner satisfaction.

Answer Key for Unit 3 Review Questions

1. B) Shared ownership and interval-based usage
2. B) A fractional ownership interest in real property
3. B) Increased flexibility to book various locations and times
4. C) Resort management company or board of directors
5. B) Annual maintenance fees
6. C) Access to a wide range of properties and services
7. B) Coordinating high-demand periods equitably among owners
8. B) Shared ownership divided among a small number of owners with extended usage rights
9. C) To fund long-term capital improvements and unexpected repairs
10. A) Federal Trade Commission (FTC)

Answer Key for Unit 4 Case Study

Case Study: Evergreen Manufactured Home Park

1. Maintenance:

How would you prioritize the maintenance tasks identified during your inspection?

1. Safety and Health Hazards:
   - Address immediate safety and health hazards first. This includes fixing the leaking roof of the community center to prevent structural damage and addressing drainage issues causing water pooling to avoid mold and mosquito breeding grounds.
2. Critical Repairs:
   - Prioritize repairs that could lead to more significant problems if left unattended, such as plumbing issues, electrical faults, and significant structural repairs.
3. Preventive Maintenance:
   - Schedule preventive maintenance tasks, such as HVAC servicing, gutter cleaning, and regular inspections of all homesites to identify and mitigate potential issues before they become major problems.
4. Tenant Comfort:
   - Attend to repairs that directly impact tenant comfort, such as fixing leaky faucets, repainting common areas, and ensuring all shared facilities are in good working order.
5. Aesthetic Improvements:
   - Lastly, focus on aesthetic improvements that enhance the park's curb appeal, such as landscaping, painting, and upgrading playground equipment.

What steps can you take to prevent future maintenance issues and ensure the park remains in good condition?

1. Regular Inspections:
   - Conduct regular inspections of all homesites and common areas to identify maintenance needs early.
2. Preventive Maintenance Plan:
   - Implement a preventive maintenance plan that includes routine tasks like HVAC servicing, plumbing inspections, and pest control.
3. Maintenance Logs:
   - Keep detailed logs of all maintenance activities to track recurring issues and plan future maintenance needs more effectively.
4. Quality Repairs:
   - Ensure repairs are done by qualified professionals to prevent recurring problems and reduce long-term maintenance costs.
5. Resident Involvement:
   - Encourage residents to report maintenance issues promptly and provide an easy reporting system, such as an online portal or a dedicated phone line.
6. Education:
   - Educate residents on basic maintenance practices they can perform to help maintain their homes and the community.

2. Community Management:

What strategies can you use to improve communication and foster a sense of community among residents?

1. Regular Newsletters:
   - Send out regular newsletters to keep residents informed about community news, upcoming events, and important updates.
2. Community Meetings:
   - Hold regular community meetings to provide a platform for residents to voice their concerns, share ideas, and stay informed about park management activities.
3. Social Events:
   - Organize social events like barbecues, holiday parties, and community clean-up days to encourage interaction and build a sense of community.
4. Open Communication Channels:
   - Maintain open lines of communication through various channels, such as a community website, email, and social media groups.
5. Resident Feedback:
   - Implement a system for collecting resident feedback, such as suggestion boxes or online surveys, and act on the suggestions where feasible.
6. Resident Involvement:
   - Encourage residents to participate in community activities and decision-making processes to foster a sense of ownership and involvement.

How would you handle the complaints about noise and disturbances to ensure a peaceful living environment for all residents?

1. Investigate Complaints:
   - Start by investigating the complaints to understand the nature and extent of the disturbances.
2. Clear Policies:
   - Establish and communicate clear policies regarding noise and disturbances, including quiet hours and acceptable noise levels.
3. Mediation:
   - Facilitate mediation sessions between residents involved in disputes to find mutually acceptable solutions.
4. Enforcement
   - Enforce community rules consistently and fairly, applying consequences for violations as outlined in the community guidelines.
5. Resident Education:
   - Educate residents on the importance of respecting their neighbors and maintaining a peaceful community environment.
6. Proactive Measures:
   - Implement proactive measures such as installing noise-reducing features in problem areas and promoting community awareness about noise policies.

3. Regulatory Compliance:

What steps would you take to ensure the park complies with the new zoning regulations?

1. Consult with Experts:
   - Consult with zoning experts, legal advisors, and local authorities to fully understand the new regulations and their implications.
2. Assessment:
   - Conduct a thorough assessment of the park's current infrastructure to identify areas that need upgrades or modifications to comply with the new regulations.
3. Planning:
   - Develop a detailed plan for implementing the necessary changes, including timelines, budgets, and resources needed.
4. Permits and Approvals:
   - Obtain all required permits and approvals from local authorities before starting any construction or modifications.
5. Implementation:
   - Execute the compliance plan systematically, ensuring all upgrades are made according to the plan and within the specified timelines.
6. Regular Monitoring:
   - Regularly monitor the progress of the compliance activities to ensure they are on track and address any issues promptly.

How can you communicate these changes to residents and involve them in the process to minimize disruption?

1. Informative Meetings:
   - Hold informative meetings to explain the new regulations, the reasons for the changes, and the benefits for the community.
2. Clear Communication:
   - Provide clear and concise written communication, such as letters or newsletters, detailing the planned changes and their timelines.
3. Resident Involvement:
   - Involve residents in the planning process by seeking their input and addressing their concerns. This can be done through surveys, suggestion boxes, or town hall meetings.
4. Regular Updates:
   - Keep residents regularly updated on the progress of the compliance activities, including any changes to schedules or plans.
5. Minimize Disruption:
   - Plan the implementation of changes in a way that minimizes disruption to residents, such as scheduling work during times when most residents are at work or school.
6. Feedback Channels:
   - Provide channels for residents to give feedback and ask questions throughout the compliance process, ensuring their concerns are heard and addressed.

Answer Key for Unit 4 Review Questions

1. B) Manufactured homes on leased land with shared amenities
2. B) Affordability and community living
3. B) Families, retirees, and individuals seeking affordable housing
4. B) Stigma and potential depreciation
5. B) Regular maintenance and ensuring safety
6. B) To build trust and address resident concerns promptly
7. B) Efficient rent collection and regular financial reporting
8. B) To ensure legal compliance and avoid penalties
9. B) Assessment of major components and estimation of future repair costs
10. B) Adhering to the Fair Housing Act

Answer Key for Unit 5-A Case Study: Riverview Apartments

Marketing:

What additional marketing strategies could you implement to increase interest in the property?

- Utilize social media advertising with targeted ads to reach potential tenants.
- Partner with local businesses and community organizations to promote the property.

- Offer referral incentives to current tenants for bringing in new tenants.

How can you highlight the property's unique features to make it stand out in the rental market?

- Emphasize amenities such as the community pool, gym, and proximity to local attractions.
- Use high-quality photos and virtual tours to showcase the units and common areas.
- Highlight recent upgrades and renovations in the property listings.

Tenant Screening:

What factors should you consider when deciding between the two potential tenants?

- Evaluate the stability of their income and employment history.
- Consider their rental history and references from previous landlords.
- Balance credit score against other factors like rental history and personal references.

How can you ensure that the tenant screening process is fair and compliant with fair housing laws?

- Apply the same screening criteria and process uniformly to all applicants.
- Avoid asking questions or making decisions based on race, color, religion, sex, national origin, familial status, or disability.
- Document the screening process and decisions for transparency and accountability.

Maintenance:

How would you prioritize the maintenance tasks identified during your inspection?

- Address urgent safety and health hazards, such as the broken pool pump, immediately.
- Follow with preventive maintenance tasks to avoid future problems, like HVAC servicing and pest control.
- Lastly, attend to aesthetic improvements and non-urgent repairs to enhance tenant satisfaction.

What steps can you take to prevent future maintenance issues and ensure the property remains in good condition?

- Implement a routine maintenance schedule for regular inspections and upkeep of common areas and units.
- Establish a system for prompt reporting and addressing of maintenance issues by tenants.
- Use high-quality materials and professional services for repairs to ensure long-lasting solutions.

Answer Key for Unit 5-B Case Study: Harmony Condominium Association

Dispute Resolution:

What steps can you take to resolve the current disputes among residents regarding noise levels and use of common areas?

- Investigate the complaints by talking to involved parties and gathering information about the incidents.
- Enforce existing rules regarding noise and common area usage, possibly introducing stricter guidelines for late-night activities.
- Mediate a meeting between the conflicting parties to reach a mutually agreeable solution.

How can you implement a system to handle future disputes effectively?

- Establish a formal complaint procedure that allows residents to report issues easily.
- Create a mediation committee consisting of board members and residents to address disputes.
- Develop clear and enforceable community rules that outline acceptable behavior and consequences for violations.

Reserve Fund Management:

What strategies can you use to ensure the reserve fund is adequately funded?

- Conduct a reserve study to determine the necessary reserve levels and adjust the budget accordingly.
- Gradually increase monthly assessments to build the reserve fund over time.
- Explore special assessments or loans for major immediate repairs if necessary.

How would you prioritize the repairs needed for the swimming pool and roof given the current financial constraints?

- Address the most critical safety and structural issues first, such as the roof repairs.
- Schedule the swimming pool repairs for a later date when funds are more readily available.
- Communicate the prioritization plan to residents to maintain transparency and understanding.

Regulatory Compliance:

What steps should you take to ensure compliance with the new state regulations regarding energy-efficient lighting and safety inspections?

- Conduct an audit to identify all areas requiring energy-efficient lighting upgrades.
- Schedule regular safety inspections and document all findings and actions taken.
- Budget for the upgrades and inspections, possibly spreading costs over several months to manage financial impact.

How can you communicate these changes to residents and involve them in the process to minimize disruption?

- Hold informational meetings to explain the new regulations and their benefits.
- Provide written updates through newsletters or emails detailing the implementation plan and timelines.
- Involve residents in the process by seeking their input on preferred lighting options and scheduling inspections at convenient times.

Answer Key for Unit 5-C Case Study: Greenview Cooperative

Managing Shareholder Relationships:

What steps can you take to resolve the current conflicts among shareholders regarding common area usage and noise complaints?

- Investigate the complaints by talking to involved parties and gathering information about the incidents.
- Implement and enforce clear rules regarding common area usage and noise levels, including designated quiet hours.
- Mediate a meeting between the conflicting parties to reach a mutually agreeable solution.

How can you improve communication and foster a sense of community among shareholders?

- Regularly update shareholders through newsletters, emails, and bulletin boards about community events and important decisions.
- Organize social events and community meetings to encourage interaction and build relationships among shareholders.
- Establish a suggestion box or feedback system to involve shareholders in decision-making processes and address their concerns.

Fee Collection and Financial Management:

What strategies can you use to ensure the timely and efficient collection of maintenance fees?

- Offer multiple payment options, such as online payments, direct debit, and checks, to accommodate different preferences.
- Implement a consistent fee collection policy with clear deadlines and penalties for late payments.
- Send regular reminders and statements to keep shareholders informed of their payment status.

How would you address delinquent accounts and improve overall financial management for the cooperative?

- Establish a clear policy for handling delinquent accounts, including late fees and payment plans.
- Communicate with delinquent shareholders to understand their situation and work out feasible payment arrangements.

- Regularly review and adjust the budget to ensure adequate funding for operations and reserve contributions.

Legal Compliance:

What steps should you take to update the cooperative's bylaws to comply with new state regulations?

- Review the new state regulations in detail and identify the specific changes needed in the bylaws.
- Draft the necessary amendments to the bylaws and present them to the board of directors for approval.
- Schedule a special meeting or include the amendments in the agenda of the next shareholders' meeting for a vote.

How can you effectively communicate these changes to shareholders and ensure their approval?

- Hold informational meetings to explain the reasons for the changes and their benefits to the community.
- Provide written summaries of the proposed changes and the implications for shareholders.
- Encourage shareholder participation in the voting process through reminders and clear instructions on how to vote.

Answer Key Unit 5-D Case Study: The Hammocks Community Association Fraud Scheme

1. **Implement Regular Independent Financial Audits:**
   - Conduct annual or bi-annual independent audits performed by certified public accountants (CPAs) who are not affiliated with the board or management.
   - Regular audits help detect discrepancies early, deter fraudulent behavior, and provide objective oversight of financial records.
2. **Ensure Transparent Financial Reporting:**
   - Provide homeowners with detailed monthly or quarterly financial reports, including income statements, balance sheets, and budget-to-actual comparisons.
   - Make financial documents easily accessible through secure online portals or during scheduled HOA meetings to promote accountability.
3. **Establish Strong Internal Controls:**
   - Implement dual-signature requirements for large disbursements and payments to ensure no single individual has unchecked control over funds.
   - Segregate financial duties so that different individuals handle budgeting, record-keeping, and financial approvals, reducing the risk of fraud.
4. **Encourage Active Homeowner Participation:**
   - Foster an engaged community by encouraging residents to attend board meetings, participate in financial committees, and ask questions about the HOA's financial health.

– Ensure meetings are properly noticed and accessible, following state laws regarding open meetings and homeowner rights.

1.1 Answer Key for Unit 5-E Case Study: Lakeview HOA

Managing Resident Relationships:

What steps can you take to resolve the current conflicts among residents regarding drivers speeding in the community and use of common areas?

- Investigate the complaints by talking to involved parties and gathering information about the incidents.
- Implement and enforce clear rules regarding speed limits and usage hours for common areas like the clubhouse.
- Mediate a meeting between the conflicting parties to reach a mutually agreeable solution.

How can you improve communication and foster a sense of community among residents?

- Regularly update residents through newsletters, emails, and community meetings about important news and events.
- Organize social events and activities to encourage interaction and build relationships among residents.
- Establish a suggestion box or feedback system to involve residents in decision-making processes and address their concerns.

Maintenance Fee Collection and Financial Management:

What strategies can you use to ensure the timely and efficient collection of maintenance fees?

- Offer multiple payment options, such as online payments, direct debit, and checks, to accommodate different preferences.
- Implement a consistent fee collection policy with clear deadlines and penalties for late payments.
- Send regular reminders and statements to keep residents informed of their payment status.

How would you address delinquent accounts and improve overall financial management for the HOA?

- Establish a clear policy for handling delinquent accounts, including late fees and payment plans.
- Communicate with delinquent homeowners to understand their situation and work out feasible payment arrangements.
- Regularly review and adjust the budget to ensure adequate funding for operations and reserve contributions.

Maintenance and HOA Reserve Funds:

What steps should you take to ensure the reserve fund is adequately funded for future repairs?

- Conduct a reserve study to assess the condition of major components and estimate future repair costs.

- Adjust the budget to include regular contributions to the reserve fund based on the reserve study's recommendations.
- Consider implementing special assessments or increasing monthly fees if necessary to meet funding requirements.

How can you effectively communicate the reserve funding plan to residents and gain their support?

- Hold informational meetings to explain the reserve study findings and the importance of adequate reserve funding.
- Provide written summaries of the reserve funding plan and its benefits to the community.
- Encourage resident participation in the decision-making process and address any concerns or questions they may have.

Answer Key for Unit 5 Review Questions

1. B) Enhancing property value through effective management
2. B) Condominium associations
3. B) More complex tenant interactions and community dynamics
4. B) Creating detailed listings with high-quality photos
5. B) To ensure reliable and responsible tenants
6. B) Regular inspections and preventive maintenance
7. A) Making key decisions about property management and maintenance
8. B) To build trust and accountability
9. B) Assessment of major components and estimation of future repair costs
10. B) Collective ownership of the property through shares
11. B) Addressed through fair and transparent processes
12. B) Clear scope of services and compensation
13. B) Making decisions that reflect the interests of the community
14. B) To build trust and keep residents informed
15. B) Implementing a consistent and efficient collection process
16. B) Regular inspections and addressing potential issues early
17. B) To ensure funds are available for future repairs and replacements
18. B) Consistent and fair application of rules
19. B) Using clear performance metrics and regular reviews
20. B) To formalize the relationship and outline expectations and compensation

Answer Key for Unit 6-A Case Study: Whispering Pines Apartment Gang Issues

Strategies to Curb Criminal Activity:

1. **Collaborating with Law Enforcement:**
   - **Partnership with Police:** The property manager at Whispering Pines could collaborate with local law enforcement to create a stronger police presence on

the property. Organizing regular patrols, engaging off-duty police officers as part of the security team, and setting up a neighborhood watch program could deter criminal activity.
   - **Criminal Trespass Orders:** Implementing criminal trespass orders would allow law enforcement to remove individuals who do not reside at the property but engage in criminal behavior. This strategy can also help monitor non-residents who may frequent the property for illegal activities.
2. **Enhancing Security Measures:**
   - **Improving Surveillance:** Upgrading the security infrastructure by installing high-definition surveillance cameras in strategic areas such as entrances, parking lots, hallways, and common areas is a critical step. Cameras should be equipped with night vision and cover all areas prone to gang activity.
   - **Access Control Systems:** Implementing keycard or biometric access control systems at all entry points can prevent unauthorized individuals from entering the property. This would limit the ease of access for gang members and other criminal elements who do not reside in the complex.
   - **Increased Lighting:** Ensuring that all common areas, including parking lots, hallways, and recreational spaces, are well-lit can reduce opportunities for criminal behavior. Studies show that well-lit areas deter illegal activities and make residents feel safer.
   - **Hiring Private Security:** Engaging a reputable private security firm to patrol the complex 24/7 can act as a deterrent. Security guards can regularly patrol the premises, intervene during disturbances, and collaborate with law enforcement when necessary.
3. **Tenant Screening and Lease Enforcement:**
   - **Stricter Tenant Screening:** Strengthening tenant screening processes is a proactive approach to preventing criminal activity. Background checks, credit checks, and criminal history reviews should be conducted for all prospective tenants to filter out individuals with a history of illegal activity.
   - **Lease Enforcement:** Implementing a zero-tolerance policy for criminal activity and ensuring that lease agreements clearly outline the consequences for tenants involved in illegal behavior would be critical. Violations should result in eviction, and lease clauses should support the property manager's ability to swiftly remove tenants who contribute to the unsafe environment.
4. **Community Engagement and Support Programs:**
   - **Resident Engagement Programs:** Organizing community-building events such as neighborhood watch meetings, social gatherings, and family-oriented activities can strengthen the sense of community. When residents feel invested in the community, they are more likely to report suspicious activities and help keep the environment safe.
   - **Collaboration with Social Services:** The property manager could also work with local social services to provide support for residents affected by gang violence or drug activity. Offering resources like addiction counseling, youth intervention programs, and mental health services can address some of the

root causes of gang involvement and help rehabilitate individuals before the situation escalates.
  - **Tenant Support Hotline:** Establishing a confidential hotline for residents to report criminal activity anonymously could encourage more tenants to come forward without fear of retaliation from gang members. This information can be shared with law enforcement to address issues more effectively.
5. **Physical Property Improvements:**
  - **Crime Prevention Through Environmental Design (CPTED):** Implementing CPTED principles can significantly improve the safety of the property. This includes strategies like trimming overgrown bushes that can provide hiding places, installing fencing or gates around the perimeter, and ensuring that common areas are open and visible to both residents and law enforcement.
  - **Repairing and Cleaning the Property:** Restoring the property by repairing vandalism, cleaning graffiti, and maintaining a clean, orderly environment can signal that the property management is taking safety and upkeep seriously. The broken windows theory suggests that visible signs of disorder, such as broken windows or graffiti, can contribute to further criminal activity. Ensuring the property looks well-maintained may discourage such behavior.

Answer Key for Unit 6-B Case Study: Inverwood Heights Residential Complex

1. **HVAC System Issues:**
  - The management team should conduct a full inspection of the HVAC system, focusing on ductwork, vents, and thermostats to identify the cause of inconsistent heating.
  - They should schedule regular maintenance for the HVAC system, including cleaning filters, checking for leaks, and ensuring the system operates efficiently to prevent future heating problems.
2. **Elevator Maintenance:**
  - The property management should hire certified elevator technicians to inspect and repair the elevators, addressing any mechanical issues that pose safety risks.
  - Regular elevator inspections will ensure compliance with safety regulations, extend the lifespan of the elevators, and reduce the frequency of breakdowns.
3. **Lighting and Trash Chute Systems:**
  - Installing energy-efficient LED lighting in common areas can improve visibility, reduce energy costs, and address tenant complaints about poor lighting.
  - Implementing a scheduled cleaning and maintenance program for the trash chute system will prevent blockages, reduce odors, and ensure sanitary conditions in the building.

4. **Pool Mechanical System:**
   - The management should work with a qualified pool technician to diagnose the root cause of the mechanical system failures and implement preventive maintenance practices to avoid costly repairs.
   - Regular testing of water chemistry, proper filter maintenance, and adhering to local health regulations will ensure the pool system operates safely and efficiently.
5. **Future Planning and Budgeting:**
   - The property management should set aside replacement reserves for major repairs like HVAC upgrades, elevator replacements, and pool system repairs, ensuring they are financially prepared for long-term needs.
   - When planning for EV charging stations, the management should assess tenant demand, local zoning regulations, and the electrical capacity of the building to ensure a smooth installation.

Answer Key for Unit 6 Review Questions

1. B) Streamlining operations and communication
2. C) Installing access control systems and smart locks
3. B) AppFolio
4. C) To track income, expenses, and overall financial health
5. C) Income statements and cash flow analysis
6. A) To allocate funds for unexpected property repairs
7. C) Personal Protective Equipment (PPE) protocols
8. B) Conducting skills assessments and background checks
9. B) Verbal warning
10. B) General liability insurance
11. B) Property insurance
12. B) Damage to the tenant's personal property
13. B) Fire safety and hazard control
14. C) Lead-Based Paint Hazard Reduction Act
15. C) Resident marketing
16. C) Fair Housing Act
17. B) Provide disclosures to tenants about potential lead hazards
18. A) Provide equal access to amenities for disabled residents
19. B) Expanded business centers with office space
20. B) By offering expanded business centers, high-speed internet, and private office spaces

Glossary of Key Terms

Access Control Systems Security systems that regulate entry and exit to a property or specific areas within a property. Examples include keycard entry systems, security gates, and biometric access controls.

Americans with Disabilities Act (ADA) A federal law that requires reasonable accommodations for individuals with disabilities, ensuring accessibility and non-discrimination in housing and public accommodations.

Antitrust Laws Regulations that promote competition and prevent monopolistic practices in the marketplace. In property management, antitrust laws are relevant in areas such as price-fixing and market allocation agreements.

Apartments Apartments are rental units within a larger building or complex, owned by a single entity or individual. Tenants lease these units, and the property manager oversees the entire building's operations, maintenance, and tenant relations.

Background Check A process used to verify the accuracy of an applicant's history, including criminal records, employment history, and credit status.

Board of Directors Elected representatives of a condominium association, cooperative, or HOA responsible for decision-making, budgeting, and enforcing community policies.

Budgeting The process of creating a financial plan to allocate resources for maintenance, repairs, and other property management expenses.

Building Owners and Managers Association (BOMA) An international organization that provides advocacy, education, and resources for commercial property managers and building owners.

Capital Improvement Major property upgrades or additions that enhance the property's value, extend its life, or adapt it for new uses. Examples include concrete restoration, flooring replacement, pool resurfacing, roof replacements, new HVAC systems, and community amenity upgrades.

Certified Property Manager (CPM) A professional designation offered by the Institute of Real Estate Management (IREM) that signifies expertise and professionalism in property management.

D. A. Vaughn, *Essentials of Residential Property Management*, Springer Texts in Business and Economics, https://doi.org/10.1007/978-3-031-92329-6

Common Areas Areas within a community that are shared by all residents, such as streets, sidewalks, playgrounds, and recreational facilities. Property managers are responsible for maintaining these areas.

Community Association Institute (CAI) An organization dedicated to the needs of community associations, including HOAs, condominium associations, and cooperatives, offering certifications like Association Management Specialist (AMS) and Professional Community Association Manager (PCAM).

Compliance Adherence to local, state, and federal laws and regulations governing property management and landlord-tenant relationships.

Condominium Association A governing body composed of unit owners responsible for the management of shared areas, enforcement of rules, and overall community governance in a condominium property.

Cooperative (Co-op) A multifamily property where residents own shares in a corporation that owns the building, rather than owning individual units outright. Shareholders hold proprietary leases, giving them the right to occupy a specific unit.

Credit Check An evaluation of an applicant's credit history to assess their financial reliability and risk as a tenant.

Cybersecurity The practice of protecting digital systems, networks, and sensitive data from unauthorized access, breaches, or attacks. In property management, cybersecurity involves safeguarding tenant data and operational systems.

Deeded Ownership A form of timeshare ownership in which individuals hold a fractional interest in the property as real estate, granting them perpetual ownership rights that can be sold, transferred, or inherited.

Dispute Resolution The process of resolving conflicts between landlords and tenants, or among tenants, through mediation, arbitration, or legal action.

Duties and Rights of Tenants and Landlords The legal obligations and privileges granted to both tenants and landlords under the lease agreement and applicable landlord-tenant laws.

Exchange Program A service offered by organizations like RCI or Interval International that allows timeshare owners to trade their usage intervals for stays at other properties within the exchange network.

Fair Housing Act (FHA) A federal law that prohibits discrimination in housing based on race, color, religion, sex, national origin, familial status, and disability.

Fiduciary Duty The legal obligation of board members and property managers to act in the best interest of the community or property owners they represent.

Financial Statement A report that outlines the financial status of a multifamily property or community association, including income, expenses, and reserve fund balances.

Fire Safety Plans Comprehensive strategies that outline emergency procedures, fire prevention measures, and evacuation routes to ensure the safety of residents and compliance with fire safety regulations.

Fractional Ownership A high-end timeshare model in which ownership is divided among a smaller group of individuals, offering extended usage rights and a more exclusive experience compared to traditional timeshares.

Emergency Repairs Immediate and necessary repairs required to address urgent issues that pose a risk to safety or property integrity.

Emergency Preparedness Planning and training to handle emergencies such as natural disasters, fires, or security threats. It involves creating emergency response plans, conducting drills, and ensuring residents and staff are informed and prepared.

Employee Handbook A document that outlines company policies, procedures, employee rights and responsibilities, and workplace expectations. It serves as a guide for both employees and management to ensure consistency and compliance.

Enforcement of Rules and Regulations The process by which community managers and boards ensure compliance with established community rules, often involving fines, notices, and, if necessary, legal action.

Eviction The legal process of removing a tenant from a rental property due to violations of the lease agreement or non-payment of rent.

Governing Documents Legal documents such as the Declaration, Bylaws, Articles of Incorporation, and Rules and Regulations that establish the structure and rules of condominium associations, cooperatives, and HOAs.

Hazard Control Practices designed to identify, eliminate, or reduce environmental and safety hazards in residential communities, such as asbestos, radon, mold, and lead-based paint.

Homeowner Association (HOA) An organization in a planned community or subdivision that enforces rules for properties and common areas, funded by dues from homeowners.

Human Resources Management (HRM) The practice of recruiting, hiring, training, evaluating, and managing employees within an organization to ensure a productive and compliant workforce.

HUD Code The Manufactured Home Construction and Safety Standards established by the U.S. Department of Housing and Urban Development (HUD), which regulate the design, construction, and installation of manufactured homes.

HVAC (Heating, Ventilation, and Air Conditioning) A system used to regulate temperature, airflow, and indoor air quality in buildings. It consists of components such as furnaces, boilers, air conditioners, and ventilation ducts, and is critical for maintaining a comfortable living environment.

Indemnification Clause A lease provision stating that one party agrees to compensate the other for certain damages or losses. In leases, this often relates to liability for injuries or damages caused by tenants.

Insurance Coverage Various types of insurance policies designed to protect residential properties, property owners, and managers from financial losses due to damage, liability claims, or other unforeseen events.

Landlord-Tenant Law Legal statutes and regulations that govern the rights and responsibilities of landlords and tenants.

Lead-Based Paint Hazard Reduction Act A federal law that addresses the risks of lead-based paint in residential properties, requiring disclosures, inspections, and mitigation efforts to protect residents from lead poisoning.

Lease Agreement A legal contract between a landlord and tenant that outlines the terms and conditions of the rental arrangement, including rent, term, and use of the property.

Liability Insurance Insurance coverage that protects property owners from legal claims and financial losses related to injuries or damages occurring on the property.

Life Safety Measures and protocols implemented to protect residents from fire, hazardous conditions, and other life-threatening situations. Life safety involves fire detection systems, emergency exits, and hazard mitigation.

Lot Rent The fee paid by a homeowner to rent the land on which the manufactured home is placed. Lot rent typically covers the cost of using the site, utilities, and shared community amenities.

Maintenance Plan A scheduled approach to maintaining a property, including routine inspections, preventive maintenance, and addressing repair needs.

Manufactured Home A factory-built, residential dwelling that meets the federal Manufactured Home Construction and Safety Standards (HUD Code). It is constructed in a controlled environment and transported to its permanent site.

Main Electrical Distribution The main component of a building's electrical system, responsible for distributing electricity from the utility provider to various circuits within the building. For multi-unit properties, each unit may have its own panel, while larger buildings may use centralized systems.

Maintenance Fee Regular payments made by residents in condominiums, cooperatives, HOA, or Timeshare to cover the cost of maintaining common areas and community services.

Manufactured Home Park A community designed for manufactured homes, where tenants typically own the home and rent the lot space. Parks often include shared amenities and services such as utilities, maintenance, and recreational areas.

Marketing Plan A strategic approach to promoting rental properties to potential tenants through various channels, including online listings, social media, and traditional advertising.

National Apartment Association (NAA) An organization representing the interests of multifamily housing professionals, offering certifications such as Certified Apartment Manager (CAM) and National Apartment Leasing Professional (NALP).

National Association of Residential Property Managers (NARPM) An organization dedicated to supporting property managers specializing in single-family residential properties, offering certifications like Residential Management Professional (RMP) and Master Property Manager (MPM).

Plumbing System The network of pipes, drains, valves, and fixtures that supply water for domestic use and remove wastewater. Regular maintenance of the plumbing system is essential for preventing leaks, clogs, and water damage.

Preventive Maintenance Regular, scheduled maintenance tasks aimed at preventing major repairs and extending the life of property components and systems.

Property Maintenance The ongoing upkeep of a property to ensure it remains in good condition and meets health and safety standards.

Property Management The administration, operation, and oversight of real estate properties on behalf of the owner, including tasks such as tenant relations, maintenance, and financial management.

Property Management Agreement A legal contract between a property manager and the community association or property owner that defines the manager's responsibilities, compensation, and scope of services.

Property Management Software Software platforms specifically designed to assist property managers in managing daily operations, such as rent collection, lease management, maintenance requests, financial reporting, and tenant communications.

Proprietary Lease A legal agreement in cooperatives that grants shareholders the right to occupy a specific unit and outlines responsibilities and rights within the co-op.

Remote Work Accommodations Modifications and amenities provided by residential properties to support residents who work from home. This includes offering expanded business centers, high-speed internet, coworking spaces, and private office areas.

Rental Market Analysis The process of evaluating the local rental market to determine competitive rental rates and assess demand for rental properties.

Rental Term The duration of the lease agreement, including the start and end dates, and any renewal options.

Repair Request A formal request submitted by a tenant or property manager to address a specific maintenance or repair need.

Reserve Fund A savings account or other highly liquid asset set aside to finance major repairs and capital improvements in multifamily communities, such as roof replacements, painting, and infrastructure upgrades.

Right-to-Use Agreement A timeshare model where individuals purchase a contractual right to occupy a property for a specific number of years, without acquiring actual ownership of the real estate.

Risk Management The process of identifying, assessing, and prioritizing risks, followed by implementing strategies to minimize and control the impact of unforeseen events. It includes methods such as risk avoidance, risk reduction, risk transfer, and risk retention.

Rules and Regulations The established guidelines and policies set by property owners, landlords, or community associations to govern the use, maintenance, and behavior within a residential property or community. These rules ensure compliance with legal requirements, promote safety, and maintain property value by outlining resident responsibilities, permitted activities, and enforcement procedures.

Safety and Security Protocols Established procedures and technologies used to protect residents and property from crime, unauthorized access, and security breaches. These protocols often include surveillance systems, security personnel, and emergency response plans.

Security Deposit A sum of money collected from the tenant at the beginning of the lease to cover potential damages or unpaid rent.

Severability Clause A provision in a lease or contract that ensures if one part of the agreement is found to be invalid or unenforceable, the remaining provisions will continue to be in effect.

Sewer System A municipal or private infrastructure system that collects and transports wastewater from residential properties to treatment facilities. In rural areas, properties may rely on septic systems for this purpose.

Smart Home Technology Advanced home automation systems that allow tenants and property managers to control and monitor household systems, such as lighting, heating, and security, remotely.

Sustainable Building Practices Environmentally responsible construction and property management practices aimed at reducing energy consumption, minimizing waste, and promoting resource efficiency in residential properties.

Technology-Driven Amenities Modern amenities in residential communities that utilize advanced technology to enhance resident convenience and lifestyle, such as smart home systems, electric vehicle charging stations, and high-speed internet.

Tenant-Landlord Law Regulations governing the rights and responsibilities of both landlords and tenants, applicable to apartment management and leasing.

Tenant Relations The management of interactions and relationships with tenants, including communication, dispute resolution, and ensuring tenant satisfaction.

Tenant Screening The process of evaluating potential tenants to ensure they are reliable and responsible, typically involving background checks, credit checks, and reference verification.

Timeshare A shared ownership model in which multiple individuals own or have usage rights to a property for specific time intervals, typically on a weekly basis, either through deeded ownership or a right-to-use agreement.

Trash Chute System A vertical waste disposal system commonly found in multi-unit residential buildings, allowing residents to dispose of trash easily from each floor. Regular cleaning and maintenance are necessary to prevent blockages and maintain sanitation.

Vendor Management The process of selecting, contracting, and overseeing vendors who provide maintenance and repair services for the property.

Vacation Club A membership-based timeshare system that provides access to a portfolio of properties and services, offering greater flexibility and variety withut conferring ownership rights.

Warranty of Habitability A legal doctrine that requires landlords to maintain rental properties in a condition fit for human habitation, meeting basic health and safety standards.

Work Order A formal document detailing the tasks to be completed for maintenance or repair work, often used to track progress and costs.

MIX
Papier aus verantwortungsvollen Quellen
Paper from responsible sources
FSC® C105338
www.fsc.org

If you have any concerns about our products,
you can contact us on
ProductSafety@springernature.com

In case Publisher is established outside the EU,
the EU authorized representative is:
Springer Nature Customer Service Center GmbH
Europaplatz 3, 69115 Heidelberg, Germany

Printed by Libri Plureos GmbH
in Hamburg, Germany